Abnormal

MICHEL FOUCAULT

Abnormal

LECTURES AT THE COLLÈGE DE FRANCE

1974–1975

Edited by Valerio Marchetti and Antonella Salomoni
General Editors: François Ewald and Alessandro Fontana

English Series Editor: Arnold I. Davidson

TRANSLATED BY GRAHAM BURCHELL

PICADOR

NEW YORK

www.picadorusa.com

Library of Congress Cataloging-in-Publication Data

Foucault, Michel.
   [Anormaux. English]
   Abnormal : lectures at the Collège de France, 1974–1975 / Michel Foucault ;
   edited by Valerio Marchetti and Antonella Salomoni ; English series editor,
   Arnold I. Davidson ; translated by Graham Burchell.—1st Picador ed.
     p. cm.
   Includes bibliographical references and indexes.
   ISBN 0-312-20334-9
   1. Abnormalities, Human—Social aspects—History. 2. Philosophical
anthropology—History. 3. Power (Social sciences)—History. I. Marchetti,
Valerio, 1939– II. Salomoni, Antonella. III. Davidson, Arnold Ira. IV. Title.

B2430.F723A613   2003
194—dc21

2003049892

First published in France by Éditions de Seuil/Gallimard under the title *Les Anormaux: Cours au Collège de France, 1974–1975*

First Picador Edition: December 2003

10 9 8 7 6 5 4 3 2 1

CONTENTS

FOREWORD

MICHEL FOUCAULT TAUGHT AT the Collège de France from January 1971 until his death in June 1984 (with the exception of 1977, when he took a sabbatical year). The title of his chair was the History of Systems of Thought.

On the proposal of Jules Vuillemin, the chair was created on 30 November 1969 by the general assembly of the professors of the Collège de France and replaced that of the History of Philosophical Thought held by Jean Hyppolite until his death. The same assembly elected Michel Foucault to the new chair on 12 April 1970.[1] He was forty-three years old.

Michel Foucault's inaugural lecture was delivered on 2 December 1970.[2]

Teaching at the Collège de France is governed by particular rules. Professors must provide twenty-six hours of teaching a year (with the possibility of a maximum of half this total being given in the form of seminars).[3] Each year they must present their original research and this obliges them to change the content of their teaching for each

---

1 Michel Foucault concluded a short document drawn up in support of his candidacy with these words: "We should undertake the history of systems of thought." "Titres et travaux," in *Dits et écrits*, ed. Daniel Defert and François Ewald (Paris: Gallimard), vol. 1, p. 846.
2 It was published by Gallimard in May 1971 with the title *L'Ordre du discours*, Paris, 1971. English translation: "The Order of Discourse," trans. Ruper Swyer, appendix to M. Foucault, *The Archeology of Knowledge* (New York: Pantheon, 1972).
3 This was Foucault's practice until the start of the 1980s.

course. Courses and seminars are completely open; no enrollment or qualification is required and the professors do not award any qualifications.[4] In the terminology of the Collège de France, the professors do not have students but only auditors.

Michel Foucault's courses were held every Wednesday from January to March. The huge audience made up of students, teachers, researchers, and the curious, including many who came from outside France, required two amphitheaters of the Collège de France. Foucault often complained about the distance between himself and his "public" and of how few exchanges the course made possible.[5] He would have liked a seminar in which real collective work could take place, and he made a number of attempts to bring this about. In the final years he devoted a long period to answering his auditors' questions at the end of each course.

This is how Gérard Petitjean, a journalist from *Le Nouvel Observateur*, described the atmosphere at Foucault's lectures in 1975:

When Foucault enters the amphitheater, brisk and dynamic like someone who plunges into the water, he steps over bodies to reach his chair, pushes away the cassette recorders so he can put down his papers, removes his jacket, lights a lamp and sets off at full speed. His voice is strong and effective, amplified by loudspeakers that are the only concession to modernity in a hall that is barely lit by light spread from stucco bowls. The hall has three hundred places and there are five hundred people packed together, filling the smallest free space . . . There is no oratorical effect. It is clear and terribly effective. There is absolutely no concession to improvisation. Foucault has twelve hours each year to explain in a public course the direction taken by his research in the year just ended. So everything is concen-

---

4 Within the framework of the Collège de France.
5 In 1976, in the vain hope of reducing the size of the audience, Michel Foucault changed the time of his course from 17.45 to 9.00. Cf. the beginning of the first lecture (7 January 1976) of "*Il faut défendre la société.*" Cours au Collège de France, 1976, Paris, 1997. English translation: "*Society Must Be Defended*": Lectures at the Collège de France, 1975-1976, trans. David Macey (New York: Picador, 2003).

trated and he fills the margins like correspondents who have too much to say for the space available to them. At 19.15 Foucault stops. The students rush toward his desk, not to speak to him but to stop their cassette recorders. There are no questions. In the pushing and shoving, Foucault is alone. Foucault remarks: "It should be possible to discuss what I have put forward. Sometimes, when it has not been a good lecture, it would need very little, just one question, to put everything straight. However, this question never comes. The group effect in France makes any genuine discussion impossible. And as there is no feedback, the course is theatricalized. My relationship with the people there is like that of an actor or an acrobat. And when I have finished speaking, a sensation of total solitude..."[6]

Foucault approached his teaching as a researcher: explorations for a future book as well as the opening up of fields of problematization were formulated as an invitation to possible future researchers. This is why the courses at the Collège de France do not duplicate the published books. They are not sketches for the books even though both books and courses share certain themes. They have their own status. They arise from a specific discursive regime within the set of Foucault's "philosophical acts." In particular they set out the program for a genealogy of knowledge/power relations, which are the terms in which he thinks of his work from the beginning of the 1970s, as opposed to the program of an archeology of discursive formations that previously framed his work.[7]

The courses also performed a role in contemporary reality. Those who followed his courses were not only held in thrall by the narrative that unfolded week by week and seduced by the rigorous exposition, they also found a perspective on contemporary reality. Michel Fou-

6 Gérard Petitjean, "Les Grands Prêtres de l'université française", *Le Nouvel Observateur*, 7 April 1975.
7 Cf. especially, "Nietzsche, Genealogy, History," M. Foucault, *The Essential Works of Foucault 1954-1984, vol. 2. Aesthetics, Method, and Epistemology*, James D. Faubion, ed., translated by Robert Hurley et al., New York, 1998.

cault's art consisted in using history to cut diagonally through contemporary reality. He could speak of Nietzsche or Aristotle, of expert psychiatric opinion or the Christian pastoral, but those who attended his lectures always took from what he said a perspective on the present and contemporary events. Foucault's specific strength in his courses was the subtle interplay between learned erudition, personal commitment, and work on the event. With their development and refinement in the 1970s, cassette recorders quickly found their way to Foucault's desk. The courses—and some seminars—have thus been preserved.

This edition is based on the words delivered in public by Foucault. It gives a transcription of these words that is as literal as possible.[8] We would have liked to present it as such. However, the transition from an oral to a written presentation calls for editorial intervention: at the very least it requires the introduction of punctuation and division into paragraphs. Our principle has been always to remain as close as possible to the course actually delivered.

Summaries and repetitions have been removed whenever it seemed to be absolutely necessary. Interrupted sentences have been restored and faulty constructions corrected. Ellipses indicate that the recording is inaudible. When a sentence is obscure, there is a conjectural integration or an addition between square brackets. An asterisk directing the reader to the bottom of the page indicates a significant divergence between the notes used by Foucault and the words actually uttered. Quotations have been checked and references to the texts used are indicated. The critical apparatus is limited to the elucidation of obscure points, the explanation of some allusions, and the clarification of critical points. To make the lectures easier to read, each lecture is preceded by a brief summary that indicates its principal articulations.[9]

The text of the course is followed by the summary published by the *Annuaire du Collège de France*. Foucault usually wrote these in June,

---

8 We have made use of the recordings made by Gérard Burlet and Jacques Lagrange in particular. These are deposited in the Collège de France and the IMEC.
9 At the end of the book, the criteria and solutions adopted by the editors of this year's course are set out in the "Course context."

some time after the end of the course. It was an opportunity for him to pick out retrospectively the intention and objectives of the course. It constitutes the best introduction to the course.

Each volume ends with a "context" for which the course editors are responsible. It seeks to provide the reader with elements of the biographical, ideological, and political context, situating the course within the published work and providing indications concerning its place within the corpus used in order to facilitate understanding and to avoid misinterpretations that might arise from a neglect of the circumstances in which each course was developed and delivered.

A new aspect of Michel Foucault's "œuvre" is published with this edition of the Collège de France courses.

Strictly speaking it is not a matter of unpublished work, since this edition reproduces words uttered publicly by Foucault, excluding the often highly developed written material he used to support his lectures. Daniel Defert possesses Michel Foucault's notes and he is to be warmly thanked for allowing the editors to consult them.

This edition of the Collège de France courses was authorized by Michel Foucault's heirs who wanted to be able to satisfy the strong demand for their publication, in France as elsewhere, and to do this under indisputably responsible conditions. The editors have tried to be equal to the degree of confidence placed in them.

FRANÇOIS EWALD AND ALESSANDRO FONTANA

INTRODUCTION*

Arnold I. Davidson

READING MICHEL FOUCAULT'S LECTURES is such a singular experience that it takes effort to remember that they were part of a course, a public event of teaching. *Abnormal,* like Foucault's other courses at the Collège de France, anticipates, intersects with, and develops themes and analyses found in his published books, especially *Surveiller et punir* and *La Volonté de savoir.* The announced topic of this course is the emergence of the abnormal individual in the nineteenth century. Foucault shows that the domain of the abnormal is constituted historically on the basis of three elements or figures: the human monster, the individual to be corrected, and the onanist. If these figures remained separate until the end of the eighteenth century or the beginning of the nineteenth, a technology of abnormal individuals was formed precisely when "a regular network of power and knowledge" had been established that brought together or took possession of these three figures according to "the same system of regularities."[1] As Fou-

---

* I am greatly indebted to Bianca Torricelli of the Librairie Française de Florence for her help in procuring French texts during the writing of this introduction.

cault also shows, the historical trajectory of these three figures moves from the monster, the predominant figure during the course of the eighteenth century, to the more modest and discrete figure of the masturbator, "the universality of sexual deviance," that becomes by the end of the nineteenth century the central figure around which the problems of abnormality turn.[2] This is the historical basis for his wonderful comment in the Course Summary that "the *Antiphysis*, which terror of the monster once brought to the light of an exceptional day, is now slipped under small everyday abnormalities through the universal sexuality of children."[3] Given this trajectory, we should not be surprised to find that, as the course proceeds, Foucault develops in more detail some of the material that is only sketched in the first volume of *The History of Sexuality*. In addition to the extended discussion of masturbation (that no doubt would have been reworked for the announced but abandoned volume on onanism, *La Croisade des enfants*, that was part of the original project of *The History of Sexuality*), the course also contains, among other significant developments, a discussion of the discovery of the notion of the instinct in psychiatric and penal practice, an analysis of Heinrich Kaan's crucial but rarely studied 1844 book, *Psychopathia sexualis*, and a detailed examination of practices of confession, practices that will come to be focused on what Foucault calls the "moral physiology of the flesh"—all of these discussions help us to fill in the contours of *La Volonté de savoir* and to appreciate the depth of analysis at which Foucault had already arrived before he put aside his initial project for the history of sexuality. Attention should also be drawn to the extraordinary lecture of 26 February 1975, where Foucault's discussion of the differences between witchcraft and possession culminates in an analysis of the phenomenon of convulsion and leads to the claim that the convulsive flesh of the possessed will come to serve, in the history of psychiatry, as the "neurological model of mental illness."[4]

Yet if the topic of abnormality inevitably brings to mind the history of sexuality, *Abnormal* has as its most proximate neighbor *Discipline and Punish*. Foucault finished *Surveiller et punir: Naissance de la prison* in August of 1974 and it was published in February of 1975.[5] Thus this

course overlaps with the publication of that book, and allows us to
see dimensions of Foucault's work whose full force might otherwise
have escaped our notice. Consider, for example, Foucault's unforget-
table remark towards the end of Part I of *Surveiller et punir:* "The soul,
effect and instrument of a political anatomy; the soul, prison of the
body."[6] Foucault's obvious allusion to the Platonic tradition, with its
body as prison of the soul rather than the soul as prison of the body,
should not be read simply as an inversion of Platonism. Nor should
this remark be taken to imply that the soul is an illusion or a mere
effect of ideology. Foucault's "soul" is very real, yet endowed not with
the metaphysical reality of the Platonic tradition but with a historical
reality that is the correlative of "a certain technology of power on the
body" (and of the procedures of knowledge that arise from and re-
inforce these relations of power).[7] When Foucault claims that the soul
is the prison of the body, he is, first of all, analyzing a problem "not
in transcendental terms, but in terms of history," and, second, con-
ducting this historical analysis through a "political history of the
body."[8] Further examples of this type of analysis can be found in the
first lectures of *Abnormal*, where Foucault is concerned with the way
in which medico-legal practice produced a psychologico-moral double
of the legal offense, created the "dangerous individual," and, eventually, through the functioning of power of normalization, came to constitute itself as the authority responsible for the control of "abnormal
individuals." The general aim of these analyses is to mark out the
displacement of the legal subject by a set of "juridically indiscernible"
personalities, such as the delinquent, the dangerous individual, the
abnormal, all of whom are correlative to techniques of power and
knowledge.[9] Hence Foucault's conclusion, at the end of his first lecture, that "along with other processes, expert psychiatric opinion
brought about this transformation in which the legally responsible
individual is replaced by an element that is the correlate of a technique of normalization."[10] And so the historical reality of the soul
could come to take on the form of the psyche or personality, with its
gradation from normal to abnormal, where everyone could become a
dossier, a case, an object of "clinical" science, affixed to his or her

own individuality.[11] A lexical indication of Foucault's increasingly more explicit conception of power as *productive*, one of the central achievements of this period of his work, is the constant recurrence of phrases such as "the correlative of," "in correlation with," phrases that indicate the type of reality possessed by the figures of nineteenth century legal psychiatry. These are figures whose reality is never denied by Foucault, but whose existence must be understood as produced by power, and thus reality and Foucault's commitment to nominalism go hand in hand.

In his 1973-1974 course at the Collège de France, *Le Pouvoir psychiatrique*, Foucault had already criticized several notions found in *Histoire de la folie*, notions that he felt had to be put aside if one wanted to advance further in the analysis of psychiatric power. After making clear that rather than beginning from an analysis of representations, he now wants to start from apparatuses of power (*les dispositifs du pouvoir*), Foucault goes on to criticize his former use of the notion of violence. He insists that power need not be violent, in the sense of being unleashed, passionate, even though its point of application is the body, and he emphasizes that this exercise of power on the body remains rationally organized and calculated even while being the physical exercise of a force.[12] Physical and calculated without having to be violent—such is the type of power that will now be the focus of Foucault's analyses. As he puts it in *Surveiller et punir*, the subjection of the body "can very well be direct, physical, play force against force, bear on material elements, and yet not be violent; it can be calculated, organized, technically thought out, it can be subtle, make use neither of weapons nor of terror, and yet remain of a physical nature."[13] This description also fits perfectly the tactics and strategies of the power of normalization that are analyzed in *Abnormal* and still later in *La Volonté de savoir*.

This new positive conception of power is clearly linked to overcoming what Foucault calls "the model of exclusion" and its central notion of repression. In his lecture of 15 January, 1975, Foucault contrasts the exclusion of the leper with the inclusion of plague victims.

The exclusion of the leper is a model based on rigorous division, rejection, disqualification—all negative notions and practices.

> I think we still describe the way in which power is exercised over the mad, the ill, criminals, deviants, children, and the poor in these terms. Generally, we describe the effects and mechanisms of the power exercised over these categories as mechanisms and effects of exclusion, disqualification, exile, rejection, deprivation, refusal, and incomprehension; that is to say, an entire arsenal of negative concepts or mechanisms of exclusion.[14]

Although Foucault continues to believe that this model, based on the exclusion of the leper, was historically present in our society, even as late as the second half of the seventeenth century, he wants to shift his attention to another model, one which he claims to have enjoyed a much greater and longer success, namely the model of the inclusion of the plague victim. And Foucault remarks, "I think the replacement of the exclusion of lepers by the inclusion of plague victims as the model of control was a major phenomenon of the eighteenth century."[15] The exercise of continuous control over a plague infested town, with its requirement of a more and more constant and insistent observation, a perpetual examination and registration of a field of differences, its division and subdivision of power that reaches the fine grain of individuality, has as its primary effect not repression but "normalization."[16] The norm, a polemical or political concept, founds and legitimizes a certain exercise of power, and is "always linked to a positive technique of intervention and transformation."[17] As Foucault says, comparing the reaction to leprosy with the reaction to the plague: "We pass from a technology of power that drives out, excludes, banishes, marginalizes, and represses, to a fundamentally positive power that fashions, observes, knows, and multiplies itself on the basis of its own effects."[18] "Repression is only a lateral and secondary effect of this positive power, a power put into place, in its modern form, by apparatuses of "discipline-normalization.""[19] Foucault argues that it is both a "methodological and a historical error" to consider power as essentially a negative mechanism of repression—a historical error because it takes as its reference a series of historically outdated models, and a methodological error because it conceives of power as negative, as basically conservative and reproductive, as superstructural, and as linked to effects that derive from a lack of knowledge, all characteristics that are anything but productive and inventive.[20]

A reader of Foucault who picks up *Abnormal* and reads these initial lectures may have a vague feeling of *déjà lu*, since, although it is very easy to overlook, the famous chapter on the panopticon in *Surveiller et punir* opens with a description of the measures that have to be taken when a town is stricken by the plague, mentions the differences between the rituals of exclusion that leprosy gave rise to and the disciplinary schemes provoked by the plague, and culminates with the claim that Bentham's *Panopticon* is the architectural figure of this technology of power.[21] Although Foucault goes on to emphasize that the plague-stricken town represented an exceptional situation, while the panoptical establishment must be understood as "a generalizable model of functioning," a "figure of political technology that one can and should detach from any specific use," there is no doubt that the targets of the disciplinary society, modeled on the techniques of the panopticon, find their historical counterparts in the mechanisms of normalization studied in *Abnormal*.[22]

These techniques of power are never dissociated from fields of knowledge. In Part III, Chapter II of *Surveiller et punir* Foucault shows how the examination (*l'examen*) embodied a "mechanism that links a certain type of formation of knowledge to a certain form of exercise of power."[23] And as early as 1973, in his remarkable series of lectures in Rio de Janeiro, "La Vérité et les formes juridiques," Foucault already discusses how the form of power he calls "panopticism" "no longer rests on an inquiry (*une enquête*), but on something totally different that I would call the examination."[24] Whereas an inquiry was a procedure of judicial practice in which the mechanisms of knowledge were aimed at learning what had taken place, the examination no longer tried to reconstitute an event, but "something or rather someone that one has to watch over (*surveiller*) without interruption and completely:

> This new knowledge is no longer organized around the questions: "Was this done? Who did it?"; it is no longer ordered in terms of presence or absence, of existence or nonexistence. It is ordered around the norm, in terms of what is normal or not, correct or not, of what one should or should not do.[25]

The examination is that form of knowledge and power that gives rise to the "human sciences," and thus that contributes to the constitution of the domain of the abnormal. The examination of the "dangerous individual," for example, implied a control not primarily of what individuals did, but of what they might do, what they are capable of doing. "Dangerousness" meant that the individual "must be considered by society at the level of his potentialities (*ses virtualités*) and not at the level of his acts," not as someone who had actually violated a law, but as someone whose potential behavior had to be subject to control and correction.[26] Similarly, the "delinquent" must be distinguished from the law-breaker, since what is relevant to his characterization is "less his act than his life... legal punishment bears on an act; punitive technique on a life."[27] Moreover, the delinquent is not only the legal author of his act, but is "linked to his offense by an entire bundle of complex threads (instincts, drives, tendencies, character)."[28] So "the correlative of the penitentiary apparatus... is the delinquent, biographical unity, core of 'dangerousness,' representative of a type of abnormality."[29] It is in following this line of analysis that Foucault concludes, in *Abnormal*, that "expert psychiatric opinion makes it possible to transfer the point of application of punishment from the offense defined by the law to criminality evaluated from a psychologico-moral point of view."[30] And all of those categories mentioned at the beginning of *Abnormal*, from psychological immaturity and poorly structured personality to infantilism and profound affective disequilibrium, had their role in the historico-political development of the examination in which everyone reaches the threshold of description to become a "case," a singularity, an identity, fabricated by these new techniques of individualization.[31]

Foucault's work from the early 1970s, his courses, lectures, interviews, and books, provides a wealth of material from which one could begin to write a genealogy of the examination, a genealogy that would intersect with the history of confession sketched in the chapter "Scientia sexualis" of *La Volonté de savoir*. In that chapter Foucault had to show how the will to know made "the rituals of confession function within the schemes of scientific regularity."[32] The genealogy of the examination would have to follow a similar path, starting from the penitential examination of the flesh and culminating in the psychiatric examination of the entire realm of drives and desires. The continuities and discontinuities between these two types of procedure would be part of that complex history of the relation between religious and scientific technologies that was so central to large parts of Foucault's work. As Foucault shows in *Abnormal*, before the Council of Trent, sins against the sixth commandment were understood in juridical terms, infractions of the relational rules between persons, of the juridical ties between persons. Hence the traditional list of fornication, adultery, sodomy, bestiality, etc.[33] Then, beginning in the sixteenth century, there is a considerable modification of the focal point to which the examination is attached:

> From the sixteenth century on, the fundamental change in the confession of the sin of lust is that the relational aspect of sexuality is no longer the important, primary, and fundamental element of penitential confession. It is no longer the relational aspect that is now at the very heart of questioning concerning the Sixth Commandment, but the movements, senses, pleasures, thoughts, and desires of the penitent's body itself, whose intensity and nature is experienced by the penitent himself. The old examination was essentially the inventory of permitted and forbidden relationships. The new examination is a meticulous passage through the body, a sort of anatomy of the pleasures of the flesh (*la volupté*). The body with its different parts and different

sensations, and no longer, or much less, the laws of legitimate union, constitutes the organizing principle of the sins of lust. The body and its pleasures, rather than the required form for legitimate union become, as it were, the code of the carnal.[34]

As Foucault puts it in a very different context, what is at stake here is not at all the "internalization of a catalogue of prohibitions," substituting for the prohibition of the act the prohibition of the intention: it is a question of "the opening up of a domain...which is that of thought, with its irregular and spontaneous flow, with its images, its memories, its perceptions, with the movements and the impressions that are communicated from the body to the soul and the soul to the body."[35] How the concupiscence of the flesh became the psyche of the abnormal, how the libido of the theologians became that of the human sciences, is a process that passes through the displacements of the examination from, so to speak, the confessional to the couch, an examination that was always both a form of knowledge and a technique of power. Here too it is a matter of tracing "the interference between two modalities of production of the truth": the penitential examination and the medico-psychological examination, the confession of the flesh and the clinico-therapeutic codification of the questionnaire.[36] It is in the midst of this interference that the abnormal individual begins to come into existence.

Abnormal adds yet another layer to the virtually inexhaustible fields of study that Foucault's work has bequeathed to us. "Abnormality" has entered our everyday discourse with a conceptual force that seems both natural and inevitable. One can only hope that the next time we are tempted to invoke the label "abnormal," rather than appearing familiar, this gesture will become problematic, even difficult. This kind of difficulty is one of the most powerful effects of what one might call the Foucault-experience: the experience of the critical work of thought on itself.

1. Michel Foucault, *Abnormal. Lectures at the Collège de France 1974-1975*. (New York, 2003) p. 61.
2. *Ibid.*, pp. 62-63.
3. *Ibid.*, p. 328.
4. *Ibid.*, p. 224. See also Valerio Marchetti "'La Chair et les corps,'" *Critique*, May 2002.
5. Michel Foucault, *Dits et écrits*, vol. 1: *1954-1975*. (Paris, 2001). See the "Chronologie," pp. 61-62.
6. Michel Foucault, *Surveiller et punir: Naissance de la prison* (Paris, 1975), p. 38.
7. *Ibid.*
8. Michel Foucault. "Titres et travaux," in *Dits et écrits*, vol. 1: *1954-1975*, p. 873; and, for the later phrase, Michel Foucault, *Abnormal*, p. 214.
9. Michel Foucault, *Abnormal*, p. 21.
10. *Ibid.*, p. 25.
11. Michel Foucault, *Surveiller et punir*, pp. 224-225.
12. Michel Foucault, Lecture of 7 November 1973, *Le Pouvoir psychiatrique*. Forthcoming.
13. Michel Foucault, *Surveiller et punir*, p. 34.
14. Michel Foucault, *Abnormal*, pp. 43-44.
15. *Ibid.*, p. 44.
16. *Ibid.*, p. 49.
17. *Ibid.*, p. 50.
18. *Ibid.*, p. 48.
19. *Ibid.*, p. 52.
20. *Ibid.*, pp. 49-52.
21. Michel Foucault, *Surveiller et punir*, pp. 228-33. See also Michel Foucault, "La Prison vue par un philosophe français," in *Dits et écrits*, vol.1: *1954-1975*, pp. 1596-97.
22. Michel Foucault, *Surveiller et punir*, p. 239.
23. *Ibid.*, p. 219.
24. Michel Foucault, "La Vérité et les formes juridiques," in *Dits et écrits*, vol. 1: *1954-1975*. p. 1462.
25. *Ibid.*, p. 1463.
26. *Ibid.*, p. 1461. See also Michel Foucault, "L'Évolution de la notion d'"individu dangereux' dans la psychiatrie légale du XIXᵉ siècle," in *Dits et écrits*, vol. 2: *1976-1988* (Paris, 2001), pp. 443-64.
27. Michel Foucault, *Surveiller et punir*, p. 292.
28. *Ibid.*, p. 293.
29. *Ibid.*, p. 295.
30. Michel Foucault, *Abnormal*, p. 16.
31. Michel Foucault, *Surveiller et punir*, pp. 225-27.
32. Michel Foucault, *Histoire de la sexualité*, vol 1: *La Volonté de savoir* (Paris, 1976), p. 87.
33. Michel Foucault, *Abnormal*, pp. 184-185.
34. *Ibid*, p. 186. See also Michel Foucault, *La Volonté de savoir*, pp. 51-56, 142-43.
35. Michel Foucault, "Le Combat de la chasteté," *Dits et écrits*, vol. 2: *1976-1988*. pp. 1125-26. See also Michel Foucault, *Abnormal*, p. 189.
36. Michel Foucault, *La Volonté de savoir*, p. 87.

one

8 JANUARY 1975

Expert psychiatric opinion in penal cases. ~ What kind of discourse is the discourse of expert psychiatric opinion? ~ Discourses of truth and discourses that make one laugh. ~ Legal proof in eighteenth-century criminal law. ~ The reformers. ~ The principle of profound conviction. ~ Extenuating circumstances. ~ The relationship between truth and justice. ~ The grotesque in the mechanism of power. ~ The psychological-moral double of the offense. ~ Expert opinion shows how the individual already resembles his crime before he has committed it. ~ The emergence of the power of normalization.

I WOULD LIKE TO begin this year's course by reading to you two expert psychiatric opinions in penal cases. The first is from 1955, exactly twenty years ago. It is signed by at least one of the prominent figures in penal psychiatry of that time and it concerns a case that some of you may still recall. It is the case of a woman and her lover who killed the woman's young daughter. The man, the woman's lover, was accused of complicity in the murder, or, at least, of incitement to murder the child, since it was established that the woman killed her child with her own hands. Here, then, is what the expert psychiatric opinion had to say about the man whom, if you don't mind, I will call A, because I have not yet been able to determine whether it is legally permissible to publish the testimony of a medico-legal expert that includes the names of those involved.[1]

The experts are obviously uncomfortable with giving their psychological judgment on A in view of the fact that they cannot take a position on his moral culpability. Nevertheless, we will start from the hypothesis that, in some way or another, A exercised an influence over the mind of the girl, L, that led her to murder her child. Based on this hypothesis, then, this is how we picture the events and people involved. A is from an irregular and socially unstable background. He was an illegitimate child who was raised by his mother. His father acknowledged him only much later, and he lived with his half-brothers without there ever being any real family cohesion. This was even more the case when, after his father died, he found himself alone again with his mother, a rather disturbed woman. In spite of everything, he started secondary school. His origins must have had an effect on his natural pride: In short, individuals of this kind never feel well integrated into the world in which they find themselves; hence their love of paradox and of everything that creates disorder. They feel less out of place in a somewhat revolutionary climate of ideas [I remind you that this is 1955; M.F.] than in a more settled environment and philosophy. This is what happens with all intellectual reforms, with all coteries; it is the story of Saint-Germain-des-Prés, of existentialism,[2] and so forth. Genuinely strong personalities may emerge in any movement, especially if they maintain a certain ability to adapt. They may thus achieve celebrity and found a stable school. But most cannot rise above mediocrity and seek to attract attention to themselves by wearing outlandish clothes or by performing extraordinary actions. In these people we find Alcibiadism[3] and Herostratism.[4] Obviously, they no longer cut off the tail of their dog or burn the temple of Ephesus, but they sometimes allow themselves to be corrupted by hatred of bourgeois morality to the point of denying its laws and resorting to crime in order to inflate their personality, especially when this personality is naturally insipid. Naturally, in all of this there is an element of romantic daydreaming (*bovarysme*),[5] of man's ability to imagine

himself other than he is, and especially as more beautiful and
great than he is by nature. This is why A could think himself
a superman. However, it is odd that he was not influenced by
his military experience, although he himself maintains that going
to Saint-Cyr was character-forming. Nonetheless, military uni-
form did not seem to normalize Algarron's attitude to any great
extent.[6] Besides, he was always in a hurry to leave the army to
go on his escapades. Another of A's psychological traits [that is,
after *bovarysme*, Herostratism, and Alcibiadism; M.F.] is Don
Juanism.[7] He spent literally all of his free time collecting mis-
tresses who were generally easy women like the young L. Then,
showing a real lack of judgment, he held forth to them on topics
they were hardly able to understand due to the low level of
their education. He enjoyed presenting them with enormous—
hénaurmes in Flaubert's spelling system—paradoxes, to which
some listened openmouthed and to which others lent only half
an ear. Just as a culture that was too advanced for his worldly
and intellectual condition had not been very good for A, so the
young L followed his lead in a distorted and tragic fashion. Here
we are dealing with *bovarysme* at a new, lower level. She swal-
lowed A's paradoxes, which had somehow intoxicated her. He
seemed to her to have reached a higher intellectual plane. A
talked about the need for a couple to do something extraordinary together in order to create an indissoluble bond: to kill a
taxi driver, for example, or to kill a child for no reason, or
merely to demonstrate their resolution. So the young L decided
to kill Catherine. At least, this is what she claims. While A does
not entirely accept this, he does not completely reject it since
he admits to having expounded paradoxes to her, perhaps im-
prudently, that she, lacking a critical mind, may well have
turned into a rule of action. Thus, without taking a position on
the reality and degree of A's culpability, we can see how his
influence on the young L could have been pernicious. However,
our particular question is one of determining and presenting A's
responsibility from a penal point of view. We again insist that

there should be no misunderstanding of terms. We are not seeking to determine the extent of A's moral responsibility for the
crimes committed by the young L: That is a matter for the magistrates and jurors. From a medico-legal point of view, we merely
seek to determine whether the abnormalities of A's character
have a pathological origin and whether they create a mental
disorder that is enough to affect his penal responsibility. The
answer will, of course, be negative. Clearly A was wrong not to
confine himself to his courses at military school and, in love, to
his weekend adventures, but nevertheless his paradoxes do not
amount to delirious ideas. Of course, if A had not just impru-
dently propounded to the young L theories that were too complex for her to understand, if he intentionally pushed her to
murder the child, whether in order perhaps to get rid of her,
or to prove to himself his power of persuasion, or out of a pure
perverse game, like Don Juan's in the scene of the poor man,[8]
then he is fully responsible. Our conclusions, which may be
attacked from every side, can only be put forward in this conditional form. We run the risk in this case of being accused of
exceeding our task and usurping the role of the jury by taking
a position for or against the actual culpability of the accused, or
again, of being reproached for being excessively laconic if we
had said bluntly what, when it comes to it, should have sufficed:
namely, that A presents no symptoms of mental illness and,
generally speaking, is fully responsible.

This is a text from 1955. Forgive me for the length of these documents (although you can see at once why they raise questions). I
would like now to quote from some much shorter documents, or
rather, from an assessment of three men accused of blackmail in a
sexual case. I will read the reports on at least two of the men.[9]
One of the men, let us call him X,

although not outstanding intellectually, is not stupid; he links his
ideas together well and has a good memory. Morally, he has been

homosexual since he was twelve or thirteen years old, and to begin with this vice could only have been a compensation for the
teasing he suffered when, as a child raised by the social services,
he lived in the Manche [the department; M.F.]. Perhaps his effeminate appearance aggravated this tendency toward homosexuality, but it was the lure of money that led him to blackmail. X
is completely immoral, cynical, and even a chatterbox. Three
thousand years ago he would certainly have been an inhabitant of
Sodom, and the heavenly flames would have justly punished him
for his vice. We should recognize, however, that Y [the object of
the blackmail; M.F.] would have deserved the same punishment.
Because he is, after all, elderly, relatively rich, and had nothing to
offer X other than a place in a club for inverts for which he was
the cashier, gradually getting back the money invested in this
purchase. This Y, successively or simultaneously the active or pas-
sive lover of X, we do not know, arouses X's contempt and nau-
sea. X loves Z. One has to have seen the effeminate appearance of
both of them to understand how such a word can be used. It is a
case of two men so effeminate that they would have had to live in
Gomorrah rather than Sodom.

And so I could go on. As for Z:

He is a quite mediocre individual with a good memory and
linking his ideas together well. Morally, he is a cynical and
immoral individual. He wallows in depravity and is manifestly
deceitful and reticent. One must literally practice a meiotic with
regard to him [meiotic is written *maïotique*, doubtless something
to do with a jersey (*maillot*)! M.F.].[10] But the most typical feature of his character seems to be an idleness whose importance
can hardly be described. It is evidently less tiring to change
records and find clients in a nightclub than it is to really work.
Furthermore, he himself recognizes that he became homosexual
from material necessity, from the attraction of money, and that
having acquired a taste for money he persists in it.

Conclusion: "He is particularly repugnant."

You can see that there is both very little and a great deal that could be said about this kind of discourse. For, after all, in a society like ours, discourses that possess all three of the following properties are rare: The first property is the power to determine, directly or indirectly, a decision of justice that ultimately concerns a person's freedom or detention, or, if it comes to it (and we will see cases of this), life and death. So, these are discourses that ultimately have the power of life and death. Second property: From what does this power of life and death derive? From the judicial system perhaps, but these discourses also have this power by virtue of the fact that they function as discourses of truth within the judicial system. They function as discourses of truth because they are discourses with a scientific status, or discourses expressed exclusively by qualified people within a scientific institution. Discourses that can kill, discourses of truth, and, the third property, discourses—you yourselves are the proof and witnesses of this[11]—that make one laugh. And discourses of truth that provoke laughter and have the institutional power to kill are, after all, in a society like ours, discourses that deserve some attention. They especially deserve our attention since, while the first of these expert opinions in particular concerned, as you have seen, a relatively serious, and so relatively rare case, what is at issue in the second case, which is from 1974 (it took place last year), is clearly the daily fare of penal justice and, I would say, of everyone subject to trial. These everyday discourses of truth that kill and provoke laughter are at the very heart of our judicial system.

This is not the first time that the functioning of judicial truth has not only raised questions but also caused laughter. You know that at the end of the eighteenth century—I spoke about it two years ago, I think[12]—the way in which the proof of truth was administered in penal justice gave rise to both irony and criticism. You recall that in the both scholastic and arithmetical kind of judicial proof, which in the penal law of the eighteenth century was called legal proof, an entire hierarchy of quantitatively and qualitatively weighted proofs was distinguished.[13] There were complete proofs and incomplete proofs, full proofs and semifull proofs, whole proofs and half proofs, indications and cavils. And then all these elements of proof were combined and added up to arrive at a certain quantity of proofs that the law, or rather custom, defined as the minimum necessary to get a conviction. At that point, on the basis of this arithmetic, of this calculus of proof, the court had to make its decision. And, to a certain extent at least, the court was bound in its decision by this arithmetic of proof. In addition to this legalization, this legal definition of the nature and quantity of the proof, apart from this legal formalization of the proof, there was the principle that punishment had to be proportional to the quantity of proofs assembled. That is, it was not enough to say that a full, whole, and complete proof must be reached in order to fix a punishment. Rather, classical law said: If the sum does not add up to that minimum degree of proof on the basis of which the full and entire penalty can be applied, if the addition remains in some way uncertain, if there is simply three-quarters proof and not a full proof in the total sum, nevertheless this does not mean that one should not punish. To a three-quarters proof corresponds a three-quarters penalty, to a semi proof, a semi penalty.[14] In other words, one is not suspected with impunity. The least element of proof, or, in any case, a certain element of proof, will be enough to entail a certain element of penalty. At the end of the eighteenth century this practice of truth provoked the criticism and irony of reformers like Voltaire, Beccaria, Servan, and Dupaty.[15]

It was to this system of legal proof, of the arithmetic of proof, that the principle called profound conviction (*intime conviction*)[16] was opposed. When we see this principle at work today, and when we see the reaction of people to its effects, we have the impression that it authorizes conviction without proof. But, in fact, the principle of profound conviction had a perfectly precise historical meaning in the way it was formulated and institutionalized at the end of the eighteenth century.[17]

First of all, it meant that one must no longer convict before reaching total certainty. That is to say, there must no longer be proportionality between the proof (*démonstration*) and the penalty. The penalty must conform to the law of all or nothing; a proof (*preuve*) that is not complete cannot entail a partial penalty. However light a penalty may be, it must be fixed only when the total, complete, exhaustive, and entire proof of the guilt of the accused has been established. This is the first meaning of the principle of profound conviction: the judge must convict only if he is profoundly convinced of guilt, and not merely if he has suspicions.

Second, the meaning of this principle is that not only proofs defined and qualified by the law can be accepted as valid. Rather, provided that it is probative—that is to say, provided it is by nature able to secure the support of any mind whatsoever open to truth, of any mind capable of judgment and therefore open to truth—any evidence must be admitted. It is not the legality of the proof, its conformity to the law, that makes it a proof: it is its demonstrability. The demonstrability of evidence makes it admissible.

Finally, and this is the third meaning of the principle of profound conviction, the criterion for recognizing that proof has been established is not the canonical table of good proofs, it is conviction: the conviction of any subject whosoever, of an indifferent subject. As a thinking subject, the subject is open to knowledge and truth. That is to say, with the principle of profound conviction we pass from the arithmetico-scholastic and ridiculous regime of classical proof to the common, honorable, and anonymous regime of truth for a supposedly universal subject.

Now this regime of universal truth, which penal justice has seemed to accept since the eighteenth century, in the way it is actually brought into play, in fact accommodates two phenomena, two facts, or two important practices that constitute, I think, the real practice of judicial truth and, at the same time, destabilize it with regard to the strict and general formulation of the principle of profound conviction.

First, you know that despite the principle that one must never punish before having arrived at proof, at the judge's profound conviction, in fact in practice a certain proportionality is always retained between the degree of certainty and the severity of the penalty imposed. You know perfectly well that when there is not complete certainty about an offense or crime, the judge—whether magistrate or jury—tends to translate this uncertainty into a mitigation of the penalty. A penalty that is mitigated to a greater or lesser extent, but a penalty nonetheless, corresponds to a certainty that has not been completely established. That is to say, even now in our system, and despite the principle of profound conviction, strong presumptions never go wholly unpunished. This is how extenuating circumstances operate.

For what, in principle, was the intention behind the notion of extenuating circumstances? In general, they were intended to modulate the rigor of the law as formulated in 1810 in the penal code. When the legislature defined extenuating circumstances in 1832, its real objective was not to allow a softening of the penalty; rather, it was to prevent the juries from acquitting when they did not want to apply the full rigor of the law. In the case of infanticide, in particular, provincial juries were in the habit of not convicting at all, because if they had convicted they would have been obliged to apply the law, which was the death penalty. They acquitted in order to avoid applying the death penalty. It was in order to provide juries and penal justice with the right degree of severity that, in 1832, juries were given the possibility of modulating the application of the law by appealing to extenuating circumstances.

However, despite the legislature's explicit objective, what actually took place? Juries became more severe. But equally it turned out that the new basis made it possible to overturn the principle of profound conviction. When juries found themselves having to decide on someone's guilt for which there was considerable evidence but still not certainty, they applied the principle of extenuating circumstances and handed out a penalty that was slightly or considerably less than the penalty provided for by the law. Presumption, the degree of presumption, was thus registered in the severity of the penalty.

In the Goldman case,[18] which took place some weeks ago, if the scandal exploded at the very heart of the judicial institution, if the public prosecutor was astonished by the jury's verdict, which carried the penalty he had himself demanded, at bottom it was because the jury did not adopt the practice, which is absolutely against the law, of resorting to extenuating circumstances when one is not quite sure of guilt. What happened in the Goldman case? Essentially, the jury applied the principle of profound conviction, or rather, if you like, it applied the law itself. That is to say, it thought that it had a profound conviction and applied the penalty demanded by the prosecution. The prosecutor was so accustomed to seeing the jury fix a lesser penalty than that demanded by the prosecution, in cases where there is doubt, that he was astonished by the severity of the penalty. In his aston-ishment he revealed this absolutely illegal custom, or at least a custom that is contrary to the principle of profound conviction and that en-sures that extenuating circumstances are intended to indicate the un-certainty of the jury. In principle, extenuating circumstances should never be used to register the uncertainty of the jury; if there is any uncertainty, the jury must purely and simply acquit. In fact, behind the principle of profound conviction you have, therefore, a practice that continues to modulate the penalty according to the uncertainty of proof, exactly as in the old system of legal proofs.

Another practice also leads to distortion of the principle of pro-found conviction and to the reconstitution of something like legal proof, or at least that in some respects resembles the way in which justice functioned in the eighteenth century. Of course, we do not see this quasi reconstitution, this pseudo reconstitution, in the reconsti-tution of an arithmetic of proofs, but rather in the fact that—contrary to the principle of profound conviction, which means that any evi-dence can be admitted and collated and must be weighed only by the conscience of the judge, jury, or magistrate—some evidence has in itself an effect of power, a demonstrative value, greater than other evidence and independently of its own rational structure. To what is this effect due if it is not the rational structure of the evidence? Well, it is due to the status of the subject who presents the evidence. In the present system of French justice, police reports or the testimony of police officers, for example, have a kind of privilege vis-à-vis any other report or testimony because they are statements made by a sworn-in functionary of the police. On the other hand, experts' reports—inasmuch as their expert status confers a scientific value or rather a scientific status on those who pronounce them—have a certain privilege vis-à-vis any other element of judicial proof. These are not legal proofs as understood in classical law at the end of the eighteenth century, but they are nevertheless privileged judicial statements that include statutory presumptions of truth, presumptions that are inherent in them according to who it is that states them. In short, they are statements with specific effects of truth and power: a sort of supralegality of certain statements in the production of judicial truth.

I would like to dwell for a moment on this truth-justice relationship because it is, of course, one of the fundamental themes of Western philosophy.[19] It is, after all, one of the most immediate and fundamental presuppositions of all judicial, political, and critical discourse that there is an essential affiliation between stating the truth and the practice of justice. Where the institution appointed to govern justice and the institutions qualified to express the truth encounter each other, or more concisely, where the court and the expert encounter each other, where judicial institutions and medical knowledge, or scientific knowledge in general, intersect, statements are formulated having the status of true discourses with considerable judicial effects. However, these statements also have the curious property of being foreign to all, even the most elementary, rules for the formation of scientific discourse, as well as being foreign to the rules of law and of being, in the strict sense, grotesque, like the texts I have just read.

When I say these are grotesque texts I use the word *grotesque*, if not in an absolutely strict sense, at least in a somewhat restricted and serious sense. I am calling "grotesque" the fact that, by virtue of their status, a discourse or an individual can have effects of power that their intrinsic qualities should disqualify them from having. The grotesque, or, if you prefer, the "Ubu-esque,"[20] is not just a term of abuse or an insulting epithet, and I would not like to use it in that sense. I think that there is a precise category, or, in any case, that we should define a precise category of historico-political analysis, that would be

the category of the grotesque or Ubu-esque. Ubu-esque terror, grotesque sovereignty, or, in starker terms, the maximization of effects
of power on the basis of the disqualification of the one who produces
them. I do not think this is an accident or mechanical failure in the
history of power. It seems to me that it is one of the cogs that are an
inherent part of the mechanisms of power. Political power, at least in
some societies, and anyway in our society, can give itself, and has
actually given itself, the possibility of conveying its effects and, even
more, of finding their source, in a place that is manifestly, explicitly,
and readily discredited as odious, despicable, or ridiculous. This grotesque mechanism of power, or this grotesque cog in the mechanism
of power, has a long history in the structures and political functioning
of our societies. There are striking examples of it in Roman history,
especially in the history of the Roman Empire, where the almost
theatrical disqualification of the origin of power in, and the coupling
of every effect of power with, the person of the emperor was precisely
a mode, if not of governing exactly, at least of domination: a disqualification that ensured that the person who possessed *maiestas*, that
is to say, more power than any other power was, at the same time,
in his person, his character, and his physical reality, in his costume,
his gestures, his body, his sexuality and his way of life, a despicable,
grotesque, and ridiculous individual. From Nero to Elagabalus, the
mechanism of grotesque power, of vile sovereignty, was perennially
brought into play in the functioning of the Roman Empire.[21]

The grotesque is one of the essential processes of arbitrary sovereignty. But you know also that the grotesque is a process inherent to
assiduous bureaucracy. Since the nineteenth century, an essential feature of big Western bureaucracies has been that the administrative
machine, with its unavoidable effects of power, works by using the
mediocre, useless, imbecilic, superficial, ridiculous, worn-out, poor,
and powerless functionary. The administrative grotesque has not been
merely that kind of visionary perception of administration that we
find in Balzac, Dostoyevsky, Courteline, or Kafka. The administrative
grotesque is a real possibility for the bureaucracy. Ubu the "pen
pusher" is a functional component of modern administration, just as

being in the hands of a mad charlatan was a functional feature of Roman imperial power. And what I say about the Roman Empire, what I say about modern bureaucracy, could also be said about many other mechanical forms of power, such as Nazism or Fascism. The grotesque character of someone like Mussolini was absolutely inherent to the mechanism of power. Power provided itself with an image in which power derived from someone who was theatrically got up and depicted as a clown or a buffoon.

It seems to me that there is in this every degree of what could be called the unworthiness of power, from despicable sovereignty to ridiculous authority. We know that ethnologists—I am thinking in particular of Clastres's very fine analyses[22]—have clearly identified the phenomenon in which the person to whom power is given is at the same time ridiculed or made abject or shown in an unfavorable light, through a number of rites and ceremonies. Is this a case of a ritual for limiting the effects of power in archaic or primitive societies? Perhaps. However, I would say that if these rituals still exist in our societies, their function is completely different. I do not think that explicitly showing power to be abject, despicable, Ubu-esque or simply ridiculous is a way of limiting its effects and of magically dethroning the person to whom one gives the crown. Rather, it seems to me to be a way of giving a striking form of expression to the unavoidability, the inevitability of power, which can function in its full rigor and at the extreme point of its rationality even when in the hands of someone who is effectively discredited. This problem of the infamy of sovereignty, of the discredited sovereign, is, after all, Shakespeare's problem: It is precisely the problem posed by the royal tragedies, without, it seems to me, the sovereign's infamy ever having been theorized.[23] But, once again, in our society, from Nero, perhaps the founding figure of the despicable sovereign, down to the little man with trembling hands crowned with forty million deaths who, from deep in his bunker, asks only for two things, that everything else above him be destroyed and that he be given chocolate cakes until he bursts, you have the whole outrageous functioning of the despicable sovereign.[24]

I have neither the strength, nor the courage, nor the time to devote this year's course to such a theme. But I would like at least to take up again this problem of the grotesque with regard to the texts I have just read. I do not think it should be considered a pure and simple insult to recognize the grotesque and to pose the problem of the existence and function of the grotesque in these texts. At its extreme point, where it accords itself the right to kill, justice has installed a discourse that is Ubu's discourse; it gives voice to Ubu science. To express things more solemnly, let us say that the West, which, no doubt since Greek society, since the Greek city-state, has not ceased to dream of giving power to the discourse of truth in a just city, has ended up in its system of justice conferring unrestrained power on the parody, on the parody that is recognized as such, of scientific discourse. We leave it to others, then, to pose the question of the effects of truth that may be produced in discourse by the subject who is supposed to know.[25] As for myself, I would rather study the effects of power produced in reality by a discourse that is at the same time both statutory and discredited. Clearly, we could pursue this analysis in different directions. We could try to identify the ideology behind the discourse I have illustrated with examples. We could also start from their institutional support, from judicial and medical institutions, in order to see how they arose. Those of you who were here in previous years will know the direction I will take. Rather than attempt an ideological or "institutional" analysis, I will try to identify and analyze the technology of power that utilizes these discourses and tries to put them to work.

To this end, as an initial approach, I will pose the following question: What takes place in that discourse of Ubu at the heart of our judicial practice, of our penal practice? The theory, therefore, of the psychiatric-penal Ubu. Essentially, I think we can say that what takes place through these discourses (of which I have given some examples) is a series of, I was going to say substitutions, but I do not think the word is right and it would be better to say doublings, because what is involved is not really a game of replacements but the introduction of successive doubles. In other words, for these psychiatric discourses on penal questions it is not a question of installing, as people say, another scene, but, on the contrary, of splitting the elements *on* the same scene. It is not a question, then, of the caesura that indicates access to the symbolic, but of the coercive synthesis that ensures the transmission of power and the indefinite displacement of its effects.[26]

First, expert psychiatric opinion allows the offense, as defined by the law, to be doubled with a whole series of other things that are not the offense itself but a series of forms of conduct, of ways of being that are, of course, presented in the discourse of the psychiatric expert as the cause, origin, motivation, and starting point of the offense. In fact, in the reality of judicial practice they constitute the substance, the very material to be punished. We know that on the basis of the penal law, that of the Napoleonic Code of 1810—and the principle was already recognized in what are called the intermediate codes of the Revolution[27]—in short, since the end of the eighteenth century, one can be sentenced only for breaches of law that have been defined as such by a law that was in force prior to the action in question. The penal law can be applied retrospectively only in certain exceptional cases. Now how does expert psychiatric opinion proceed with respect to the letter of the law that says: "Only breaches of the law defined as such by the law can be punished"? What type of objects does it bring to light? What type of objects does it present to the judge for his judicial intervention and as the target of punishment? If we go back to the words, what objects does expert psychiatric opinion reveal and attach to the offense as its double? I have taken a short series of expert opinions that all date from the years 1955-1974, but I could cite other texts. The notions found again and again throughout this set of texts are: "psychological immaturity," "a poorly structured personality," "a poor grasp of reality." These are all expressions I have found in the reports of psychiatric experts: "a profound affective imbalance," "serious emotional disturbance." Or again: "compensation," "imaginary production," "display of perverted pride," "perverse game," "Herostratism," "Alcibiadism," "Don Juanism," "*bovarysme*," et cetera. What, then, is the function of this set of notions, or this double series of notions? First of all, its function is to repeat the offense tautologically in order to register it and constitute it as an individual trait. Expert psychiatric opinion allows one to pass from action to conduct, from an offense to a way of being, and to make this way of being appear as nothing other than the offense itself, but in general form, as it were, in the individual's conduct. Second, the function of this series of notions is to shift the level of reality of the offense, since these forms of conduct do not break the law. There is no law against being affectively unbalanced or having emotional disturbances. There is no law against having perverted pride, and there are no legal measures against Herostratism. However, what is it that these forms of conduct infringe on if they do not break the law? These objects emerge against a background in which they are measured against an optimum level of development ("psychological immaturity," "poorly structured personality," "profound imbalance"), a criterion of reality ("poor grasp of reality"), moral qualities (modesty, fidelity), and ethical rules.

In short, expert psychiatric opinion makes it possible to constitute a psychologico-ethical double of the offense. That is to say, it makes it possible to delegalize the offense as formulated by the code, in order to reveal behind it its double, which resembles it like a brother or a sister, I don't know, and which makes it not exactly an offense in the legal sense of the term, but an irregularity in relation to certain rules, which may be physiological, psychological, or moral, et cetera. You will tell me that this is not so serious, and if, when they are asked to assess a delinquent, psychiatrists say, "After all, if he has stolen, it is basically because he is a thief," or, "If he has committed murder, in the end it is because he has a drive to kill." This is no more than the Molière-esque analysis of the daughter's mutism.[28] Except, in fact, it is more serious, and it is serious not just because, as I said a short while ago, it may entail a man's death. What is more serious is that in fact psychiatry does not really set out an explanation of the crime but rather the thing itself to be punished that the judicial system must bite on and get hold of.

You recall what happened in the psychiatric assessment of Algarron. The experts said: As experts we do not have to say whether he committed the crime he is accused of. However, (and this is how the final paragraph I read to you begins) let us assume he did commit it. I, as a psychiatric expert, will explain to you how he would have committed it, if he had done so. The whole analysis of this case (I have now given the name of the accused several times, but it doesn't matter) is really the explanation of how the crime could in fact have been committed. Moreover, the experts bluntly say: "We will start from the hypothesis that, in one way or another, A exerted an influence over the mind of the girl L that led her to murder her child." And at the end they say: "Without taking a position on the reality and degree of A's culpability, we can understand how his influence on the young L could have been pernicious." And you remember the final conclusion: "He must be regarded as responsible." Meanwhile, what has emerged between the hypothesis that he could have had some kind of responsibility and the final conclusion? A certain character has appeared who has been offered up, so to speak, to the judicial system: a man who is incapable of integrating himself in the world, who loves disorder, commits extravagant or extraordinary acts, hates morality, who denies its laws and is capable of resorting to crime. So that, when all is said and done, the person who will be convicted is not the actual accomplice in the murder in question, but this character who cannot integrate himself, loves disorder, and commits acts that go as far as crime. And when I say that it is this character who has actually been convicted, I do not mean that, thanks to the expert, a suspect has been sentenced instead of the guilty person (which is true, of course); I mean something more. What, in a sense, is more serious is that, in the end, even if the subject in question is guilty, what the judge is able to condemn in him on the basis of expert psychiatric opinion is no longer the crime or offense exactly. What the judge will judge and punish, the point on which he will bring to bear the punishment, is precisely these irregular forms of conduct that were put forward as the crime's cause and point of origin and the site at which it took shape, and which were only its psychological and moral double.

Expert psychiatric opinion makes it possible to transfer the point of application of punishment from the offense defined by the law to criminality evaluated from a psychologico-moral point of view. Through this attribution of a causal relationship, whose tautological character is at the same time both obvious and of little importance (unless one attempts to analyze the rational structures of such a text, which would be interesting), we have gone from what could be called the target of punishment, the point of application of a mechanism of power, that is to say, of legal punishment, to a realm of objects of a knowledge, a technique of transformation, a whole set of rational and concerted coercions.* It is true that expert psychiatric opinion contributes nothing to knowledge, but this is not what matters. Its essential role is to legitimize, in the form of scientific knowledge, the extension of punitive power to something that is not a breach of the law. What is essential is that it makes it possible to resituate the punitive action of judicial power within a general corpus of reflected techniques for the transformation of individuals.

The second function of psychiatric expertise—the first being that of twinning the offense with criminality—is to double the author of the offense with this new character of the delinquent, previously unknown to the eighteenth century. In "classical" expert opinion defined in terms of the law of 1810, ultimately the issue was simply this: We will call upon the expert only in order to know whether or not the individual accused was in a state of dementia when he committed the act. If he was in a state of dementia, then he can no longer be regarded as responsible for his actions. This is the meaning of the famous Article 63 [*rectius*: 64], which states that there is neither crime nor offense if the individual is in a state of dementia at the time of the action.[29] What happens in expert opinion as we see it at work today and in the example I have given? Do we really seek to determine whether a state of dementia allows us to consider the author of the action as someone who is no longer a juridical subject responsible for his actions? Not at all. Expert psychiatric opinion does something

---

* The manuscript says: "of a rational and concerted coercion."

quite different. First of all, it tries to establish the antecedents below the threshold, as it were, of the crime.*

I quote you the example of an expert opinion that was given by three major figures of criminal psychiatry around the 1960s and which resulted, moreover, in a man's death, since the object of the expert opinion was sentenced to death and guillotined. This is what we read about this individual:

> Besides the desire to surprise, when R was very young he ex-hibited a taste for domination, commanding and exercising his power (which is another manifestation of pride). From child-hood, he bullied his parents by making scenes at the least op-position and at school he tried to get his friends to play truant. A taste for firearms and cars and a passion for gambling were also evident at a young age. He was already showing off revolvers at school. He was found at Gibert's playing with a gun. Later he collected weapons, loaned them out, dealt in them, and en-joyed that reassuring sensation of power and superiority that carrying firearms gives to the weak. Similarly, motorcycles, then fast cars, of which he seemed to get through a great deal and always drove as fast as possible, helped to satisfy his appetite for domination, albeit imperfectly."[30]

Expert opinion like this recounts a series of what could be called misdeeds that do not break the law, or faults that are not illegal. In other words, the aim is to show how the individual already resembles his crime before he has committed it. The simple repetitive use of the adverb *already* in these analyses is in itself a way of linking together, simply through analogy, a whole series of illegalities below the thresh-old, of improper acts that are not illegal, and of piling them up in order to make them resemble the crime itself. Recounting the series of misdeeds is a way of showing how the individual resembles his

---

* The French has "of the penalty," but the sense of the sentence makes it clear that this should be "of the crime." *Trans.*

crime and at the same time revealing what could be called a para-pathological series that is close to being an illness, but an illness that is not an illness since it is a moral fault. Because in the end this series is proof of a form of conduct, a character, and an attitude that are moral defects while being neither, pathologically, illnesses nor, legally, offenses. The experts have always sought to reconstitute the dynasty of the extended series of ambiguities that lie just below the surface.

Those of you who are familiar with the Rivière dossier[31] know already how, in 1836, the practice of psychiatrists and, at the same time, of depositions called for by the court, was precisely to recon-stitute this absolutely ambiguous series of the infrapathological and the paralegal, or of the parapathological and the infralegal, which is a kind of reconstruction of the crime itself, in a scaled-down version, before it has been committed. This is what expert psychiatric opinion is used for. In this parapathological, sublegal series below the thresh-old, the subject is present in the form of desire. Expert psychiatric opinion shows how the subject is present in the form of criminal desire in all these details and minutiae, in all these vile deeds and things that are not quite regular. In the expert opinion I have just read concerning someone who was ultimately sentenced to death, the expert thus says:

> He wanted to know every pleasure, to enjoy everything in a hurry, to experience strong emotions. This was the aim that he set himself. He says that he refrained from drugs only because he feared addiction, and from homosexuality, not on principle, but due to the absence of desire. R could not tolerate any ob-stacle to his goals and whims. He could not bear opposition to his will. He employed emotional blackmail with his parents, and with strangers and those around him he used threats and vio-lence.

In other words, this analysis of the constant criminal desire makes it possible to fix what could be called the fundamental position of il-legality in the logic or movement of desire. The subject's desire is closely connected with transgression of the law:* His desire is fundamentally bad. But this criminal desire—and this is still regularly found in these experiences [*rectius*: expert opinions]—is always the correlate of a flaw, a breakdown, a weakness or incapacity of the subject. This accounts for the regular appearance of notions such as "lack of intelligence," "failure," "inferiority," "poverty," "ugliness," "immaturity," "defective development," "infantilism," "behavioral archaism," and "instability." In fact, this infracriminal, parapathological series, in which both the illegality of desire and the deficiency of the subject are set out, is in no way intended to answer the question of responsibility; rather, it is designed not to answer it, to avoid psychiatric discourse having to pose the question that is nevertheless implicitly defined by Article 64. That is to say, by situating the crime in this infracriminal and parapathological series, by means of this correlation, a kind of region of juridical indiscernibility is established around the author of the offense. With his irregularities, his lack of intelligence, his failures, and his unflagging and infinite desires, a series of elements are constituted concerning which the question of responsibility can no longer be posed, or simply cannot arise, since ultimately, according to these descriptions, the subject is responsible for everything and nothing. He is a juridically indiscernible personality over whom, in the terms of its own laws and texts, justice has no jurisdiction. Magistrates and jurors no longer face a legal subject, but an object: the object of a technology and knowledge of rectification, readaptation, reinsertion, and correction. In short, the function of expert opinion is to double the author of the crime, whether responsible or not, with a delinquent who is the object of a specific technology.

Finally, expert psychiatric opinion has, I think, a third role, in addition to that of doubling the offense with criminality after having doubled the author of the offense with the delinquent subject. Its function is to constitute, to call up, another doubling, or rather, a

---

* The manuscript says: "The logic of desire is fundamentally connected to transgression of the law."

group of further doublings. There is the constitution of a doctor who is at the same time a doctor-judge. That is to say—when the function of the doctor or psychiatrist becomes that of saying whether the subject analyzed has traits or forms of conduct that, in terms of criminality, make it probable that there will be a breach of the law in the strict sense—the value of psychiatric expertise is often, if not always, that of demonstrating potential criminality, or rather, the potential for the offense the individual is accused of. The purpose of describing his delinquent character, the basis of his criminal or paracriminal conduct since childhood, is clearly to facilitate transition from being accused to being convicted.

I will give you just one example of this concerning a fairly recent story that caused quite a stir. It involved finding out who had killed a young girl whose body was found in a field. There were two suspects. One of the suspects was a town notable and the other was an adolescent, eighteen or twenty years old. This is how the psychiatric experts described the mental condition of the notable (he was assessed by two psychiatric experts). Not having read the expert opinion, I give the summary as presented in the prosecutor's speech before the criminal court of appeals:

> The psychiatrists did not find any memory disorder. They examined confidential material on symptoms suffered by the subject in 1970. These were due to professional and financial difficulties. He claimed to have obtained his high school diploma when he was sixteen years old and to have graduated when he was twenty, to have earned two diplomas of higher education and to have completed twenty-seven months of military service in North Africa as sublieutenant. Then he took over his father's business and worked hard, his entertainment being confined to tennis, hunting, and sailing.

Now let us look at the description, by two different experts, of the young man who was also accused in this case. The psychiatrists notice "few subtleties of character," "psychological immaturity," "a poorly structured personality" (you see these are always exactly the same categories), "judgment lacking rigor," "a poor appreciation of reality," "profoundly unbalanced emotionally," and "very serious emotional disturbances." Moreover: "After alluding to his passion for reading comic strips and the books of *Satanik*, the experts took into account the onset of sexual drives normal for a youth of his physical stature [eighteen to twenty years old; M.F.]. They ended with the hypothesis that, confronted . . . with the passion aroused by the young girl, he felt a violent repugnance, judging it to be satanic." Whence the explanation of an action provoked by the profound repugnance he would have experienced.

These two assessments were submitted to the court of appeals in order to determine which of the two was guilty. Do not tell me now that it is the judges who judge and that psychiatrists only analyze the mentality, the personality, psychotic or otherwise, of the subjects in question. The psychiatrist really becomes a judge; he really undertakes an investigation, and not at the level of an individual's legal responsibility, but of his or her real guilt. Conversely, faced with the doctor, the judge will also divide into two. For when he comes to pronounce his judgment, that is to say, his decision on the punishment of someone who is not the juridical subject of an offense defined by the law but an individual who has these defined character traits, when the judge has to deal with this ethico-moral double of the juridical subject, it is not the offense he punishes. He can allow himself the luxury, the grace, or the excuse, as you like, of imposing a set of measures of correction, reform, and reinsertion on the individual. The sordid business of punishing is thus converted into the fine profession of curing. As well as serving other ends, expert psychiatric opinion serves to effect this conversion.

Before ending I would like to emphasize at least two things. Perhaps you will say to me: This is all very well, but you describe, somewhat aggressively, a medico-legal practice that is, after all, recent. Psychiatry is surely only in its infancy, and painfully and slowly it is in the process of leaving behind these confused practices, some traces of which can still be found in the grotesque texts you have maliciously selected. Now I say to you that in fact things are quite the opposite, and that if we go back to its historical origins, that is to say, to simplify things, to the first years of the application of the penal code (1810-1830), we find that expert psychiatric opinion in penal cases was a medical act absolutely isomorphous with the medical knowledge of the period in its formulations, its rules of constitution, and its general principles of formation. Today, however (and we should at least pay this tribute to doctors and some psychiatrists), I know of no doctor and few psychiatrists who would risk signing their name to texts like those I have just read. Now you can see why there is a problem if they refuse to sign them in their normal practice as doctors, or even as psychiatrists, while agreeing to write such texts and sign their names to them in judicial practice where, in the end, it is a question of a man's freedom or his life. This kind of disconnection, or involution, at the level of the scientific and rational normative structure of discourses, really poses a problem. From a situation at the beginning of the nineteenth century in which medico-legal expertise was placed on the same level as all medical knowledge of the period, there has been a movement of disconnection, a movement by which penal psychiatry has abandoned this normative structure and accepted, welcomed, and submitted itself to new rules of formation.

It is not enough to say that it is the psychiatrists or experts who are no doubt purely and simply responsible for the fact that things have evolved in this way.[32] In fact, the law itself, or decrees affecting the application of the law, clearly show where it is going and how it got where it is. At first, expert medico-legal opinion is more or less governed by the old formula of Article 64 of the penal code: there is no crime or offense if the individual was in a state of dementia at the time of his action. In practice, this rule dominated and informed expert criminal opinion throughout the nineteenth century. At the start of the twentieth century there is a circular, the Chaumié circular of 1903 [rectius: 1905], in which the role conferred on psychiatry is already considerably distorted, considerably inflected, since the circular says that the role of psychiatry is obviously not to define the legal responsibility of a criminal subject—because this is too difficult, it cannot be done—but is to establish whether he has mental abnormalities that can be connected to the offense in question. You can see that already we are entering a completely different realm that is no longer that of the legal subject responsible for his actions and who is medically judged to be responsible, but rather a realm of mental abnormality that has an imprecise relationship to the offense. And finally, in another circular from the postwar period, from the fifties (I no longer remember the exact date, I think it is 1958 but I would not swear to it; I apologize if I am mistaken), psychiatrists are asked to answer, if they can of course, the same old famous question of Article 64: Was he in a state of dementia? But above all they are asked—first question—whether the individual is dangerous. Second question: Is he accessible to penal sanction? Third question: Can he be cured or reformed? You see, then, that at the level of the law, not simply at the mental level of psychiatrists' knowledge but at the level of the law itself, there is an evolution that is perfectly clear. We have shifted from the juridical problem of the attribution of responsibility to a completely different problem. Is the individual dangerous? Is he accessible to penal sanction? Can he be cured or reformed? This is to say, henceforth, penal sanction will not be brought to bear on a legal subject who is recognized as being responsible but on an element that is the correlate of a technique that consists in singling out dangerous individuals and of taking responsibility for those who are accessible to penal sanction in order to cure them or reform them. In other words, from now on, a technique of normalization will take responsibility for the delinquent individual. Along with other processes, expert psychiatric opinion brought about this transformation in which the legally responsible individual is replaced by an element that is the correlate of a technique of normalization.[33]

I would like to try to study this appearance, this emergence of techniques of normalization and the powers linked to them by taking as a principle, as an initial hypothesis (but I will return to this at greater length next time), that these techniques of normalization, and the powers of normalization linked to them, are not simply the effect of the combination of medical knowledge and judicial power, of their composition or the plugging of each into the other, but that a certain type of power—distinct from both medical and judicial power—has in fact colonized and forced back both medical knowledge and judicial power throughout modern society. It is a type of power that finally ends up in the courtroom, by finding support, of course, in judicial and medical institutions, but which, in itself, has its own rules and autonomy. What I would like to study* is the emergence of the power of normalization, the way in which it has been formed, the way in which it has established itself without ever resting on a single institution but by establishing interactions between different institutions, and the way in which it has extended its sovereignty in our society. So, we will begin next week.

---

* The manuscript says: "do the archaeology of."

1. Cf. *L'Affaire Denise Labbé–[Jacques] Algarron*, Paris, 1956 (Bibiliothèque nationale de France, *Factums*, 16Fm 1449). From 1971 on, Michel Foucault's seminar was devoted to the study of expert psychiatric opinion; cf. Michel Foucault, "Entretien sur la prison: le livre et sa méthode," in *Dits et écrits, 1954-1988*, edition established under the direction of D. Defert and F. Ewald in collaboration with J. Lagrange (Paris: Gallimard, 1994), vol 2: *1970-1975*, p. 846. English translation: "Prison Talk," in Michel Foucault, *Power/Knowledge: Selected Interviews and Other Writings, 1972-1977*, edited by Colin Gordon, translated by Colin Gordon et al. (New York: Pantheon Books, 1980).

2. The term *existentialism* is used here in its most commonplace sense: "The name given, especially just after the Second World War, to young people who put on a show of an untidy style of dress and a distaste for an active life and who frequented certain Parisian cafés around Saint-Germain-des-Prés," *Grand Larousse de la langue française*, vol. 3 (Paris: Larousse, 1973), p. 1820.

3. According to *Le Grand Robert de la langue française: Dictionnaire alphabétique et analogique*, 2d edition, vol. 1 (Paris: Dictionnaires Le Robert, 1985), the name *Alcibiades* was often used as a synonym for "someone whose character combines great qualities and many defects (pretentiousness, pushiness)." Dictionaries of psychiatry do not record the term.

4. Cf. A. Porot, *Manuel alphabétique de psychiatrie clinique, thérapeutique et médico-légale* (Paris: s.l., 1952), p. 149: "In reference to the example of Herostratus setting fire to the Temple of Diana at Ephesus, [P.] Valette [*De l'érostratisme ou vanité criminelle* (Lyon, 1903)] created the term *Herostratism* to designate the association of maliciousness with amorality and vanity in the feebleminded and to characterize the kind of offenses resulting from these mental dispositions" (C. Bardenat's definition).

5. Cf. A. Porot, *op. cit.*, p. 54: "An expression taken from Flaubert's famous novel, *Madame Bovary*, which gave some philosophers the idea of turning it into a psychological entity," whereas Jules de Gaultier defined *bovarysme* as "man's ability to think himself other than he is."

6. Foucault here unintentionally utters the name of the individual assessed by the expert psychiatric witnesses.

7. According to *Le Grand Robert de la langue française: Dictionnaire alphabétique et analogique*, 2d edition, vol. 3 (Paris: Dictionnaires Le Robert, 1985), in psychiatry, *Don Juanism* means "the pathological search for new conquests" by a man, but the dictionaries of psychiatry do not record the term.

8. Reference to act 3, scene 2, of Molière's *Don Juan* in *Dom Juan ou le Festin de pierre*, in *Oeuvres*, vol. 5 (Paris: published by E. Despois and P. Mesnard, 1880), pp. 114-20. English translation: Molière, *Don Juan and Other Plays*, edited with an introduction and notes by Ian Maclean, translated by George Gravely and Ian Maclean (Oxford/New York: Oxford University Press, 1989), pp. 63-64.

9. What follows is taken from the conclusions of the medico-psychological examination of three homosexuals held at Fleury-Mérogis in 1973 for robbery and blackmail. Cf. "Expertise psychiatrique et justice," *Actes: Les cahiers d'action juridique* 5/6, December 1974-January 1975, pp. 38-39.

10. Foucault draws attention here to the assonance between *maïotique* (a nonexistent word) and *maïeutique* (maieutic), that is to say the Socratic or, more generally, heuristic method for discovering the truth.

11. Foucault alludes to the frequent laughter accompanying his reading of the expert psychiatric opinions.

12. See the course at the Collège de France for 1971-1972, Penal Theories and Institutions; course summary in *Dits et écrits, 1954-1988*, vol. 2: *1970-1975*, pp. 389-93. English translation: *Ethics, Subjectivity, and Truth: The Essential Works of Foucault 1954-1984*, vol. 1, edited by Paul Rabinow, translated by Robert Hurley et al. (New York: New Press, 1997), pp. 17-21.

13. Cf. D. Jousse, *Traité de la justice criminelle en France*, vol. 1 (Paris, 1771), pp. 654-837; F. Hélie, *Histoire et théorie de la procédure criminelle*, vol. 4 (Paris, 1866), pp. 334-341, nn. 1766-1769.

14. Foucault refers to the situation caused by the *ordonnances* of Louis XIV. The *ordonnance* on criminal procedure, in twenty-eight articles dating from 1670, is a code of criminal investigation (*code d'instruction criminelle*), since it was promulgated in the absence of a penal code. Cf. F. Serpillon, *Code criminelle ou Commentaire sur l'ordonnance de 1670* (Lyon, 1767); F. Hélie, *Traité de l'instruction criminelle ou Théorie du code d'instruction criminelle* (Paris, 1866).

15. Cf. C. Beccaria, *Dei delitti e delle pene* (Livorno, 1764) (French translation: *Traité des délits et des peines* [Lausanne, 1766]), and Voltaire, *Commentaire sur le Traité des délits et des peines* [Paris, 1766]; English translation: C. Beccaria Bonasena, *An Essay on Crimes and Punishments*, translated from the Italian with a commentary attributed to Monsieur de Voltaire translated from the French, 2d edition [London: 1769]); J. M. A. Servan, *Discours sur l'administration de la justice criminelle* (Geneva, 1767); C. M. J. B. Mercier Dupaty, *Lettres sur la procédure criminelle de la France, dans lesquelles on montre sa conformité avec celle de l'Inquisition et les abus qui en résultent*, s.l., 1788.

16. Cf. A. Rached, *De l'intime conviction du juge: Vers une théorie scientifique de la preuve en matière criminelle* (Paris: s.l., 1942).

17. Cf. F. Hélie, *Traité de l'instruction criminelle*, op. cit., vol. 4, p. 340 (the principle formulated 29 September 1791 and institutionalized 3 Brumaire, Year 4 [1975]).

18. Pierre Goldman appeared before the Paris court on 11 December 1974, charged with murder and theft. He was sentenced to life imprisonment. The support of a committee of intellectuals, who had denounced several irregularities in the investigation and procedural defects, led to a review of the trial. In the appeal judgment Goldman was sentenced to twelve years in prison for the three assaults he admitted. Cf. *Souvenirs obscurs d'un juif polonais né en France* (Paris: s.l., 1975) for an extract from the indictment. Pierre Goldman was murdered on 20 September 1979.

19. Cf. M. Foucault, "La vérité et les formes juridiques," 1974, in *Dits et écrits, 1954-1988*, vol. 2: *1970-1975*, pp. 538-623. English translation: "Truth and Judicial Forms" in *The Essential Works of Foucault 1954-1984*, vol. 3: *Power*, edited by James D. Faubion, translated by Robert Hurley, et al. (New York: The New Press, 2000).

20. The adjective *Ubuesque* was introduced in 1922 and derives from the play by Alfred Jarry, *Ubu roi*, Paris, 1896. English translation by Barbara Wright (London: Eyre Methuen, 1966). See the *Grand Larousse*, vol. 7 (Paris: Larousse, 1978): "The word describes someone who, by his grotesque, absurd, or ludicrous nature, recalls the figure of Ubu"; *Le Grand Robert*, 2d edition, vol. 9 (Paris: Dictionnaires Le Robert, 1985): "Someone resembling the figure of King Ubu (in his comically and extravagantly cruel, cynical, or cowardly character)."

21. Allusion to the development of literature inspired by the opposition of the senatorial aristocracy to the strengthening of imperial power. It is illustrated most notably by the *De vita Caesarum* (The Lives of the Ceasars) by Suetonius in which virtuous emperors (*principes*) are contrasted with the vicious emperors (*monstra*) represented by Nero, Caligula, Vitellius, and Heliogabalus.

22. Cf. P. Clastres, *La Société contre l'État: Recherches d'anthropologie politique* (Paris: Éditions de Minuit, 1974). English translation: P. Clastres, *Society Against the State: Essays in Political Anthropology*, translated by Robert Hurley with Abe Stein (New York: Zone Books, 1989).

23. Concerning the Shakespearean tragedies that raise the question of the transition from illegitimacy to law, see Michel Foucault, *"Il faut défendre la société": Cours au Collège de France, 1975-1976* (Paris: Éditons de Seuil/Gallimard 1997), pp. 155-56. English translation: *"Society Must Be Defended": Lectures at the Collège de France, 1975-1976* (New York: Picador, 2003).

24. See Joachim C. Fest, *Hitler*, vol. 2: *Le Führer, 1933-1945*, (Paris: s.l., 1973), pp. 387-453.

The original edition was published in Frankfurt-am-Main, Berlin, and Vienna by s.1., in 1973. English translation: *Hitler* (New York: Harcourt Brace, 1992).

25. Allusion to "Du sujet supposé savoir," in J. Lacan, *Le Séminaire*, Book 11: *Les Quatre Concepts fondamentaux de la psychanalyse* (Paris: s.1., 1973), chapter 18. English translation: "Of the Subject Who Is Supposed to Know," in J. Lacan, *The Four Fundamental Concepts of Psycho-analysis*, edited by J.-A. Miller, translated by A. Sheridan (New York: W. W. Norton, 1981).

26. Some of the ideas developed here were also expressed during a "Table ronde sur l'expertise psychiatrique" (1974), reprinted in *Dits et écrits, 1954-1988*, vol. 2: *1970-1975*, pp. 664-75.

27. Concerning the intermediate codes of the Revolution (the penal code passed by the Constituent Assembly in 1791, but also the *Code d'instruction criminelle* promulgated in 1808), see G. Lepointe, *Petit Précis des sources de l'histoire du droit français* (Paris: s.1., 1937, pp. 227-40.

28. Molière, in "Le Médecin malgré lui," Act 2, scene 4: "Une certaine malignité, qui est causée ... par l'âcreté des humeurs engendrées dans la concavité du diaphragme, il arrive que ces vapeurs ... *ossabardus, nequeys, nequer, potarinum, quipsa milus*, voilà justement ce qui fait que votre fille est muette." ("A certain malignancy, caused by the acridity of the humors engendered in the concavity of the diaphragm, these vapors ... *ossabardus, nequeys, nequer, potarinum, quipsa milus*, are precisely why your daughter is mute"), in *Oeuvres*, vol. 6 (Paris: E. Despois and P. Mesnard, 1881), pp. 87-88. English translation: Molière, *The Doctor in Spite of Himself and The Bourgeois Gentlemen*, translated by Albert Bernel (New York: Applause Books, 1987), p. 26.

29. Article 64 of the penal code says: "There is neither crime nor offense when the defendant was in a state of dementia at the time of the action, or when he was constrained by a force that he could not resist." Cf. E. Garçon, *Code pénal annoté*, vol. 1 (Paris: s.1., 1952), pp. 207-26; R. Merle and A. Vitu, *Traité de droit criminel*, 6th edition, vol. 1. (Paris: s.1., 1984), pp. 759-66 (the first edition was published in 1967).

30. This is the case of Georges Rapin. Cf. *infra*, the lecture of 5 February.

31. *Moi, Pierre Rivière, ayant égorgé ma mère, ma soeur et mon frère ... Un cas de parricide de XIX siècle*, presented by Michel Foucault (Paris: s.1., 1973). Michel Foucault, ed., *I, Pierre Rivière, Having Slaughtered My Mother, My Sister, and My Brother ... : A Case of Parricide in the Nineteenth Century* (New York: s.1., 1975). The complete dossier, discovered by Jean-Pierre Peter, was studied in the Monday seminar of the academic year 1971-1972, which focused upon "the study of medico-legal practices and concepts." See the report at the end of the course summary cited above: *Dits et écrits, 1954-1988*, vol. 2: *1970-1975*, p. 392. English translation: "Penal Theories and Institutions," in *Ethics, Subjectivity, and Truth: The Essential Works of Foucault, 1954-1984*, vol 1, pp. 20-21.

32. Foucault will again take up this theme in "L'Évolution de la notion d' 'individu dangereux' dans la psychiatrie légale du XIXᵉ siècle" (1978), in *Dits et écrits, 1974-1988*, vol. 3: *1976-1979*, pp. 443-64. English translation: "About the Concept of the 'Dangerous Individual' in Nineteenth-Century Legal Psychiatry," in *The Essential Works of Foucault 1954-1984*, vol. 3: *Power*, pp. 176-200.

33. The circular of the Minister of Justice, Joseph Chaumié, was promulgated on 12 December 1905. The new code of criminal procedure came into force in 1958 (the reference is to article 345 of the *Code d'instruction général d'application*). The schema used by Foucault can be found in A. Porot, *Manuel alphabétique de psychiatrie*, op. cit., pp. 161-63.

two

15 JANUARY 1975

Madness and crime. ~ Perversity and puerility. ~ The dangerous individual. ~ The psychiatric expert can only have the character of Ubu. ~ The epistemological level of psychiatry and its regression in expert medico-legal opinion. ~ End of the antagonistic relationship between medical power and judicial power. ~ Expert opinion and abnormal individuals (les anormaux). ~ Criticism of the notion of repression. ~ Exclusion of lepers and inclusion of plague victims. ~ Invention of positive technologies of power. ~ The normal and the pathological.

AT THE END OF last week's lecture someone asked me if really I was not mistaken and had given a lecture on expert medico-legal opinion rather than the promised lecture on abnormal individuals. These are not at all the same things, but you will see that starting from the problem of expert medico-legal opinion I will come to the problem of abnormal individuals.

What I tried to show was that in terms of the famous Article 64 of the 1810 penal code, in which there is no crime or offense if the individual is in a state of dementia when the crime is committed, expert opinion must make it possible, or at least *should* make it possible, to distinguish clearly between the dichotomies of illness and responsibility, between pathological causality and the freedom of the legal subject, between therapy and punishment, medicine and penalty, hospital and prison. One must choose, because madness wipes out the crime. Madness cannot be crime, just as crime cannot be, in itself, an act rooted in madness. It is the principle of the revolving door: In terms of the law, when pathology comes in, criminality must go out. In the event of madness, the medical institution must take over from the judicial institution. Justice cannot take possession of the mad, or rather, when it recognizes someone as mad, justice must relinquish jurisdiction and release him or her.

For this division and for the principle of this division, clearly set down in the texts, modern expert opinion has in fact substituted other mechanisms that are gradually combined throughout the nineteenth century and which arise relatively early from what I would say was a kind of general complicity. For example, in the years 1815-1820, we see assize court juries finding people guilty and then, despite their guilt stated in the verdict, asking that they be placed in a psychiatric hospital because they are ill. Juries thus began to tighten the relationship, the affiliation, the kinship of madness and crime. However, to a certain extent the judges themselves, the magistrates, accept this coupling, since they sometimes say that an individual may just as well be placed in a psychiatric hospital, despite having committed a crime, because he is, after all, no more likely to leave a hospital than he is a prison. When extenuating circumstances were introduced in 1832 it became possible to pass sentences that were not modulated according to the circumstances of the crime, but according to the description, assessment, and diagnosis of the criminal himself. Thus there is the gradual elaboration of that kind of medico-judicial continuum whose effects and principal form of institutionalization are seen in expert medico-legal opinion.

Broadly speaking, we can say that modern expert opinion has replaced the mutual exclusion of medical and judicial discourses by a game that could be called the game of dual, medical and judicial, qualification. This practice, this technique of dual qualification, organizes the realm of that very strange notion, "perversity," that begins to emerge in the second half of the nineteenth century and that will dominate the entire field of this double determination and authorize the appearance of a range of manifestly obsolete, laughable, and puerile terms or elements in the discourse of experts who are justified as scientists. When you go through these expert medico-legal opinions, such as those I read to you last week, you are struck by terms like *laziness, pride, stubbornness,* and *nastiness.* You are given biographical elements that do not in any way explain the action in question but are kinds of miniature warning signs, little scenes of childhood, little childish scenes that are presented as already analogous to the crime. It is a kind of scaled-down criminality for children characterized by the language used by parents or by the morality of children's books. In fact, the puerility of the terms, notions, and analysis at the heart of modern expert medico-legal opinion has a very precise function: it makes possible an exchange between juridical categories defined by the penal code, which stipulates that one can only punish when there is malice or a real intention to harm, and medical notions like "immaturity," "weak ego," "undeveloped superego," "character structure," and so on. You can see how notions like those of perversity make it possible to stitch together the series of categories defining malice and intentional harm and categories constituted within a more or less medical, or at any rate, psychiatric, psychopathological, or psychological discourse. The whole field of notions of perversity, converted into their puerile vocabulary, enables medical notions to function in the field of judicial power and, conversely, juridical notions to function in medicine's sphere of competence. This set of notions functions, then, as a switch point (*échangeur*), and the weaker it is epistemologically, the better it functions.

Another operation performed by expert opinion is the replacement of the institutional alternative "either prison or hospital," "either atonement or cure," by the principle of homogeneity of social response. It makes it possible to put in place or, in any case, to justify the existence of a sort of protective continuum throughout the social body ranging from the medical level of treatment to the penal institution strictly speaking, that is to say, the prison and, if it comes to it, the scaffold. After all, beneath all these modern discourses on the penal system that have been put together since the nineteenth century, you know there is the endlessly reiterated phrase "You will end up on the scaffold." But if the phrase "You will end up on the scaffold" is a real possibility (so that more or less all of us have heard it, from the first time we failed to get a good report), and if it has a historical basis, it is because the continuum, ranging from the first correctional hold over an individual to the ultimate sanction of death, was effectively constituted by a vast practice, by an immense institutionalization of the repressive and the punitive that is discursively sustained by criminal psychiatry and by the practice of expert psychiatric opinion in particular. In short, society responds to pathological criminality in two ways or offers a homogeneous response with two poles: one expiatory and the other therapeutic. These are the two poles of a continuous network of institutions. But in the end, what are these two poles a response to? To be sure, they are not a response to illness, for if it were only a question of illness we would have specifically therapeutic institutions. But nor are they a response to crime exactly, since for this punitive institutions would suffice. This continuum with its therapeutic and judicial poles, this institutional mixture, is actually a response to danger.

This institutional system is aimed at the dangerous individual, that is to say, at the individual who is not exactly ill and who is not strictly speaking criminal. In expert psychiatric opinion (and the 1958 circular eventually states it quite explicitly, I believe) the individual whom the expert has to diagnose and with whom he has to struggle, in his questioning, analysis, and diagnosis, is the potentially dangerous individual. So that in the end we have two notions that can immediately be seen to be both close to and distant from each other: on the one hand, there is the notion of "perversion" that will enable the series of medical concepts and the series of juridical concepts to be stitched together and, on the other, there is the notion of "danger," of the "dangerous individual," which will make possible the justification and theoretical foundation of an uninterrupted chain of medico-judicial institutions. Danger and perversion constitute, I think, the essential theoretical core of expert medico-legal opinion.

But if this is indeed the theoretical core of expert medico-legal opinion, then I think a number of things become comprehensible. The first, of course, is this truly grotesque and Ubu-esque characteristic that I tried to bring out last week through the expert opinions I read to you, all of which, I repeat, come from the biggest names in legal psychiatry. Since I am not now quoting from these expert opinions I can give you the names of their authors (you will not be able to connect the authors' names to the expert opinions). They are Cénac, Gouriou, Heuyer, and Jénil-Perrin.[1] The theoretical core constituted by the coupling of perversion and danger enables us to explain the existence and support of this truly grotesque, Ubu-esque character of penal discourse. You can see in fact that the joining of the medical and the judicial secured by expert medico-legal opinion, this function of the medical and the judicial, is brought about only by means of the reactivation of what I would call elementary categories of morality that are attached to the notion of perversity; those, for example, of "pride," "stubbornness," "nastiness," and so on. That is to say, joining together the medical and the judicial implies, and can only be brought about by, the reactivation of an essentially parental-puerile, parental-childish discourse that is the discourse of parent to child, of the child's moralization. It is a childish discourse, or rather, a discourse basically addressed to children that is necessarily in the form of the ABC. And, from a different angle, it is a discourse not only organized around the field of perversity, but also around the problem of social danger. That is to say, it will also be a discourse of fear whose function is to detect danger and to counter it. It is, then, a discourse of fear and of moralization, a childish discourse, a discourse whose epistemological organization, completely governed by fear and moralization, can only be derisory, even regarding madness.

The Ubu-esque character of penal discourse is not just something bound up with the kind of person who utters it, or with an undeveloped feature of expert opinion and the knowledge associated with it. It is positively connected to the role of penal expert opinion as a "switch point." It is directly linked to the functions of this expert opinion. Returning to Ubu for the last time (we will leave him here): If we accept that Ubu is the exercise of power through the explicit disqualification of the person who wields it, that the political grotesque is the nullification of the person holding power by the very ritual that displays this power and the person wielding it—as I tried to show last week—then we can see how the psychiatric expert can only be Ubu himself. He can exercise the terrible power he is asked to take on—which in the end is to determine, or to play a large part in determining, an individual's punishment—only through a childish discourse that disqualifies him as scientist at the very moment he is appealed to as a scientist, and through a discourse of fear, which makes him ridiculous as soon as he speaks in court about someone accused of a crime who is in the dock and consequently deprived of any power. The scientist, who is sheltered, protected, and even regarded as sacred by the entire institution and sword of justice, speaks the language of children and the language of fear. The infantile language of expert opinion functions precisely to bring about the exchange of effects of power between judicial and medical institutions through the disqualification of the figure in whom these institutions are joined together. In other words, expert opinion is the countess of Ségur sheltering between Esquirol on one side and Fouquier-Tinville on the other.[2] In any case, you can see why, from Pierre Rivière to Rapin,[3] or in the expert opinions I cited the other day, we always encounter the same type of discourse. What do these expert opinions reveal? The illness? Not at all. Responsibility? Not at all. Freedom? Not at all. There are always the same images, the same actions, the same attitudes, the same puerile scenes: "He played with wooden weapons." "He cut the heads off cabbages." "He was a trial to his parents." "He played truant from school." "He didn't learn his lessons." "He was lazy." And then: "I conclude from this that he was responsible." At the heart of a mechanism in which judicial power solemnly clears a space for medical knowledge, it is Ubu who appears and who, while both alarmed and ignorant, now enables this double mechanism to function. Buffoonery and the function of expert are one and the same: it is as a functionary that the expert is really a clown.

On the basis of this I think we may be able to reconstruct two correlative historical processes. In the first place, there is the very odd historical regression that we see taking place from the nineteenth century to the present. Initially, expert psychiatric opinion—the expert opinion of Esquirol, Georget, and Marc—was simply the transposition into the judicial institution of a medical knowledge constituted elsewhere; in the hospital, in clinical experience.[4] What we see now, however, is an expert opinion that is, as I said last week, absolutely detached from the psychiatric knowledge of our time. Because, whatever one may think of present-day psychiatric discourse, what expert psychiatric opinion says is, of course, a long way below the epistemological level of psychiatry. But what is it that reappears in this sort of regression, disqualification, or decomposition of psychiatric knowledge in expert opinion? It is easy to identify what reappears. It is something like the following, a text from the eighteenth century. It is a *placet*, a mother's request that her son be admitted to Bicêtre in 1758 [*rectius:* 1728]. I take this from the work being undertaken by Christiane Martin on *lettres de cachet*. You will recognize exactly the same type of discourse as that currently used by psychiatrists.

The supplicant [the woman requesting the *lettre de cachet* for her son's confinement; M.F.] remarried after three months of widowhood in order to save a little by working as a haberdasher. She thought to do well by taking her son back into her home.... The libertine promised to please her in order to get a certificate as an apprentice haberdasher. The supplicant dearly loved her child in spite of all the distress he had [already] caused her. She made him an apprentice and kept him at home. Unfortunately for her and her [other] children, he stayed for two years, during which time he regularly stole from her and would have ruined her if he had remained any longer. The supplicant thought he would be better behaved with others since he was acquainted with trade and able to work, so she placed him with M. Cochin, a man of integrity with a haberdashery at the Saint-Jacques gate. For three months the libertine hid his character and then stole six hundred *livres* that the supplicant had to repay in order to save her son's life and the honor of her family....

This rogue, not knowing how to ensnare his mother, pretended to want to become a member of a religious order, and to this end he deceived various honest people who, accepting in good faith what the scoundrel said to them, showered his mother with good reasons for going along with his wish and told her that she would have to answer to God for what happened to her son if she opposed his vocation.... The supplicant, while acquainted with her son's bad conduct for several years, nonetheless fell into the trap and generously [*rectius:* generally] gave him everything he needed to enter the Yverneaux monastery.... The wretch remained there only three months, saying that he did not like this order and would prefer to be a Premonstratensian.[5] Wanting to be above reproach, the supplicant gave her son everything he demanded so that he could enter the house of the Premonsratensians. There he donned the habit, but this wretch, who in fact sought only to deceive his mother, soon revealed his treachery and the Premonstratensians were obliged to expel him after six months as a novice.

Finally, it continues and ends in this way: "The supplicant [that is to say, the mother; M.F.] appeals to your kindness, my lord, and very humbly begs you [she is addressing the police lieutenant; M.F.] to give her a *lettre de cachet* for the confinement of her son and to deport him to the Islands at the first opportunity, failing which she and her husband will never be at peace, nor their life secure."[6]

Perversity and danger. You can see how today we find again, at the same level, reactivated in a modern institution and knowledge, a vast practice that judicial reform at the end of the eighteenth century was supposed to have got rid of. This is not just the result of a kind of archaism. Rather, as crime becomes increasingly pathologized and the expert and judge swap roles, this form of control, assessment, and effect of power linked to the characterization of an individual becomes increasingly active.

Besides this regression and reactivation of what is now a centuries-old practice, the other historical process that deals with it, as it were, is an indefinite demand for power in the name of the modernization of justice. That is to say, since the beginning of the nineteenth century we have seen doctors constantly and ever more insistently laying claim to judicial power, and judges laying claim to medical power. Right at the start of the nineteenth century the problem of the doctor's power in the judicial apparatus was essentially a problem of antagonism, in the sense that doctors, for reasons it would take too long to explain now, demanded the right to exercise their knowledge within the judicial institution. The judicial system was fundamentally opposed to this as an invasion, a confiscation, and a disqualification of its own competence. However, from the end of the nineteenth century, and this is important, we see instead judges gradually beginning to share the demand for the medicalization of their profession, function, and decisions. Then there is the coupled demand for the judicial institutionalization, as it were, of medical knowledge: "As a doctor, I am judicially competent," doctors repeat from [the beginning of] the nineteenth century. However, in the second half of the nineteenth century you hear judges saying for the first time: "We demand a therapeutic function just as much as a function of judgment and atonement." At the second international congress of criminology that took place in 1892, I think (I don't know, let's say around 1890, the date escapes me for the moment), we hear quite serious proposals for the suppression of the jury.[7] The jury, it is argued, [is made up of] people who are neither doctors nor judges and who consequently are competent neither in law nor in medicine. A jury of this kind can only be an obstacle, an opaque element, a resistant block within the judicial institution as it ought to be ideally. How would the true judicial institution be composed? It would be made up of a jury of experts under the juridical responsibility of a magistrate. That is to say, all the public judicial bodies set up by the penal reforms of the end of the eighteenth century are to be bypassed so that doctors and magistrates can finally join together, but in a union without outsiders. Of course, at this time the demand was only indicative of a movement, and it immediately aroused considerable opposition from doctors and especially from magistrates. Nonetheless, it remains the case that it served as the focal point for a series of reforms that were established in their essentials at the end of the nineteenth century and during the twentieth century and which effectively organize a sort of medico-judicial power whose principal elements or manifestations are the following.

First, there is the requirement that every individual who comes before the assize courts has to have been examined by a psychiatric expert. As a result, the individual never appears in court with just his crime. He arrives with the psychiatric expert's report and comes before the court burdened with both his crime and this report. There is a question concerning whether this measure, which is universal and obligatory for the assize courts, should also become the general rule in the criminal courts, where it is only applied in some cases, but not yet universally.

The second sign of the implementation of a medico-judicial power is the existence of special courts for children in which the information given to the judge, who both investigates and judges, is essentially psychological, social, and medical. This information consequently bears much more on the context of the individual's existence, life, and discipline than on the act for which he has been brought before the children's court. The child is brought before a court of perversity and danger rather than before a criminal court.

Equally, within the prison administration, medico-psychological services are established that are required to report on the individual's development while serving his sentence, that is to say, on the level of perversity and level of danger he still represents at a given moment during his sentence, it being understood that if he has reached a sufficiently low level of danger and perversity he could be freed, at least conditionally.

A series of institutions of medico-legal surveillance surrounding childhood, youth, young people in danger, and so on could also be mentioned.

All in all, then, we have a partly dual, medical and judicial, system, set up since the nineteenth century, in which expert opinion, with its very strange discourse, constitutes the central mechanism, the infinitely feeble and infinitely solid little peg holding it together.

And now I come to the subject of this year's course. It seems to me that the expert medico-legal opinion we see at work today is a particularly striking example of the irruption, or more probably, the insidious invasion within judicial and medical institutions, exactly at the frontier between them, of a mechanism that is precisely neither medical nor judicial. If I have spoken at such length about expert medico-legal opinion, it was to show that it performed the function of stitching together the judicial and the medical, that it constituted their seam. However, I have constantly tried to show that it was as foreign to the judicial institution as to the internal norms of medical knowledge; not only foreign, but also derisory. Expert medical opinion violates the law from the start; with its first words expert psychiatric opinion in penal cases makes medical and psychiatric knowledge look ridiculous. It is consistent with neither law nor medicine. Although it has a major role in their institutional adaptation, at their join, at the frontier between them, it would be absolutely unjust to judge modern law (or, at any rate, law as it functioned at the beginning of the nineteenth century) by such a practice, and it would be unjust to assess medical knowledge and even psychiatric knowledge in the light of this practice. Ultimately, it is a question of something else. Expert medico-legal opinion comes from somewhere else. It derives neither from law nor from medicine. No historical examination will find penal expert opinion deriving from the evolution of law or from the evolution of medicine, or even from their joint evolution. It is something that inserts itself between them, securing their join, but which comes from elsewhere with different terms, different norms, and different rules of formation. Essentially, both justice and psychiatry are adulterated in expert medico-legal opinion. They do not deal with their own object; they do not work in accordance with their own norms. Expert medico-legal opinion does not address itself to delinquents or innocents or to those who are sick as opposed to those who are well. It addresses itself, I believe, to the category of "abnormal individuals." Or, if you prefer, expert medico-legal opinion is not deployed in a field of opposition, but in a field of gradation from the normal to the abnormal.

The strength, the vigor, and the penetrative and disruptive power of expert medico-legal opinion with regard to the legality of the judicial institution, and the normativity of medical knowledge, is due precisely to the fact that it offers them different concepts, addresses itself to a different object, and introduces different techniques that form a sort of third, insidious, and hidden term, carefully cloaked on all sides and at every point by the legal notions of "delinquency," "recidivism," et cetera, and the medical concepts of "illness," et cetera. Expert medico-legal opinion offers in fact a third term, that is to say, I want to show that probably it does not derive from a power that is either judicial or medical, but from a different type of power that for the moment I will provisionally call the power of normalization. With expert medico-legal opinion we have a practice concerned with abnormal individuals that introduces a certain power of normalization and which, through its own strength and through the effects of the joining together of the medical and the judicial that it ensures, tends gradually to transform judicial power as well as psychiatric knowledge and to constitute itself as the authority responsible for the control of abnormal individuals. Inasmuch as expert medico-legal opinion constitutes the medico-judicial as the body responsible for the control of the abnormal, of the abnormal individual, rather than for the control of crime or illness, it raises an important theoretical and political problem. In this respect it also refers back to a genealogy of this curious power, the genealogy that I would like now to trace.

Before moving on to concrete analysis next week, I would like to present now a few methodological reflections. Actually, I am not, of course, the first to speak about the history of this power of normalization applied primarily to sexuality, about the techniques of the normalization of sexuality since the seventeenth century. A number of books have been dedicated to the subject and fairly recently a book by Van Ussel has been translated into French that is called *La Répression de la sexualité* or *Histoire de la répression de la sexualité*.[8] What I want to do differs from this and a number of other works written along the same lines not exactly in its method, but in its point of view. There is a difference in what these analyses and my own analysis presuppose and imply in their theory of power. It seems to me, in fact, that the principal, the central notion in the analyses to which I refer is the notion of "repression."[9] That is to say, in these analyses there is an implicit reference to a power whose major function is repression, which is effective essentially at a superstructural level, is part of the superstructure, and whose mechanisms are essentially linked to ignorance and blindness. I would like to suggest a different conception of power, a different type of analysis of power, through the analyses I will be undertaking of the normalization of sexuality since the seventeenth century.

To clarify things straightaway I will take two examples that seem to me still to disturb contemporary analyses. You will see immediately that with these two examples I call into question my own earlier analyses.[10]

Everyone knows how lepers were excluded at the end of the Middle Ages, or even throughout the Middle Ages.[11] The leper's exclusion was a social practice that included first of all a rigorous division, a distancing, a rule of no contact between one individual (or group of individuals) and another. Second, it involved casting these individuals out into a vague, external world beyond the town's walls, beyond the limits of the community. As a result, two masses were constituted, each foreign to the other. And those cast out were cast out in the strict sense into outer darkness. Third, and finally, the exclusion of lepers implied the disqualification—which was perhaps not exactly moral, but in any case juridical and political—of individuals thus excluded and driven out. They entered death, and you know that the exclusion of lepers was regularly accompanied by a kind of funeral ceremony during which individuals who had been declared leprous were declared dead (which meant that their possessions could be passed on) and they departed for the foreign, external world. In short, there were practices of exclusion, of casting out, of "marginalization" as we would say today. I think we still describe the way in which power is exercised over the mad, criminals, deviants, children, and the poor in these terms. Generally, we describe the effects and mechanisms of the power exercised over these categories as mechanisms and effects of exclusion, disqualification, exile, rejection, deprivation, refusal, and incomprehension; that is to say, an entire arsenal of negative concepts or mechanisms of exclusion. I believe, and I continue to believe, that this practice or this model of the exclusion of lepers really was a model put to work in our society even later than the Middle Ages. In any case, when, toward the middle of the seventeenth century, the great hunt for beggars, vagabonds, the idle, libertines, and so forth began—with the sanctions of either driving this floating population from the towns or confining them in the *hôpitaux généraux*—I think it was still this model of the exclusion of lepers that the royal administration put to work.[12] However, there is another model of control that seems to me to have enjoyed a much wider and longer success.*

It seems that the model of the "exclusion of lepers," the model of the individual driven out in order to purify the community, finally disappeared roughly at the end of seventeenth and the beginning of the eighteenth centuries. However, something else, a different model, was not established but reactivated. This model is almost as old as the exclusion of lepers and concerns the problem of plague and the spatial partitioning and control (*quadrillage*) of plague-infested towns. It seems to me that essentially there have been only two major models for the control of individuals in the West: one is the exclusion of lepers and the other is the model of the inclusion of plague victims. And I think that the replacement of the exclusion of lepers by the inclusion of plague victims as the model of control was a major phenomenon of the eighteenth century. To explain this I would like to remind you how quarantine was enforced in a town in which the plague had broken out.[13] A certain territory was marked out and

---

* The manuscript says: "It may be that this model was historically active at the time of the 'great confinement' or the hunting down of beggars, but it went into permanent decline when it was taken over by another model that seems to me to have had..."

closed off: the territory of a town, possibly that of a town and its suburbs, was established as a closed territory. However, apart from this analogy, the practice with regard to plague was very different from the practice with regard to lepers, because the territory was not the vague territory into which one cast the population of which one had to be purified. It was a territory that was the object of a fine and detailed analysis, of a meticulous spatial partitioning (*quadrillage*).

The plague town—and here I refer to a series of regulations, all absolutely identical, moreover, that were published from the end of the Middle Ages until the beginning of the eighteenth century—was divided up into districts, the districts were divided into quarters, and then the streets within these quarters were isolated. In each street there were overseers, in each quarter inspectors, in each district someone in charge of the district, and in the town itself either someone was nominated as governor or the deputy mayor was given supplementary powers when plague broke out. There is, then, an analysis of the territory into its smallest elements and across this territory the organization of a power that is continuous in two senses. First of all, it is continuous due to this pyramid of control. From the sentries who kept watch over the doors of the houses from the end of the street, up to those responsible for the quarters, those responsible for the districts and those responsible for the town, there is a kind of pyramid of uninterrupted power. It was a power that was continuous not only in this pyramidal, hierarchical structure, but also in its exercise, since surveillance had to be exercised uninterruptedly. The sentries had to be constantly on watch at the end of the streets, and twice a day the inspectors of the quarters and districts had to make their inspection in such a way that nothing that happened in the town could escape their gaze. And everything thus observed had to be permanently recorded by means of this kind of visual examination and by entering all information in big registers. At the start of the quarantine, in fact, all citizens present in the town had to give their name. The names were entered in a series of registers. The local inspectors held some of these registers, and others were kept by the town's central administration. Every day the inspectors had to visit every house, stopping outside and summoning the occupants. Each individual was assigned a window in which he had to appear, and when his name was called he had to present himself at the window, it being understood that if he failed to appear it had to be because he was in bed, and if he was in bed he was ill, and if he was ill he was dangerous and so intervention was called for. It was at this point that individuals were sorted into those who were ill and those who were not. All the information gathered through the twice-daily visits, through this kind of review or parade of the living and the dead by the inspector, all the information recorded in the register, was then collated with the central register held by the deputy mayors in the town's central administration.[14]

You can see that this kind of organization is in fact absolutely antithetical to, or at any rate different from, all the practices concerning lepers. It is not exclusion but quarantine. It is not a question of driving out individuals but rather of establishing and fixing them, of giving them their own place, of assigning places and of defining presences and subdivided presences. Not rejection but inclusion. You can see that there is no longer a kind of global division between two types or groups of population, one that is pure and the other impure, one that has leprosy and the other that does not. Rather, there is a series of fine and constantly observed differences between individuals who are ill and those who are not. It is a question of individualization; the division and subdivision of power extending to the fine grain of individuality. Consequently, we are far from the global division into two masses characteristic of the exclusion of lepers. You can see also that there is none of that distancing, severing of contact, or marginalization. Rather, there is a close and meticulous observation. While leprosy calls for distance, the plague implies an always finer approximation of power to individuals, an ever more constant and insistent observation. With the plague there is no longer a sort of grand ritual of purification, as with leprosy, but rather an attempt to maximize the health, life, longevity, and strength of individuals. Essentially, it is a question of producing a healthy population rather than of purifying those living in the community, as in the case of leprosy. Finally, you can see that there is no irrevocable labeling of one part of the population but rather constant examination of a field of regularity within which each individual is constantly assessed in order to determine whether he conforms to the rule, to the defined norm of health.

You know that there is an extremely interesting body of literature in which the plague appears as the moment of panic and confusion in which individuals, threatened by visitations of death, abandon their identities, throw off their masks, forget their status, and abandon themselves to the great debauchery of those who know they are going to die. There is a literature of plague that is a literature of the decomposition of individuality; a kind of orgiastic dream in which plague is the moment when individuals come apart and when the law is forgotten. As soon as plague breaks out, the town's forms of lawfulness disappear. Plague overcomes the law just as it overcomes the body. Such, at least, is the literary dream of the plague.[15] But you can see that there was another dream of the plague: a political dream in which the plague is rather the marvelous moment when political power is exercised to the full. Plague is the moment when the spatial partitioning and subdivision (*quadrillage*) of a population is taken to its extreme point, where dangerous communications, disorderly communities, and forbidden contacts can no longer appear. The moment of the plague is one of an exhaustive sectioning (*quadrillage*) of the population by political power, the capillary ramifications of which constantly reach the grain of individuals themselves, their time, habitat, localization, and bodies. Perhaps plague brings with it the literary or theatrical dream of the great orgiastic moment. But plague also brings the political dream of an exhaustive, unobstructed power that is completely transparent to its object and exercised to the full. You can see that there is a connection between the dream of a military society and the dream of a plague-stricken society, between both of these dreams born in the sixteenth and seventeenth centuries. From the seventeenth to eighteenth centuries I do not think it was the old model of leprosy that was important politically, the final residue or one of the last major manifestations of which was no doubt the great "confinement" and the exclusion of beggars and the mad and so forth. Another, very different model replaced the model of leprosy in the seventeenth century. Plague replaces leprosy as a model of political control, and this is one of the great inventions of the eighteenth century, or in any case of the Classical Age and administrative monarchy.

Broadly I would say that the replacement of the model of leprosy by the model of plague essentially corresponds to a very important historical process that I will call, in a word, the invention of positive technologies of power. The reaction to leprosy is a negative reaction; it is a reaction of rejection, exclusion, and so on. The reaction to plague is a positive reaction; it is a reaction of inclusion, observation, the formation of knowledge, the multiplication of effects of power on the basis of the accumulation of observations and knowledge. We pass from a technology of power that drives out, excludes, banishes, marginalizes, and represses, to a fundamentally positive power that fashions, observes, knows, and multiplies itself on the basis of its own effects.

I would say that generally the Classical Age is praised because it succeeded in inventing a considerable number of scientific and industrial techniques. We know that it also invented forms of government; it developed administrative apparatuses and political institutions. All this is true. But, and I think less attention has been given to this, the Classical Age also invented techniques of power of a kind that ensured that power did not function by means of deduction, but by means of production and the maximizing of production. It invented techniques of a power that does not act by excluding but rather through a close and analytical inclusion of elements, a power that does not act by separating into large confused masses, but by distributing according to differential individualities, a power that is linked not to ignorance but rather to a series of mechanisms that secure the formation, investment, accumulation, and growth of knowledge. [The Classical Age invented techniques of power] that can be transferred to very different institutional supports, to State apparatuses, institutions, the family, and so forth. The Classical Age developed therefore what could be called an "art of governing," in the sense in which "government" was then understood as precisely the "government" of children, the "government" of the mad, the "government" of the poor, and before long, the "government" of workers. Taking the term *government* in this wide sense, we should understand three things. First, of course, the eighteenth century, or the Classical Age, invented a juridico-political theory of power centered on the notion of the will and its alienation, transfer, and representation in a governmental apparatus. The eighteenth century, or the Classical Age, also set up a State apparatus that extended into and was supported by different institutions. And then—and it is on this that I would like to focus, or which I would like to serve as background to my analysis of the normalization of sexuality—it refined a general technique of the exercise of power that can be transferred to many different institutions and apparatuses. This technique constitutes the other side of the juridical and political structures of representation and is the condition of their functioning and effectiveness. This general technique of the government of men comprises a typical apparatus (*dispositif*), which is the disciplinary organization I spoke to you about last year.[16] To what end is this apparatus directed? It is, I think, something that we can call "normalization." This year, then, instead of considering the mechanics of the disciplinary apparatus, I will be looking at their effects of normalization, at what they are directed toward, the effects they can achieve and that can be grouped under the rubric of "normalization."

A few words more, if you will allow me a few minutes. I would like to say this, I would like to refer you to a text that is found in the second edition of George Canguilhem's book, *On the Normal and the Pathological* (starting on page 145). In this text on the norm and normalization, there is a set of ideas that seem to me to be both historically and methodologically fruitful. First of all, Canguilhem refers to the development in the eighteenth century of a general process of social, political, and technical normalization that takes effect in the domain of education, with the school; in medicine, with hospital organization; and also in the domain of industrial production. The army could no doubt be added to this list. So we have a general process of normalization during the eighteenth century and the multiplication of its effects regarding childhood, the army, production, and so forth.

In the same text there is also the important idea that the norm is not at all defined as a natural law but rather by the exacting and coercive role it can perform in the domains in which it is applied. The norm consequently lays claim to power. The norm is not simply and not even a principle of intelligibility; it is an element on the basis of which a certain exercise of power is founded and legitimized. Canguilhem calls it a polemical concept. Perhaps we could say it is a political concept. In any case—and this is the third important idea—the norm brings with it a principle of both qualification and correction. The norm's function is not to exclude and reject. Rather, it is always linked to a positive technique of intervention and transformation, to a sort of normative project.[17]

It is this set of ideas, this simultaneously positive, technical, and political conception of normalization that I would like to try to put to work historically by applying it to the domain of sexuality. And you can see that behind this, the basic target of my criticism, or what I would like to get free from, is the idea that political power—in all its forms and at whatever level we grasp it—has to be analyzed within the Hegelian horizon of a sort of beautiful totality that through an effect of power is misrecognized or broken up by abstraction or division. It seems to me that it is both a methodological and a historical error to consider power as an essentially negative mechanism of repression whose principal function is to protect, preserve, or reproduce the relations of production. It also seems to me wrong to consider power as something situated at a superstructural level relative to the play of forces. Finally, it is wrong to consider power as essentially linked to the effects of ignorance. It seems to me that this kind of traditional and "omni-circulating" conception of power, found in historical writing and in present-day political and polemical texts, is actually constructed on the basis of a number of outdated historical models. It is a composite notion that is inadequate for the real world in which we have been living for a considerable length of time, that is, since at least the end of the eighteenth century.

From where is this conception of power borrowed that sees power impinging massively from the outside, as it were, with a continuous violence that some (always the same) exercise over others (who are also always the same)? It comes from the model of, or if you like, from the historical reality of, slave society. The idea that power has the essential function of prohibiting, preventing, and isolating, rather than allowing the circulation, change, and multiple combination of elements, seems to me a conception of power that also refers to an outdated historical model, in this case the model of caste society. By making power a mechanism whose function is not to produce but to deduct, to impose obligatory transfers of wealth and, consequently, to deprive some of the fruit of their work; in short, the idea that the essential function of power is to seal off the process of production and to make a certain social class profit from it, in an absolutely identical renewal of the relations of power, does not seem to me to refer at all to the real functioning of power at the present time, but to how we may suppose or reconstruct it as functioning in feudal society. Finally, in referring to a power that, with its administrative machinery of control, is superimposed on forms, forces, and relations of production established at the level of an already given economy, by describing power in this way, it seems to me that we are still using an outdated historical model that in this case is the model of the administrative monarchy.

In other words, it seems to me that by making the major characteristics we attribute to political power into an instance of repression, a superstructural level, and an instance whose essential function is to reproduce and preserve the relations of production, we do no more than constitute, on the basis of historically outdated and different models, a sort of daguerreotype of power that is really based on what we think we can see in power in a slave society, a caste society, a feudal society, and in a society like the administrative monarchy. It hardly matters whether this is a failure to recognize the reality of these societies; it is in any case a failure to grasp what is specific and new in what took place during the eighteenth century and the Classical Age, that is to say, the installation of a power that, with regard to productive forces, relations of production, and the preexisting social system, does not play a role of control and reproduction but rather a really positive role. What the eighteenth century established through the "discipline of normalization," or the system of "discipline-normalization," seems to me to be a power that is not in fact repressive but productive, repression figuring only as a lateral or secondary effect with regard to its central, creative, and productive mechanisms.

It seems to me that the eighteenth century also succeeded in creating—and the disappearance at the end of the eighteenth century of the monarchy, of what we call the Ancien Régime, is precisely the confirmation of this—a power that is not part of the superstructure but that is integrated in the play, distribution, dynamic, strategy, and effectiveness of forces; a power, therefore, that is invested directly in the distribution and play of forces. It seems to me that the eighteenth century established a power that is not conservative but inventive, a power that possesses within itself the principles of transformation and innovation.

Finally, it seems to me that with the disciplines and normalization, the eighteenth century established a type of power that is not linked to ignorance but a power that can only function thanks to the formation of a knowledge that is both its effect and also a condition of its exercise. So I will try to employ this positive conception of the mechanisms and effects of this power when analyzing how, from the seventeenth to the end of the nineteenth century, normalization was attempted in the domain of sexuality.

---

1. On M. Cénac, P. Gouriou, G. Heuyer, and Jénil-Perrin, cf. A. Porot and C. Bardenat, *Psychiatrie medico-légale* (Paris: s.1., 1959), pp. 60, 92, 154, 270. With particular attention to Cénac's contribution to what Foucault calls the "institutional mixture," see his much discussed report, "Le témoignage et sa valeur au point de vue judiciaire," presented in 1951 at the forty-ninth session of the congress of French psychiatrists and neurologists (*Rapports* [Paris: s.1., 1952], pp. 261-299), and his "Introduction théorique aux fonctions de la psychanalyse en criminologie" (signed with Jacques Lacan) on the occasion of the thirteenth conference of French-speaking psychoanalysts in 1950 and published in *Revue française de psychanalyse*, 15/1 (1951), pp. 7-29 (then reworked in J. Lacan, *Écrits*, [Paris: s.1., 1966], pp.125-149).

2. To understand Foucault's allusion, we must remember that Sophie Rostopchine, the Countess of Ségur (1799-1874), was the author of a number of works for young people that were written in the childish language of mothers. A. Q. Fouquier-Tinville was public prosecutor in the revolutionary court during the Terror. J. E. D. Esquirol (1722-1795) was the founder, along with P. Pinel, of clinical psychiatry and was head doctor at the Maison Royale de Charenton in 1825.

3. On Pierre Rivière, cf. lecture of January 8 and lecture of February 12, both in this volume. Georges Rapin murdered his mistress in the Fontainebleau forest on 29 May 1960. He was defended by René Floriot, was condemned to death and executed on 26 July 1960.

4. On the reports produced by J. E. D. Esquirol, E. J. Georget and C. C. H. Marc from the 1820s, cf. lecture of February 5 in this volume. Cf. the summary of the Collège de France course for 1970-1971: *La Volonté de Savoir*, from *Dits et écrits, 1954-1988*, in four volumes: vol 1: *1954-1969*, vol. 2: *1970-1975*, vol. 3: *1976-1979*, vol. 4: *1980-1988*, edition established under the direction of D. Defert and F. Ewald in collaboration with J. Lagrange (Paris: Gallimard, 1994), vol. 2, p. 244. English translation: *The Will to Knowledge* in *The Essential Works of Foucault 1954-1984*, vol. I: *Ethics, Subjectivity and Truth*, edited by Paul Rabinow, translated by Robert Hurley et al. (New York: New Press, 1997), vol. 1 p.15: "This year's seminar was generally confined to the study of the penal system in France in the nineteenth century. It dealt, this year, with the first development of penal psychiatry in the period of the Restoration. The material used was largely the text of the medico-legal expert opinion submitted by the contemporaries and disciples of Esquirol."

5. An order of canons regular established in 1120 and subject to Augustinian rule. It was suppressed during the Revolution.

6. The document quoted here comes from the inventory of *lettres de cachet* produced by Christiane Martin on Michel Foucault's request. Christiane Martin died before completing the work. It is published in A. Farge and Michel Foucault, *Le Désordre des familles. Lettres de cachet des Archives de la Bastille* (Paris: s.1., 1982), pp. 294-296.

7. The debate on the suppression of the jury took place at the Second International Congress of Criminal Anthropology in 1889. The proceedings are published in *Archives de l'anthropologie criminelle et des sciences pénales*, vol. 4 (s.1.: Paris: 1889), pp. 517-660.

8. J. Van Ussel, *Geschiedenis van het seksuele probleem* (Meppel: s.1., 1968). German translation: *Sexualunterdrückung. Geschichte der Sexualfeindschaft* (Hamburg: s.1., 1970). French translation: *Histoire de la répression sexuelle*, translated by C. Chevalot (Paris: s.1., 1972).

9. Cf. the chapter "L'hypothèse répressive," in Foucault's *La Volonté de savoir* (Paris: Gallimard, 1976), pp. 23-67. English translation: "The Repressive Hypothesis," part 2 in M. Foucault, *The History of Sexuality, vol. 1: An Introduction* (London: Allen Lane, 1979), translated by R. Hurley.

10. Foucault is referring to the analysis of the forms of punitive tactics presented in the Collège de France course of 1972-1973: *La Société Punitive* (*The Punitive Society*), especially the lecture of January 3, 1973. Cf. the course summary in M. Foucault, *The Essential Works* vol. 1, pp. 23-37.

11. These rules of exclusion, drawn up in councils from 583 on and taken up by a capitulary of Charlemagne in 789, appear frequently in customary law texts and synodal statutes from the twelfth and thirteenth centuries. Thus, around 1400-1430, in some dioceses of northern and eastern France, lepers had to undergo a ceremony officially putting them outside of society. Led to church to the singing of *Libera me*, just as for the dead, the leper listened to Mass hidden beneath a catafalque before undergoing a simulated burial and being accompanied to his new residence. The extinction of leprosy led to the disappearance of this liturgy after 1580. See A. Bourgeois, "Lépreux et maladreries," in *Mémoires de la commission départementale des monuments historiques du Pas-de-Calais*, 14/2 (Arras, s.1., 1972).

12. Cf. M. Foucault, *Histoire de la folie à l'âge classique* (Paris: Gallimard, 1972), pp. 13-16, 56-91. English translation: *Madness and Civilization: A History of Insanity in the Age of Reason*, translated by Richard Howard (London/New York: Vintage, 1989), pp. 3-7, 38-64.

13. Cf. J. A. F. Ozanam, *Histoire médicale générale et particulière des maladies épidémiques, contagieuses et épizootiques, qui ont régné en Europe depuis les temps les plus reculés jusqu'à nos jours*, 2nd edition, vol. 4 (Paris, 1835), pp. 5-93.

14. Cf. M. Foucault, *Surveiller et Punir. Naissance de la prison* (Paris: Gallimard, 1975), pp. 197-201. English translation: *Discipline and Punish: The Birth of the Prison*, translator Alan Sheridan (London/New York: Allen Lane, 1977), pp. 195-199.

15. This literature begins with Thucydides, Istoriai (History of the Peloponnesian War),vol. 2, 47, 54, and Lucretius, *De natura rerum* (On the Nature of the Universe), vol. 6, 1138, 1246, and continues with A. Artaud, *Le Théâtre et son double* (Paris, Gallimard, 1938). English translation: *The Theater and Its Double*, translated by Mary Caroline Richards (New York: Grove Press, 1958), and A. Camus, *La Peste* (Paris: s.1., 1946) English translation: *The Plague*, translated by S. Gilbert (London: s.1., 1948).

16. See the Collège de France course for 1973-1974: *Le Pouvoir psychiatrique*, (Psychiatric Power) especially the lectures of November 21 and 28 and December 5, 1973. Cf. the course summary in M. Foucault, *The Essential Works*, vol. 1, pp. 39-50.

17. G. Canguilhem, *Le Normal et le Pathologique* (Paris: P.U.F., 1972), pp. 169-172—for the reference to the normal as a polemical concept. English translation: *On the Normal and the Pathological*, translated by Carolyn R. Fawcett, with an introduction by Michel Foucault (Dordrecht/Boston/London, D. Reidel, 1978), pp. 145-158 (p.146 for the reference to the normal as a "polemical concept"). Cf. M. Foucault, "La vie: l'expérience et la science," (1985) in *Dits et écrits*, vol. 4, pp. 774-776. English translation: "Life: Experience and Science," in *The Essential Works of Foucault 1954-1984*, vol. 2, *Aesthetics, Method, and Epistemology*, edited by James Faubion, translated by Robert Hurley, et al. (New York: New Press, 1998), pp. 465-466.

three

22 JANUARY 1975

Three figures that constitute the domain of abnormality: the human monster, the individual to be corrected; the masturbating child. ~ The sexual monster brings together the monstrous individual and the sexual deviant. ~ Historical review of the three figures. ~ Reversal of their historical importance. ~ Sacred embryology and the juridico-biological theory of the monster. ~ Siamese twins. ~ Hermaphrodites: minor cases. ~ The Marie Lemarcis case. ~ The Anne Grandjean case.

TODAY I WOULD LIKE to begin the analysis of the domain of abnormality as it functions in the nineteenth century. I would like to try to show that this domain was constituted on the basis of three elements. These three elements begin to be distinguished and defined in the eighteenth century and then come together in the nineteenth century to give rise to the domain of abnormality that gradually overlays them, appropriates them, and, as it were, colonizes them to the point of absorbing them. These three elements are essentially three figures or, if you like, three circles in which the problem of abnormality is gradually posed.

The first of these figures is what I will call the "human monster." The frame of reference of the human monster is, of course, law. The notion of the monster is essentially a legal notion, in a broad sense, of course, since what defines the monster is the fact that its existence and form is not only a violation of the laws of society but also a violation of the laws of nature. Its very existence is a breach of the law at both levels. The field in which the monster appears can thus be called a "juridico-biological" domain. However, the monster emerges within this space as both an extreme and an extremely rare phenomenon. The monster is the limit, both the point at which law is overturned and the exception that is found only in extreme cases. The monster combines the impossible and the forbidden.

I want to pay particular attention to this notion because it gives rise to a number of ambiguities that will haunt the figure of the abnormal man for a long time, even when the abnormal man of eighteenth-century practice and knowledge has reduced, appropriated, and absorbed the monster's specific traits. The monster, in fact, contradicts the law. It is the breach of the law taken to its furthest degree. And yet, although it is a breach of the law (in the raw state, so to speak), the monster does not bring about a legal response from the law. It could be said that the monster's power and its capacity to create anxiety are due to the fact that it violates the law while leaving it with nothing to say. It traps the law while breaching it. When the monster violates the law by its very existence, it triggers the response of something quite different from the law itself. It provokes either violence, the will for pure and simple suppression, or medical care or pity. But the law itself does not respond to the attack on it represented by the monster's existence. One of the first ambiguities is that the monster is a breach of the law that automatically stands outside the law. The second is that the monster is, so to speak, the spontaneous, brutal, but consequently natural form of the unnatural. It is the magnifying model, the form of every possible little irregularity exhibited by the games of nature. In this sense we can say that the monster is the major model of every little deviation. It is the principle of intelligibility of all the forms that circulate as the small change of abnormality. The recurring problem of the nineteenth century is that of discovering the core of monstrosity hidden behind little abnormalities, deviances, and irregularities. This is the problem posed by Lombroso's studies of delinquents, for example.[1] What is the great natural monster that looms up behind the little thief? Paradoxically, the monster is a principle of intelligibility in spite of its limit position as both the impossible and the forbidden. And yet this principle of intelligibility is strictly tautological, since the characteristic feature of the monster is to express itself as, precisely, monstrous, to be the explanation of every little deviation that may derive from it, but to be unintelligible itself. Thus, it is this tautological intelligibility, this principle of explanation that refers only to itself that lies at the heart of analyses of abnormality.

The ambiguities of the human monster, which are widely diffused at the end of the eighteenth century and the beginning of the nineteenth century, are present, toned down and muffled of course, but nonetheless firmly implanted and really effective in the problematic of abnormality and the judicial and medical techniques that revolve around abnormality in the nineteenth century. In a word, we can say that until the end of the nineteenth century and perhaps until the twentieth century—remember the expert opinions I read out—the abnormal individual is essentially an everyday monster, a monster that has become commonplace. For a long time the abnormal individual will be something like a pale monster. This is the first figure I want to consider.

The second figure in the genealogy of abnormality and the abnormal individual could be called the "individual to be corrected." He, too, is a character who appears very clearly in the eighteenth century, but later than the monster who, as you will see, has a very long ancestry behind him. The individual to be corrected is essentially a very specific individual of the seventeenth and eighteenth centuries, of the Classical Age. His frame of reference is obviously much narrower than that of the monster. The monster's frame of reference was nature and society, the system of the laws of the world: The monster was a cosmological or anticosmological being. The frame of reference of the individual to be corrected is much narrower: It is the family exercising its internal power or managing its economy, or, even more, in its relations with the institutions adjoining or supporting it. The individual to be corrected emerges in the play of relations of conflict and support that exist between the family and the school, workshop, street, quarter, parish, church, police, and so on. This, then, is the field in which the individual to be corrected appears.

The individual to be corrected also differs from the monster in that obviously he appears much more frequently. The monster is by definition the exception; the individual to be corrected is an everyday phenomenon. He is so much an everyday phenomenon that—and this is his first paradox—he is, so to speak, typically regular in his irregularity. As a result, the figure exhibits a number of ambiguities that we will encounter again, long after the eighteenth century, in the problematic of the abnormal man. First of all, because the individual to be corrected is a very frequent phenomenon, because he is very close to the rule, it is always very difficult to define him. There is a kind of familiar, everyday obviousness that renders him immediately recognizable; but he is so familiar that we do not have any definite evidence that an individual is this character. Consequently, being unable to provide any proof, we can never really demonstrate that an individual is incorrigible. He verges precisely on undecidability. We can offer no evidence or proof of incorrigibility. This is the first ambiguity.

Another ambiguity is that the individual to be corrected appears to require correction because all the usual techniques, procedures, and attempts at training within the family have failed to correct him. What defines the individual to be corrected is that he is incorrigible. However, paradoxically, insofar as he is incorrigible, he calls up around him a number of specific interventions over and above the customary and family techniques of training and correction, that is to say, a new technology of rectification, of supercorrection. Thus a kind of game between incorrigibility and rectifiability emerges around the individual to be corrected. An axis of rectifiable incorrigibility emerges on which we will later find the abnormal individual and which will serve as a support for all the specific institutions developed for abnormal individuals in the nineteenth century. The pale, commonplace monster, the abnormal individual of the nineteenth century, is also an incorrigible who will be placed in the center of an apparatus of correction. This, then, is the second ancestor of the nineteenth-century abnormal individual.

The third figure is the "masturbator." The masturbator, the child masturbator, is a completely new figure of the nineteenth century (but who can be found at the end of the eighteenth century) and whose field of appearance is the family or even something narrower than the family: his frame of reference is no longer nature and society, as it was for the monster, nor the family and its entourage, as it was for the individual to be corrected. It is a much narrower space. It is the bedroom, the bed, the body; it is the parents, immediate supervisors, brothers and sisters; it is the doctor: it is a kind of microcell around the individual and his body.

The figure of the masturbator appears at the end of the eighteenth century with a number of specific characteristics distinct from those of both the monster and the individual to be corrected. The first is that the masturbator is not at all an exceptional figure in eighteenth-century thought, knowledge, and pedagogical techniques; he is, rather, a frequently encountered individual. He seems to be an almost universal individual. Now this absolutely universal individual, or rather, the practice of masturbation that is recognized as being universal is, at the same time, said to be an unknown or ignored practice that no one has spoken about, that no one knows and whose secret is never revealed. Masturbation is the universal secret shared by everyone but disclosed to no one. It is the secret all possess that never emerges into self-consciousness or universal discourse (we will come back to this later), its general formula being (and I barely distort what can be found in books on masturbation at the end of the eighteenth century): Almost no one knows what everyone does. There is something here that is absolutely decisive in the organization of nineteenth-century anthropological knowledge and techniques. This secret shared by everyone and told to no one is posited in its quasi universality as the possible root, even as the real root, of almost every possible evil. Masturbation is a kind of polyvalent causality to which one can attach, and to which doctors in the eighteenth century will immediately attach, the entire panoply, the entire arsenal of physical, nervous, and psychiatric illnesses. Finally, in the pathology of the end of the eighteenth century, there will be practically no illness that cannot, in one way or another, be laid at the door of this etiology, that is to say, of this sexual etiology. In other words, this almost universal element found in practically everyone is at the same time the explanatory principle of the most extreme changes of nature; it is the explanatory principle of pathological singularity. The fact that almost everyone masturbates explains why some suffer from extreme illnesses that affect no one else. It is the kind of etiological paradox with regard to sexuality and sexual abnormalities that we find at the heart of the nineteenth or twentieth century. There is, then, nothing surprising in this. What is surprising, if you like, is that this kind of paradox and this general form of analysis is posited in such an axiomatic form as early as the last years of the eighteenth century.

To situate this kind of archeology of abnormality we will say that the nineteenth-century abnormal individual is the descendant of these three individuals: the monster, the incorrigible, and the masturbator. For a long time, in medical practice, judicial practice, and in knowledge and the institutions around it, the nineteenth-century abnormal individual is distinguished by a kind of monstrosity that is increasingly faded and diaphanous and by a rectifiable incorrigibility increasingly surrounded by apparatuses of rectification. Finally, it is marked by this common and particular secret of the general and universal etiology of the worst peculiarities. Thus, the genealogy of the abnormal individual directs us to these three figures: the monster, the incorrigible, and the onanist.

Before beginning this week with the monster, I would like to make a few remarks. The first is that there are, of course, connections between these three figures whose distinctive features in the eighteenth century I have indicated, and these connections are established very quickly in the second half of the eighteenth century. For example, we see the emergence of a figure basically unknown to earlier periods: the sexual monster. The monstrous individual and the sexual deviant link up. We find the reciprocal theme that masturbation can cause not only the worst illnesses, but also the worst physical deformities and finally the worst kinds of monstrous behavior. Similarly, at the end of the eighteenth century, we see correctional institutions focusing increasingly on sexuality and masturbation as fundamental to the problem of the incorrigible. Consequently, the monster, the incorrigible, and the masturbator are characters who begin to exchange some of their traits and whose profiles begin to be superimposed on each other. However—and this is a fundamental point that I want to stress—I think that these three figures nonetheless remain absolutely distinct and separate until the end of the eighteenth and the beginning of the nineteenth century. A technology of human abnormality, a technology of abnormal individuals appears precisely when a regular network of knowledge and power has been established that brings the three figures together or, at any rate, invests them with the same system of regularities. It is only then that a field of abnormalities will really be constituted in which the ambiguities of the monster, the incorrigible, and the masturbator will be rediscovered, but within a homogeneous and relatively less stable field. Prior to this, however, it seems to me that in the period with which I am concerned—the end of the eighteenth and the beginning of the nineteenth centuries—these three figures remain separate. They remain separate essentially because the systems of power and knowledge to which they refer remain separate from each other.

Thus, the monster falls under what in general terms could be called the framework of politico-judicial powers. His features will take shape and be transformed at the end of the eighteenth century inasmuch as these politico-judicial powers are transformed. The figure of the incorrigible will be defined, take shape, and be transformed and developed along with the reorganization of the functions of the family and the development of disciplinary techniques. The masturbator emerges and takes shape within a redistribution of the powers that surround the individual's body. To be sure, these levels of power are not independent of one another, but they do not function in the same way. There is no single technology of power to bring them together and ensure that they function coherently together. That is why we find these three figures separate from one another. Similarly, the bodies of knowledge to which they refer are also separate. The monster refers to a natural history organized essentially around the absolute and insurmountable distinctions between species, genus, and kingdoms, et cetera. The incorrigible refers to a type of knowledge that is slowly constituted in the eighteenth century in pedagogical techniques; in techniques of collective education and the learning of skills. Finally, the masturbator appears late, in the last years of the eighteenth century, linked to a nascent biology of sexuality that will not have a scientific kind of consistency until the period from 1820 to 1830. Consequently, to organize the control of abnormality as a technique of power and knowledge in the nineteenth century it will be necessary to systematize, codify, and link together these bodies of knowledge and power that functioned separately in the eighteenth century.

A final remark. Quite clearly there is a pronounced kind of historical tendency in the nineteenth century that reverses the relative importance of these three figures. At the end of the eighteenth century, or anyway during the eighteenth century, the most important and dominant figure, the figure that emerges in the judicial practice of the early years of the nineteenth century—and with what forcefulness!—is obviously the monster. The monster is problematic, challenging both the medical and the judicial system. It is around the monster that the entire problematic of abnormality is set out in the period from 1820 to 1830 with regard to the monstrous crimes of people like the woman of Sélestat, Henriette Cornier, Léger, Papavoine, et cetera, which we will have occasion to speak about later.[2] The monster is the fundamental figure around which bodies of power and domains of knowledge are disturbed and reorganized. Then, gradually, increasing importance is attributed to the more modest, discreet, and less scientifically supercharged figure, the figure apparently most indifferent to power, that is to say, the masturbator or, if you like, the universality of sexual deviance. At the end of the nineteenth century the masturbator has overlaid the other figures, and most of the problems concerning abnormality are concentrated on this figure.

So much, then, for the establishment of these three figures. In the next three or four sessions I want to begin to study the formation, transformation, and paths taken by these three figures from the eighteenth century until the second half of the nineteenth century, that is to say, the period in which first of all they are formed and then, at a certain moment, they are taken up within the problem, technique, and knowledge of abnormality.

Today we will start with the monster[3] as a juridical rather than a medical notion. Roman law, which is obviously the background to this problematic of the monster, carefully, although not entirely clearly, distinguished two categories: that of deformity, disability, and deficiency (the deformed, disabled, and defective are called the *portentum* or the *ostentum*), and then the monster in the strict sense.[4] What is the monster in a both juridical and scientific tradition? From the Middle Ages to the eighteenth century, the period that concerns us, the monster is essentially a mixture. It is the mixture of two realms, the animal and the human: the man with the head of an ox, the man with a bird's feet—monsters.[5] It is the blending, the mixture of two species: the pig with a sheep's head is a monster. It is the mixture of two individuals: the person who has two heads and one body or two bodies and one head is a monster. It is the mixture of two sexes: the person who is both male and female is a monster. It is a mixture of life and death: the fetus born with a morphology that means it will not be able to live but that nonetheless survives for some minutes or days is a monster. Finally, it is a mixture of forms: the person who has neither arms nor legs, like a snake, is a monster. Consequently, the monster is the transgression of natural limits, the transgression of classifications, of the table, and of the law as table: this is actually what is involved in monstrosity. However, I do not think that it is this alone that constitutes the monster. For medieval thought, and definitely for seventeenth- and eighteenth-century thought, the breach of natural law is not enough to constitute monstrosity. Monstrosity requires a transgression of the natural limit, of the law-table, to fall under, or at any rate challenge, an interdiction of civil and religious or divine law. There is monstrosity only when the confusion comes up against, overturns, or disturbs civil, canon, or religious law. The difference between disability and monstrosity is revealed at the meeting point, the point of friction, between a breach of the natural law-table and a breach of the law instituted by God or by society, at the point where these two breaches of law come together. Disability may well be something that upsets the natural order, but disability is not monstrosity because it has a place in civil or canon law. The disabled person may not conform to nature, but the law in some way provides for him. Monstrosity, however, is the kind of natural irregularity that calls law into question and disables it. Law must either question its own foundations, or its practice, or fall silent, or abdicate, or appeal to another reference system, or again invent a casuistry. Essentially, the monster is the casuistry that is necessarily introduced into law by the confusion of nature.

Thus the monster is said to be a being in which the mixture of two kingdoms can be seen, because where do we look for the cause when we detect the presence of the animal and human species in one and the same individual? We look for a breach of human and divine law in the progenitors, that is to say, for fornication between a human individual and an animal.[6] It is because there was a sexual relationship between a man and an animal that a monster appears in which the two kingdoms are mixed. In that respect we are referred to a breach of civil or religious law. However, at the same time as natural disorder refers to a breach of religious and civil law, the law finds itself acutely embarrassed. We see this in the problem, for example, of whether an individual with a human body and an animal's head, or with an animal's body and a human head, should be baptized. Canon law, which provided for many disabilities and incapacities, cannot resolve this problem. Consequently, the disorder of nature upsets the juridical order and the monster appears. Similarly, the birth of a shapeless being that will inevitably die, for example, but which nonetheless lives for some moments, hours, or days, also poses a problem for the law.[7] It is a breach of the natural order and a juridical enigma at the same time. In the law of inheritance, for example, in jurisprudence, there are interminable discussions of cases, the most typical of which is the following. A man dies and his wife is pregnant. He leaves a will in which he says: If the child whom my wife is bearing is born he will inherit all my possessions. If, however, the child is not born or is born dead, if he is stillborn, then my possessions will go to my family.[8] Who will inherit his possessions if the child born is a monster? Should we regard the child as having been born or not? The law is set an insoluble problem as soon as this monstrous child, this kind of mixture of life and death, is born. When a monster with two bodies or two heads is born, should we give it one or two baptisms?[9] Should we consider it a case of one child or two?[10] I have found the trace of a story of two Siamese twin brothers, one of whom had committed a crime. (Unfortunately I have not been able to find out where the documents of the case, of the trial, are to be found, nor how one can find this out).[11] The problem was whether one or both of them should be executed. If one were executed, then the other would die; but if the innocent brother was allowed to live, then the other also had to be allowed to live.[12] This is how the problem of monstrosity really appeared. The monster was also someone with two sexes whom one didn't know whether to treat as a boy or a girl, whether or not he/she should be allowed to marry and with whom, whether he/she could become the holder of an ecclesiastical living, whether he/she could take religious orders, and so on.[13]

All these problems of legal teratology are summarized in a very interesting book that seems to me to be of absolutely fundamental importance for understanding the question of the birth and development of the juridico-natural, juridico-medical problem of the monster. It is a book written by a priest called Cangiamila. In 1745 he published a text called *Traité d'embryologie sacrée* which sets out the juridico-natural, juridico-biological theory of the monster.[14] In the eighteenth century, then, the monster appears and functions precisely at the point where nature and law are joined. It brings with it natural transgression, the mixture of species, and the blurring of limits and of characteristics. However, it is a monster only because it is also a legal labyrinth, a violation of and an obstacle to the law, both transgression and undecidability at the level of the law. In the eighteenth century the monster is a juridico-natural complex.

I have been talking about the monster in the eighteenth century, but this juridico-natural functioning of the monster is, I believe, very ancient, and we find it again in the nineteenth century. We come across it, transposed and transformed, in the expert opinions I read out. However, it seems to me that the new theory of the monster found in the nineteenth century begins to be worked out in the eighteenth century with regard to a particular type of monster. Moreover, I think that in each epoch, for legal and medical reflection at least, there have been privileged forms of monsters. In the Middle Ages it was obviously the bestial man, that is to say, the mixture of two kingdoms, the monster that is both man and beast. It seems striking to me, but it will have to be studied more closely, that the form of monstrosity especially privileged during the Renaissance, both in literature generally and in medical, legal, and religious books, was Siamese twins. The one who is two and the two who are one. In analyses at the end of the sixteenth and the beginning of the seventeenth centuries we almost always, or at least very regularly, come across a curious reference to the individual who has one head and two bodies, or one body and two heads. It is the image of the kingdom and also of Christianity divided into two religious communities. There are some very interesting discussions in which there is a close connection between the religious and medical problematics. In particular, there is the case of two Siamese twin brothers [*rectius*: sisters] who were baptized, or rather who were brought to the baptismal font. One was baptized and then the second died before she could be baptized. A big discussion takes place, and the Catholic priest who performed the baptism says: There is no difficulty. If the other is dead, it is because she would have been Protestant. We also have the image of the Kingdom of France, half of which is saved by baptism and the other half lost and damned. In any case, it is typical that Siamese twins are the most frequent theme in legal, medical, and religious cases at the end of the sixteenth and the beginning of the seventeenth centuries.[15]

However, in the Classical Age I think a third type of monstrosity is privileged: hermaphrodites. The new figure of the monster, which appears at the end of the eighteenth century and is at work at the start of the nineteenth century, is elaborated, or begins to be elaborated, around the question of hermaphrodites. No doubt this should be examined more closely, but broadly speaking we can accept, or at least people will tell you, that from the Middle Ages to the sixteenth century, and until at least the start of the seventeenth century, hermaphrodites were considered to be monsters and were executed, burnt at the stake and their ashes thrown to the winds. Suppose we accept this. In fact, in 1599, for example, at the very end of the sixteenth century, there is a case of the punishment of someone convicted as a hermaphrodite apparently without anything else being involved other than the fact of being a hermaphrodite. It was someone called Antide Collas, denounced as a hermaphrodite. He/she lived in Dôle and, after examining him/her, the doctors concluded that this individual really had both sexes, but that he/she could only have both sexes because he/she had had relations with Satan and it was this relationship that had added a second sex to his/her original sex. When interrogated, the hermaphrodite confessed to having had relations with Satan and was burnt alive in Dôle in 1599. It seems that this is one of the last cases in which a hermaphrodite was burnt for being a hermaphrodite.[16]

Very soon afterward a different type of jurisprudence appears. This is set out at great length in Brillon's *Dictionnaire des arrêts des parlements de France*[17] and shows that, from the seventeenth century at least, a hermaphrodite was not convicted just for being a hermaphrodite. Individuals recognized as hermaphrodites were asked to choose their sex, their dominant sex, and to conduct themselves accordingly, especially by wearing appropriate clothes. They were subject to criminal law and could be convicted for sodomy only if they made use of their additional sex.[18] In fact, a number of hermaphrodites were convicted for the supplementary use of their additional sex. Héricourt, in *Les Lois ecclésiastiques de France*, published in 1761 [*rectius:* 1771], refers to a case from the start of the seventeenth century.[19] A hermaphrodite was convicted because, after having chosen the male sex, he used his other sex with a man and was therefore burned.[20] Or again, right at the start of the seventeenth century, two hermaphrodites were burned alive and their ashes scattered in the wind simply because they lived together and so, it was assumed, must have made use of both of their sexes with each other.[21]

The history of hermaphrodites from the seventeenth century to the end of the eighteenth century is, I think, interesting. I will take two cases. One is from 1614-1615 [*rectius*: 1601[22]] and the other from 1765. The first case was known at the time as "the Rouen hermaphrodite."[23] It concerned someone who was baptized as Marie Lemarcis and who gradually became a man, wore men's clothes, and married a widow who was already the mother of three children. There was a denunciation. Marie Lemarcis, who had taken the name of Martin Lemarcis, came before the court and the first judges called for a medical examination by a doctor, an apothecary, and two surgeons. They found no sign of virility. Marie Lemarcis was sentenced to be hung, burned, and her ashes scattered in the wind. His wife, or the woman who lived with him or her, was sentenced to witness the execution of her husband and to be thrashed at the town's crossroads. Because it was a capital penalty, there was a right of appeal that took place at the Rouen court with a new expert opinion. The new experts agreed with the first experts that there was no sign of virility; only one, Duval, recognized signs of virility. The verdict of the Rouen court is interesting because it releases the woman, orders her to wear women's clothes, and prohibits her from living with anyone of either sex, "on pain of death." So there is a ban on all sexual relations but no conviction for the fact of being a hermaphrodite or for the nature of hermaphroditism. Nor is there a conviction for having lived with a woman, even though it seems that the hermaphrodite's dominant sex was that of a woman.

This case seems to me to be important for a number of reasons, and first of all because it gave rise to an open debate between two doctors. One of these doctors, Riolan, was the specialist on monsters at the time and had written a number of books on monstrosity. The other, who gave the expert opinion, was the famous doctor Duval, to whom I have just referred.[24] Duval's expert opinion is very interesting because it presents what could be called the very first rudiments of a clinical approach to sexuality. Duval does not conduct the examination traditionally performed by matrons, doctors, and surgeons. He undertakes a detailed examination with palpitation and, in particular, in his report he gives a detailed description of how he found the organs. This is, I think, the first medical text in which the sexual organization of the human body is not given in its general form but rather in clinical detail and with regard to a particular case. Until then, medical discourse only spoke of sexual organs in general, in their whole conformation, with regard to no one in particular and with considerable reserve in the language used. Here, we have a detailed, individual description in which things are called by their names.

Duval not only does this, he also gives us the theory of medical discourse on sexuality. We should not really be surprised, he says, that the organs of sexuality or reproduction have never been named in medical discourse. Doctors usually hesitate before naming these things since, in a tradition that goes back to Antiquity when women were especially despised because of their debauchery, it was quite normal for a master of knowledge to be unable to speak of a woman's sexual organs. But then came the Virgin Mary who, Duval says, "carried our Savior in her womb." From that moment "holy matrimony" was instituted, all "lewdness was ended" and the "vicious customs of women were abolished." A number of consequences follow from this. The first is that "the womb that was previously mainly blamed in women" now had to be recognized as "the most lovable, noble, holy, venerable and miraculous temple of the universe." Second, men's inclination for the woman's womb was no longer determined by lewdness, but became a sort of tangible "divine precept."[25] Third, the role of women became venerated. Since Christianity women have been entrusted with the care and protection of household goods and their transmission to descendants. There is yet another consequence, or rather a general consequence of all of this: we must now know the womb because it has become this sacred object and because religion has made woman sacred through marriage and the economic system of the transmission of household goods. Why? In the first place, so that women can avoid having to suffer great pain and, even more, so that fewer die in childbirth. Above all, it will reduce the number of children who die at birth or even before they are born. In an obviously wild estimate, Duval says that every year there are a million children who could see the light of day if the knowledge of doctors was sufficiently developed for mothers to be able to give birth in the right way. How many children have not seen the light of day, their mothers dead and buried in the same tombs, he says, due to this "shameful silence"! In this text from 1601 you can see the direct link between the themes of the sacred religious and economic function of women on the one hand, and the mercantilist, strictly economic theme of national strength linked to the size of the population on the other. Women are precious because they reproduce; children are precious because they replenish a population, and no "shameful silence" must stand in the way of knowing what will enable these lives to be saved. Duval writes: "Oh, cruelty! Oh, what great shame! Oh, supreme impiety to recognize that for so many souls to see the light of this world ... requires from us only an apparatus." We lack this apparatus because of words that "some consider sensitive because they could provoke lewdness," which is a very "poor answer when weighed against so many evils and such great inconveniences."[26] I think this text is significant because it gives us not only a medical description of the sexual organs, a clinical description of a particular case, but also the theory of the old medical silence about the sexual organs and the theory of the present need for an explicit discourse.

I will make a short digression at this point. Everyone says that until the sixteenth century and the beginning of the seventeenth century verbal license, the boldness of discourse, made it possible to name a sexuality that later, in the Classical Age, fell under a regime of silence, or at any rate of metaphor. I think this is both very true and very false. It is quite false if you speak of language in general, but it is quite true when you distinguish carefully between types of discursive formation or practice. While it is true that, beginning in this period, the expression of sexuality in literary language had to conform to a regime of censorship or displacement, nonetheless in the same period there was an exactly opposite movement in medical discourse.

Prior to this, medical discourse had been completely impermeable, completely closed to that kind of expression and description. The need for a scientific discourse on sexuality and its anatomical organization appears, and is theorized, with the case of the Rouen hermaphrodite.

The other reason for the importance of this case is that it clearly asserts that a hermaphrodite is a monster. We find this in Riolan's discourse where he says that the hermaphrodite is a monster because he/she is counter to the order and general rule of nature that has divided humankind into two: male and female.[27] Thus, if someone has both sexes, then he/she must be regarded as a monster. However, since the hermaphrodite is a monster, the reason for performing an examination, according to Riolan, will be to determine what clothes he/she must wear and whether, and to whom, he/she can be married.[28] On the one hand, then, we have the clearly formulated demand for a medical discourse on sexuality and its organs and then, on the other, the still traditional conception of hermaphrodites as monsters, but monsters, as we have seen, whose monstrosity nonetheless escapes the conviction and sentencing that were previously the rule.

Let us now turn to 1765. One hundred and fifty years later there is a case that is almost the same as the Rouen case. It is the case of Anne Grandjean, baptized as a girl.[29] However, as someone who wrote a statement in her support said, "as she approached her fourteenth birthday, a certain instinct for pleasure drew her to her girlfriends."[30] Disturbed by her attraction to young girls, she decided to wear boys' clothes, move to another town, and settle in Lyon, where she married someone called Françoise Lambert. After being exposed, she was brought before the courts. She was seen by the surgeon who concluded that she was a woman and could be tried since she had lived with another woman. She had, then, used the sex that was not dominant in her, and the first judges sentenced her to the pillory with this inscription: "She profaned the marriage sacrament."[31] The pillory, whip, and cane. In this case, too, there was an appeal before the Dauphiné court. Her case was dismissed, that is to say, she was released, with the requirement that she wear women's clothes and that she associate with neither Françoise Lambert nor any other woman. You can see that the judicial process and verdict in this case are more or less the same as in 1601, the only difference being that whereas Françoise Lambert [*rectius:* Anne Grandjean] was banned from spending her time with women, and only with women, in the previous case it was with anyone of "whatever" sex.[32] Marie Lemarcis was banned from sexuality and sexual relationships.[33]

The Grandjean case, despite being almost completely isomorphic with the 1601 case, nevertheless marks a very important development. First of all, it is important because of the fact that the hermaphrodite is no longer defined in medical discourse as a mixture of two sexes, as was still the case with Riolan.[34] In the memoirs written and published by Champeaux concerning the Grandjean case, he refers explicitly to an article of about the same time, "Hermaphrodit," in the *Dictionnaire de médecine,* where it says: "I consider all the stories about hermaphrodites as so many fables."[35] For Champeaux, and for most doctors at the time, there is no mix of the sexes; there is never the simultaneous presence of two sexes in a single organism and a single individual.[36] But there are individuals "who have a [predominant] sex, but the generative parts of which are so badly formed that they cannot engender [in themselves or outside of themselves]."[37] Consequently, what we call a hermaphrodite is only a defective structure accompanied by impotence. There are those who have male organs and some female forms (that we will define as secondary characteristics), and there are very few of these, according to Champeaux.[38] Then there are those who are women with female organs and some forms, some secondary characteristics, that are male, and Champeaux says that there are many of these.[39]

Thus, monstrosity as the mix of sexes, as transgression of everything that separates one sex from another, disappears.[40] However, and here the notion of monstrosity that we find at the start of the nineteenth century begins to be developed, there is no mixing of the sexes: There are only eccentricities, kinds of imperfection, errors of nature. These eccentricities, these poor structures, errors, and stammerings of nature are, or at any rate may be, the source or the pretext for a number of forms of criminal conduct. Champeaux says that it is not the fact of being a hermaphrodite that should arouse or provoke our condemnation of the woman Grandjean. Rather, it is the simple fact that for a woman she has perverse tastes, that she loves women, and it is this monstrosity, which is not a monstrosity of nature but a monstrosity of behavior, that calls for condemnation. Monstrosity, therefore, is no longer the undue mixture of what should be separated by nature. It is simply an irregularity, a slight deviation, but one that makes possible something that really will be a monstrosity, that is to say, the monstrosity of character. Champeaux says, "Why then assume a supposed sexual division in these lustful women," who are only women after all, "and attribute an inclination toward such criminal debauchery to the first natural impressions of their own sex? This would be to excuse the horrible crimes of those men, the shame of humanity, who reject a natural alliance in order to satisfy their brutality with other men. Will it be said that they experience only coldness with women, and that an instinct for pleasure, the cause of which they do not know, draws them, despite themselves, to their own sex? Woe betide whoever is persuaded by such reasoning."[41]

You can see how in this case the juridico-natural complex of hermaphroditic monstrosity begins to break up. On the basis of what is no more than an imperfection, a deviation—we could say, in anticipation, a somatic abnormality—the attribution of a monstrosity emerges that is no longer juridico-natural but juridico-moral; a monstrosity of conduct rather than the monstrosity of nature.[42] And in the end it is indeed this theme of the monstrosity of conduct that organized and was at the center of the discussion of the Grandjean case. Anne Grandjean's supporter, the lawyer Vermeil, insisted on the significance of organic deformity despite the general opinion of the doctors.[43] (Vermeil did not defend Anne Grandjean because he was not a criminal lawyer at the time, but he published a statement in her defense.) Against the doctors, Vermeil tried to claim that there was a mix of sexes, and therefore true hermaphroditism, in Anne Grandjean. In this way he could absolve her of the moral monstrosity she was accused of by the doctors who no longer recognized the monstrous character of hermaphroditism or who no longer recognized that hermaphroditism involved a real mixture of the sexes. The proof that this was what was at stake is found in a poem published in support of Anne Grandjean and that circulated under her name. It is a love poem about the woman she lived with. Sadly, it was probably written by someone other than Anne Grandjean. It is a long poem in poor verse whose entire meaning consists, I believe, in showing, along with Anne Grandjean's defenders, that the feelings she had for the woman she lived with were not monstrous but perfectly natural.[44]

Anyway, when we compare the first and later case, the Rouen case and the Lyon case, the one from 1601 and the one from 1765, we can see a change that is, so to speak, the autonomization of a moral monstrosity, of a monstrosity of behavior that transposes the old category of the monster from the domain of somatic and natural disorder to the domain of pure and simple criminality. From then on we see the emergence of a kind of specific domain that will become the domain of monstrous criminality or of a monstrosity that does not produce its effects in nature and the confusion of species, but in behavior itself.

This is, of course, no more than a sketch. It is the beginning of a process that develops between 1765 and 1820-1830, when the problem of monstrous conduct, of monstrous criminality, will explode. This is only the point of departure of this movement and transformation. However, to sum everything up in a couple of words I would say that until the middle of the eighteenth century monstrosity had a criminal status inasmuch as it was a transgression of an entire system of laws, whether natural laws or juridical laws. Thus it was monstrosity in itself that was criminal. The jurisprudence of the seventeenth and eighteenth centuries tried as far as possible to remove the penal consequences of this inherently criminal monstrosity. However, I think it still remained essentially and fundamentally criminal until late in the eighteenth century. It is, then, monstrosity that is criminal. Then, toward 1750, in the middle of the eighteenth century (for reasons that I will try to analyze later), we see something emerge, that is to say, the theme of the monstrous nature of criminality, of a monstrosity that takes effect in the domain of conduct, of criminality, and not in the domain of nature itself. Until about the middle of the eighteenth century, monstrosity necessarily indicated criminality and was not yet what it later became, that is to say, a possible qualifier of criminality. At the end of the end of the eighteenth and the beginning of the nineteenth centuries, the figure of the monstrous criminal, of the moral monster, suddenly appears with great exuberance. It appears in extraordinarily different forms of discourse and practice. In literature, the moral monster looms up in the gothic novel at the end of eighteenth century. It breaks out with Sade. It also appears with a whole series of political themes that I will talk about next week. It appears in the judicial and medical world. Our problem is to know how this transformation was brought about. What prevented the formation of this category of monstrous criminality? What was it that prevented aggravated criminality from being seen as a kind of monstrosity? How was it that the extremity of crime and the aberration of nature were not linked together? Why was it that we had to wait until the end of the eighteenth and the beginning of the nineteenth centuries for the appearance of this heinous figure of the criminal monster in whom the most extreme breach of the law joins up with the aberration of nature? And it is not the aberration of nature that in itself is a breach of the law, but the breach of the law that refers—as if to its origin, cause, excuse, or framework, it matters little—to something that is the aberration of nature itself.

This is what I would like to try to explain next week. Of course, the principle of this transformation is to be found, I believe, in a kind of economy of the power to punish and the transformation of this economy.

1. Foucault is referring here to the whole of Lombroso's activity in the field of criminal anthropology. See, in particular, C. Lombroso, *L'Uomo delinquente studiato in rapporto all'antropologia, alla medicina legale ed alle discipline carcerarie* (Milan, 1876). French translation (from the 4ᵗʰ edition of the Italian): *L'Homme criminel* (Paris: s.l., 1997).

2. Cf. lectures of 29 January and 5 February, in this volume.

3. Foucault's analysis of the figure of the monster in this course is fundamentally based upon the work of E. Martin, *Histoire des monstres depuis l'Antiquité jusqu'à nos jours* (Paris, 1880).

4. Ibid., p. 7: "The expressions *portentum* and *ostentum* will designate a simple abnormality, and that of *monstrum* will be applied exclusively to any being which does not have human form." The foundation for the Roman law is *Digesta* 1.5.14: "Non sunt liberi qui contra formam humani generis converso more procreantur: veluti si mulier monstrosum aliquid aut prodigiosum enixa sit. Partus autem, qui membrorum humanorum official ampliavit, aliquatenus videtur effectus et ideo inter liberos connumerabitur." *Digesta Iustiniani Augusti*, vol. 2, edited by T. Mommsen (Berolini, 1870), p. 16.

5. E. Martin, *Histoire des monstres*, pp. 85-110.

6. Cf. A. Pareaus, *De monstris et prodigiis*, in *Opera*, latinitate donata I. Guilleameau labore et diligentia (Paris, 1582), p. 751. French translation: A. Paré, *Des monstres et prodiges*, in *Les Œuvres*, 7th edition (Paris, 1617), p. 1031: "Monsters are born, some half in the form of a beast and the other half human, or some completely resembling animals. These are the products of sodomites and atheists who couple, against nature, with beasts. Many horrendous monsters, shameful to see and to speak of, are generated in this way. Each time dishonesty is effected in deed, not just in word, the result is most unfortunate and abominable; and infamy and disgrace to the man or woman who couples with beasts, whence come these monstrous half men, half beasts."

7. Cf. F. E. Cangiamila, *Embriologia sacra ovvero dell'uffizio de' sacerdoti, medici e superiori circa l'eterna salute de' bambini racchiusi nell'utero libri quattro* (Palermo, 1745), and *Embryologia sacra sive De officio sacerdotum, medicorum et aliorum circa aeternam parvulorum in utero existentium salutem libri quatuor* (Panormi, 1758). Translated into French, by J. A.-T. Dinouart, as *Abrégé de l'embryologie sacrée ou Traité des devoirs des prêtres, des médecins et autres, sur le salut éternel des enfants qui sont dans le ventre de leur mère* (Paris, 1762). The chapter on the baptism of monsters ends by noting that although the monster, "completely formless and frightful in its physical aspect, soon dies naturally," there is legislation that "explicitly prohibits the suffocation of these monsters and orders the curate to be called in order to examine them and make a judgment" (pp. 192-93).

8. Cf. P. Zacchia, *Questionum medico-legalium tomus secondus* (Lyon, 1726), p. 526. On the question of inheritance in cases of the birth of a *monstrum* in modern European jurisprudence, see E. Martin, *Histoire des monstres*, pp. 177-210.

9. F. E. Cangiamila, *Abrégé de l'embryologie sacrée*: "Two questions can be posed here: 'When can we say that a monster has a rational soul, so that he can be baptized?'; 'When is there only one soul and when are there two, so that one can give one or two baptisms?' " (pp. 188-89).

10. "If a monster has two bodies which, despite being joined, each possess its own limbs ... two separate baptisms must be given because there are certainly two men and two souls present. In the case of pressing danger, the single formula in the plural may be used: i.e. 'I baptize you,' 'Ego vos baptiso,' " ibid., pp. 190-91.

11. We have not found the documentation to which Foucault refers.

12. The case is cited by H. Sauval, *Histoire et Recherches des antiquités de la ville de Paris*, vol. 2 (Paris, 1724), p. 564: "Since he had killed a man with a knife, he was tried and sentenced to death, but because of his brother, who took no part in the murder, he was not

executed, it not being possible to put one to death without killing the other at the same time."

13. The juridical sources of the discussion—*Digesta Iustiniani,* I.5.10 (*Quaeritur*); XXII.5.15 (*Repetundarum*); XXVIII.2.6. (*Sed est quaesitum*)—are found in *Digesta Iustiniani Augusti,* pp. 16, 652, and 820. Regarding the question of marriage, the *Summae* of the Middle Ages are unanimous. See for example: H. de Segusio, *Summa aurea ad vetustissimos codices collata* (Basel, 1573), col. 488. For the priesthood: S. Maiolus, *Tractatus de irregularitate et aliis canonicis impedimentis in quinque libros distributos quibus eclesiasticos ordines suscipere et susceptos administrare quisque prohibetur* (Rome, 1619), pp. 60-63.

14. F. E. Cangiamila, *Embriologia sacra ovvero dell'uffizio de' sacerdoti, medici e superiori circa l'eterna salute de' bambini racchiusi nell'utero libri quattro* (Palermo, 1745), and *Embryologia sacra sive De officio sacerdotum, medicorum et aliorum circa aeternam parvulorum in utero existentium salutem libri quatuor* (Panormi, 1758). Foucault uses the second French edition, considerably expanded and approved by the Royal Academy of Surgery: *Abrégé de l'embryologie sacrée ou Traité des devoirs des prêtres, des médicins, des chirurgiens, et des sages-femmes envers les enfants qui sont dans le sein de leur mère* (Paris, 1766). His analysis of the "juridical-natural" or "juridical-biological" theory of the monster is essentially based on chapter eight, "Du baptème des monstres," of book 3, pp. 188-93.

15. Foucault's judgment is based upon H. Sauval, *Histoire et Recherches des antiquités,* vol. 2, p. 563: "So many babies born coupled and joined together have been seen in Paris that a book could be written about it, there being so many reported cases, not to mention those that go unreported." Some are "among the most rare and monstrous" (ibid., pp. 563-66). Regarding the medical literature, see A. Paré, *Des monstres et prodiges,* critical edition with a commentary by J. Céard (Geneva: s.l., 1971) pp. 9-20 (with Céard's complete bibliography of authors who have dealt with Siamese twins in their works on monsters, pp. 203-18). It should also be noted that the term *"frères siamois"* (Siamese twins) was only introduced into medical literature in the nineteenth century.

16. The case of Antide Collas is reported in E. Martin, *Histoire des monstres,* p. 106: "Toward the end of 1599 . . . a woman of Dôle, named Antide Collas, was accused of having a physical characteristic that, judging from the details contained in the trial documents, must have been similar to that of Marie le Marcis. Doctors were called to undertake an examination. They established that the malformation of her sexual organs was the result of vile commerce with demons. Since these conclusions supported the accusation, Antide Collas was returned to prison. She was put to the question and tortured. She resisted for some time but, overcome by her horrible suffering, ended up deciding to confess: "She confessed," the chronicler says, "that she had had criminal relations with Satan and she was burned alive on the public square of Dôle."

17. P.-J. Brillon, *Dictionnaire des arrêts ou Jurisprudence universelle des parlements de France et autres tribunaux* (Paris, 1711, 3 vols.; Paris, 1727, 6 vols.; and Lyon, 1781-1788, 7 vols.). Foucault uses the first edition, whose second volume (pp. 366-67) presents six questions regarding hermaphroditism.

18. Ibid., p. 367: "Hermaphrodites . . . are known by their dominant sex. Some have claimed that the accusation of the crime of sodomy could be leveled against hermaphrodites who, having chosen the male sex that is dominant in them, have assumed the role of a woman. A young hermaphrodite was condemned to be hanged and burned for this crime by the decision of the Paris parliament in 1603." Nonetheless, several sources (for example, the *Dictionnaire universel française et latin vulgairement appelé Dictionnaire de Trévoux,* vol. 4 [Paris, 1771]) do not cite sodomy as the reason for that sentence.

19. L. de Héricourt, *Les Lois ecclésiastiques de France dans leur ordre naturel et une analyse des livres du droit canonique, considérées avec les usages de l'Église gallicane* (Paris, 1719). Foucault uses the last edition (1771).

20. Ibid., vol. 3, p. 88: "By the decision of the Paris parliament in the year 1603, a hermaphrodite who had chosen the male sex dominant in him was convicted for having used his other sex and was condemned to be hanged and burned."

21. The case is reported in E. Martin, *Histoire des monstres*, pp. 106-07: "In 1603 . . . a young hermaphrodite was accused of having relations with another person with the same physical configuration. As soon as the facts became known, the authorities seized the two unfortunates and a trial was initiated. . . . Upon proof of their guilt they were condemned to death and executed."

22. Concerning correction of the dating, see the following note.

23. The trial began on 7 January and ended on 7 June 1601. The case is reported in J. Duval, *Des hermaphrodits, accouchemens des femmes, et traitement qui est requis pour les relever en santé et bien élever leurs enfants* (Rouen, 1612), pp. 383-447 (revised edition: *Traité des hermaphrodits, parties génitales, accouchements des femmes* [Paris, 1880], pp. 352-415).

24. J. Riolan, *Discours sur les hermaphrodits, où il est démontré, contre l'opinion commune, qu'il n'y a point de vrais hermaphrodits* (Paris, 1614); J. Duval, *Réponse au discours fait par le sieur Riolan, docteur en médecine et professeur en chirurgie et pharmacie à Paris, contre l'histoire de l'hermaphrodit de Rouen* (Rouen, n.d. [1615]).

25. J. Duval, *Réponse au discours fait par le sieur Riolan*, pp. 23-24.

26. Ibid., pp. 34-35.

27. Cf. J. Riolan, *Discours sur les hermaphrodits*, pp. 6—10 ("what is a hermaphrodite and is it a monster[?]").

28. Ibid.: "how to recognize hermaphrodites in order to give them the sex appropriate to their nature" (pp. 124—30); "how to treat hermaphrodites in order to restore to them a whole nature, capable of generation" (pp.130-34).

29. Concerning the Anne Grandjean case, cf. F.-M. Vermeil, *Mémoire pour Anne Grandjean connu sous le nom de Jean-Baptiste Grandjean, accusé et appelant, contre Monsieur le Procureur général, accusateur et intimé. Question: «Un hermaphrodite, qui a épousé une fille, peut-il être réputé profanateur du sacrement de mariage, quand la nature, qui le trompait, l'appelait à l'état de mari?»* (Paris, 1765); C. Champeaux, *Réflexions sur les hermaphrodites relativement à Anne Grand-Jean, qualifiée telle dans un mémoire de Maître Vermeil, avocat au Parlement* (Avignon, 1765). The case was publicized in Europe thanks to the summation of these rare documents by G. Arnaud [de Ronsil], *Dissertation sur les hermaphrodites*, in *Mémoires de chirurgie*, vol. 1 (London, Paris, 1768), pp. 329-90, who published them in full and translated them into German under the title *Anatomisch-chirurgische Abhandlung über die Hermaphroditen* (Strasbourg, 1777).

30. Vermeil, *Mémoire pour Anne Grandjean*, p. 4.

31. Ibid., p. 9.

32. See also the manuscript note on the attorney Vermeil's copy of the *Mémoire*, kept in the Bibliothèque Nationale de France: "recording the sentence of la Tournelle of 10 January 1765, in which the public prosecutor annulled Anne Grandjean's marriage, instructed her to wear women's clothes, and prohibited her from living with Françoise Lambert or anyone else of the same sex."

33. "[The court] clearly prohibited [them] from living with anyone of either sex on pain of death" (Duval, *Traité des hermaphrodits*, p. 410).

34. Cf. Riolan, *Discours sur les hermaphrodits*, p. 6.

35. C. Champeaux, *Réflexions sur les hermaphrodites*, p. 10. Cf. the article "Hermaphrodit," in *Dictionnaire universel de médecine*, vol. 4 (Paris, 1748): "I consider all the stories about hermaphrodites to be so many fables. I will note here that in all the people that have been presented to me as hermaphrodites I have only seen a clitoris of exorbitant thickness and length, the lips of which are prodigiously swollen, and nothing of a man." This dictionary is the French translation—by Denis Diderot—of R. James, *A Medicinal Dictionary* (London, 1743-1745).

36. Champeaux, *Réflexions sur les hermaphrodites*, p. 10.

37. Ibid., p. 36

38. Ibid., pp. 7, 11-15.

39. Ibid., pp. 7, 15-36.

40. Ibid., pp. 37-38.

41. Ibid., pp. 26-27.

42. "So many observations so unanimously established should doubtless be considered as a body of incontestable proof, that some irregularities of nature in the distinctive human parts pertaining to sex do not change the species at all, and still less the inclinations of the individual in which this defective physical configuration is found," ibid., pp. 35-36.

43. G. Arnaud, *Dissertation sur les hermaphrodites:* "Thus Grandjean's error was an error common to everyone. If she is criminal, we should blame everyone. For it is this common error that has strengthened our belief in the accused. Let us better say that this error is what justifies her today. Nature alone is at fault in this case, and how can we make the accused responsible for the wrongs of nature?" (p. 351).

44. E.-Th. Simon, *L'Hermaphrodite ou Lettre de Grandjean à Françoise Lambert, sa femme* (Grenoble, 1765).

four

29 January 1975

The moral monster. ~ Crime in classical law. ~ The spectacle of public torture and execution (la supplice). ~ Transformation of the mechanisms of power. ~ Disappearance of the ritual expenditure of punitive power. ~ The pathological nature of criminality. ~ The political monster: Louis XVI and Marie-Antoinette. ~ The monster in Jacobin literature (the tyrant) and anti-Jacobin literature (the rebellious people). ~ Incest and cannibalism.

TODAY I WANT TO talk about a character, the moral monster, who appears on the threshold of the nineteenth century and whose destiny will be extremely important right until the end of the nineteenth and the beginning of the twentieth centuries.

Until the seventeenth or eighteenth century I think we can say that monstrosity as the natural manifestation of the unnatural brought with it an indication of criminality.* At the level of the rules governing natural species and distinctions between natural species, the monstrous individual was always associated, if not systematically at least virtually, with a possible criminality. Then, starting in the nineteenth century, the relationship is reversed and monstrosity is systematically suspected of being behind all criminality. Every criminal

---

* The manuscript says: "of criminality, the value of which was modified but not yet canceled in the middle of the eighteenth century."

could well be a monster, just as previously it was possible that the monster was a criminal.

The problem, then, is how this transformation was brought about. What was it that brought about this transformation? To answer this I think we should first divide up the question and ask how it was that in the seventeenth century, and late into the eighteenth century, the reading of monstrosity was not reversible. How was it that the potentially criminal character of monstrosity could be admitted without establishing or positing the reciprocal proposition of the potentially monstrous character of criminality? The aberration of nature was inscribed in the transgression of law, but not the reverse. That is to say, the extremity of crime was not likened to the aberration of nature. Punishment of an involuntary monstrosity was admitted, but not the spontaneous mechanism of a confused, disturbed, and contradictory nature behind crime. Why?

I want to reply to this subsidiary question first of all. It seems to me that we should look for the reason in what could be called the economy of punitive power. In classical law—and I will be brief since I think I have already referred to this several times[1]—a crime was voluntary harm done to another, but it was not only this. Neither was it only a wrong and a damage done to the interests of the whole society. The crime was crime insofar it attacked the sovereign; it attacked his rights and his will present in the law and it thereby attacked his strength and physical body. In every crime, therefore, there was a clash of forces, a revolt, or insurrection against the sovereign. There was a fragment of regicide in the smallest crime. You can see that according to this law of the fundamental economy of the right to punish, punishment was neither simple restitution for damage done, as is clear, nor something demanded in the name of the fundamental rights and interests of society. Punishment was always something more: It was the sovereign's vengeance, his revenge, and the return of his strength. Punishment was always a vendetta, and the sovereign's personal vendetta. The sovereign confronted the criminal anew, but what took place in the ritual deployment of his strength on the scaffold was the ceremonial reversal of the crime. In the crim-

inal's punishment one witnessed the ritual and well-ordered reconstitution of power in its integrity. There was nothing like a common
unit of measurement between crime and punishment. There was no
common locus of crime and punishment, no common element found
in both one and the other. The problem of the relationship between
crime and punishment was not posed in terms of measure, of a
measurable equality or inequality. Rather, there was a sort of joust
between them, a sort of rivalry. The excess of punishment had to
respond to the excess of the crime and triumph over it. There was a
necessary imbalance, therefore, at the very heart of the act of punishment. There had to be a kind of surplus on the side of punishment.
This surplus was terror; the terrorizing character of the punishment.
The terrorizing character of the punishment should be understood in
terms of the constitutive elements of terror. First of all, the terror
inherent in the punishment had to take up the crime again; the crime
had to be somehow presented, represented, actualized, or reactualized
in the punishment itself. The very horror of the crime had to be there
on the scaffold. In addition, a fundamental element of the terror was
the splendor of the sovereign's vengeance that had to be presented as
insurmountable and invincible. Finally, terror had to involve intimi-
dation against any future crime. Consequently, public torture (*la
supplice*) naturally had its place in this unbalanced economy of punishments. The principal element of this economy was not then the
law of measure: it was the principle of excessive demonstration. The
corollary of this principle was what could be called communication
in the atrocious. What bound crime and punishment together was not
a common measure but atrocity. The atrocious character of the crime
was the form, or rather the intensity, it acquired when it reached a
certain degree of rarity, violence, or scandal. A crime that reached a
certain point of intensity was considered atrocious, and the atrociousness of the penalty had to respond to the atrocious crime. In the
atrociousness of the penalty, the atrociousness of the crime had to be
turned into the excess of triumphant power; retort, then, and not
measure.[2]

Crime and punishment communicate with each other only through this kind of imbalance that revolved around rituals of atrocity. You can see, then, that the enormity of crime could not be a problem precisely because, however enormous a crime might be, however atrocious it appeared, there was always power left over; there was something specific to the intensity of sovereign power that always enabled it to respond to any crime, however atrocious. There was no unanswered crime inasmuch as the power responsible for responding to it always had available an excess of power that could nullify it. That is why power never had to withdraw or hesitate before an atrocious crime: Sovereign power had a stock of intrinsic atrocities that enabled it to erase the crime.

This was how the great scenes of public torture and execution took place in the seventeenth or even the eighteenth century. You recall, for example, the atrocious crime committed against William of Orange.* When William of Orange was assassinated, the response was an equally atrocious public torture and execution. It took place in 1584 and is recounted by Brantôme. The assassin was tortured for eighteen days: "On the first day he was taken to a place where there was a cauldron of boiling water into which the arm that struck the blow was plunged. The following day the arm was cut off and, after it fell at his feet, he was constantly kicking it from top to bottom of the scaffold. On the third day he was tortured with pincers gripping his breast and forearms. The fourth day he was similarly tortured from behind with pincers gripping his arms and buttocks, and in this way the man was tortured over eighteen days, on the last of which he was broken on the wheel and beaten with a wooden club. At the end of six hours he was still asking for water that was not given to him. Finally, the lieutenant in charge of criminal executions was asked to finish him off and strangle him so that his soul did not despair."[3]

We still find examples of this same ritual excess of power at the end of the seventeenth century. The following example is taken from the jurisprudence of Avignon. It took place in the Papal States and so is not exactly the same as that which took place in France, but it

---

* William I, *the Silent*, Prince of Orange. 1533-1584. *Trans.*

gives us the general style and structural principles that govern public torture and execution. The *massola* consisted of the following. The condemned man was tied to the stake, blindfolded. Around the scaffold were placed stakes with iron hooks. The confessor spoke in the penitent's ear and, "after he had been blessed, the executioner, with an iron club like those used in an abattoir, struck the unfortunate with all his strength on the side of his head and killed him." It is precisely after death that the public torture begins, because in the end it was less a question of punishing the guilty or of expiating the crime than of producing a ritual display of the infinite power to punish: the ceremony of punitive power, unfolding on the basis of itself and when its object has disappeared, thus works away on a corpse. After the unfortunate has fallen dead, the executioner "who has a big knife, cuts his throat, which covers him with blood and produces a spectacle that is horrible to behold; he cuts the tendons from the two heels and then opens the belly and takes out the heart, the liver, the spleen and the lungs and attaches them to some iron hooks; he dissects them and cuts them into pieces that he puts on the other hooks as he works, just as one does with an animal. Behold who can."[4]

You can see, then, that the mechanisms of power are so strong and their excess is so ritually calculated that punishment never has to inscribe the crime, however outrageous, in terms of something like a nature. The mechanisms of power are strong enough to absorb, display, and nullify the enormity of crime in rituals of sovereignty. To that extent, it is not necessary, it is not even possible, for outrageous crime to have anything like a nature. Outrageous crime does not have a nature; in fact, there is only a battle, rage, and fury that starts with the crime and revolves around it. There is no mechanics of crime that could be the object of a possible knowledge; there is only a strategy of power that deploys its force around and with regard to the crime. It is for this reason that until the end of the seventeenth century the question of the criminal's nature did not arise. The economy of power was such that the question need never arise, or rather, it existed only very marginally in a way that I will briefly indicate. In some texts, and in particular in a text by Bruneau of 1715, *Observations et maximes sur les matières criminelles*, we read the following: The judge must study the accused. He must study his mind, his habits, the strength of his physical qualities, his age and his sex. As far as he can, he must "enter within" the criminal so as to penetrate, if possible, his soul.[5] Clearly, a text like this appears to deny everything I have just been saying to you in a somewhat schematic and offhand way. However, when we look more closely we see that the judge must have knowledge of the criminal, must enter into the criminal, not at all so that he can understand the crime, but only so as to know if it was committed. What this means is that the judge must be familiar with the criminal's soul in order to question him appropriately, so that he can catch him out with his questions, so that he can weave around him the specious cunning of questioning and force the truth from him. The judge's knowledge must lay siege to the criminal as a subject who possesses the truth and never as a criminal who has committed the crime. For all this knowledge serves no purpose in fixing the punishment once he has confessed. It is not the criminal subject but the knowing subject who is thus besieged by this knowledge. Thus, I think we can say that until the end of eighteenth century the economy of punitive power was such that there was no need to raise a question about the nature of crime, and especially about the nature of an outrageous crime.

How, then, was the transformation brought about? We pass now to the second part of the question. More precisely, in what way did the exercise of the power to punish crimes need, at a given moment, to refer to the criminal's nature? How, at a certain point, was the division between lawful and unlawful acts yoked to a distribution of normal and abnormal individuals? I would like to indicate at least the direction my response will take. We know, as all historians say, that the eighteenth century saw the invention of a series of scientific and industrial technologies. Furthermore, we also know that in the eighteenth century a number of political forms of government were defined, or at least schematized and theorized. Equally, we know that in this century State apparatuses and the institutions linked to them were set up, or developed and perfected. But it should be stressed, and this seems to me to be at the origin of the transformation I am trying to identify, that something else was developed in the eighteenth century. There was the elaboration of what could be called a new economy of the mechanisms of power: a set of procedures and analyses that enabled the effects of power to be increased, the costs of its exercise reduced and its exercise integrated in mechanisms of production. By increasing the effects of power I mean that there was the discovery in the eighteenth century of a number of means by which, or at least, the principle in accordance with which power could be exercised in a continuous manner, rather than in the ritual, ceremonial, discontinuous way it was exercised under feudalism and continued to be exercised in the absolute monarchies. That is to say, it is no longer exercised through ritual, but through permanent mechanisms of surveillance and control. Increasing the effects of power means that mechanisms of power lose the incomplete character they had in feudal regimes and continued to have in the regimes of absolute monarchy. Instead of being brought to bear on arbitrarily defined points, zones, individuals, or groups, mechanisms of power were discovered in the eighteenth century that could be exercised without gaps and that could penetrate the social body in its totality. Finally, increasing the effects of power means making them inevitable in principle, that is to say, detaching them from the arbitrariness of the sovereign and his good will so as to turn them into a sort of absolutely fatal and necessary law, weighing in principle on everyone in the same way. So, there is an increase in the effects of power and also a reduction of the cost of power: the eighteenth century saw the refinement of a whole series of mechanisms for exercising power at less financial and economic cost than in the absolute monarchies. The cost of power is also reduced in the sense of reducing the possibilities of resistance, discontent, and revolt that could be provoked by monarchical power. Finally, these mechanisms of power reduce the extent, level, and surface covered by the disobedient and illegal conduct that monarchical and feudal power had to tolerate. Then, as well as increasing the effects of power and reducing its economic and political costs, these mechanisms enable power to be integrated in processes of production: Instead of power working essentially through a levy' on production, the eighteenth century invented mechanisms of power that could be directly superimposed on the processes of production, accompanying them throughout their development and functioning like a sort of permanent control and increase of production. You can see that I am only summarizing schematically what I explained two years ago with regard to the disciplines.[6] Broadly speaking, we can say that the bourgeois revolution was not just the conquest by a new class of State apparatuses that had been gradually constructed by the absolute monarchy. Nor was it just the organization of an institutional system. The bourgeois revolution of the eighteenth century and the beginning of the nineteenth century was the invention of a new technology of power whose essential elements were the disciplines.

Having said this (and referring again to previous analyses), it seems to me that the penal system and the organization of punitive power can serve as an example of this new technological system of power. First of all, at the end of the eighteenth century there is a punitive power that depends on such a tight network of surveillance that crime in principle can no longer avoid punishment. An incomplete justice gives way to an apparatus of justice and police, of surveillance and punishment, in which there is no longer any discontinuity in the exercise of punitive power. Second, the new technology of punitive power links crime and punishment together in a necessary and obvious way through a number of procedures at the forefront of which are public proceedings and the rule of profound conviction. Henceforth, for every crime there must be a corresponding penalty that must be publicly applied following a proof that is accessible to all. Finally, the third characteristic of this new technology of punitive power is that punishment must be exercised in such a way that one only punishes as much as is necessary, and no more than is necessary, to prevent repetition of the crime. All that excess, the whole giant economy of the ritual and magnificent expenditure of punitive power now gives way to an economy of measure instead of imbalance and excess. A unit of measurement common to crime and punishment had to be found so that the punishment both fits the crime and prevents its reoccurrence. Judges and criminal law theorists call this unit of measurement of the new technology of punitive power "interest," or the crime's motive, the element that is the crime's raison d'être, the principle of its appearance, repetition, imitation by others, and greatest frequency. In short, interest is the basis both of real crimes actually committed and of similar possible crimes that may be committed by others. This natural basis of crime, this motive for crime, is what has to serve as the unit of measurement. The mechanisms of punishment must work on this element in order to neutralize the basis of crime, in order to set something against it that is at least as strong, or just a little bit stronger. Consequently, punishment must be brought to bear on this element according to a precisely calculated system. Penal theory and the new legislation of the eighteenth century define the motive for the crime, or interest as the motive for the crime, as the element common to crime and punishment. Instead of the grand extravagant rituals in which the atrociousness of the penalty repeated the atrociousness of the crime, there will be a calculated system in which, instead of repeating and striking at the crime itself, punishment is brought to bear on the interest motivating the crime by introducing a similar, analogous interest that is just a little stronger than the interest that was the basis of the crime itself. This interest-motive component of the crime is the new economic principle of punitive power and replaces the old principle of atrocity.

You can see that this generates a new set of questions. Henceforth, the important question is not the circumstances of the crime—an old legal notion—or the question of the criminal's intention posed by casuists. The question now concerns the mechanism and play of interests that could have made the person accused of a crime into a criminal. Therefore, it does not concern the circumstances of the crime or even the subject's intention but the immanent rationality of criminal conduct, its natural intelligibility. What is the natural intelligibility that is both the basis for the crime and that makes it possible to determine an exactly appropriate punishment? Crime, then, is no longer only the violation of civil and religious laws; it is no longer only a violation of civil and religious laws that is thereby a potential violation of the laws of nature themselves. Crime now has a nature. Through the operations of the new economy of punitive power, crime is now filled out with what it never had and could never have in the old economy of punitive power; it is provided with a nature. Crime has a nature and the criminal is a natural being defined by his criminality at the level of his nature. You can see that this new economy of power requires an absolutely new knowledge; a naturalist's knowledge, as it were, of criminality. The natural history of the criminal as a criminal will have to be created.

The third set of questions or demands we encounter is that if it is true that crime has a nature, if crime must be analyzed and punished—and it must be analyzed in order to be punished—as a conduct with a natural intelligibility, then we must ask what kind of interest it is that violates the interest of everyone else and goes so far as to expose itself to the worst dangers by risking punishment. Is not this interest, this natural element and immanent intelligibility of the criminal act, an interest blind to its own ends? Is it not an intelligibility that something, a natural mechanism, has driven out of control? Perhaps an interest that drives an individual to crime and the risk of punishment, and of a fatal and necessary punishment in the new system, is one that is so strong that it fails to calculate its consequences and cannot see beyond itself? Is it not an interest that contradicts itself by asserting itself? And anyway, is not an interest that does not conform to the nature of all interests an irregular, deviant interest? For it should not be forgotten that the original contract that citizens are supposed to have signed together, or to which they are supposed to have subscribed individually, clearly showed that it is in the nature of interest to join with the interest of others and renounce its solitary assertion. So, when the criminal takes up his egoistic interest, withdraws it from the legislation founded by the contract, and makes it prevail over the interest of everyone else, does he not restore nature? Does he not return to its history and intrinsic necessity? As a result of this, do we not encounter in the criminal a character who is the return of nature within a social body that has given up the state of nature through the pact and obedience to the laws? And will not this natural individual be quite paradoxical, since he ignores the natural development of interest? He is unaware of the necessary tendency of interest and that the supreme point of his interest is to accept the game of collective interests. Is he not a natural individual who brings with him the old man of the forests with all the fundamental presocial archaisms and who is, at the same time, an unnatural individual? In short, is not the criminal precisely nature against nature? Is this not the monster?

In fact, the question of the potentially pathological nature of criminality appears for the first time within this general climate, within this horizon, in which the new economy of punitive power is formulated in a new theory of punishment and criminality.* According to a tradition found in Montesquieu but going back to the sixteenth century, the Middle Ages, and also to Roman law, the criminal, and especially the frequency of crimes, represents a disease of the social body.[7] The frequency of criminality represents a disease, but a disease of the collectivity, of the social body. Although superficially similar, there is a great difference between this tradition and the theme that appears at the end of the eighteenth century in which it is not crime that is a disease of the social body but rather the criminal who as such is someone who may well be ill. This is expressed quite clearly at the time of the French Revolution in discussions that took place around 1790-1791, when the new penal code was being worked out.[8] I will quote some texts. Take, for example, Prugnon who said: "Murderers are exceptions to the laws of nature, their entire moral being is extinguished. . . . They are out of the ordinary."[9] Or again, in another text: "A murderer is [really] a sick being whose tainted organization has corrupted all the affections. A bitter and burning humor consumes him."[10] In *Médicine expectante,* Vitet says that perhaps some crimes are in themselves kinds of illness.[11] In volume 16 of the *Journal de médecine,*

---

* The manuscript adds: "The affiliation of crime with all that still confused domain of the pathological, of illness, of the natural aberration and disorder of the mind and the body. In the crime one must see an indicator of abnormalities. This explains why one sees a displacement of the traditional theme at the end of the eighteenth century."

Prunelle proposes an inquiry in the Toulon baths to establish whether or not the criminals currently confined in Toulon are ill. This is, I think, the first inquiry on the possible medicalization of criminals.[12]

This set of texts and projects, especially Prunelle's, marks, I think, the point at which what could be called a pathology of criminal conduct begins to be organized. Henceforth—in virtue of the principles of the functioning of penal power, in virtue, that is, not of a new theory of law, of a new ideology, but of the rules intrinsic to the economy of punitive power—crime will of course continue to be punished in the name of the law according to evidence displayed to all, but the individuals punished will always be referred back to the virtual horizon of illness; they will be judged as criminals but assessed, appraised, and measured in terms of the normal and the pathological. The question of the illegal and the question of the abnormal, or of the criminal and the pathological, are now bound up with each other, not on the basis of a new ideology that may or may not arise from a State apparatus, but according to a technology defining the new rules of the economy of punitive power.

I would now like to begin the history of this moral monster whose conditions of possibility I have tried to indicate. To start with, I will present the first outline, the first face of this moral monster called forth by the economy of punitive power. Strangely, and in a way that seems to me quite typical, the first moral monster to appear is the political monster. That is to say, crime is pathologized, I believe, on the basis of a new economy of power, and there is a kind of supplementary proof of this in the fact that the political criminal is the first or at least the most important and striking moral monster to appear at the end of the eighteenth century. Actually, in the new theory of criminal law I have been talking about, the criminal is someone who breaks the pact to which he has subscribed and prefers his own interest to the laws governing the society to which he belongs. He thereby reverts to the state of nature since he has broken the original contract. The man from the forest reappears in the criminal. However, he is a paradoxical man of the forest since he fails to understand the calculation of interest that made him subscribe to the pact along with his fellow men. Since crime is thus a kind of breach of the pact, since it is the assertion and the condition of a personal interest opposed to all other interests, you can see that crime is basically a kind of abuse of power. The criminal is always in some way a little despot who at his own level advances his personal interest like the despot. Thus, around 1760, thirty years before the Revolution, there is clearly formulated the theme, which will be so important during the French Revolution, of a fundamental kinship between the criminal and the tyrant, between the lawbreaker and the despotic monarch. On both sides of the broken pact there is a kind of symmetry, a kind of kinship between the criminal and the despot who, as it were, greet each other like two individuals who reject, disregard, or break the fundamental pact and make their interest the arbitrary law that they seek to impose on others. In 1790, precisely when the new penal code is under discussion, Duport, who is far from representing an extreme position, says: "The despot and the malefactor both disturb public order. In our eyes, an arbitrary order and a murder are equal."[13]

This theme of the link between the sovereign above the law and the criminal beneath it, the theme of these two outlaws, the sovereign and the criminal, is found first of all, before the French Revolution, in the pallid and commonplace form of the arbitrariness of the tyrant being an example for possible criminals, or of his fundamental illegality being permission for crime. Why should one not allow oneself to break the laws when the sovereign, who should promote, enforce, and apply them, allows himself the possibility of overturning them, suspending them, or at least of not applying them to himself? The result is that the more despotic the power, the more criminals there are. A tyrant's great power does not get rid of malefactors but multiplies them. From 1760 to 1780-1790 this theme is found constantly in all the theorists of criminal law.[14] However, with the Revolution, and especially after 1792, the theme of the kinship or possible connection between the criminal and the sovereign is found in a much more pointed, violent, and immediate form. In fact, it is not just the connection between the criminal and the sovereign that we see in this period, but rather a kind of reversal of roles in a new differentiation between the criminal and the sovereign.

What is a criminal after all? A criminal is someone who breaks the pact, who breaks it from time to time whenever he needs or wants to, when his interest dictates, when in a moment of violence or blindness the motive of his interest prevails despite the most elementary rational calculation. The criminal is a temporary despot, a despot of the moment, through blindness, fantasy, passion, or whatever. By contrast, the despot asserts the predominance of his interest and will; he makes it prevail permanently. The despot is a criminal by his status whereas the criminal is a despot by accident. When I say by status I am exaggerating because the despot cannot have any status in society. The despot can promote his will over the entire social body only through a permanent state of violence. The despot is therefore someone who—beyond status and the law, but in a way that is completely bound up with his very existence—permanently exercises and advances his interest in a criminal way. The despot is the permanent outlaw, the individual without social ties. The despot is the man alone. The despot is someone who, by his very existence and merely by his existence, performs the greatest crime, the crime par excellence, of a total breach of the social pact by which the very body of society can exist and maintain itself. The despot is someone whose existence is united with crime, whose nature is therefore contrary to nature. The despot is the individual who promotes his violence, his whims, and his irrationality as the general law or *raison d'Etat*. This means that from his birth to his death, or for as long as he exercises his despotic power, the king—or at least the tyrannical king—is quite simply a monster in the strict sense. The first juridical monster to emerge in the new regime of the economy of punitive power, the first monster to appear, to be identified and defined, is not the murderer, the transgressor, or the person who breaks the laws of nature, but the person who breaks the fundamental social pact. The first monster is the king. The king, I believe, is the general model from which, through successive historical shifts and transformations, the countless little monsters who people nineteenth-century psychiatry and legal psychiatry are historically derived. In any case, it seems to me that the fall of Louis XVI and the problematization of the figure of the king mark a decisive point in this history of human monsters. All human monsters are descendants of Louis XVI.

The appearance of the monster as king and of the king as monster is seen very clearly, I think, at the end of 1792 and the beginning of 1793, when the question arises of the king's trial and of the penalty to be applied to him, and even more of the form his trial should take.[15] The legislative committee proposed that he should suffer the public torture and execution meted out to traitors and conspirators. A number of Jacobins, and principally Saint-Just, responded that Louis XVI should not be sentenced to the penalty for traitors and conspirators precisely because there was provision for this penalty in the law. The penalty was therefore a consequence of the social contract and it could only be legitimately applied to someone who had sub-scribed to the social contract and who, to that extent, while having broken the pact at a particular moment, now accepted that it worked against him, on him, or with regard to him. The king, however, had never subscribed to the social pact. There could be no question therefore of applying to him clauses in or deriving from this pact. No law of the social body could apply to him. The king was the absolute enemy and should be regarded as an enemy by the entire social body. He therefore had to be crushed as one crushes an enemy or a monster. And yet, Saint-Just said, this is too much, because if one asks the entire social body to crush Louis XVI and get rid of him as its mon-strous enemy, one opposes the entire social body to Louis XVI. That is to say, one admits, as it were, a relationship of symmetry between an individual and the social body. Now Louis XVI never recognized the existence of the social body and only ever applied his power by ignoring its existence. He only ever applied his power to particular individuals, as if the social body did not exist. Having consequently suffered the king's power as individuals rather than as a social body, individuals would have to get rid of Louis XVI as individuals. A hostile individual relationship must therefore serve as the basis for the death of Louis XVI. At the level of legal theory (which was very important), this meant that anyone had the right to crush Louis XVI, even without the general consent of others. Anyone could kill the king: "Against tyranny" Saint-Just says, "men have a personal right."[16]

The discussion on the king's trial, which took place between the end of 1792 and the beginning of 1793, is very important not only because of the emergence of the first great juridical monster—the political enemy, the king—but also because the arguments will be transposed and applied in a different domain in the nineteenth century, and especially in the second half of the century, when psychiatric and criminological analyses, from Esquirol to Lombroso,[17] characterize the humdrum, everyday criminal as a monster. From then on, the monstrous criminal gives rise to the following question: Should we really apply the laws to him? As a being of a monstrous nature and the enemy of the whole society, should not society get rid of him without calling upon the might of the law? The monstrous criminal, the born criminal, has never actually subscribed to the social pact: Is he then a matter for the law? Should the laws be applied to him? The problems that arise in the discussions of the manner in which Louis XVI should be sentenced will be transposed in the second half of the nineteenth century to born criminals, to anarchists who also reject the social pact, to all monstrous criminals and all those nomadic figures who circulate around the social body but whom the social body does not recognize as belonging to it.

These legal arguments were echoed in a representation that is also important, I believe. It is a caricatural, polemical representation of the monstrous king who is criminal through a kind of intrinsic, unnatural nature. In this period the problem of the monstrous king is posed and a series of books are written that are veritable annals of royal crime, from Nimrod to Louis XVI, from Brunehaut to Marie-Antoinette.[18] There is Levasseur's book, for example, on the *Tigres couronnés*[19] Prudhomme on the *Crimes des reines de France*[20] and Mopinot's *Effrayantes histoires des crimes horribles qui ne sont communs qu'entre les familles des rois*, which was published in 1793 and is a very interesting text because it constructs a sort of genealogy of royalty. According to

Mopinot, the institution of royalty arose in the following way. At the origin of humanity were two kinds of people: those devoted to agriculture and animal husbandry and those who had to protect them because ferocious wild animals threatened to eat the women and children, destroy the harvests, and devour the herds, et cetera. Hunters were required to protect the agricultural community from wild beasts. Then a time came when the hunters had been so effective that there were no more wild beasts. The hunters consequently became useless and, disturbed by their uselessness, which would deprive them of their privileges as hunters, they transformed themselves into wild beasts and turned against those they were protecting. They in turn attacked the herds and families they should have been protecting. They were the wolves of mankind. They were the tigers of primitive society. Kings are nothing else but these tigers, these hunters of earlier times who took the place of the wild beasts prowling around the first societies.[21]

In this period of books on the crimes of royalty, Louis XVI and Marie-Antoinette are also portrayed in pamphlets as the monstrous, bloodthirsty couple, both jackal and hyena.[22] Whatever the purely conjunctural character of these texts and their emphases, this literature is nonetheless important for the themes inscribed in the figure of the human monster that continue to appear throughout the nineteenth century. The theme of the human monster crystallizes around Marie-Antoinette in particular. In the pamphlets of the time, Marie-Antoinette takes on a number of features peculiar to monstrosity. First of all, there is of course the fact that she is basically foreign, that is to say, she is not part of the social body.[23] She is therefore the wild beast with regard to the social body of the country in which she reigns; she is in any case a being in the state of nature. Furthermore, she is the hyena, the ogress, "the tigress," who, Prudhomme says, "once she has seen ... blood, cannot get enough of it."[24] So, we have the cannibalistic, anthropophagic side of the sovereign, greedy for the blood of the people. Then there is also the scandalous, debauched woman who abandons herself to the most outrageous licentiousness in two privileged forms.[25] First of all, she is incestuous, since we learn from these texts and pamphlets that when she was still a child she was deflowered by her brother, Joseph II, that she became the mistress of Louis XV, and then that she was the lover of her brother-in-law, the Dauphin being the son of the Comte d'Artois. To give an idea of this theme, I will quote a passage from one of these texts, *La Vie privée, libertine et scandaleuse de Marie-Antoinette,* which appeared in Year I and is concerned with the relations between Marie-Antoinette and Joseph II: "He was the most ambitious sovereign, the most immoral man, the brother of Léopold, who had the first fruits of the French queen. The introduction of the imperial priapus into the Austrian canal stoked up, so to speak, the passion for incest, the filthiest pleasures, hatred of France [*rectius*: the French], aversion toward the duties of wife and mother, in a word, everything that reduces humanity to the level of ferocious beasts."[26] She is incestuous then and, second, as well as being incestuous, she is guilty of the other great sexual transgression: She is homosexual. Here as well there are relationships with archduchesses, sisters, and cousins, with the women of her entourage, and so on.[27] The coupling of the two great forbidden consumptions (*consommations*), incest and cannibalism, seems to me typical of this first presentation of the monster within the horizon of the practice and thought of juridical imagination at the end of the eighteenth century, but with this qualification: In this first figure of the monster, Marie-Antoinette, the dominant theme seems to be sexual debauchery, and incest in particular.

In the same period, however, opposite the royal monster we find the other great figure of the monster in the anti-Jacobin, counterrevolutionary literature. Here it is not the monster of the abuse of power, but the monster that breaks the social pact by revolt. The monster is no longer the king but the revolutionary people who are the mirror image of the bloodthirsty monarch. The people in revolt are the hyena that attacks the social body. In the revolutionary period, in monarchist and Catholic literature, and also in English literature, there is a sort of reverse image of the Marie-Antoinette depicted in Jacobin and revolutionary pamphlets. The other profile of the monster is seen principally in connection with the September massacres: the popular monster that breaks the social pact from below, whereas Marie-Antoinette and the sovereign broke it from above. Madame Roland, for example, describing the September massacres, said: "If you knew the dreadful details of the raids! The women brutally raped before being torn apart by these tigers, the guts cut up and carried like ribbons, blood-soaked human flesh eaten."[28] In *L'Histoire du clergé pendant la Révolution*, Barruel tells the story of a countess of Pérignon being roasted with her two daughters on the Dauphine square, and of six priests who were also burnt alive on the square for refusing to eat her roasted body.[29] Barruel also tells of the sale of human flesh pâté at the Palais Royal.[30] Bertrand de Molleville[31] and Maton de la Varenne[32] recount a series of tales: the famous story of Mademoiselle de Sombreuil drinking a glass of blood in order to save her father's life,[33] or the story of the man who had to drink blood from the heart of a young man in order to save his two friends,[34] or again, of those who carried out the September massacres and who drank eau-de-vie into which Manuel had poured gunpowder, and who ate bread rolls dipped in wounds.[35] Here again there is the figure of debauchery and cannibalism, but cannibalism prevails over debauchery. The two themes of sexual and alimentary prohibition are quite clearly intertwined in the first two major figures of the monster and the political monster. These two figures arise from a precise conjuncture, but they also take up ancient themes: the debauchery of kings, the libertinage of the great, and the violence of the people. These are all old themes, but what is interesting is that they are reactivated and revived in this first great figure of the monster. There are a number of reasons for this.

First of all, the reactivation of these themes and the new picture of bestial savagery are linked to the reorganization of political power and the new rules for its exercise. It was not by chance that the monster appeared in connection with the trial of Louis XVI and the September massacres, which were, as you know, a sort of popular demand for a justice that was more violent, speedy, direct, and fair than institutional justice. The two figures of the monster appeared around the problem of law and the exercise of punitive power. These figures are also important for another reason. They were echoed widely in all the literature of the age, literature in the most traditional sense of the term, or in any case the literature of terror. It seems to me that the sudden irruption of the literature of terror at the end of the eighteenth century, in the years roughly contemporary with the Revolution, are connected to this new economy of punitive power. It is the unnatural nature of the criminal, the monster, that appears at this moment. It also appears in two forms in this literature. On the one hand, we see the monster of the abuse of power: the prince, the lord, the wicked priest, and the guilty monk. Then, in this same literature of terror, there is also the monster from below who returns to wild nature: the brigand, the man of the forest, the brute with his limitless instinct. These are the figures found in the novels of Ann Radcliffe, for example.[36] Consider the *Château des Pyrénées*,[37] which is entirely constructed around the conjunction of these two figures: the fallen lord who seeks vengeance through the most dreadful crimes and who, to this end, uses brigands who accept him as their chief in order to protect themselves and their own interests. Double monstrosity: The *Château des Pyrénées* connects the two great figures of monstrosity and, moreover, inserts them in a very typical landscape and setting, since the story unfolds in a place that is both castle and mountain. It is an inaccessible, hollowed-out mountain carved into a genuinely strong castle. The feudal castle, scene of the ultrapowerful lord and thus the manifestation of this criminal power beyond the law, is part and parcel of the savagery of nature itself, where the brigands have taken refuge. In this figure of the *Château des Pyrénées* we have, I believe, a dense image of these two forms of monstrosity as they appear in the political thematic and imagination of the age. The novels of terror should be read as political novels.

Of course, these two forms of the monster are also found in Sade. In most of his novels, in *Juliette* at any rate, there is this regular coupling of the monstrosity of the powerful with the monstrosity of the man of the people, the monstrosity of the minister with the monstrosity of revolt, and their mutual complicity. Juliette and La Dubois are obviously at the center of this series of couples of ultrapowerful monstrosity and rebellious monstrosity. In Sade, libertinage is always linked to the corruption of power. The monster is not simply an intensified nature that is more violent than others. In Sade the monster is an individual to whom money or reflection or political power offer the possibility of turning against nature. In his monsters nature turns against itself through this excess of power and ends up nullifying its natural rationality to become no more than a sort of monstrous rage, venting itself not just on others but also on itself. The self-destruction of nature in a sort of unrestrained monstrosity, a fundamental theme in Sade, is always brought about through the presence of a number of ultrapowerful individuals; through the ultrapowerful nature of the prince, lord, minister, money, or rebel. There are no politically neutral or average monsters in Sade: Either they come from the dregs of the people and have risen up against established society, or they are princes, ministers, or lords who wield a lawless superpower over all social powers. In any case, power—the excess of power, the abuse of power, despotism—is always the operative element of libertinage in Sade. It is this superpower that transforms simple libertinage into monstrosity.

I would add that these two figures of the monster—the monster from below and the monster from above, the cannibalistic monster represented above all by the figure of the people in revolt, and the incestuous monster represented above all by the figure of the king— are important because in the nineteenth century we find them at the very heart of the juridico-medical theme of the monster. In their very twinship, these two figures will haunt the problematic of abnormal individuality. It should not be forgotten (and I will come back to this at greater length next week) that at the end of the eighteenth century and especially at the beginning of the nineteenth century the first major cases of legal medicine were not at all cases of crimes committed in a state of flagrant and manifest madness. It was not this that created a problem. What created a problem, what constituted the point of formation of legal medicine, was precisely the existence of these monsters recognized as monsters precisely because they were both incestuous and cannibalistic, or because they transgressed the two great alimentary and sexual prohibitions. As you know, the first recorded monster is the woman of Sélestat, whose case was analyzed by Jean-Pierre Peter in a psychoanalytic review. In 1817 she killed her daughter, cut her up, and cooked her thigh with white cabbage.[38] Some years later there is the case of Léger, a shepherd whose solitude produced a regression to the state of nature. He killed a young girl, raped her, cut out her sexual organs and ate them, and tore out her heart and sucked it.[39] Then, around 1825, there is the case of the soldier Bertrand who, in the Montparnasse cemetery, opened the graves and took out the corpses of women, sexually violated them, and then cut them open with a knife and hung their entrails like garlands on the crosses of the graves and the branches of the cypresses.[40] These figures of monstrosity, of sexual and cannibalistic monstrosity, were the points of organization, the starting points, of all legal medicine. These themes, in this double figure of the sexual transgressor and the cannibal, are found throughout the nineteenth century. They are constantly found on the borders of psychiatry and the penal system and give stature to the great figures of criminality of the end of the nineteenth century: Vacher in France, the Düsseldorf Vampire in Germany, Jack the Ripper in England. The latter had the advantage of not only disemboweling prostitutes but of probably being a relative of Queen Victoria, bringing together the monstrosity of the people and the monstrosity of the king in this blurred figure.

These two figures of the cannibal (the popular monster) and the incestuous (the princely monster) later served as the grid of intelligibility for and means of access to a number of disciplines. I am thinking, of course, of ethnology; not perhaps the ethnology of fieldwork, but the ethnology of academic reflection on so-called primitive populations. If we look at how the academic discipline of anthropology was formed and take, for example, Durkheim as, if not the point of origin, then at least the first major crystallization of this university discipline, we can see that the problems of anthropophagy and incest underlie his problematic. Totemism functions as the vantage point from which to question primitive societies. What is the problem posed by totemism? It is the problem of the community of blood, of the animal that is the bearer of the group's values, energy, and vitality, of its very life. It is the problem of the ritual consumption of this animal. Thus, it is the problem of the absorption of the social body by each individual, or of the absorption of each individual by the totality of the social body. According to Durkheim himself, what we see behind totemism is ritual cannibalism as the moment of the community's exaltation. For Durkheim these moments are simply moments of maximum intensity that only punctuate a stable and regular state of the social body.[41] What characterizes this stable state is precisely the fact that the blood of the community is prohibited, that one cannot touch those who belong to the same community, and that one cannot touch the women in particular. The great totemic festival, the great festival haunted by anthropophagy, only imparts a regular rhythm to a society governed by the law of exogamy, that is to say, by the prohibition of incest. Occasionally eating food that is absolutely prohibited, that is to say, man himself, and then regularly forbidding oneself sexual relations with one's own women—this is the dream of cannibalism and the rejection of incest. It was these two problems that, for Durkheim, and after him as well, organized, or at least crystallized, the whole development of this discipline. What do you eat and whom don't you marry? With whom do you enter into blood ties and what do you have the right to cook? Alliance and cuisine: You are well aware that these are the questions that still obsess theoretical and academic ethnology today.

It is with these questions of incest and cannibalism that one approaches all the little monsters of history, all those outer fringes of society and economy that constitute primitive societies. Broadly speaking, I think we can say that anthropologists and theorists of anthropology who privilege the point of view of totemism, that is to say, ultimately of anthropophagy, end up producing an ethnological theory that leads to the extreme dissociation and distancing of primitive societies from our societies, precisely because one connects them with their primitive anthropophagy. This is Lévy-Bruhl's position.[42] Alternatively, if you refer totemic phenomena back to rules of alliance, that is to say, if you dissolve the theme of anthropophagy in order to privilege the analysis of rules of alliance and symbolic circulation, you produce a theory of ethnology that is a theory of the intelligibility of primitive societies and the rehabilitation of the so-called savage. This is the position taken by Lévi-Strauss.[43] However, you can see that we are always caught in the cleft stick of cannibalism-incest, that is to say, in the dynasty of Marie-Antoinette. Cannibalism and incest constitute the great outside, the great otherness that has been defined by our juridico-political interiority since the eighteenth century.

As you know, what is valid for ethnology is valid a fortiori for psychoanalysis, since if anthropology has tended to follow a line that has led it from the historically primary problem of totemism, that is to say, from the problem of anthropophagy, to the more recent problem of the prohibition of incest, we can say that the history of psychoanalysis has followed the reverse direction and that the grid of intelligibility proposed for the neuroses by Freud was incest.[44] Incest: the crime of kings, the crime of excessive power, the crime of Oedipus and his family. This is the intelligibility of neurosis. Afterward, with Melanie Klein, there follows the grid of intelligibility of psychosis.[45] What was the basis for the formation of this grid? It was the problem of devouring, of the introjection of good and bad objects, of cannibalism that is no longer the crime of kings but of the starving.

It seems to me that the human monster who began to be delineated by the new economy of punitive power in the eighteenth century is essentially a figure in which these two great themes of the incest of kings and the cannibalism of the starving are combined. These two themes formed at the end of the eighteenth century in the new regime of the economy of punishment and in the particular context of the French Revolution, with the two great forms of the outlaw in bourgeois thought and politics, that is to say, the two figures of the despotic sovereign and the people in revolt, now permeate the field of abnormality. The two great monsters that watch over the domain of abnormality and are still not sleeping—ethnology and psychoanalysis attest to this—are the two great subjects of prohibited consumption (*consommation*): the incestuous king and the cannibalistic people.[46]

1. See the course at the Collège de France entitled *La Société Punitive*, especially the lecture of 10 January 1973.

2. Throughout the following discussion Foucault takes up and develops some of the themes touched on in *Surveiller et Punir: Naissance de la prison*, chapter 2: "L'éclat des supplices." English translation: *Discipline and Punish: The Birth of the Prison* (New York: Pantheon, 1975), pp. 47-57.

3. P. de Bourdeille, seigneur de Brantôme, *Mémoires contenant les vies des hommes illustres et grands capitaines étrangers de son temps*, vol. 2 (1665; revised edition Paris, 1722), p. 191.

4. A. Bruneau, *Observations et Maximes sur les matières criminelles*, second edition (Paris, 1715), p. 259.

5. Foucault here summarizes Bruneau, *Observations*, p. iii, r-v.

6. See the course entitled *La Société Punitive* and the course summary in *Dits et écrits, 1954 - 1988*, vol. 2, pp. 456-70. English translation: *The Essential Works*, vol. 1, pp. 23-37.

7. See, for example, the article by L. de Jaucourt, "Crime (droit naturel)," in *Encyclopédie raisonée des sciences, des arts et des métiers*, vol. 4 (Paris, 1754), pp. 466b-468a, which is based on Montesquieu's *Esprit des Lois*, English translation: *The Spirit of the Laws* (1748).

8. Foucault is referring in particular to M. Lepeletier de Saint-Fargeau, "Extrait du rapport sur le projet de Code pénal, fait au nom des comités de constitution et de législation criminelle," *Gazette nationale, ou le Moniteur universel*, 150 (May 30, 1791), pp. 525-528; "Discussion sur la question de savoir si la peine de mort sera conservée," *Gazette nationale*; 151 (May 31, 1791), pp. 522-526, 537; *Gazette nationale*; 155 (June 4, 1791), pp. 572-574. Cf. *De l'abrogation de la peine de mort. Fragments extraits du rapport sur le projet de Code pénal présenté à l'Assemblée constituante* (Paris, 1793). The *Projet du Code pénal* is published in M. Lepeletier de Saint-Fargeau, *Œuvres* (Brussels, 1826), pp. 79-228.

9. L. P. J. Prugnon, *Opinion sur la peine de mort* (Paris, 1791), pp. 2-3: "One of the legislator's first concerns must be the prevention of crime, and he must answer to society for all those he did not prevent but could have prevented. He must then have two aims: the first, to express all the horror inspired by great crimes and the second, to terrify by example. Yes, it is the example, and not the man punished, that must be seen in public torture and execution. The soul is pleasantly moved and, if I may say so, refreshed at the sight of a human association without public torture and the scaffold. I believe that indeed it is the most delightful of all meditations. But where is hidden the society that could banish executioners with impunity? Crime inhabits the earth and the great mistake of modern writers is to attribute their own calculations and logic to murderers. Such is the sophism generated by books, that the writers did not see that these men were an exception to the laws of nature, that their entire moral being had been extinguished. Yes, the apparatus of torture and execution, even when seen from afar, terrifies criminals and stops them; the scaffold is closer to them than eternity. They are beyond the pale of the ordinary; without this fear, would they murder? Thus we must arm ourselves against the heart's first judgment and mistrust the prejudices of virtue." This passage can also be read in the *Archives parlementaires de 1787 à 1860. Recueil complet des débats législatifs et politiques des chambres française*, vol. 26 (Paris, 1887), p. 619.

10. See the speech in the session of the National Assembly of 30 May 1791 (*Gazette nationale, ou le Moniteur universel*, 153 [2 June 1791], p. 552) summarized in A. J.-F. Duport, *Opinion sur la peine de mort* (Paris, 1791), p. 8.

11. In part eight of the section "Maladies mentales" of L. Vitet's *Médecine expectante*, vol. 5 (Lyon, 1803), pp. 156-374, there is no mention of crime as illness. In Year VI of the Revolution, Louis Vitet, author of *Le Médecin du peuple* (Lyon, 1805), was involved in drafting legislation for special schools for medicine. Cf. M. Foucault, *Naissance de la clinique. Une archéologie du regard médical* (Paris: P.U.F., 1963), pp. 16-17. English translation: s.l., *The Birth of the Clinic: An Archeology of Medical Perception*, translated by A. M. Sheridan Smith (London: Tavistock, 1973), p. 17.

12. The article was not published in volume sixteen of the *Journal de médecine, chirurgie, pharmacie* (1808). Cf. C. V. F. G. Prunelle, *De la médecine politique en générale et de son objet. De la médecine légale en particulier, de son origine, de ses progrès et des secours qu'elle fournit au magistrat dans l'exercice de ses fonctions* (Montpellier, 1814).

13. We have not been able to find this quotation.

14. These theorists of criminal law are listed by Foucault in *Dits et Écrits, 1954 - 1988*, vol. 2, p. 458. English translation: the summary of the course "The Punitive Society," *Essential Works*, vol. 1, pp. 23-37.

15. The documents have been collected and presented by A. Soboul, *Le Procès de Louis XVI*, (Paris: s.l., 1966).

16. Similar arguments are put forward by Louis Antoine Lion Saint-Just in his "Opinions concernant le jugement de Louis XVI" (November 13 and December 27, 1792), in *Œuvres* (Paris, 1854). Cf. M. Lepeletier de Saint Fargeau, *Opinion sur le jugement de Louis XVI*, (Paris, 1792) and *Œuvres*, pp. 331-346.

17. On the psychiatric and criminological analyses of Esquirol, see the lecture of February 5, in this volume; on Lombroso, see the lecture of January 22, in this volume.

18. Foucault here alludes to the "historical observations on the origin of kings and on the crimes that sustain their existence" of A. R. Mopinot de la Chapotte, *Effrayante histoire des crimes horribles qui ne sont communs qu'entre les familles des rois depuis le commencement de l'ère vulgaire jusqu'à la fin du XVIIIᵉ siècl* (Paris, 1793), pp. 262-303. On Nimrod, founder of the Babylonian empire, see Gen. 10. 8-12. Brunehaut, born about 534, was the youngest daughter of Athanagild, king of the Spanish Visigoths.

19. Levasseur, *Les Tigres couronnés ou Petit Abrégé des crimes des rois de France*, fourth edition (Paris, 1794). On the notion of "tigridomanie," see A. Mathey, *Nouvelles Recherches sur les maladies de l'esprit* (Paris, 1816), p. 117 and p. 146.

20. L. Prudhomme [L. Robert], *Les Crimes des reines de France, depuis le commencement de la monarchie jusqu'à Marie-Antoinette* (Paris, 1791), and *Les Crimes de Marie-Antoinette d'Autriche dernière reine de France, avec les pièces justificatives de son procès*, (Paris, vol. 2 [1793-1794]).

21. Cf. A. R. Mopinot de la Chapotte, *Effrayante histoire*, pp. 262-266.

22. For example: *La Chasse aux bêtes puantes et féroces, qui, après avoir inondé le bois, les plaines, etc., se sont répandues à la cour et à la capitale* (1789); *Description de la ménagerie royale d'animaux vivants, établie aux Tuileries près de la Terrasse nationale, avec leurs noms, qualités, couleurs et propriétés* (1789).

23. *L'Autrichienne en goguettes ou l'Orgie royale*, (1791).

24. L. Prudhomme, *Les Crimes de Marie-Antoinette*, p. 446.

25. *Bordel royal, suivi d'un entretien secret entre la reine et le cardinal de Rohan après son entrée aux États-generaux* (1789); *Fureurs utérines de Marie-Antoinette, femme de Louis XVI* (Paris, 1791).

26. *Vie de Marie-Antoinette d'Autriche, reine de France, femme de Louis XVI, roi des Français, depuis la perte de son pucelage jusqu'au premier mai 1791* (Paris, I [1791]), p. 5. Cf. *La Vie privée, libertine et scandaleuse de Marie-Antoinette d'Autriche, ci-devant reine des Français, depuis son arrivée en France jusqu'à sa détention au Temple*, s.l.n.d.

27. *Les Bordels de Lesbos ou le Génie de Sapho* (Saint Petersburg, 1790).

28. *Lettres de Madame Roland*, vol. 2, (Paris: C. Perroud, 1902), p. 436.

29. A. Barruel, *Histoire du clergé pendant la Révolution française* (London, 1797), p. 283.

30. The story is recounted by P. Caron, *Les Massacres de septembre* (Paris: s.l., 1935), pp. 63-64, which gives the source of the gossip and the denials of contemporaries.

31. A. F. Bertrand de Molleville, *Histoire de la Révolution de France*, 14 volumes (Paris, IX-XI [1800-1803]).

32. P. A. L. Maton de la Varenne, *Les Crimes de Marat et des autres égorgeurs, ou Ma Résurrection. Où l'on trouve non seulement la preuve que Marat et divers autres scélérats, membres des autorités publiques, ont provoqué tous les massacres des prisonniers, mais encore des matériaux précieux pour l'histoire de la Révolution française* (Paris, III [1794-1795]) and, *Histoire particulière des événements qui ont eu lieu en France pendant les mois de juin, juillet, d'août et de septembre 1792, et qui ont opéré la chute du trône royal* (Paris, 1806), pp. 345-353.

33. Cf. A. Granier de Cassagnac, *Histoire des girondins et des massacres de septembre d'après les*

documents officiels et inédits, vol. 2 (Paris, 1860), p. 226. The story of Mademoiselle de Sombreuil has given rise to a vast literature; see P. V. Duchemin, *Mademoiselle de Sombreuil, l'héroïne au verre de sang (1767-1823)* (Paris: s.l., 1925).

34. Cf. J. G. Peltier, *Histoire de la révolution du 10 août 1792, des causes qui l'ont produite, des événements qui l'ont précédée, et des crimes qui l'ont suivie*, vol. 2, (London, 1795), pp. 334-335.

35. P. A. L. Maton de la Varenne, *Les Crimes de Marat et des autres égorgeurs . . .* , p. 94.

36. See, for example, A. W. Radcliffe, *The Romance of the Forest* (London, 1791).

37. The novel *Les Visions du château des Pyrénées* (Paris, 1803), attributed to A. E. Radcliffe, is apocryphal.

38. J. P. Peter, "Ogres d'archives," *Nouvelle Revue de psychanalyse* 6 (1972), pp. 252-258. The case of Sélestat (Schlettstadt in Alsace) was publicized in France by Ch. Ch. H. Marc, who published in the *Annales d'hygiène publique et de médecine légale*, 8/1 (1832), pp. 397-411, the translation of the medico-legal examination of F. D. Reisseisen, which originally appeared in German in the *Jahrbuch der Staatsartzneikunde* of J. H. Kopp (1817). Cf. Ch. Ch. H. Marc, *De la folie considérée dans ses rapports avec les questions médico-judiciaires*, vol. 2 (Paris, 1840), pp. 130-146.

39. E. J. Georget, *Examen médical des procès criminels des nommés Léger, Feldtmann, Lecouffe, Jean-Pierre et Papavoine, dans lesquels l'aliénation mentale a été alléguée comme moyen de défense. Suivi de quelques considérations médico-légales sur la liberté morale* (Paris, 1825), pp. 2-16. Cf. J. P. Peter, "Ogres d'archives," pp. 259-267, and "Le corps du délit," *Nouvelle Revue de psychanalyse* 3 (1971), pp. 71-108.

40. See the lecture of March 12 in this volume.

41. E. Durkheim, "La prohibition de l'inceste et ses origines," *L'Année sociologique* 2, (1898), pp. 1-70. Cf. E. Durkheim, *Incest: The Nature and Origin of the Taboo*, translated by A. Ellis (New York: s.l., 1963).

42. L. Lévy-Bruhl, *La Mentalité primitive* (Paris: s.l., 1922); English translation: *Primitive Mentality*, translated by Lillian A. Clare (London/New York: s.l., 1923). *Le Surnaturel et la Nature dans la mentalité primitive* (Paris: s.l., 1932); English translation: *Primitives and the Supernatural*, translated by Lillian A. Clare (London: s.l., 1936).

43. C. Lévi-Strauss, *Les Structures élémentaires de la parenté* (Paris: s.l., 1947); English translation: *The Elementary Structures of Kinship* translated by J. H. Bell, J. R. von Sturmer and R. Needham, (London, s.l., 1968), and *Le Totémisme aujourd'hui* (Paris: s.l., 1962); English translation: *Totemism* translated by R. Needham (London: s.l., 1964).

44. S. Freud, *Totem und Tabu: Über einige Übereinstimmungen im Seelenleben der Wilden und der Neurotiker* (Leipzig/Vienna: s.l., 1913). French translation: *Totem et Tabou: Quelques concordances entre la vie psychique des sauvages et celle des névrosés* (Paris: s.l., 1993). English translation: *Totem and Taboo* translated by J. Strachey (London: s.l., 1960).

45. M. Klein, "Criminal tendencies in normal children," *British Journal of Medical Psychology* (1927); French translation: "Les tendances criminelles chez les enfants normaux," in *Essais de psychanalyse*, 1921—1945 (Paris, 1968), pp. 269—71.

46. On the "privileged place" occupied by psychoanalysis and ethnology in Western knowledge, see chapter 10, section 5 of M. Foucault, *Les Mots et les Choses: Une archéologie des sciences humaines* (Paris: Gallimard, 1966), pp. 385—98. English translation: *The Order of Things: An Archeology of the Human Sciences* (New York: Random House, 1970).

five

5 FEBRUARY 1975

*In the land of the ogres. ~ Transition from the monster to the
abnormal* (l'anormal). *~ The three great founding monsters of
criminal psychiatry. ~ Medical power and judicial power with
regard to the notion of the absence of interest. ~ The
institutionalization of psychiatry as a specialized branch of public
hygiene and a particular domain of social
protection. ~ Codification of madness as social danger. ~ The
motiveless crime* (crime sans raison) *and the tests of the
enthronement of psychiatry. ~ The Henriette Cornier case. ~ The
discovery of the instincts.*

IT SEEMS TO ME, then, that the character of the monster with his
two profiles, cannibalistic and incestuous, dominated the early years
of penal psychiatry or criminal psychology. The mad criminal makes
his appearance first and foremost as a monster, as an unnatural nature.

The history I would like to relate this year, the history of abnormal
individuals (*les anormaux*), begins quite simply with King Kong; that
is to say, from the outset we are in the land of the ogres. The dynasty
of abnormal Tom Thumbs has its roots in the figure of the ogre.[1]
Historically they are his natural descendants, the only paradox being
that the little abnormal individuals, the abnormal Tom Thumbs, end
up devouring the great monstrous ogres who served as their fathers.
The problem I would now like to consider is how it came about that
over the years the stature of these monstrous giants was gradually

reduced so that if the monstrous character still appears at the end of the nineteenth century, as in fact he does, it is as no more than a sort of exaggerated, paroxysmal form of a general field of abnormality that constitutes the daily fare of psychiatry, on the one hand, and of criminal psychology, penal psychiatry, on the other? How, then, could the species of great exceptional monstrosity end up being divided up into this host of little abnormalities, of both abnormal and familiar characters? How did criminal psychiatry pass from a form in which it questioned great cannibalistic monsters to a practice of questioning, analyzing, and measuring bad habits, little perversities, and childish naughtiness?

There is, then, a transition from the monster to the abnormal. This transition cannot be explained by assuming something like an epistemological necessity or scientific tendency according to which psychiatry would pose the problem of the smaller only after having posed the problem of the bigger, the less visible after the more visible, the less important after the more important. Nor should we seek the origin of the processes that led from the monster to the abnormal in the appearance of techniques or technologies like psychotechnology, psychoanalysis, or neuropathology. Rather, it is these phenomena, the appearance of these techniques, which arise from a transformation of the monster into the abnormal.

That is the problem. Let us take, then, the three major founding monsters of criminal psychiatry.* The first is the woman of Sélestat about whom I have spoken several times and who, as you know, killed her daughter, cut her into pieces, cooked her thigh with cabbage, and ate it.[2] Then there is the case of Papavoine, who killed two little children in the Bois de Vincennes and who may have thought they were descendants of the children of the Duchess of Berry.[3] Finally, there is Henriette Cornier, who cut the throat of her neighbor's little girl.[4]

---

* A fragment of the rest of the sentence follows here, but its sense cannot be reconstructed, as part of it is inaudible on the recording: "...the line of these three great monsters that has not...very long."

You can see how, in one way or another, these three monsters tally with the major theme of the monster I spoke about last week: cannibalism, decapitation, and the issue of regicide. All three of them stand out against the background of this landscape in which, at the end of the eighteenth century, the monster was still a legal category and a political fantasy rather than a psychiatric category. The fantasy of devouring and the fantasy of regicide can be found either explicitly or implicitly in these three accounts. You can see why these three characters were immediately charged with a great intensity. And yet it seems to me that it is the third, and only the third, Henriette Cornier, who finally crystallized the problem of criminal monstrosity. Why Henriette Cornier? Why this case and not the other two, or anyway, more than the other two?

I must have said it twenty times, so I will repeat it for the last time: What is astonishing in the first of these cases, the Sélestat case, and what prevents it creating a real problem for the psychiatrists, is quite simply that this poor, wretched woman killed her daughter, cut her up, cooked her, and devoured her at a time, in 1817, when there was a serious famine in Alsace. So when the prosecution charged her, it was able to claim that she was not mad because she had killed and eaten her child for a motive that everyone accepts, that is to say, hunger. Had she not been hungry, had there not been famine, and had she not been wretched, then one might wonder about the reasonable or unreasonable character of her action. But given that she was hungry and that hunger is a motive (certainly, completely valid for eating one's child!), then the question of madness need not arise. Consequently, some good advice: It is better to be rich if you eat your children! The case was thus defused from the psychiatric point of view.

The Papavoine case was an important one that was later hotly debated but at the time it was also defused as a juridico-psychiatric problem. When Papavoine was questioned about this apparently absurd and motiveless murder of two children whom he did not know, he claimed to have thought that he recognized them as two children of the royal family. He wove a number of themes, beliefs, and assertions around this, which could be immediately handed over and inscribed on the register of delirium, illusion, false belief, and therefore madness. The crime was consequently reduced to madness just as, conversely, the Sélestat woman's crime was reduced, as it were, to reasonable and almost lucid interest.

Things are much more difficult in the Henriette Cornier case, however. The case somehow seems to elude both the ascription of reason and of madness. Inasmuch as reason cannot be ascribed it escapes law and punishment. However, because it is also difficult to recognize and demonstrate the advent of madness in this particular case, it eludes the doctors as well and is referred on to psychiatric authority. What actually takes place in this case? A woman who was still young, who had had children and abandoned them, and who was abandoned in turn by her first husband, found work as a domestic for some families in Paris. One day, after having repeatedly threatened to kill herself and having shown signs of sadness, she called on her neighbor and offered to look after her little daughter aged eighteen [*rectius*: nineteen] months for a while. The neighbor hesitated and then accepted the offer. Henriette Cornier took the little girl into her room and there, with a big knife she had ready, cut right through her neck. She stayed for quarter of an hour with the little girl's corpse, its trunk on one side and the head on the other. When the mother came looking for her little girl, Henriette Cornier told her: "Your daughter is dead." The mother, who was upset but at the same time did not believe her, tried to enter the room. At that point, Henriette Cornier took an apron, put the head in it, and threw it out of the window. She was arrested immediately and when asked, "Why?" she replied, "An idea."[5] Nothing more could be got from her.

Neither the identification of an underlying delirium, as in the Papavoine case, nor an elementary, crude interest, as in the Sélestat case, have a role in this case. Yet it seems to me that in their different ways both the Papavoine and the Sélestat case call to mind the general profile of the Cornier case and share in the kind of singularity that Henriette Cornier presents in the pure state. It seems to me that these cases, these kinds of acts, create a problem for criminal psychiatry. In fact, to say they pose a problem for criminal psychiatry is not really correct. Actually, these cases do not pose a problem for criminal psychiatry so much as constitute it, or rather, they are the ground on which criminal psychiatry is able to constitute itself as such. Both of these cases provoke scandal and embarrassment. A series of maneuvers develops around these cases on both sides of these enigmatic acts. Some of these maneuvers arise on the side of the accusation and the judicial mechanism and attempt to mask somehow the absence of a motive for the crime and to discover or assert the criminal's motive and rational state. On the other side, the maneuvers of the defense and of psychiatry seek to make the absence of motive, the absence of interest, function as the cornerstone for psychiatric intervention.

To show you the mechanism at work in the Cornier case and other similar cases, a mechanism that is, I believe, not only very important for the history of abnormal individuals and for the history of criminal psychiatry, but also for the history of psychiatry *tout court* and ultimately for the human sciences, I will set out my exposition in the following way. To start with, I will look at the general reasons for what could be called a double attentiveness around the absence of interest. By double attentiveness I mean the attentiveness of the judges, the judicial apparatus and the penal mechanism with regard to these cases and, on the other hand, the attentiveness of the medical apparatus, of medical knowledge and the new medical power with regard to these same cases. How do judicial power and medical power, notwithstanding their different interests and tactics, come together around these cases in such a way that they mesh? Then, after setting out these general reasons, I will attempt to see how they actually functioned in the Cornier case by taking this case as an example of all those cases that are more or less of the same type.

So, first of all, I will consider the general reasons for the double, medico-judicial concern, medical on one side and judicial on the other, with the problem of what could be called the absence of interest. First there is the concern of the penal mechanism, of the judicial apparatus. What is it that at this moment fascinates the judges in an act that does not appear to be motivated by a decipherable and intelligible interest? I have attempted to show that essentially this scandal, this fascination and questioning, could not occur and could have no place in the old penal system for which the only excessive crime that goes beyond all conceivable limits is a crime such that no punishment, however cruel, can expunge it, nullify it, and afterward restore the sovereignty of power. Is there a crime so violent that no public torture and execution could ever answer it? In fact, power always found tortures and executions that were more than able to respond to the savagery of a crime. Crimes, therefore, posed no problems. However, in the new penal system in which crime is measurable, and in which it is therefore possible to match it with a measured punishment, the possibility of punishment is fixed and determined, as I tried to show last week, by uncovering the underlying interest of the criminal and his conduct. Crime is to be punished at the level of the interest that underpinned it. It is not a question of punishment expiating a crime, except metaphorically. No punishment can make the crime disappear, since the crime exists. What can be nullified, however, are the mechanisms of interest at work in the criminal that gave rise to the crime and which could give rise to similar crimes in others. Consequently, you can see that interest is both a sort of internal rationality of the crime that makes it intelligible and, at the same time, what justifies the punitive hold one has over it, what gives a hold on the crime or on all similar crimes: what makes crime punishable. The interest of a crime is its intelligibility that at the same time makes it punishable. The crime's rationality, thus understood as the decipherable mechanism of interest, is required by the new economy of punitive power, which was not at all the case in the old system of an always excessive and always unbalanced expenditure of torture and execution.

Therefore, the mechanism of punitive power now implies two things. The first is an explicit assertion of rationality. Previously, any crime could be punished if the subject's dementia could not be demonstrated. It was only if the question of the subject's dementia arose that, secondarily, one raised questions about the crime's rationality. Now, when a crime is only punished at the level of the interest that provoked it, when the real target of punitive action or of the exercise of punitive power is the criminal's own mechanism of interest, or, in other words, when it is no longer the crime that is punished but the criminal, then you can see that the postulate of rationality is given greater force. It is not enough to say: Since dementia has not been proven, that will do, we can punish. Now one can only punish if one explicitly, I would say positively, postulates the rationality of the act that is punished. So, there is an explicit assertion of rationality, a positive requirement of rationality, rather than, as in the previous system, a mere supposition. Second, one must not only explicitly assert the rationality of the subject to be punished, but in this new system one must also regard the intelligible mechanism of the interests underlying the act and the rationality of the subject who committed it as superposable. These two systems of reasons, the motives (*raisons*) for committing the act, which make the act intelligible, and the subject's reason (*raison*), which makes him punishable, must in principle be superposable. You can see, then, the system of strong hypotheses now required by punitive power. In the old regime, in the old system that coincided exactly with the Ancien Régime, only minimal hypotheses were needed at the level of the subject's reason. It was enough that there was no proof of the subject's dementia. There now has to be an explicit postulate of rationality; rationality is explicitly required. Furthermore, one must accept that the motives that make the crime intelligible can be superimposed on the rationality of the subject to be punished.

This compact body of hypotheses is at the heart of the new punitive structure. Now—and it is here that the entire penal mechanism finds itself in difficulty and, as a result, fascinated by the motiveless act— if the very exercise of punitive power requires these weighty hypotheses, what do we find at the level of the code, that is to say, at the level of the law, which does not define the real exercise of punitive power but rather the application of the right to punish? There is merely the famous Article 64, which says: There is no crime if the subject, the defendant, is in a state of dementia at the time of the act. That is to say, inasmuch as it legislates for the applicability of the right to punish, the code only ever refers to the old system of de-

mentia. It requires only one thing, that the subject's dementia has not
been demonstrated. As a result, the law can be applied. But in reality
the code expresses in law the structural principles of a punitive power
that demands much more, since it requires rationality, the rational
state of the subject who committed the crime, and the intrinsic rationality of the crime itself. In other words, there is—and this is
characteristic of the whole of the penal mechanism from the nineteenth century until now—a mismatch between the codification of
punishments, the legal system that defines the applicability of the
criminal law, on the one hand, and what I would call the punitive
technology, or the exercise of punitive power, on the other. Because
of this mismatch, because the exercise of punitive power requires a
rationality for the act that is to be punished, which the code and
Article 64 completely ignore, you can see why there is a constant
tendency at the very heart of the penal mechanism to drift away from
the code and Article 64. But a drift toward what? Toward a certain
form of knowledge, a certain form of analysis, which makes it possible
to define or characterize the rationality of an act and to distinguish
between an act that is rational and intelligible and one that is irra-
tional and unintelligible. But at the same time you can see that if
there is a constant and necessary drift due to the mechanics of the
exercise of punitive power, a drift away from the code and the law
toward a psychiatric reference, if, in other words, reference to a
knowledge, to a psychiatric knowledge, is always increasingly pre-
ferred over reference to the law, this can only be due to the existence,
at the very heart of this structure, of the ambiguity, which you will
have been able to detect in what I have been saying, between the
reason of the subject who commits the crime and the intelligibility of
the act to be punished. The criminal subject's reason is the condition
of the application of the law. The law cannot be applied if the subject
is not rational: That is what Article 64 says. But exercise of the right
to punish says: I can punish only if I understand why he committed
the act, how he committed the act, that is to say, if I can enter into
the analyzable intelligibility of the act in question. Hence the radically
uncomfortable position of psychiatry as soon as it is dealing with a

motiveless act committed by a subject endowed with reason; or again, every time that it deals with an act whose analytic principle of intelligibility cannot be found, but which is the act of a subject whom one cannot demonstrate to be in a state of dementia. We inevitably find ourselves in a situation in which the exercise of punitive power can no longer justify itself, since we find no intrinsic intelligibility of the act through which the exercise of punitive power connects up with the crime. Conversely, however, because the subject's state of dementia cannot be demonstrated, the law will be applied; the law must be applied, since in terms of Article 64, the law must always be applied if a state of dementia has not been demonstrated. In such cases, and in the Henriette Cornier case in particular, the law is applicable, while punitive power no longer has a justification for being exercised. Hence the central predicament of the penal mechanism and its kind of collapse, paralysis, and blockage. Operating according to both the law that defines the applicability of the right to punish on one side, and the modalities of the exercise of punitive power on the other, the penal system is caught in the blockage of these two mechanisms, each jamming the other. Consequently it can no longer judge; it is obliged to come to a halt and put questions to psychiatry.[6]

You can see also that this predicament entails what could be called an effect of reluctant permeability in the sense that the penal apparatus cannot avoid calling upon a scientific, medical, or psychiatric analysis of the crime's motives. From another angle, however, while calling for this analysis, it cannot find a way to insert this analysis within the code and the letter of the code, since it is an analysis pitched at the level of the intelligibility of an act and the code knows only dementia, that is to say, the subject's disqualification on the grounds of madness. The result of this is that there is permeability with regard to psychiatry, and even more, an appeal to psychiatry, but an inability of power to inscribe the psychiatric discourse, called for by the penal apparatus itself, within the penal regime. There is an incomplete receptiveness, a request for a discourse and an essential deafness to it once it has been given, a game of demands and rejections, and it is this, I believe, that characterizes the specific predicament of the penal apparatus when it is confronted by what we can call, with all the ambiguity of the word, crimes without reason. That is what I wanted to say concerning the reason or reasons why the penal apparatus both threw itself on these cases and was at the same time embarrassed by them.

I want now to turn to the medical apparatus and consider the different reasons for its fascination with these famous motiveless crimes for which Henriette Cornier is our example. I think something should be kept in mind that I failed to stress enough last year.[7] This is that psychiatry, as it was constituted at the end of the eighteenth century and above all at the beginning of the nineteenth century, was not identified as a branch of general medicine. From the beginning until perhaps almost the middle of the nineteenth century, psychiatry did not function as a specialist medical knowledge or theory but much more as a specialized branch of public hygiene. Before being a medical specialism, psychiatry was institutionalized as a particular domain of social protection against all the dangers to society that may arise from the fact of illness, or from everything that could directly or indirectly be accorded the status of illness. Psychiatry was institutionalized as social safety, as hygiene of the whole social body (not forgetting that the first journal in France to specialize in psychiatry was the *Annales d'hygiène publique*[8]). It was a branch of public hygiene, so you can see that in order to exist as an institution of knowledge, that is to say, as a well-founded and justifiable medical knowledge, psychiatry had to undertake two simultaneous codifications. First of all, it had to codify madness as illness; pathologize its disorders, errors, and illusions, and undertake analyses—symptomatologies, nosographies, prognoses, observations, clinical files, et cetera—to bring this public hygiene, or the social safety it was responsible for, as close as possible to medical knowledge and thereby enable this system of protection to function in the name of medical knowledge. However, you can see that a second, simultaneous codification was also required. Madness had to be codified at the same time as danger, that is to say, psychiatry had to make madness appear as the bearer of a number of dangers, as the bearer of risks, and as a result of this psychiatry, as the knowledge of mental illness, could function as public hygiene. Roughly, on the one hand, psychiatry made an entire part of public hygiene function as medicine and, on the other, it made the knowledge, prevention, and possible cure of mental illness function as an absolutely necessary form of social precaution against a number of fundamental dangers linked to the very existence of madness.

The history of this double codification extends throughout the nineteenth century. We can say that the high points of the history of psychiatry in the nineteenth, but also in the twentieth, century are precisely when the two codifications effectively coincide, or when there is one and the same type of discourse, one and the same type of analysis and one and the same body of concepts enabling madness to be constituted as illness and seen as danger. Thus, at the beginning of the nineteenth century the notion of monomania makes it possible to classify a series of dangers within a wholly medical type of nosography, or anyway, one that is completely isomorphic with other medical nosographies, so within a discourse that is morphologically medical. Thus there is the clinical description of something like homicidal or suicidal monomania. Social danger is in this way codified within psychiatry as illness. As a result, psychiatry can effectively function as a medical science responsible for public hygiene. Similarly, in the second half of the nineteenth century there is a notion that is as comprehensive as monomania and that in a sense plays the same role, but with a very different content: the notion of "degeneration."[9] The notion of degeneration provides a way of isolating, covering, and cutting out a zone of social danger while simultaneously giving it a pathological status as illness. We could ask whether the notion of schizophrenia does not play the same role in the twentieth century.[10] To the extent that some think schizophrenia to be an illness that is coextensive with our entire society, the discourse on schizophrenia is indeed a way of codifying a social danger as illness. The function of public hygiene always reappears in the high points of psychiatry or, if you prefer, in its weak concepts.

Apart from these general codifications, psychiatry seems to need and has constantly paraded the specifically dangerous character of the mad as mad. In other words, since psychiatry has functioned as knowledge and power within the general domain of public hygiene or protection of the social body, it has always sought to discover the secret of the crimes that all madness is in danger of harboring, or the kernel of madness that must haunt all individuals who may be dangerous for society. In short, to function in the way I have indicated, psychiatry has had to establish that madness belongs essentially and fundamentally to crime and crime to madness. This kinship is absolutely necessary and one of the constitutive conditions of psychiatry as a branch of public hygiene. Psychiatry carried out two major operations in establishing this kinship. One, which I spoke about last year, consists in constructing an analysis of madness within the asylum that moves away from the traditional analysis to one in which the essential core of madness is no longer delirium but rather intractability, resistance, disobedience, insurrection, or, literally, the abuse of power. You recall what I said last year concerning the fact that for nineteenth-century psychiatry the madman is essentially always someone who takes himself for a king, that is to say, someone who wants to assert his power against and over all established power, whether it be the power of the institution or of the truth.[11] Thus, psychiatry functions within the asylum as the detection of possible danger, or rather as the operation by which the perception of possible danger is joined to every diagnosis of madness. However, it seems to me that a somewhat similar process takes place again outside the asylum. That is to say, outside the asylum psychiatry has always sought—at any rate, in a particularly intense and strained manner in the nineteenth century since what was essentially at stake was its very constitution—to detect the danger harbored by madness, even when it is a scarcely perceptible, gentle, and inoffensive madness. To justify itself as a scientific and authoritative intervention in society, as the power and science of public hygiene and social protection, mental medicine must demonstrate that it can detect a certain danger, even when it is not yet visible to anyone else; and it must demonstrate that it can perceive this danger through its capacity as a medical knowledge.

Given these conditions, you can see why, from the outset and in the process of its historical constitution, psychiatry very quickly became interested in the problem of criminality and criminal madness. It did not become interested in criminal madness at the end of the day and it was not because, after having gone through every other possible domain of madness, it came across this superfluous and excessive madness that consists in killing. In fact, it was interested straightaway in madness that kills because its problem was to constitute itself and advance its claims as a power and knowledge of protection within society. It had, then, an essential interest in criminal madness, an interest that was constitutive in the strong sense of the word, just as it paid particular attention to all those forms of behavior in which the crime cannot be predicted. No one could predict it; no one could guess it in advance. When crime suddenly irrupts, unprepared, implausibly, without motive and without reason, then psychiatry steps forward and says: Even though no one else is able to detect in advance this crime that suddenly erupts, psychiatry, as knowledge, as science of mental illness, as knowledge of madness, will be able to detect precisely this danger that is opaque and imperceptible to everyone else. In other words, it is clear that psychiatry cannot fail to have a vital interest in motiveless crimes, in this danger that suddenly irrupts in society and which no intelligibility explains, in these literally unintelligible and unpredictable crimes that offer no handhold to any means of detection. Psychiatry can say that it can recognize them when they occur and even predict them, or enable them to be predicted, by diagnosing in time the strange illness that consists in committing them. This is, so to speak, the outstanding feat of the enthronement of psychiatry. You are familiar with all those tales in which it is said: If your foot is small enough for the glass slipper, you will be queen; If your finger is thin enough for the golden ring, you will be queen; If your skin is so delicate that the smallest pea placed under a pile of feather mattresses will bruise it and you will be covered in bruises the following morning, if you are capable of all these things, then you will be queen. Psychiatry set itself this kind of test of recognition of its royalty, of its sovereignty, of its knowledge and power: I can identify an illness; I can discover the signs of what has never been recognized. Imagine a crime that is unforeseeable, but which could be recognized as the particular sign of madness that a doctor could diagnose and foresee. Give it to me, says psychiatry, I can recognize it as I can recognize a motiveless crime, a crime that is therefore the absolute danger, hidden deep in the body of society. If I can analyze a motiveless crime, then I will be queen. The literally frenetic interest that psychiatry has in motiveless crimes at the beginning of the nineteenth century should, I think, be understood as its test of enthronement, the feat by which its sovereignty is recognized.

We see, then, a very strange and remarkable complementarity established between problems internal to the penal system and the demands or desires of psychiatry. On one side, the motiveless crime is an absolute embarrassment for the penal system. Faced with a motiveless crime, punitive power can no longer be exercised. But the motiveless crime is an immensely coveted object for psychiatry, for if one gets to identify and analyze this kind of crime it will be the test of the strength and knowledge of psychiatry and the justification of its power. You can see, then, how the two mechanisms engage with each other. Penal power will constantly say to medical knowledge: I am confronted by a motiveless act. So I beg you, either find some reasons for this act and then my punitive power can be exercised, or, if you don't find any reasons, the act will be mad. Give me a proof of dementia and I will not apply my right to punish. In other words: Give me grounds for exercising my punitive power or grounds for not applying my right to punish. This is the question put to medical knowledge by the penal apparatus. And medical knowledge-power will answer: See how indispensable my science is, since I can perceive danger where no motive reveals it. Show me your crimes and I will be able to show you that for many of them there is no motive. That is to say, I can show you that there is potential crime in all madness and thus the justification of my own power. This, then, is how the two engage with each other, this need and this desire, or this embarrassment and this covetousness. That is why Henriette Cornier was such an important stake in this history that unfolded in the first third or, if we take the widest dates, the first half of the nineteenth century.

What happened exactly in the Henriette Cornier case? I think that these two mechanisms can clearly be seen at work. The expressions *crime without reason, crime without motive,* and *crime without interest* can all be found in the accusation drawn up by the prosecution. So great is the embarrassment of the judges in exercising their punitive power on a crime to which, nonetheless, the law manifestly applies, that they immediately grant the request of Henriette Cornier's defense for a psychiatric expert opinion. The psychiatric assessment is undertaken by Esquirol, Adelon, and Léveillé. They produce a very strange report in which they say: Listen, we have seen Henriette Cornier several months after her crime. It must be acknowledged that several months after her crime she displays no clear sign of madness. To this one might say: That's fine, the judges can proceed to judge her. But they do not say this at all. They notice a passage in Esquirol's report in which he says: We have only examined her over some days or for a relatively short time. If you give us more time we will be able give you a clearer answer. The paradoxical thing is that the public prosecutor accepts Esquirol's proposal, or uses it as an excuse to say: Please continue, and give us a second report in three months time. This shows that there is this kind of request, this appeal and fatal reference to psychiatry at the point when application of the law must become the exercise of power. In the second expert opinion, Esquirol, Adelon, and Léveillé say: Things are the same. She continues to exhibit no signs of madness. You have given us a little more time and we have discovered nothing. However, if we had been able to assess her at the very moment of the act, then perhaps we would have been able to discover something.[12] Clearly, it was more difficult to respond to this request. However, at this point Henriette Cornier's defense introduced another psychiatrist on its own behalf, Marc, who, referring to a number of similar cases, retrospectively reconstituted what he judged to have happened. He did not provide an expert opinion on Henriette Cornier, but gave a consultation that appears in the defense documents.[13] It is these two collections of documents that I would now like to begin to analyze.

We have, then, a motiveless act. What will judicial power do when faced with this act? What will the indictment and the prosecution say? Second, what will the doctor and the defense say? The absence of interest in the act clearly exhibited in the immediate account and by the simplest evidence is recodified in the indictment. How? The indictment says: Actually, there was of course no interest. Or rather, it does not say this, it does not pose the question of interest, but says: What do we see when we consider how Henriette Cornier's life has unfolded? We see a certain way of being, a certain habitual way of behaving and a mode of life that exhibits little that is good. She separated from her husband. She gave herself up to debauchery. She has had two illegitimate children. She abandoned her children to the public assistance, and so on. None of this is very pretty. That is, if it is true to say that there is no reason for her act, at least everything she is can be found within her act, or again, her act is already present in a diffused state in her whole life. Her debauchery, her illegitimate children, and the abandonment of her family are all already the preliminaries, the analogy of what will happen when she well and truly kills a child who lived alongside her. You can see how, for the problem of the act's reason and intelligibility, the indictment substitutes something else: the subject's resemblance to her act, or even the act's imputability to the subject. Since the subject so resembles her act, then the act really is hers and we have the right to punish the subject when we come to judge the act. You can see how we are surreptitiously referred back to the famous Article 64, which defines the conditions under which there cannot be imputability and so how, negatively, an act cannot be imputed to a subject. This is the first recodification found in the indictment. However, the indictment clearly notes that Henriette Cornier shows none of the traditional signs of illness. There is no sign of what the psychiatrists call melancholy and no trace of delirium. On the contrary, not only is there no trace of delirium, there is perfect lucidity. The indictment and prosecution establish this lucidity on the basis of a number of elements. First, her lucidity is demonstrated by premeditation before the act itself. When questioned, she acknowledged that at a certain point she decided that at some time she would kill her neighbor's little daughter. She went to the neighbor with the express purpose of kill-ing the girl: It was a decision made beforehand. Second, she had arranged her room so as to be able to commit the crime, since she had placed a chamber pot at the foot of the bed to catch the blood that would flow from her victim's body. Finally, she went to her neighbor on a false pretext she had established in advance. She had insisted that the child be given to her. She had more or less lied. She displayed pseudo affection and tenderness for the child. Therefore, all this was a calculated act of cunning. The same is true at the moment of the act. When she carried off this child that she had nonetheless decided to kill, she covered her with kisses and caressed her. She caressed the child when she met the concierge as she was mounting the stairs to her room: "She covered her with hypocritical caresses," says the indictment. Finally, according to the indictment, immediately after the deed, "she was fully aware of the gravity of what she had done." The proof of this is what she said, one of the phrases she uttered after the murder: "This deserves the death penalty." She had, then, a precise awareness of the moral value of her act. Not only was she aware of the moral value of her deed, but still she lucidly sought to escape it, first by hiding at least one part of her victim's body as best she could, since she threw the head out of the window, and then, when the mother wanted to enter the room, by saying to her: "Go away, go away at once, you could be a witness." She thus tried to avoid having a witness to her act. All this, according to the prose-cution case, clearly indicates the criminal's, Henriette Cornier's, lu-cidity.[14]

This was how the indictment's approach covers up or glosses over the disturbing absence of a motive that was what had nonetheless led the public prosecutor to appeal to the psychiatrists. At the point of indictment, when it was decided to call for Henriettte Cornier's head, the indictment covered up this absence of a reason, of a motive, with the presence of reason itself (*la raison*), of reason understood as the subject's lucidity and so as the act's imputability to the subject. The specific maneuver of the indictment is, I believe, this presence of reason itself (*la raison*) that doubles, covers up, and conceals the absence of any intelligible motive (*de raison intelligible*) for the crime. The indictment concealed the gap that prevented the exercise of punitive power and consequently authorized application of the law. The question posed had been: Was the crime really without interest? The indictment did not answer this question even though this was the question posed by the public prosecutor. The indictment replied: The crime was committed with complete lucidity. The request for an expert opinion was motivated by the question of whether the crime was without interest, but when the procedure of indictment was put into operation and it was necessary to call for the exercise of punitive power, then the psychiatrists' response could no longer be accepted. The prosecution fell back on Article 64 and the indictment said: The psychiatrists can continue to say what they like, but in this act everything exudes lucidity. Consequently, who says lucidity says awareness and not dementia, says imputability and application of the law. You can see, in fact, how the mechanisms I attempted to reconstruct earlier in a general way come into play in this procedure.

What do we see when we look at the defense? The defense takes up exactly the same elements, or rather the absence of the same elements, that is, the absence of an intelligible motive for the crime. It takes them up and tries to put them to work as pathological elements. The defense and Marc's expert opinion try to turn the absence of interest into a manifestation of illness: The absence of motive becomes the presence of madness. The defense and the expert opinion do this in the following way. First, the absence of motive is inserted into a sort of general symptomatology so as to show that Henriette Cornier is first and foremost just simply ill rather than mentally ill. Every illness has a beginning. Thus something is sought that could indicate the beginning of something like an illness in Henriette Cornier. Actually, it is shown that she went from being cheerful to being sad. All the signs and elements of debauchery and the libertine's life, et cetera, which the indictment had employed to make the accused resemble her crime, are taken up by the defense and Marc's expert opinion in order to introduce a difference between the earlier life of the accused and her life at the time she committed the crime. There is no more libertinism and debauchery, no more cheerful and joyful humor; she becomes sad, almost melancholic, and she is often in a state of stupor and does not reply to questions. A crack appears and there is no resemblance between the act and the person. Even better, one person does not resemble the other; one phase of life does not resemble another. There is a break, the onset of illness. Second, there is always the same attempt to insert what happened in the symptomatology—I would say an acceptable symptomatology—of any illness: finding a physical correlate. In fact, Henriette Cornier was menstruating at the time of the crime, and as everyone knows. . . . [15] Except that, if what the indictment saw as immorality is to be recodified and put to work in a nosological, pathological field, if this criminal conduct is to be medically saturated and any possibility of a murky and ambiguous relationship between the pathological and the blameworthy rejected, then there must be some kind of moral requalification of the subject. This is the second major task of the defense and Marc's consultation. In other words, Henriette Cornier must be presented as a moral consciousness utterly different from the act she committed, and the illness must be presented as unfolding, or rather as passing like a meteor across her manifest and permanent moral consciousness. At this point, with always the same elements and the same signs, the defense and the consultation say the following: What does it prove when Henriette Cornier said "this deserves death" after committing murder? Actually, it proves that, as a moral subject, in general her moral consciousness remained absolutely impeccable. She was perfectly aware of the law and the moral significance of her act. As a moral consciousness she remained what she was and therefore her act cannot be imputed to her as a moral consciousness, or even as a legal subject to whom culpable actions can be imputed. In the same way, taking up the famous words, "You could be a witness," Marc and the defense, especially the defense, refer to the different depositions of the child's mother, Madame Belon, and note that in fact she did not hear Henriette Cornier say: "Go away, you *could be* (*serviriez*) a witness." She heard her say: "Go away, you *will be* (*servirez*) a witness." And if Henriette Cornier really did say, "You will be a witness," this means: Go away, run and fetch the police and testify to them that a shocking crime has been committed.[16] The absence of the second *i* in *servirez* proves that Henriette Cornier's moral consciousness was perfectly intact. One side sees in "you could be a witness" the sign of her cynical lucidity, and the other sees in "you will be a witness" the sign of the constancy of her moral consciousness that somehow remained intact through the crime itself.

In the analysis given by the defense and Marc's consultation we have then a condition of illness, a moral consciousness that is intact, an undisturbed field of morality, and a kind of ethical lucidity. Except that, as soon as Marc or the defense emphasize this lucidity as the fundamental element of innocence and the act's nonimputability to Henriette Cornier, it can be seen that either the specific mechanism of the act without interest or the meaning of the notion of an act without interest must be overturned. For this act without interest, that is to say without raison d'être, must be such that it breaches the barriers presented by Henriette Cornier's intact moral consciousness. Thus we are no longer dealing with a motiveless act, or rather we are indeed dealing with an act that is without motive at a certain level. However, at another level, we must acknowledge that in this act which upsets, breaches, and thus gets through the barriers of morality by overcoming them, there is something like an energy intrinsic to the act's absurdity, a dynamic that is both the bearer of this absurdity and is borne by it. We must acknowledge an intrinsic force. In other words, the analyses put forward by the defense and Marc imply that if the act in question really does fall outside the mechanism of interests, it does so only inasmuch as it arises from a specific dynamic that is capable of pushing aside the mechanism of interest. If we go back to Henriette Cornier's famous phrase, "I know this deserves death," we can see what is at stake in the problem. Because if Henriette Cornier could say, "I know this deserves death" as soon as she has committed the act, does not this prove that her interest, the interest every individual has in living, was not strong enough to block this need or drive, this intrinsic dynamic of the act that made her kill? You can see how the entire structure of the penal system is embarrassed, almost trapped, by such an act, since a fundamental principle of penal law, from Beccaria to the 1810 code, was that between another individual's death and one's own, one will always prefer to forgo the death of one's enemy in order to preserve one's own life. But if we are dealing with someone confronted by someone else who is not even her enemy, and who then accepts to kill him or her in the knowledge that her own life is thereby condemned, are we not dealing with an absolutely specific dynamic that the Beccarian dynamic, the dynamic of Ideology, the eighteenth-century dynamic of interests, is unable to understand? Thus we enter an entirely new field. The fundamental principles that organized the exercise of punitive power are questioned, challenged, disturbed, put back into play, cracked, and undermined by this nonetheless paradoxical thing of the dynamic of an act without interest that pushes aside the most fundamental interests of every individual.

Thus, in the defense plea of the lawyer Fournier, and in Marc's expert opinion, we see the emergence of a kind of fluctuating domain that is not yet a definite field of elementary knowledge. In his consultation, the doctor, Marc, refers to an "irresistible direction," an "irresistible affection," an "almost irresistible desire," and an "atrocious tendency about whose origin we can say nothing." He says that Cornier was irresistibly driven to "bloodthirsty acts." You can see how far we are from the mechanism of interest underlying the penal system. The lawyer, Fournier, speaks of "an influence that Henriette Cornier herself deplores," of "the energy of a violent passion," of "the presence of an extraordinary agent foreign to the usual laws of human organization," of "a fixed, unchanging determination that marches without pause toward its aim," and he speaks of "the influence that shackled all Henriette Cornier's faculties and that, in a general way, imperiously directs all monomaniacs."[17] You can see that all these names, terms, and adjectives, et cetera, designating this dynamic of the irresistible revolve around something named elsewhere in the text:

instinct. It is named in the text: Fournier speaks of a "barbarous instinct," and Marc speaks of an "instinctive act" or even of an "instinctive propensity." It is named in the defense plea and it is named in the consultation, but I would say that it is not conceptualized. It is not yet conceptualized and it cannot and could not be conceptualized because there is nothing in the rules of formation of psychiatric discourse of the time that allows this absolutely new object to be named. As long as madness was conceived in terms of error, illusion, delirium, false belief, and nonobedience to the truth—as it still was at the beginning of the nineteenth century—then there was no place within psychiatric discourse for instinct as a brute, dynamic element. It could indeed be named, but it was neither constructed nor conceptualized. That is why whenever they name this instinct, whenever they designate it, Fournier and Marc constantly seek to take it back, reabsorb it, or dissolve it somehow by presuming something like delirium, because at this time, in 1826, delirium is still the constitutive hallmark, or at least the major qualification, of madness. Marc actually says this with regard to this instinct that he names and whose intrinsic and blind dynamic in Henriette Cornier he identifies: He calls it an "act of delirium." But this has no meaning, since either we are dealing with an act produced by a delirium, which is not the case (Marc cannot say what delirium Henriette Cornier suffers from), or an act of delirium means an act that is so absurd that it is like the equivalent of a delirium, but is not a delirium. So what is this act? Marc cannot name or express it: He cannot conceptualize it. Thus he speaks of an "act of delirium." As for the lawyer, Fournier, he gives an analogy that is very interesting but to which we should not lend more historical meaning than it has. Fournier says of Henriette Cornier's act: Essentially, she acted as if she was in a dream, and she awoke from her dream only after committing the act. Perhaps this metaphor already existed among psychiatrists; in any case, it will certainly be taken up again. This reference to the dream, this comparison with the dream, should not be seen as a kind of premonition of the relationships between dream and desire that will be defined at the end of the nineteenth century. Actually, when Fournier says, "She is as in a dream state," it is really to reintroduce surreptitiously the old notion of madness-dementia, that is to say, a madness in which the subject is not aware of the truth and to whom access to the truth is barred. If she is as in a dream, then her consciousness is not the true consciousness of the truth and can therefore be attributed to someone in a demented state.

In spite of being transcribed in these forms, that is, by Fournier as dream and by Marc as this bizarre notion of an act of delirium, I think that there is nonetheless the sudden emergence here of an object, or rather of a whole domain of new objects, of a whole series of elements that will be named, described, analyzed, and, bit by bit, integrated, or rather developed, within nineteenth-century psychiatric discourse. These objects or elements are impulses, drives, tendencies, inclinations, and automatisms. In short, they are all those notions and elements that, in contrast with the passions of the Classical Age, are not governed by a prior representation but rather by a specific dynamic in relation to which representations, passions, and affects have secondary, derivative, or subordinate status. With Henriette Cornier we see the mechanism that transforms an act that was a legal, medical, and moral scandal because it lacked a motive, into an act that poses medicine and law specific questions inasmuch as it arises from a dynamic of instinct. We have gone from a motiveless act to the instinctive act.

This takes place at a time—and I mention this merely to indicate the historical connections—when Geoffroy Saint-Hilaire was demonstrating that the monstrous forms of some individuals are only the product of a disturbance in the action of natural laws.[18] At the same time, with regard to a number of cases, of which the Henriette Cornier case is certainly the purest and most interesting, legal psychiatry was discovering that monstrous acts, that is to say, the motiveless acts of certain criminals, were in reality not just products of a lack indicated by the absence of motive, but were produced by a certain morbid dynamic of the instincts. We are here, I believe, at the point of discovery of the instincts. I know that "discovery" is not a good word, but it is not the discovery that interests me but rather the conditions of possibility for the appearance, construction, and regulated use of a concept within a discursive formation. Hence the importance of this mesh on the basis of which the notion of instinct can appear and be formed; for the instincts will become, of course, the major vector of the problem of abnormality, or even the operative element through which criminal monstrosity and simple pathological madness find their principle of coordination. Basing itself on the instincts, nineteenth-century psychiatry is able to bring into the ambit of illness and mental illness all the disorders and irregularities, all the serious disorders and little irregularities of conduct that are not, strictly speaking, due to madness. On the basis of the instincts and around what was previously the problem of madness, it becomes possible to organize the whole problematic of the abnormal at the level of the most elementary and everyday conduct. This transition to the minuscule, the great drift from the cannibalistic monster of the beginning of the nineteenth century, is finally converted into the form of all the little perverse monsters who have been constantly proliferating since the end of the nineteenth century. This transition from the great monster to the little pervert could only have been accomplished by means of this notion of instinct and its use and functioning in the knowledge and operations of psychiatric power.

This is, I think, the second interesting feature of this notion of instinct and its crucial character. With the notion of instinct we have a completely new problematic, a completely new way of posing the problem of what is pathological in the order of madness. Thus, in the years following the Henriette Cornier case, we see the appearance of a series of questions that were inadmissible in the eighteenth century. Is it pathological to have instincts? Is it or is it not an illness to allow instincts to act, to allow the development of the instinctual mechanism? Or is there a particular economy or mechanics of instincts that is pathological, an illness or abnormal? Are there instincts that are in themselves the carriers of something like an illness or an infirmity or a monstrosity? Are there abnormal instincts? Can we control instincts? Can we correct instincts? Can we rectify instincts? Is there a technology for curing instincts? In this way instinct becomes the major theme of psychiatry and occupies an increasingly prominent place, taking over the old domain of delirium and dementia that was the core of knowledge and practice concerning madness until the beginning of the nineteenth century. The impulses, drives and obsessions, the emergence of hysteria—madness with absolutely no delirium or error—the use of epilepsy as a model for the pure and simple liberation of automatisms, and the general question of motor or mental automatisms, and so on, come to occupy an ever more extensive and important place at the heart of psychiatry. It is not only this field of new problems that emerges with the notion of instinct, but also the possibility of inserting psychiatry in a biological problematic and not just in a medical model that it had utilized for a long time. Are human instincts the same as animal instincts? Is the morbid human instinct a repetition of an animal instinct? Is the abnormal human instinct the resurrection of archaic human instincts?

The insertion of psychiatry within evolutionist pathology and the injection of evolutionist ideology into psychiatry could not take place on the basis of the old notion of delirium and only became possible with this notion of instinct. All this became possible when instinct became the major problem of psychiatry. Finally, in the last years of the nineteenth century, psychiatry is flanked by two major technologies that, as you know, block it on one side and relaunch it on the other. On one side, there was the technology of eugenics with the problem of heredity, racial purification, and the correction of the human instinctual system by purification of the race. From its founders up to Hitler, eugenicism was a technology of the instincts. On the other side, confronting eugenics, there was the other great technology of the instincts, the other major means advanced simultaneously, in a quite remarkable synchrony, for the correction and normalization of the instincts—psychoanalysis. Eugenics and psychoanalysis are the two great technologies that arose at the end of the nineteenth century to give psychiatry a hold on the world of instincts.

Forgive me; I have taken as long as usual. I have dwelt on the Henriette Cornier case and the emergence of the instincts for methodological reasons. I have tried to show how a certain transformation took place at a certain point through a number of cases, Henriette Cornier's being simply exemplary. This transformation essentially made possible an immense process that has still not come to an end; the process that enabled psychiatric power centered on illness within the mental asylum to exercise a general jurisdiction, both within and outside the asylum, not over madness, but over the abnormal and all abnormal conduct. The point of origin of this transformation, its historical condition of possibility, was the emergence of the instincts. The mainspring, the gear mechanism, of this transformation was the problematic, the technology of the instincts. I wanted to show that this was not in any way due to a discovery internal to psychiatric knowledge any more than it was due to an ideological effect. If my demonstration is accurate, since it aims to be a demonstration, what was the basis for the appearance of all these epistemological—as well as technological—effects? They appeared on the basis of a certain play, a certain distribution and meshing of mechanisms of power, some of which were characteristic of the judicial institution and others of the medical institution, or rather of medical power and knowledge. The transformation was produced in the interplay between these two powers, in the play of their differences and their meshing together, in the need each had for the other and the support they found in each other. The reason we have passed from a psychiatry of delirium to a psychiatry of the instincts, with all the consequences of this transition for the generalization of psychiatry as a social power, is, I believe, this interlocking of power.

Next week the course will take place despite the vacation and I will attempt to show the trajectory of the notion of instinct in the nineteenth century, from Henriette Cornier up to the birth of eugenics, through the organization of the notion of degeneration.

1. Reference to Charles Perrault's *Petit Poucet* from the *Contes de ma mère l'oye* (known in English as *Tom Thumb*, from *Mother Goose's Fairy Tales*).
2. See the lecture of 29 January.
3. Concerning the case of L. A. Papavoine, see the three files kept in the *Factums* of the Bibliothèque nationale de France (8 Fm 2282-2288), which contain the following documents: *Affaire Papavoine, 1* (Paris, 1825); *Plaidoyer pour Auguste Papavoine accusé d'assassinat, 2* (Paris, 1825); *Affaire Papavoine. Suite des débats. Plaidoyer de l'avocat général, 3* (Paris, 1825); *Papavoine (Louis-Auguste), accusé d'avoir, le 10 octobre 1824, assassiné deux jeunes enfants de l'âge de 5 à 6 ans, dans le bois de Vincennes* (Paris, [1825]); *Procès et Interrogatoires de Louis-Auguste Papavoine, accusé et convaincu d'avoir, le 10 octobre 1824, assassiné deux enfants, âgés l'un 5 ans et l'autre de 6, dans le bois de Vincennes* (Paris, 1825); *Procédure de Louis-Auguste Papavoine* (Paris, [no date]); *Procès criminel de Louis-Auguste Papavoine. Jugement de la cour d'assises* (Paris, [no date]). The dossier was studied for the first time by E. J. Georget, *Examen médical*, pp. 39-65.
4. The H. Cornier case was presented by Ch. Ch. H. Marc, *Consultation médico-légale pour Henriette Cornier, femme Berton, accusée d'homicide commis volontairement et avec préméditation. Précédée de l'acte d'accusation* (Paris, 1826). The text is summarized in *De la folie*, vol. 2, pp. 71-116; E. J. Georget, *Discussion médico-légale sur la folie ou aliénation mentale, suivie de l'examen du procès criminel d'Henriette Cornier, et des plusieurs autres procès dans lesquels cette maladie a été alléguée comme moyen de défense* (Paris, 1826), pp. 71-130; N. Grand, *Réfutation de la discussion médico-légale du Dr Michu sur la monomanie homicide à propos du meurtre commis par H. Cornier* (Paris, 1826). Extracts from the medico-legal reports can be found in the series of articles on the trial in the *Gazette des tribunaux* (February 21 and 28; and June 18, 23 and 25, 1826).
5. Ch. Ch. H. Marc, *De la folie*, vol. 2, p. 84 and p. 114.
6. Cf. the analysis of Article 64 of the penal code put forward by Ch. Ch. H. Marc *De la folie*, pp. 425-433.
7. See the course summary, previously cited, *Le Pouvoir psychiatrique*. English translation: "Psychiatric Power," in *The Essential Works of Michel Foucault*, vol. 1, *Ethics, Subjectivity and Truth*.
8. The *Annales d'hygiène publique et de médecine légale* appeared from 1829 until 1922.
9. On the theory of "degeneration" see in particular B. A. Morel, *Traité des dégénérescences physiques, intellectuelles et morales de l'espèce humaine et des causes qui produisent ces variétés maladives* (Paris, 1857), and *Traité des maladies mentales*, (Paris, 1860); V. Magnan, *Leçons cliniques sur les maladies mentales* (Paris, 1891); V. Magnan and P. M. Legrain, *Les Dégénérés. État mental et syndromes épisodiques* (Paris, 1895).
10. The notion was introduced by E. Bleuler, *Dementia praecox oder Gruppe der Schizophrenien* (Leipzig-Vienna, s.1., 1911).
11. Foucault refers here specifically to the course previously cited, *Le Pouvoir psychiatrique*. Allusion to E. Georget, *De la folie* (Paris, 1820), 282, who wrote: "If you say … to someone claiming to be a king that he is not, he will answer you with abuse."
12. The first report of J. E. D. Esquirol, N. P. Adelon, and J. B. F. Léveillé was published, almost in its entirety, by E. J. Georget, *Discussion médico-légale sur la folie …*, pp. 85-86. The second report, drawn up after observation over three months, was printed textually. Ibid., pp. 86-89.
13. Ch. Ch. H. Marc, *De la folie*, vol. 2, pp. 88-115.
14. Ibid., pp. 71-87.
15. Ibid., pp. 110-111, where reference is made to Ch. Ch. H. Marc, "Aliéné," in *Dictionnaire des sciences médicales*, vol. 1 (Paris, 1812), p. 328.
16. Ch. Ch. H. Marc, *De la folie*, vol. 2, p.82.
17. The defense plea of Louis Pierre Narcisse Fournier is summarized by E. J. Georget in

Discussion médico-légale sur la folie . . . , pp. 97-99. See *in extenso* in the *Factums* of the Bibliothèque nationale de France (8 Fm 719), the *Plaidoyer pour Henriette Cornier, femme Berton accusée d'assassinat, prononcé à l'audience de la cour d'assises de Paris, le 24 juin 1826, par N. Fournier, avocat stagiaire près la Cour Royale de Paris* (Paris, 1826).

18. E. Geoffroy Saint-Hilaire, *Histoire générale et particulière des anomalies de l'organisation chez l'homme et les animaux,* four volumes (Paris, 1832-1837); see vol. 2, (1832), pp. 174-566. The treatise has the subtitle: *Ouvrage comprenant des recherches sur les caractères, la classification, l'influence physiologique et pathologique, les rapports généraux, les lois et les causes des monstruosités, des variétés et vices de conformation, ou Traité de tératologie.* E. Geoffroy Saint-Hilaire's preparatory works should also be noted: *Philosophie anatomique,* (Paris, 1822) (chapter 3: "Des monstruosités humaines"), and *Considérations générales sur les monstres, comprenant une théorie des phénomènes de la monstruosité* (Paris, 1826) (taken from volume eleven of the *Dictionnaire classique d'histoire naturelle*).

six

12 FEBRUARY 1975

Instinct as grid of intelligibility of motiveless crime and of crime that cannot be punished. ~ Extension of psychiatric knowledge and power on the basis of the problematization of instinct. ~ The 1838 law and the role claimed by psychiatry in public security. ~ Psychiatry and administrative regulation, the demand for psychiatry by the family, and the constitution of a psychiatric-political discrimination between individuals. ~ The voluntary-involuntary axis, the instinctive and the automatic ~ The explosion of the symptomatological field. ~ Psychiatry becomes science and technique of abnormal individuals. ~ The abnormal: a huge domain of intervention.

I HAVE BEEN STRICKEN with a fear that may be a little obsessional. A few days ago, when recalling what I said about the woman of Sélestat who killed her daughter, cut off her leg, and ate it with cabbage, I had the idea that I told you she was convicted. Do you remember? No? Did I say she was acquitted? You don't remember that, either? I spoke about it at least? All the same, if I said she was convicted, it was a mistake: She was acquitted. This changes her fate a great deal, if not her daughter's, but it doesn't really change what I wanted to say concerning this case in which what seemed to me important was the determined attempt to find the motives that would enable the crime to be understood and, potentially, punishable.

I thought I said that she was convicted because there was a famine, she was wretched and so she had an interest in eating her daughter since she had nothing to eat. This argument was actually used, but it failed to prevail and she was in fact acquitted. She was acquitted because her lawyers argued that she still had some food left and consequently had no interest in eating her daughter. She could have eaten lard before eating her daughter and her self-interest did not come into it. In any case, these were the grounds for her acquittal. Please forgive me if I made a mistake; the truth is now established, or reestablished.

Let us now return to where I left off last week with the analysis of the Henriette Cornier case. With Henriette Cornier we have a kind of reserved, pallid, pure, and silent monster whose case brings out for the first time in a fairly clear and explicit way the notion, or rather the element, of instinct. Psychiatry discovers instinct, but jurisprudence and penal practice discover it as well. What is this instinct? It is an element that can function on two levels or, if you like, it is a kind of cog that enables two mechanisms to mesh: the penal mechanism and the psychiatric mechanism. More precisely, it enables the power mechanism—the penal system with its need for knowledge—to engage with the knowledge mechanism—psychiatry with its need for power. For the first time, through the element of instinct that is constituted at this point, these two machines effectively engage in a way that is equally productive for both the penal and the psychiatric realms. In fact, the notion of instinct enables the legal scandal of a crime without interest or motive, and consequently an unpunishable crime, to be reduced to intelligible terms. Then, from a different angle, it makes possible the scientific transformation of the absence of a motive for an act into a positive pathological mechanism. This, I believe, is the role of instinct as an element in the game of knowledge-power.

The Henriette Cornier affair is, of course, an extreme case. For the first thirty or forty years of the nineteenth century, mental medicine invokes instinct only when it can do nothing else. In other words, psychiatry has recourse to instinct only in extreme cases, when there is an absence of the delirium, dementia, or mental alienation that broadly define its object. Moreover, we need only consider the point at which instinct enters the great taxonomic architecture of psychiatry at the beginning of the nineteenth century to see the extraordinarily limited place it occupies. Instinct occupies a clearly demarcated and marginal place in this edifice in which there are a number of kinds of madness: continuous, intermittent, total, and partial (that is to say, madness that only affects a particular area of behavior). In partial madness, there are kinds of madness that affect intelligence but not the rest of behavior, or kinds that affect the rest of behavior but not intelligence. It is only within the latter category that we find madness that does not affect behavior in general but only a particular type of behavior: murderous behavior, for example. It is in this very precise region that we see instinctive madness emerge as the last stone, as it were, in the pyramidal edifice of the taxonomy. Instinct thus occupies, I think, a very important place politically. By this I mean that the problem of instinct and instinctive madness is very important in the conflicts and demands and the distributions and redistributions of power at the beginning of the nineteenth century. However, epistemologically it is a very mixed and minor element.

The problem I want to try to resolve today is this: How was this epistemologically regional and minor element able to become an absolutely fundamental element that came to define and more or less cover the entire field of psychiatric activity? Even more, this element of the instinctive will not only cover or, anyway, run through the whole of this domain, but is also the source of the extension and growth of psychiatric power and knowledge, the constant pushing back of its frontiers and the almost indefinite extension of its domain of intervention. It is this generalization of psychiatric power and knowledge on the basis of the problematization of instinct that I want to study today.

I want to situate this transformation in relation to what I think can be regarded as its causes, the elements that determined it. Schematically, we can say that the transformation is brought about through the pressure of three processes, all of which involve the insertion of psychiatry within mechanisms of power that are external to it. The first process that I will rapidly consider is the fact that, in France at least, psychiatry was given a place within new administrative rules around the 1840s (in other countries, the process was similar but chronologically or legislatively slightly different). I spoke a little about this new administrative regulation last year with regard to the constitution of psychiatric power within the asylum.[1] This year I want to speak about it from the point of view of psychiatric power outside the asylum. This new administrative regulation is essentially crystallized in the famous 1838 law.[2] I said a few words about the 1838 law last year and you know that, among other things, it defines what we call the compulsory hospitalization order, that is to say, confinement of the insane (*aliéné*) in a psychiatric hospital on the request, or rather on the order, of the administration, and more precisely on the order of the prefectorial administration.[3] How does the law of 1838 regulate the hospitalization order? First of all, the hospitalization order must specify commitment to a specialized establishment, that is to say, one that is intended first to receive and second to cure those who are ill. The medical character of the confinement, since it is a question of curing, and its specialized medical character, since it concerns an establishment set apart for the mentally ill, is thus precisely defined in the 1838 law. The 1838 law consecrated psychiatry as a medical discipline, but also as a specialized discipline within the field of medical practice. Second, a hospitalization order for one of these establishments is obtained by a prefectorial decision accompanied by medical certificates that precede the decision (but without the decision being in any way bound by these certificates). A medical certificate may be, if you like, a letter introducing an individual to the prefectorial administration and requesting his or her confinement. But this is not necessary.

Once confinement has been decided by the prefectorial administration, the specialized establishment and its doctors must produce a medical report on the condition of the confined subject, but without the conclusions of the report being in any way binding on the administration. It is perfectly possible for someone to be confined by an administrative order, doctors to conclude that the subject is not insane, and the compulsory hospitalization to continue. The third feature of the hospitalization order deriving from the 1838 law is that hospitalization, the text says, must really be motivated by the mentally deranged condition of an individual, but it must be a mental derangement of a kind that is likely to jeopardize public order and safety. You can see that the doctor's role, or rather the interlocking of the medical function and the administrative apparatus, is defined in a way that is at the same time clear and yet ambiguous. In fact, the 1838 law sanctions the role of psychiatry as a particular scientific and specialized technique of public hygiene. However, it places psychiatry and the psychiatrist under the obligation to address a problem that is completely new with regard to the traditional scientific structure of psychiatry.

Previously, when interdiction (*interdiction*) was the major judicial procedure concerning madness, for example, the problem was always one of knowing whether the subject in question harbored an apparent or unapparent condition of dementia that would make him incapable as a legal subject and disqualify him as a subject of rights[4]: Is he suffering from a condition of consciousness or unconsciousness, from an alienation of consciousness, that prevents him from continuing to exercise his fundamental rights? As soon as the 1838 law comes into force, however, the question posed to psychiatry becomes the following: We have before us an individual who is capable of disturbing public order or endangering public safety. What does psychiatry have to say about this possibility of disorder or danger? The administrative decision asks psychiatry about the possibility of disturbance, disorder, and danger. When the psychiatrist treats a patient subject to a hospitalization order, he must respond both in terms of psychiatry and in terms of disorder and danger, but without his conclusions having any binding force on the prefectorial administration. The psychiatrist has to comment on the connections between the madness or the illness and the possibility of disturbance, disorder, and danger. It is no longer a question, then, of stigmata of incapacity at the level of consciousness, but rather of sources of danger at the level of behavior. You can see, then, how a whole new type of objects necessarily appears by virtue of the new administrative role or relationship in which psychiatry finds itself. Psychiatric analysis, investigation, and surveillance tends to shift from what those who are ill think about what they do and what they can understand, to what they are liable to do; it shifts from what those who are ill may consciously will to the possibility of involuntary behavior. Consequently, what is important is completely reversed. The singular, extreme, and monstrous case of monomania was a madness that could be terribly dangerous in its singularity. If psychiatrists attached so much importance to monomania, it was because they paraded it as proof that, after all, there really could be cases in which madness became dangerous. Psychiatrists needed this in order to define and establish their power within the systems regulating public hygiene. Now, however, psychiatrists no longer have to demonstrate and display this link between danger and madness in monstrous cases. It is the administration itself that singles out the madness-danger link, since the administration only makes a hospitalization order when someone really is dangerous or when his mental derangement or illness represents a danger either to himself or to public safety. There is no longer any need for monomaniacs. The political need, the political proof that was sought in the epistemological constitution of monomania, is now more than satisfied by the administration. Those subject to hospitalization orders are automatically picked out as being dangerous. With the hospitalization order, the administration carried out by itself a de facto synthesis of danger and madness that previously had to be demonstrated theoretically by reference to monomania. The administration carries out this synthesis not only in cases of exceptional and monstrous subjects; it carries it out for everyone subject to compulsory hospitalization. One consequence of this is that homicidal monomania ceases to be the major politico-juridico-scientific problem that it was at the beginning of the century because the desire to murder or, at any rate, the possibility of danger, disorder, and death, is now coextensive with the whole of the asylum population. Everyone in the asylum potentially carries the danger of death. Thus the great exceptional monster who has killed, such as the woman of Sélestat, Henriette Cornier, Léger, and Papavoine, is replaced by the typical figure, the reference figure, of the little obsessive: the gentle, docile, anxious, and kind obsessive who naturally would like to kill, and who knows that he will or could kill, but who very politely asks his family, the administration, or the psychiatrist to confine him so that he at least has the good fortune not to kill.

Thus, against the Henriette Cornier case we can set a case recorded by Gratiolet and commented upon by Baillarger in 1847 (the case itself is from 1840 [*rectius*: 1839], that is to say, immediately after the 1838 law).[5] A farmer from Lot called Glenadel felt the desire to kill his mother from his earliest years (that is, from when he was about fifteen years old, and so for twenty-six years since he was more than forty years old at the time of the case). When his mother died from natural causes his desire to kill was transferred to his sister-in-law. In order to escape from these two dangers, from his desire to kill, he naturally enlisted in the army, which enabled him to avoid killing his mother at least. He was allowed leave on several occasions but never took it so as to avoid killing his mother. Finally he was discharged. He tried not to return home and did so only when he heard of the death of his sister-in-law. Unfortunately, the news was wrong, his sister-in-law was alive and he ended up living nearby her. Whenever the desire to kill became too insistent or too violent he tied himself to his bed with a vast array of chains and padlocks. At this point, after some time, around 1840, he agreed with his family, or they agreed with him, that a court official should come, accompanied by a doctor, I think, to ascertain his condition and determine what could be done and whether he could be confined. We have the protocol of the visit by the court official.[6] He got him to recount his life and asked him, for example, how he wanted to kill his sister-in-law. Glenadel was chained to his bed and all the family was together around him, including his sister-in-law and the official.[7] Glenadel was asked: "How do you want to kill your sister-in-law?" He looked at his sister-in-law with tearful eyes and answered: with "the most gentle instrument." He was asked if his brother's and his nephew's grief wouldn't stop him? He answered that he would of course be sorry to cause pain to his brother and nephews but, in any case, he would not have to see their grief. If in fact he committed the murder, he would immediately be put in prison and then executed, the thing he desired most in the world, for behind his desire to kill was his desire to die. At this point he was asked whether, in view of this double desire to kill and to die, he would not like more secure bindings and heavier chains, and he gratefully replied: "What pleasure you would give me!"[8]

I think this case is interesting. Not that this is the first appearance in psychiatric literature of what I would call the polite monomaniac.[9] Esquirol had already referred to a number of them.[10] However, this observation has a particular value due to the theoretical psychiatric consequences Baillarger draws from it, to which I will return shortly, but also because it is a scientifically, morally, and legally perfect case. There was in fact no real crime to cloud it. The patient is perfectly aware of his condition; he knows exactly what has happened; he gauges the intensity of his desire, his drive, his instinct; he knows its irresistibility; he demands the chains himself and, perhaps, his confinement. He is therefore perfect in his role of someone ill who is aware of his illness and willingly submits to juridico-administrative-psychiatric authority. Second, there is a good and pure family. Faced with the patient's desire, it recognizes the irresistibility of his drive and puts him in chains.

Then, as a good family, obedient to the recommendations of the administration and feeling that there is a danger, it calls upon a court official to establish his condition in accordance with the proper procedures. As for the official, I think, but again without being sure, that he, too, is a good official and that he brings a doctor in order to draw up a good file for either a compulsory hospitalization order or a voluntary admission (no doubt the latter in this case) to the nearest psychiatric asylum. We have, therefore, perfect collaboration between medicine, justice, family, and the sick person. The patient is consenting, the family is concerned, the court official is vigilant, and the doctor is scientific: All this surrounds, encircles, shackles, and captures the famous desire to kill and be killed that appears here nakedly as an ambiguous or double will to death. The patient is both a danger to himself and to others, and it is around this absolute, pure, but perfectly visible, little black fragment of danger that everyone gathers. We are, if you like, in the element of psychiatric holiness. In the center, laid bare, appears the newborn death instinct. On one side, there is the sick individual who is its bearer, its generator, and on the other, there is the forbidden woman who is its object. Behind stand the judicial ox and the psychiatric ass. It is the nativity of the divine child, of the death instinct that is now becoming the chief and fundamental object of the psychiatric religion. When I say "death instinct" I am not of course referring to anything like the premonition of a Freudian notion.[11] I mean simply that what appears quite clearly here will become the privileged object of psychiatry, namely, instinct, and instinct inasmuch as it is the bearer of the purest and most absolute form of danger, death—the death of the person who is ill and the death of those around him—a danger that calls for a double, administrative and psychiatric, intervention. I think a very important episode in the history of psychiatry is bound up with this figure of instinct as the bearer of death. I will attempt to explain why, or how, this is in my view the second or real birth of psychiatry, after the basically protopsychiatric episode of the theory or medicine of mental alienation. This, then, is what I wanted to say about the first process that leads to the generalization of instinct and the generalization of psychiatric power and knowledge: the insertion of psychiatry in a new administrative regime.

The second process that explains this generalization is the reorganization of familial demand. Here again we must refer to the 1838 law. With this law there is a change in the nature and rules of the family's relationship to psychiatric and judicial authorities. The family is no longer needed to obtain an internment. The two procedures previously available to the family no longer exist or, at any rate, are not used in the same way. Previously there were two ways of proceeding. One, pure and simple internment in the name of paternal power, was rapid and sudden but legally dubious. The other, the heavy and complex procedure of interdiction, required a meeting of the family council followed by a slow judicial process at the end of which the subject could be interned by the appropriate court. Henceforth, with the 1838 law, those close to the sick person can request a voluntary admission (which, of course, is not the hospitalization that the sick person wants, but what those around him want for him). The immediate circle then, that is to say, essentially the close family, can ask for internment, but to get a voluntary admission they must first obtain a medical certificate supporting their application (the prefect does not need this, but the family can only get a voluntary admission with a medical certificate). After internment, the doctor of the establishment must get the prefect's endorsement and, in addition, draw up a confirmation of the medical certificate given at the time of admission. Thus, the family is directly connected to medical knowledge and power, and there is minimal recourse to the judicial administration, or even to the administration *tout court*. The family has to ask the doctor both for the necessary documents to justify internment and also for the later confirmation of the internment's validity. A consequence of this is that the form of familial demand changes with regard to psychiatry. Henceforth it is no longer the family in the wide sense (the group constituted as the family council), but rather the close family that asks the doctor directly to define the individual's danger to the family, rather than to define the patient's legal incapacity. Second, the request also has a new content. For the point to which psychiatric diagnostic and prognostic knowledge now attaches itself is precisely the danger constituted by the mad person within the family, that is to say within intrafamilial relationships. Psychiatry no longer has to define the condition of the patient's consciousness or free will, as was the case with interdiction. Psychiatry has to psychiatrize a range of conducts, disorders, threats, and dangers at the level of behavior rather than of delirium, dementia, or mental alienation. Internal disruptions of relationships between parents and children, brothers and sisters, and husband and wife, become the domain of investigation, the point of decision and the site of intervention for psychiatry. The psychiatrist consequently becomes the official overseeing the most everyday intrafamilial dangers. The psychiatrist becomes the family doctor in both senses of the term: He is the doctor who is called for by the family, who is constituted as a doctor by the will of the family; but he is also the doctor who has to treat something that takes place within the family. He is a doctor who has medical responsibility for the potential disorders and difficulties that develop on the family stage. Psychiatry is thus inserted as a technique of both correction and restitution, as a technique of what could be called an immanent family justice.

I think the text that best characterizes this very important mutation in the relationship between psychiatry and the family is Ulysse Trélat's *La Folie lucide* of 1861.[12] The book begins more or less with the lines I will read out. We can see clearly that the psychiatrist is not concerned with mentally ill individuals as such, any more than he is concerned with the family; rather, he is concerned with all the disruptive effects that the former may induce in the latter. The psychiatrist intervenes as a doctor of relationships between the mentally ill and the family. What do we find when we study the mentally disturbed? When we study the mentally disturbed, Ulysse Trélat says, we do not look for what it is that constitutes mental alienation, or even for its symptoms. We discover "the infinite torments imposed on excellent, lively, and productive natures by individuals suffering from a sometimes incurable [*rectius*: indestructible] illness." The other members of the family are "excellent, lively, and productive natures" confronted with "individuals suffering from a sometimes incurable [*rectius*: indestructible] illness." In fact, Trélat says, mentally ill individuals are "violent, destructive, harmful, aggressive." The mentally ill individual "kills everything that is good."[13] Ending the book's preface, Trélat writes, "I have not written it out of hatred for the mentally deranged, . . . but in the interest of the family."[14]

Here again, a new domain of objects appears with this mutation of the relationships between psychiatry and the family. In contrast to the homicidal monomaniac, as well as Baillarger's obsessive, we can see a new character and a new domain of objects that he embodies. Broadly speaking, this is the pervert. The obsessive and the pervert are two new characters. Here is a description from 1864. It comes from Legrand du Saulle's *La Folie devant les tribunaux*. This is by no means the first character of this type in psychiatry, but it is quite typical of the new psychiatrized character around the middle of the eighteenth [*rectius:* nineteenth] century. It is a description of someone called Claude C., who is the child of "respectable parents" but who very quickly displays "extraordinary disobedience":

He took a kind of pleasure in breaking and destroying every- thing that fell into his hands; he struck children of his own age when he thought he was the stronger; if he had a little cat or a bird under his control, he seemed to take pleasure in making them suffer and torturing them. As he grew older he became increasingly naughty; he feared neither his father nor his mother and felt a marked aversion toward the latter in particular, al- though she was very good to him. He insulted and struck her whenever she did not give him what he wanted. Nor did he like an older brother who was as good as Claude was wicked. When left alone he thought only of doing wrong, of breaking a useful piece of furniture, of stealing what he thought was valu- able; several times he tried to start a fire. By the time he was five years old he had become the terror of the other children of the neighborhood to whom he did every possible harm when he thought no one could see him.... After complaints were made about him [he was five years old, was he not? M.F.], M., the prefect, sent him to an insane asylum where, says M. Bottex, we have been able to observe him for more than five years. There, closely supervised and restrained by fear, he rarely had the chance to cause harm, but nothing could alter his natural insincerity and perversity. Caresses, encouragement, threats, and punishments were all employed without success. He barely learned some prayers. He failed to learn how to read although he was given lessons for several years. One year after leaving the asylum [he is then eleven years old; M.F.], we learn that he has become even more wicked and dangerous, because he is stronger and no longer afraid of anyone. Thus, he is always striking his mother and threatening to kill her. A younger brother is always his victim. Last of all, a wretched legless cripple in a little cart came begging to the door of his parents' house when they were absent and Claude C. overturned this poor unfortunate, struck him, and ran off after breaking his cart! ... We will have to place him in a house of correction. His misdeeds will probably cause him to spend his life in prison and he will be lucky not to end up ... on the scaffold![15]

This case seems to me to be interesting both in itself and for the way in which it is analyzed and described. Clearly, it can be compared to other medical observations of the same or broadly similar kind. I am thinking, of course, of the medical observations and reports produced on Pierre Rivière.[16] In the Pierre Rivière case you find many of the elements that are found in the present case: killing birds, spitefulness toward younger brothers and sisters, absence of love for the mother, et cetera. However, in Pierre Rivière all these elements functioned as thoroughly ambiguous signs since either they indicated the ineradicable nastiness of a character (and so Pierre Rivière's culpability or the imputability of his crimes) or, and without anything changing, they figured in some of the medical reports as early signs of madness and thus as evidence that his crimes could not be imputed to him. In any case, the elements were drawn up differently: Either they were elements foreshadowing crime or they were the early signs of madness. They signified nothing in themselves. In the present case, however, we are dealing with a file on a boy who was in a psychiatric asylum for five years, between the ages of five and ten years old, precisely because of these elements themselves apart from any reference to either a major dementia or a major crime. These elements—spitefulness, perversity, and various kinds of disturbance and disorder within the family—function in and by themselves as symptoms of a pathological state that requires internment. In themselves they are a reason for intervention. All these elements that were previously either criminalized or, through reference to an internal madness, pathologized, are now medicalized by right, autochthonously, from the outset.

One is a potential subject for medicalization as soon as one is naughty: This is the first point of interest about this medical observation.

The second point of interest is that the psychiatrist's intervention occupies a kind of superordinate position with regard to other levels of control: with regard to the family, neighborhood, and house of correction. Psychiatry insinuates itself, as it were, between these different disciplinary elements. No doubt the doctor's intervention and the measures he takes are quite specific. However, what is it that defines and demarcates everything that falls under his responsibility and which becomes the target of his intervention, all the elements that from the outset and by right are now medicalized? It is the disciplinary field defined by the family, the school, the neighborhood, and the house of correction. This is now the object of medical intervention. Psychiatry thus doubles these elements, goes back over them, transposes them, and pathologizes them; at least, it pathologizes what could be called the leftovers of these disciplinary elements.

The third point of interest about this text is that the essential vein of the description is concerned with relationships within the family, and essentially with love relationships, or rather their absence. If we consider the medical observations of the alienists of the preceding period, those of Esquirol and his contemporaries, we can see that they frequently concern the relationship between the mentally ill and their families. Indeed, they often concern relationships between mentally ill criminals and their families. However, it is always when these relationships are good that they are invoked in order to prove that the sick person is mad. The best evidence for Henriette Cornier's madness was that she had a good relationship with her family. For Esquirol, what made a man's obsession about killing his wife an illness was precisely the fact that the subject suffering from this obsession was at the same time a good husband. Thus, madness is indicated when there are positive feelings within the family. What is the basis for the pathologization of intrafamilial relationships in the present case? Pathologization is now based on precisely the absence of these good sentiments; not loving one's mother, hurting one's little brother, beating one's big brother. This is all now pathological in itself. Instead of it being the positive nature of relationships in the family that indicate madness, it is now the absence of such relationships that is pathological.

There is a description in Esquirol that could refer to this case, but for the moment I do not want to give a precise date for the formation of this new field of psychiatric intervention. I merely want to characterize it on the basis of the host of medical descriptions to be found at this time. In other words, what comes to light is the constitution of a pathology of bad family feelings. I will give another example of this problem of bad feelings. In Trélat's *La Folie lucide*, there is a fine example of the appearance, in the eyes of a psychiatrist, of the bad family feeling that punctures, as it were, the normally and normatively good framework of family feelings, and emerges as a pathological irruption. In this case it is a matter of signs of love being repaid with vileness. It is an example in which, "the virtue of the young woman sacrificed would be worthy of a higher purpose.... As often happens, the fiancée could only see the elegant stature of the man whose titled name she would take but had let herself ignore his weak mind and base habits. Less than eight hours had passed [since the marriage; M.F.] when the new wife, as beautiful, fresh, and spiritual as she was young, discovered that the count [her young husband; M.F.] spent his mornings and gave all his attention to making little balls with his excrement, lining them up in order of size in front of his clock on the mantelpiece. The poor child saw all her dreams evaporating."[17] Obviously it makes one laugh, but I think it is one of countless examples where lack of feeling in the family, the repayment of good conduct with bad, emerges as the bearer of pathological values in itself, without any reference to a nosographical picture of the major forms of madness listed in the nosographies of the previous period.

The first process of the generalization of psychiatric knowledge and power involved the interlocking of psychiatry and administrative regulation. The second process was the new form of the family's demand for psychiatry (the family as a consumer of psychiatry). The third process of generalization is the appearance of a political demand for psychiatry. The other demands (or the other processes that I have tried to identify, one on the side of the administration and the other on the side of the family) were more in the way of shifts or transformations of already existing relations. The expression of the political demand directed at psychiatry is, I think, new and appears later. The first two processes can be identified around 1840-1850. The political demand appears between 1850 and 1870-1875. What is this demand? I think we can say that psychiatry is called upon to provide what could be called a discriminant (*discriminant*), a psychiatric-political discrimination between individuals or a psychiatric discrimination between individuals, groups, ideologies, and historical processes for political purposes.

As a hypothesis, I would say that after the English Revolution of the seventeenth century there was, if not the complete construction, then at least the consolidation and reformulation of a juridico-political theory of sovereignty, of the contract that founds sovereignty and of the relations between the general will and its representative organs. Whether we take Hobbes, Locke, or later French theorists, we can say that there was a juridico-political type of discourse one role of which—though not the only role, of course—was to constitute what I will call a formal and theoretical discriminant that enables one to distinguish between good and bad political regimes. These juridico-political theories of sovereignty were not constructed with exactly this end in mind, but this was how they were actually used throughout the eighteenth century. They were employed as a principle for deciphering past and distant regimes. Which are the good regimes? Which regimes are legitimate? What historical regimes can we acknowledge and in what regimes can we recognize ourselves? At the same time, they were employed as a critical principle for justifying or discrediting contemporary regimes. It was in this way that in France throughout the eighteenth century the theory of the contract or the theory of sovereignty provided contemporaries with the guiding thread for a real criticism of the political regime.[18]

At the end of the eighteenth century, after the French Revolution, the political discriminant applied to the past and the present seems to me to be less the juridico-political analysis of regimes and States than history itself. That is to say, history had to answer such questions as: Which part of the Revolution should we salvage? What can still be justified in the Ancien Régime? How can we recognize the elements in the past that should be endorsed and those that should be discarded? History was put forward as the discriminating element in order to resolve these questions, theoretically at least. Edgar Quinet's work on the history of the Third Estate and Michelet's history of the people were attempts to use history to find the guiding thread that would enable them to decipher both the past and the present and that would enable them to disqualify, dismiss, and class as politically undesirable or historically invalid a number of events, characters, and processes while confirming the validity of others.[19] History, then, acts as a political discriminant of the past and present.[20]

After the third wave of republican, democratic, nationalist, and sometimes socialist revolutions that shook Europe between 1848 and 1871, it was psychiatry, and psychology in general, that people tried to put to work as a discriminant. It was a discriminant that was theoretically much weaker than the juridico-political and historical discriminants, but it possessed at least the advantage of being coupled with an effective instrument of sanction and exclusion, since medicine as power and the psychiatric hospital as institution existed to sanction this discrimination. It is clear that psychiatry is called upon to play this role in France from 1870 onward, but this occurs even earlier in Italy.[21] Lombroso's problem was quite simply the movements in Italy that began in the first half of the nineteenth century, which were continued with Garibaldi and that Lombroso now saw as developing, or deviating, toward socialism or anarchism. How can those movements that can be endorsed be distinguished from those that should be criticized, excluded, and sanctioned? Do the first anticlerical movements for the independence and reunification of Italy legitimate the socialist and already anarchist movements that are beginning in Lombroso's time, or do the more recent movements compromise the older ones? How can this confusion of agitation and political processes be disentangled? Lombroso, who was republican, anticlerical, positivist, and nationalist, sought to establish a discontinuity between, on the one hand, those movements he acknowledged, that is, in which he could recognize himself and which he saw as having been ratified by history, and, on the other, those contemporary movements that he opposed and sought to discredit. We will possess the principle of discrimination if it can be proved that these contemporary movements are led by a biologically, anatomically, psychologically, and psychiatrically deviant class of men. Biological, anatomical, psychological, and psychiatric science makes it possible to recognize immediately the political movement that can be endorsed and the movement that must be discredited. In his applied anthropology Lombroso says that anthropology seems to provide us with a way of distinguishing the genuine, fruitful, and useful revolution from the always sterile riot and revolt. The great revolutionaries, he continues, Paoli, Mazzini, Garibaldi, Gambetta, Charlotte Corday, and Karl Marx, were almost all saints and geniuses who possessed, moreover, wonderfully harmonious physiognomies.[22] However, examining the photographs of forty-one anarchists in Paris, he noticed that 31 percent of them had serious physical defects. Of one hundred anarchists arrested in Turin, thirty-four lacked the wonderfully harmonious figure of Charlotte Corday or Karl Marx (which indicates that the political movement they represent should be historically and politically discredited since it is already physiologically and psychiatrically discredited).[23] In the same way, after 1871 and until the end of the century, psychiatry in France will be employed according to this model of the principle of political discrimination.

Here again, I would like to quote a medical observation that matches and follows up Baillarger's obsessive and Legrand du Saulle's little pervert. This time it is Laborde's notes on an old communard who was executed in 1871. This is the psychiatric portrait he gives:

R was a failure (*fruit sec*) in every sense of the word. Not that he lacked intelligence. Far from it. But his tendencies always led him to make an abortive, useless, or unhealthy use of his aptitudes. Thus, after trying without success to enter the Polytechnique and then the École Centrale, he turned to medical studies as a last resort. But he ended up without any results, as an amateur with nothing better to do than hide behind the cloak of a serious purpose. If in fact he showed some application to these studies, it was only in order to take some courses that were to his taste and that supported the atheist and materialist doctrines that he brazenly and cynically paraded and that he linked politically to the most excessive socialist and revolutionary ideas. Hatching plots, forming or joining secret societies, frequenting public meetings and clubs, displaying his subversive and negative theories about everything respectable in the family and society in an appropriately violent and cynical language, assiduously frequenting certain establishments of ill-repute with his acolytes, where people engaged in politics *inter pocula* [some of you will know Latin; I do not know what *inter pocula* means; M.F.] and orgies, shady academies of atheism, worthless socialism, and excessive revolutionism, in a word, of the most profound debauchery of the senses and intelligence, and collaborating finally in the popularization of his shameless doctrines in unhealthy, short-lived papers that were censured and prosecuted as soon as they appeared: These were R's preoccupations and, one could say, his entire existence. Given all this, it is understandable that he was often in trouble with the police. He went further and laid himself open to prosecution. . . . One day, at a private meeting of the most honorable and respectable people, notably young women with their mothers . . . he cried out, to general amazement, "Long live the revolution! Down with the priests!" This feature in a man like him is not unimportant. . . . In recent events [that is to say, the Commune; M.F.] these impulsive tendencies found a most favorable opportunity for their realization and free development. The longed-for day finally arrived when he was able to carry out the favorite object of his sinister aspirations: wielding absolute discretionary power of arrest and requisition and over the life and death of individuals. He made extensive use of this power; his appetite was violent and he must have had a proportionate satisfaction. . . .

Betrayed by chance, it is said that he had the courage to proclaim his views. Could this be because he could not do otherwise? As I have already said, R was scarcely twenty-six years old, but his tired, pale, and already lined features bore the imprint of premature old age, his look lacked frankness, due perhaps to severe myopia. In reality, the general and habitual expression of his physiognomy had a certain hardness, a certain wildness, and an extreme arrogance; his flattened and open nostrils breathed sensuality as did his somewhat thick lips partially covered by a long, bushy, black-and-tawny-tinged beard. His laughter was sarcastic, his words brief and urgent, and his mania for terrorizing led him to inflate the tone of his voice so as to make it resound more terribly.[24]

With a text like this from more than one hundred years ago, I think we reach the discursive level of those expert psychiatric opinions that we began with in the first lecture. This is the kind of description, analysis, and disqualification for which psychiatry has assumed responsibility. In any case, it seems to me that between 1840 and 1870-1875 three psychiatric frames of reference are constituted: an administrative frame of reference in which madness no longer appears against the background of common truth but against the background of a restraining order; a familial frame of reference in which madness is brought out against a background of feelings, affects, and obligatory relationships; and a political frame of reference in which madness appears against a background of stability and social immobility. A number of consequences follow from this and in particular the generalization of psychiatric knowledge and power that I spoke about at the start of the lecture.

First of all, there is a new structure of relationships between madness and instinct. With Henriette Cornier, with the homicidal monomania of Esquirol and the mental alienists, we were in a kind of frontier region constituted by the paradox of, as they put it, a sort of "delirium of the instinct," of an "irresistible instinct." Now, with the three processes I have identified, this frontier region gradually gains ground and spreads like a cancer over the whole domain of mental pathology. First, there is the notion of "moral madness" in Prichard, and of "lucid madness" in Trélat.[25] These represent only territorial gains, however, and they do nothing to resolve the problems posed by "bloodthirsty" madness. From 1845-1850 we see a change, or a double change, taking place in psychiatric theory that shows, in its way, the new operations of psychiatric power that I have tried to identify.

First, the strange notion of "partial madness" that the alienists employed so widely is abandoned. "Partial madness" was a kind of madness that only affected a sector of the personality. It inhabited a corner of consciousness and affected only a small element of behavior with no relation to the rest of the individual's psychological makeup or personality. Henceforth, psychiatric theory makes a major effort to reunify madness and demonstrate that even when madness manifests itself only in a highly localized symptom, in a very rare, particular, discontinuous, and even bizarre symptom, nonetheless mental illness only ever appears in an individual who is, as an individual, profoundly and comprehensively mad. The subject must himself be mad for even the most singular and rare symptom to appear. There is no partial madness but rather regional symptoms of a madness that is always fundamental and that, while it may not always be apparent, always affects the whole subject.

A second change appears with this reunification, with this kind of unifying deep-rootedness of madness: Reunification no longer takes place at the level of the consciousness or grasp of truth that for the alienists was the principal core of madness. Henceforth, the unification of madness through its symptoms, even the most particular and re-gional symptoms, takes place at the level of an interplay between the voluntary and the involuntary. A person who is mad is someone in whom the demarcation, interplay, or hierarchy of the voluntary and involuntary is disturbed. As a result, the axis of psychiatric question-ing is no longer orientated by the logical forms of thought but rather by specific modes of spontaneous behavior, or, at least, this axis of behavioral spontaneity, of the voluntary and involuntary in behavior, becomes primary. The clearest formulation of this complete reversal of the epistemological organization of psychiatry can be found, I think, in two articles written by Baillarger in 1845 and 1847 in which he says that the characteristic feature of someone who is mad is something like a dream state. However, for Baillarger, the dream is not a state in which one is mistaken about the truth but rather a state in which one is not master of one's will; it is a state in which one is completely taken over by involuntary processes. The dream functions as a model of all mental illness as the seat of involuntary processes. Baillarger's second fundamental idea is that this disturbance in the order and organization of the voluntary and involuntary is the basis for the development of all the other phenomena of madness. In particular, hallucinations, acute deliria, and false beliefs, that is to say, everything that comprised the essential, fundamental element of madness for eighteenth-century psychiatrists, and still for the alienists at the beginning of the nineteenth century, is now demoted to second rank, to a secondary level. Hallucinations, acute deliria, mania, fixed ideas, and maniacal desire are all the result of the involuntary exercise of the faculties prevailing over the voluntary due to a morbid accident of the brain. This will be called the "Baillarger principle."[26] We need only recall the alienists' major concern and anxiety in the previous period: How is it that we can, and even must, speak of madness, when we can find no trace of delirium? You can see that everything is now reversed. It is no longer necessary to find a little element of delirium beneath the instinctive so that it can be inscribed within madness. Rather, behind any delirium we must discover the little disturbance of the voluntary and involuntary that makes the formation of delirium understandable. The second psychiatry is founded by the Baillarger principle with the primacy of the question of the voluntary, the spontaneous, and the automatic and with the assertion that however localized the symptoms of mental illness may be, they affect the whole subject. At this point, around 1845-1847, psychiatrists take over from the alienists. Esquirol is the last of the alienists because he is the last to pose the question of madness, that is to say, of the relation to truth. Baillarger is the first psychiatrist in France (in Germany it is Griesinger at more or less the same time)[27] because he is the first to pose the question of the voluntary and the involuntary, of the instinctive and the automatic, within the process of mental illness.

A consequence of this new nuclear organization of psychiatry, of this new core, is a kind of epistemological thaw in psychiatry that develops in two directions. On one side a new symptomatological field opens up: a range of phenomena that previously had no status in the realm of mental illness can now be identified by psychiatry as symptoms. Previously, in the medicine of the alienists, a form of conduct was not a possible symptom of mental illness merely because of its rarity or absurdity, but only if it harbored a little fragment of delirium. Henceforth, the symptomatological value of conduct, what enables an element or form of conduct to be the symptom of a possible illness, is, on the one hand, the deviation of conduct from rules of order or conformity defined on the basis of administrative regularity, familial obligations, or political and social normativity. These deviations define conduct as a potential symptom of illness. The value of conduct as symptomatic also depends on where these deviations are situated on the axis of the voluntary and involuntary. Starting around the 1850s, deviation from the norm of conduct and the degree to which this deviation is automatic are the two variables that enable conduct to be inscribed either on the register of mental health or on the register of mental illness. Broadly speaking, conduct is healthy when there is minimal deviation and automatism, that is to say, when it is conventional and voluntary. When deviation and automatism increase, however, and not necessarily at the same rate or to the same degree, there is illness that must be precisely defined in terms of this increasing deviation and automatism. If this is what defines conduct as pathological, we can see how psychiatry can now take into its field of analysis an enormous mass of data, facts, and behaviors that it can describe and whose symptomatic value it can question in terms of deviations from the norm and position on the voluntary-involuntary axis. In short, a range of conduct can now be investigated and pathologized without having to refer to mental alienation. All conduct must be capable of being situated on this axis of the voluntary and involuntary, the span of which is controlled by psychiatry. It must also be possible to situate all conduct in relation to, and according to, a norm that is also controlled, or is at least seen to be controlled, by psychiatry. Psychiatry no longer needs madness in order to function; it no longer needs dementia, delirium, and mental alienation. Psychiatry can psychiatrize without referring to mental alienation. Psychiatry "disalienizes" itself. In this sense, we can say that Esquirol was still an alienist and that Baillarger and his successors are no longer alienists. The latter are psychiatrists because they are no longer alienists. For the same reason, by virtue of this disalienization of psychiatric practice, you can see that because there is no longer any need to refer to a core of delirium, dementia, or madness, from the moment there is no longer any reference to the relationship to truth, psychiatry finally sees the entire domain of all possible conduct opening up before it as a domain for its possible intervention and symptomatological evaluation. Finally, thanks to the removal of the privilege of madness, of this illusion of the privilege of madness, dementia, delirium, and so forth, thanks to this disalienization, there is nothing in human conduct that cannot, in one way or another, be questioned by psychiatry.

However, at the same time as this almost indefinite opening enables psychiatry to become the medical jurisdiction for any conduct whatsoever, reference to the voluntary-involuntary axis also makes possible a new type of coupling with organic medicine. For the alienists, psychiatry really was a medical science because it obeyed the same formal—nosographical, symptomatological, classificatory, and taxonomic—criteria. Esquirol needed the grand edifice of psychiatric classifications that so delighted him to ensure that his discourse and objects were the discourse of psychiatry and the objects of a medical psychiatry. The medicalization of the discourse and practice of the alienists passed through this kind of formal structuration isomorphous with medical discourse (if not the medical discourse of the same period, then at least of the previous period—but this is another question). With the new psychiatric problematic—that is to say, a psychiatric investigation focused on deviations from the norm along the axis of the voluntary and involuntary—mental illness, mental disorders, and all the disorders with which psychiatry concerns itself can be connected directly, at the level of their content and more simply at the level of the discursive form of psychiatry, to all the organic or functional disorders, and fundamentally to the neurological disorders that disturb voluntary conduct. Hence, at the level of content, it becomes possible to establish connections between psychiatry and medicine through the interstitial or liminal discipline of neurology, rather than through the formal organization of psychiatric knowledge and discourse. Medicine and psychiatry can now communicate through the intermediary of this domain concerned with the disintegration of the voluntary control of behavior. A neuropsychiatry with institutional support will be constituted shortly afterward. In this new field, which establishes a continuum going from medicine and functional or organic disorder to disturbance of conduct, there is, then, a continuous weave at the center of which we find, of course, epilepsy (or hystero-epilepsy, since the distinction had not been made at the time) as a neurological, functional disorder manifesting itself in the involuntary release of automatisms and susceptible to innumerable gradations. Epilepsy functions as a "switch point" in this new organization of the psychiatric field. Just as alienists sought delirium everywhere, behind every kind of symptom, so for a long time psychiatrists will seek the little epilepsy, the epileptic equivalent, or anyway the little automatism that must function as the support for every psychiatric symptom. By this route we arrive at the end of the nineteenth century and the beginning of the twentieth century at a theoretical perspective that is exactly the opposite of Esquirol's[28] in which hallucinations are defined as sensory epilepsies.[29]

So, on one side there is a sort of explosion of the symptomatological field that psychiatry undertakes to cover in pursuit of every possible disorder of conduct. As a result, psychiatry is invaded by a vast range of conduct that had previously been accorded only a moral, disciplinary, or judicial status. Any kind of disorder, indiscipline, agitation, disobedience, recalcitrance, lack of affection, and so forth can now be psychiatrized. At the same time as this explosion of the symptomatological field is taking place, psychiatry becomes firmly anchored in a medicine of the body with the possibility of a somatization that is not merely formal at the level of discourse, but a fundamental somatization of mental medicine. Thus we have a real medical science, but one that is concerned with all conduct; an authentic medical science, since it is based in neurology, and a medicine concerned with all behavior as a consequence of the explosion of the symptomatological field. Psychiatry brings two things into contact in its organization of this phenomenologically open, but scientifically modeled field. First, across the field it covers, psychiatry introduced something that until then was partly foreign to it: the norm understood as rule of conduct, informal law, and principle of conformity opposed to irregularity, disorder, strangeness, eccentricity, unevenness, and deviation. Psychiatry introduces the norm with the explosion of the symtomatological field. However, by being rooted in organic and functional medicine, psychiatry is also able to exploit the norm understood in a different sense: the norm as functional regularity, as the principle of an appropriate and adjusted functioning; the "normal" as opposed to the pathological, morbid, disorganized, and dysfunctional. Within the field organized by the new psychiatry, or by the new psychiatry that takes over from the medicine of the alienists, two usages and two realities of the norm are joined together, mutually adapted, and partially superimposed in a way that is still difficult to theorize (but that is another question). There is the norm as rule of conduct and the norm as functional regulation; the norm opposed to irregularity and disorder, and the norm opposed to the pathological and the morbid. You can see, then, how the reversal I spoke about was possible. Instead of encountering the clash between the disorder of nature and the order of law only at the far limit, in the extremely rare, exceptional, and monstrous corner of monomania, psychiatry is now entirely underpinned by this interplay between the two norms. The disorder of nature will no longer disturb and challenge the game of the law through the exceptional figure of the monster. Everywhere, all the time, in the simplest, most common, and most everyday conduct, in its most familiar object, psychiatry will deal with something that is an irregularity in relation to a norm and that must be at the same time a pathological dysfunction in relation to the normal. A mixed field of disruptions of order and functional disorders is constituted or entangled in an absolutely close weave. At this point psychiatry becomes medico-judicial not just at its limits and in exceptional cases, but all the time, in its daily life and working agenda. Between the description of social norms and rules and the medical analysis of abnormalities, psychiatry becomes essentially the science and technique of abnormal individuals and abnormal conduct. An obvious implication of this is that the connection between crime and madness becomes a regular phenomenon for psychiatry rather than the extreme case. Little crimes, of course, and little mental illnesses; tiny delinquencies and almost imperceptible abnormalities of behavior essentially constitute the organizational and fundamental field of psychiatry. Since 1850, or at least since the three processes I have tried to describe, psychiatry has functioned in a space that is, even if in a broad sense, medico-judicial, pathologico-normative through and through. Psychiatric activity essentially investigates morbid immorality or illnesses of disorder. Thus we can understand how the great monster, the extreme and final case, is effectively dissolved in a swarm of primary abnormalities, I mean in a swarm of abnormalities that constitute the primary domain of psychiatry. And there you have it. The great ogre of the end of history has become little Tom Thumb, the crowd of little abnormal Tom Thumbs with which history now begins. In this period, from 1840 to 1860-1875, a psychiatry is organized that can be defined as a technology of abnormality.

The problem now is how this technology of abnormality encountered other processes of normalization that were not concerned with crime, criminality, or monstrosity, but with something quite different: everyday sexuality. I will try to take up the theme by going back to the history of sexuality, the control of sexuality, from the eighteenth century until the point we have just reached, that is to say, roughly 1875.

1. See Foucault's course, previously cited, *Le Pouvoir psychiatrique*, lecture of 5 December 1973.

2. A "medico-legal examination of the insane per the law of June 30, 1838," with a paragraph on "hospitalization orders" and "voluntary hospitalizations" (drafted on the basis of the ministerial circular of August 14, 1840) can be found in H. Legrand du Saulle, *Traité de médecine légale et de jurisprudence médicale* (Paris, 1874), pp. 556-727. Cf. H. Legrand du Saulle, G. Berryer, and G. Ponchet, *Traité de médecine légale, de jurisprudence médicale et de toxicologie*, second edition (Paris, 1862), pp. 596-786.

3. Cf. C. Vallette, *Attributions du préfet d'après la loi du 30 juin 1838 sur les aliénés. Dépense de ce service*, (Paris, 1896).

4. See A. Laingui, *La Responsabilité pénale dans l'ancien droit (XVIᵉ-CVIIIᵉ siècle)*, (Paris: s.1., 1970), pp. 173-204 (vol. 2, chapter 1: "La démence et les états voisins de la démence"), which also refers to the documents presented by M. Foucault in order to show the indifference of jurists towards internment notices containing classifications of mental illnesses in M. Foucault, *Folie et Déraison. Histoire de la Folie a l'âge classique* (Paris: Gallimard, 1961), pp. 166-172; English translation: *Madness and Civilization: A History of Insanity in the Age of Reason*, translated by Robert Howell (1971; reprinted, London: Tavistock, 1989), pp. 74-81.

5. The case of Jean Glenadel was reported by Pierre Louis Gratiolet to Jules Gabriel François Baillarger; they summarize it in their *Recherches sur l'anatomie, la physiologie et la pathologie du système nerveux* (Paris, 1847), pp. 394-399.

6. Cf. the detailed account of the conversation between the farmer and the health officer. Ibid., pp. 394-396.

7. "I found Glenadel sitting on his bed with a rope around his neck, the other end tied to the bedstead; his arms were tied together at the wrists with another rope." Ibid., p. 394.

8. "But as I saw him in a state of great excitement, I asked if the rope tying his arms was strong enough and did he not feel strong enough to untie himself. He made an attempt and said to me: - Yes, I think so. - If I got you something that would keep your arms more tightly bound, would you accept it? - With gratitude, sir. - In that case I will ask the sergeant at the police station to give me some of what he uses to bind prisoners' hands and send it to you. - You will do me a kindness." Ibid., 398.

9. In fact, the court official wrote: "I remain convinced that Jean Glenadel suffers from a delirious monomania characterized by an irresistible inclination to murder." Ibid., pp. 398-399.

10. J. E. D. Esquirol, *Des maladies mentales considérées sous les rapports médical, hygiénique et médico-légal*, vol. 1 (Paris, 1838), pp. 376-393. Cf. E. Esquirol, *Mental Maladies. A Treatise on Insanity*, translated by E. K. Hunt (Philadelphia, 1845).

11. See the notion of the "death instinct" (*"Todestriebe"*) in S. Freud: *Jenseits der Lustprinzips* (Leipzig, Wien, Zürich: s.1., 1920); French *translation: Au-delà du principe de plaisir*, in *Essais de psychanalyse* (Paris: s.1., 1981); English translation: *Beyond the Pleasure Principle*, translated by J. Strachey (London: s.1., 1961). To understand the difference stressed by Foucault, cf. the article "Instinct" written by J. J. Virey, in *Dictionnaire des sciences médicales*, 25 (Paris, 1818), pp. 367-413, and the articles "Instinct" in J. Laplanche and J. B. Pontalis, *Vocabulaire de la psychanalyse* (1967, Paris: s.1., revised edition 1990), p. 208; English translation: *The Language of Psycho-analysis*, translated by D. Nicholson-Smith (London: s.1., 1973), and C. Rycroft, *A Critical Dictionary of Psychoanalysis* (London: s.1., 1968); French translation: *Dictionnaire de psychanalyse* (Paris: s.1., 1972), pp. 130-133.

12. U. Trélat, *La Folie lucide étudiée et considérée au point de vue de la famille et de la société* (Paris, 1861).

13. Ibid., pp. viii-ix.

14. Ibid., p. ix: "Such is the origin of this book, which is not written out of hatred for the mentally deranged, but rather less in their interest than in that of their relatives; and positively with a view toward shedding light on a dangerous terrain and, if possible, to reduce the number of unhappy unions."

15. H. Legrand du Saulle, *La Folie devant les tribunaux* (Paris, 1864), pp. 431-433, which summarizes the case from the study by A. Bottex, *De la médecine légale des aliénés, dans ses rapports avec la legislation criminelle* (Lyon, 1838), pp. 5-8.

16. See the lecture of January 8, in this volume.

17. U. Trélat, *La Folie lucide*, p. 36.

18. Cf. M. Foucault, "*Il faut défendre la société*," pp. 79-86, lecture of February 4, 1976; English translation: "*Society Must Be Defended*" (New York: Picador, 2003).

19. J. Michelet, *Le Peuple* (Paris, 1846); E. Quinet, *La Révolution*, vols. 1-2 (Paris, 1865) and *Critique de la révolution* (Paris, 1867).

20. Cf. M. Foucault, "*Il faut défendre la société*, " pp. 193-212, lecture of March 10, 1976; English translation: "*Society Must Be Defended*" pp. 235-237.

21. Foucault could refer here to the works of A. Verga and to the manual of C. Livi, *Frenologia forense* (Milan, 1868), which preceded by a few years the first work on the morbid psychology of the Commune (for example: H. Legrand du Saulle, *Le Délire de persecution* [Paris, 1871], pp. 482-516). Later on there was C. Lombroso and R. Laschi, *Il delitto politico e le rivoluzioni in rapporto al diritto, all'antropologia criminale ed alla scienza di governo* (Torino, 1890).

22. Foucault summarizes here some of the theses of C. Lombroso and R. Laschi, *Le Crime politique et les Révolutions, par rapport au droit, à l'anthropologie criminelle et à la science du gouvernement*, vol. 2 (Paris, 1892), pp. 168-188. See also chapter fifteen: "Facteurs individuels. Criminels politiques par passion," pp. 189-202; chapter sixteen: "Influence des génies dans les révolutions," pp. 203-207; and chapter seventeen: "Rébellions et révolutions. Différences et analogies."

23. Ibid., vol. 2, p. 44: "Out of forty-one Paris anarchists examined by us at the Paris Prefecture of Police, were found: mad types, one - criminal types, thirteen (31%) - semi-criminals, eight - normal, nineteen. Out of one hundred individuals arrested in Turin for the strikes of May 1, 1890, I found a similar proportion: 34% of physiognomically criminal types; 30% of recidivists for ordinary crimes. However, out of one hundred non-political criminals in Turin, the criminal type reaches the proportion of 43% and the recidivist 50%."

24. J. B. V. Laborde, *les Hommes et les Actes de l'insurrection de Paris devant la psychologie morbide* (Paris, 1872), pp. 30-36.

25. See U. Trélat, *La Folie Lucide*, and the two essays by J.C. Prichard, *A Treatise on Insanity and Other Disorders Affecting the Mind*, (London, 1835) and *On the Different Forms of Insanity in relation to Jurisprudence* (London, 1842).

26. Foucault refers principally to "L'application de la physiologie des hallucinations à la physiologie du délire considéré d'une manière générale" (1845). This article, as well as the articles "Physiologie des hallucinations" and "La théorie de l'automatisme," can be read in J.-G.-F. Baillarger, *Recherches sur les maladies mentales*, vol. 1 (Paris, 1890), pp. 269-500.

27. Cf. W. Griesinger, *Die Pathologie und Therapie der psychischen Krankheiten für Ärtzte und Studierende* (Stuttgart, 1845); French translation of the German edition of 1861: *Traité des maladies mentales. Pathologie et thérapeutique* (Paris, 1865); English translation: *Mental Pathology and Therapeutics*, translated by C. L. Robertson and J. Rutherford (London, 1867/ New York: s.l., 1965).

28. Esquirol's definition, first proposed in *Des hallucinations chez les aliénés* (1817), is found again in *Des maladies mentales* vol. 1, p. 188. See also the chapters *Des Hallucinations* and *Des hallucinations chez les aliénés* (1832), pp. 80-100, 202-204. See also the chapters "Hallucinations" and "Illusions of the insane," in *Mental Maladies* pp. 93-110 and pp. 111-119.

29. J. Falret, *De l'état mental des épileptiques* (Paris, 1861); E. Garimond, *Contribution à l'histoire*

de l'épilepsie dans ses rapports avec l'aliénation mentale (Paris, 1877); E. Defossez, *Essai sur les troubles des sens et de l'intelligence causés par l'épilepsie* (Paris, 1878); A. Tamburini, *Sulla genesi delle allucinazioni* (Reggio Emilia, 1880), and "La théorie des hallucinations," *Revue scientifique*, 1 (1881), pp. 138-142; J. Seglas, *Leçons cliniques sur les maladies mentales et nerveuses* (Paris, 1895).

seven

19 FEBRUARY 1975

The problem of sexuality runs through the field of abnormality. ~ The old Christian rituals of confession. ~ From the confession according to a tariff to the sacrament of penance. ~ Development of the pastoral. ~ Louis Habert's Pratique du sacrement de pénitence *and Charles Borromée's (Carlo Borromeo)* Instructions aux confesseurs. *~ From the confession to spiritual direction (*direction de conscience*). ~ The double discursive filter of life in the confession. ~ Confession after the Council of Trent. ~ The sixth commandment: models of questioning according to Pierre Milhard and Louis Habert. ~ Appearance of the body of pleasure and desire in penitential and spiritual practices.*

I WILL RECAPITULATE SOME of what has been said so far. Last week I tried to show how a large domain of intervention, the domain of what we can call the abnormal, opened up before psychiatry. Starting from the localized, juridico-medical problem of the monster, a sort of explosion took place around or on the basis of the notion of instinct, and then, around 1845-1850, the domain of control, analysis, and intervention, the domain of the abnormal, was opened up to psychiatry.

I want to begin the other part of my topic at this point. Almost from the outset, the field of abnormality is very quickly taken up with the problem of sexuality. This occurs in two ways. First of all, the problem or at least the identification of phenomena of heredity and degeneration is immediately applied to the general field of abnormality as an analytic grid by which the field is codified and subdivided.[1] To that extent, medical and psychiatric analysis of the functions of reproduction becomes involved in the methods for analyzing abnormality. Then, within the domain constituted by this abnormality, the characteristic disorders of sexual abnormality are, of course, identified. Sexual abnormality initially appears as a series of particular cases of abnormality and then, soon after, around 1880-1890, it emerges as the root, foundation, and general etiological principle of most other forms of abnormality. All this begins, then, very early in the period I identified last week, that is to say, 1845-1850, the period of Griesinger's psychiatry in Germany and Baillarger's in France. In 1843, in the *Annales medico-psychologiques*, there is a psychiatric report in a criminal case. (This is no doubt not the first case, but it seems to me to be one of the clearest and most significant.) The report, written by Brierre de Boismont, Ferrus, and Foville, analyzes the sexual abnormality of a pederast teacher named Ferré.[2] In 1849, in *L'Union médicale*, there is an article by Michéa entitled "Unhealthy Deviations of the Generative Appetite."[3] In 1857, the famous Baillarger writes an article on "imbecility and perversion of the generative sense."[4] Moreau de Tours, in 1860-1861, I think, writes "Aberrations of the Generative Sense."[5] And then there is the long series of Germans, with Krafft-Ebing[6] and, in 1870, the first speculative or, if you prefer, theoretical article on homosexuality, written by Westphal.[7] As you can see, the birth, or anyway the dawn or opening up, of the field of abnormality, and then the crisscrossing, if not the subdivision, of this field by the problem of sexuality, are more or less contemporaneous.[8]

I would like to try to analyze this sudden branching out of the problem of sexuality into psychiatry. Because, although it is true that at least some elements concerning sexuality immediately implied abnormality, sexuality, while not absent from the medicine of mental alienation, nonetheless occupied an extremely limited place. So what happened? What took place around 1845-1850? How was it that, at the very moment that abnormality became the legitimate domain of intervention for psychiatry, sexuality suddenly became problematic in psychiatry? I would like to try to show that actually it was not the result of what could be called the removal of censorship, the removal of a ban on speech. It was not a question of an initially timid, technical, and medical breach of a taboo of discourse, speech, or expression that had perhaps weighed on sexuality from the depths of time and certainly since the seventeenth or eighteenth century. What I think took place around 1850, and I will try to analyze this later, was not at all the metamorphosis of a practice of censorship, repression, or hypocrisy, but the metamorphosis of a quite positive practice of forced and obligatory confession. I would say that, in the West, sexuality is not generally something about which people are silent and that must be kept secret; it is something one has to confess. If there have been periods when silence on sexuality was the rule, this never total and always entirely relative silence is always only one of the functions of the positive practice of confession. The imposition of areas, conditions, and prescriptions of silence has always been connected to some technique or other of obligatory confession. Obligatory confession as a procedure of power is, I think, primary and fundamental and it is around this practice, which must be identified and understood, that the rule of silence is able to function. In other words, censorship is not the primary and fundamental process. Whether we understand censorship to be repression or merely hypocrisy, it is in any case only a negative process that is governed by a positive mechanism that I will try to analyze. If it is true that silence, or certain regions of silence, or particular ways in which silence functions, have indeed been required by the way in which confession has been prescribed at different times, it is nonetheless easy to find periods in which the obligation of a statutory, approved, and institutional confession of sexuality exists side by side with considerable freedom at the level of other forms of expression of sexuality.[9]

I know nothing about this, but since I imagine it will please a lot of people, we can suppose that the rule of silence on sexuality had very little weight prior to the seventeenth century (let us say, before the epoch of the formation of capitalist societies) and that previously everyone could say what they liked with regard to sexuality.[10] Perhaps! Perhaps it was so in the Middle Ages, and freedom of expression with regard to sexuality was much greater in the Middle Ages than in the eighteenth or nineteenth century. Nonetheless, it remains the case that, even within this kind of space of freedom, there was a thoroughly codified, demanding, and highly institutionalized avowal of sexuality: the confession. However, I would say that we cannot rely too much on the example of the Middle Ages since it has not been sufficiently explored by historians. Consider what happens now. Today, on one side we have a series of institutionalized practices for the confession of sexuality: psychiatry, psychoanalysis, sexology. Now all these scientifically and economically codified forms of the confession of sexuality are correlative to a relative liberation or freedom at the level of possible statements concerning sexuality. Confession is not a way of getting round the rule of silence despite the existence of rules, customs, and morality. Confession and freedom of expression face each other and complement each other. If we go to the psychiatrist, psychoanalyst, or sexologist so frequently to consult them about our sexuality, and to confess the nature of our sexuality, it is precisely to the extent that all kinds of mechanisms everywhere—in advertising, books, novels, films, and widespread pornography—invite the individual to pass from this daily expression of sexuality to the institutional and expensive confession of his sexuality to the psychiatrist, psychoanalyst, or sexologist. Today we have, then, a figure in which the ritualization of confession has its counterpart and correlate in a proliferating discourse on sexuality.

What I would like to attempt to do by very vaguely sketching out this little history on the discourse of sexuality is not to pose the problem in terms of the censorship of sexuality. When was sexuality censored? Since when have we had to reduce sexuality to silence? When, and under what conditions, did we begin to speak of sexuality? I would like to turn the problem around and look at the history of the confession of sexuality. Under what conditions and according to what ritual was a certain obligatory and forced discourse, the confession of sexuality, organized amid other discourse on sexuality? A survey of the ritual of penance will serve as my guiding thread.

I apologize for the schematic character of the kind of survey that I shall attempt, but I would like a few things to be kept in mind that are, I think, important.[11] First, confession was not originally part of the ritual of penance. Confession became necessary and obligatory somewhat belatedly in the ritual of penance. Second, it must be kept in mind that the effectiveness of this confession and its role in the practice of penance underwent considerable changes between the Middle Ages and the seventeenth century. I alluded to these two things two or three years ago, and I will therefore return to them very quickly.[12]

First of all, the ritual of penance did not originally include obligatory confession. What was penance in early Christianity? Penance was a status that one deliberately and voluntarily assumed at a given moment of one's life for reasons that could be linked to an enormous and disgraceful sin, but which could just as well be motivated by a quite different reason. In any case, it was a status that one took on and that one took on once and for all in a way that was usually definitive: One could only be a penitent once in one's life. The bishop, and only the bishop, had the right to confer the status of penitent on someone who requested it. This took place in a public ceremony during which the penitent was both reprimanded and exhorted. After this ceremony, the penitent entered the order of penance that involved wearing a hair shirt and special clothes; scorning personal cleanliness; being solemnly expelled from the church, from the sacraments, or in any case from communion; undergoing rigorous fasts; suspending all sexual relations, and being obliged to bury the dead. When the penitent left the state of penance (and sometimes he did not leave it and remained penitent until the end of his life), it was after a solemn act of reconciliation that removed his status as penitent but left certain traces, such as the obligation of chastity that generally lasted for the rest of his life.

You can see that the public confession of one's transgressions was not absolutely required by this ritual. Even private confession was not required, although the penitent usually gave reasons and justifications when he asked the bishop to confer the status of penitent on him. However, the idea of a general confession of all the sins of one's life, the idea that such a confession could by itself be in any way effective in the remission of sins, was absolutely excluded by the system. The remission of sins was possible only by virtue of the severity of the penalties the individual inflicted on himself, or allowed to be inflicted on him, by taking the status of penitent. At a certain point, that is to say, from about the sixth century, a completely different model of "tariffed" penance succeeded, or rather was tangled up with, this old system. The model of ordination clearly governs the system I have just described. However, penance according to a tariff has an essentially lay, judicial, and penal model. A tariffed penance was established in terms of the Germanic penal model. Tariffed penance consisted in the following. When a faithful committed a sin, he could, or rather (and at this point you can see that we begin to pass from a free possibility or free decision to an obligation), he had to find a priest and tell him the transgression he had committed. The priest responded to this transgression, which always had to be serious, by suggesting or imposing a penance that was called a "satisfaction." For each sin there had to be a corresponding satisfaction. It was the performance, and only the performance, of this satisfaction that could entail, without any further ceremony, the remission of the sin. We are, then, still within a type of system in which it was only the satisfaction—or, as we should say, the performance of penance in the strict sense—that allowed the Christian to see his sin remitted. As for the penance, it was tariffed in the sense that for every type of sin there was a catalogue of obligatory penance, just as in the lay penal system, institutional reparation was granted to the victim for every crime and offense in order to wipe out the crime. With this system of tariffed penance, which originated in Ireland and was therefore not Latin, the statement of the transgression begins to play a necessary role. In fact, from the moment that one has to give a certain satisfaction after every transgression, or at least after every serious transgression, and from the moment that the tariff for this satisfaction is given, prescribed, and imposed by the priest, then the statement of the transgression, after each transgression, becomes indispensable. Moreover, in order for the priest to apply the right penance or satisfaction, and in order for him to be able to distinguish between those transgressions that are serious and those that are not, not only must the transgression be expressed or stated, but one must also recount it, describe its circumstances and how one committed it. It is through this penance, whose origin is clearly judicial and secular, that the small kernel of confession—still very limited and with only utilitarian effectiveness—gradually begins to take shape.

A theologian of the time, Alcuin, said: "How could the priest's power absolve a transgression if the bonds that shackle the sinner are not known? Doctors would no longer be able to do anything if the sick refused to show them their wounds. The sinner must therefore seek out the priest as the sick seek out the doctor, explaining to him the cause of his suffering and the nature of his illness."[13] However, beyond this necessary implication, confession has no value and no effectiveness in itself. It merely allows the priest to fix the penalty. It is not confession that somehow brings about the remission of sins. At most, we find in the texts of the time, between the seventh and tenth centuries, that confession, and confession to the priest, is something difficult and painful that involves a feeling of shame. To that extent, confession is already a kind of penalty and the beginning of expiation. Alcuin says that this confession, which is necessary so that the priest can play his role as a quasi doctor, is a sacrifice because it induces humiliation and blushes. It causes *erubescentia*. The penitent blushes when he speaks and thus, says Alcuin, "gives God a good reason to forgive him."[14] Now a number of shifts occur from the importance and effectiveness initially attributed to the simple fact of confessing one's sins. Because if it is true that the act of confessing is already the beginning of expiation, could we not conclude that in the end a sufficiently costly and humiliating confession is penance in itself? So, instead of the great satisfactions of fasting, the hair shirt, pilgrimage, and so on, could we not substitute a penalty that would quite simply be the statement of the transgression itself? *Erubescentia*, humiliation, would constitute the very heart, the essential part, of the penalty. Thus, in the ninth, tenth, and eleventh centuries, confession to the laity becomes widespread.[15] After all, if there is no priest on hand when one has committed a sin, one can quite simply express one's sin to someone (or several people) who happens to be available, and one becomes ashamed of oneself in telling him one's sins. As a result, confession will have taken place, expiation will have come into play, and God will grant the remission of sins.

You can see that the ritual of penance, or rather the setting of a quasi juridical tariff of penance, gradually tends to shift toward symbolic forms. At the same time, the mechanism of the remission of sins, the kind of little operational element that ensures that sins will be remitted, increasingly closes around confession itself. There is a corresponding weakening of the power of the priests, and even more so of the bishops. Now, what takes place in the second half of the Middle Ages, from the twelfth century until the beginning of the Renaissance, is that the Church manages to restore ecclesiastical power over the mechanism of the confession that had, to a certain extent, deprived it of power in the operation of penance. This reinsertion of confession within a consolidated ecclesiastical power takes place at the time of the scholastics through a variety of procedures. First, the obligation of regular confession emerges in the twelfth [*rectius*: thirteenth] century: at least once a year for the laity and monthly or even weekly for the clergy.[16] Thus, one no longer confesses when one has committed an offense. One can and indeed must confess after committing a serious offense, but one must in any case confess regularly and at least annually. Second, there is the obligation of continuity. This means that one must express every sin committed since at least the previous confession. Here again, a requirement of totalization, or of partial totalization at least, replaces the occasional character of confession. Finally, and above all, there is the obligation of exhaustiveness. It is not enough to express one's sin as soon as one has committed it and because one thinks it particularly serious. One must express all one's sins, not only the serious ones, but also the less serious. For it is up to the priest to distinguish between venial and mortal sins; it is for the priest to handle the theologians' very subtle distinction between venial and mortal sins that, as you know, can be transformed into each other depending on the circumstances of the action, the time at which it took place, the persons involved, and so on. So, there is the obligation of regularity, continuity, and exhaustiveness. All this entails a formidable extension of the obligation of penance and thus of the confession (*la confession*), of confession (*l'aveu*) itself.

With this considerable extension of penance and confession there is a corresponding proportional increase in the priest's power. In fact, what guarantees the regularity of confession is not just that the faithful are obliged to confess annually, but that they must always make their annual confession to the same priest, to their own priest or the priest who has authority over them, usually the parish priest. Second, what guarantees the continuity of confession, that is to say, that one forgets nothing that has happened since the last confession, is that a wider cycle of general confession must be added to the usual rhythm of confessions. The faithful are enjoined, or required, to make a general confession several times during their lifetime in which they go back over all their sins from the start of their life. Finally, what guarantees exhaustiveness is that the priest is no longer satisfied with the spontaneous confession of the faithful who seek him out after transgressing and because they have transgressed. Exhaustiveness is guaranteed by the priest's control over what the faithful says: He prods him, questions him, and clarifies his confession by a technique of the examination of conscience. A system of questioning develops in the twelfth and thirteenth centuries that is codified in terms of the Ten Commandments, the seven deadly sins, and then, a bit later, by the commandments of the Church, the list of virtues, and so forth. The result is that in twelfth-century penance the entire confession is structured and controlled by the priest's power. But this is not all. Something more will enable confession to be more securely installed within the mechanism of ecclesiastical power. Starting in this period, the priest is no longer bound by the tariff of satisfactions but fixes the penalties himself according to the sin, the circumstances, and the person. There is no longer an obligatory tariff. Gratien's decree says: "Penalties are arbitrary."[17] Second, and especially, the priest is now the only person who holds the "power of the keys." It is no longer a matter of recounting one's sins and confessing them to someone who is not a priest under the pretext that it makes one blush. There is only penance if there is confession, but there is only confession if one confesses to a priest. This power of the keys, held by the priest alone, gives the priest the possibility of remitting sins himself, or rather of practicing the ritual of absolution, which is such that God himself remits the sins through the priest's words and gestures. At this point penance becomes a sacrament in the strict sense. The sacramental theology of penance develops in the twelfth and thirteenth centuries. Previously penance was an act by which a sinner asked God to remit his sins. Starting in the twelfth and thirteenth centuries, it is the priest himself who, by freely giving his absolution, induces the working of divine nature— absolution—through human mediation. The priest's power can now be said to be firmly and definitively anchored in the practice of confession.

The whole sacramental structure of penance, not only as it is known at the end of the Middle Ages but also enduring into our own time, is more or less fixed. It is characterized by two or three major features. First of all, confession occupies the central place in the mechanism of the remission of sins. One absolutely must confess. One must confess everything. Nothing must be left out. Second, the domain of confession is considerably extended since it is no longer a question of confessing only serious transgressions but of confessing everything. Finally, there is a corresponding increase both in the priest's power (since he now gives absolution) and of his knowledge (since he now has to control what is said within the sacrament of penance, he has to question and impose the framework of his learning, his experience, and his moral and theological knowledge). The power and knowledge of priest and church are caught up in a mechanism that forms around confession as the central element of penance. This is the central and general structure of penance as it was fixed in the Middle Ages and as it still functions today.

What I would like to consider now, so as finally to come to our subject, is what took place starting in the sixteenth century, that is to say, in a period that is not characterized by the beginning of de-Christianization, but rather, as a number of historians have shown, by a phase of in-depth Christianization.[18] The period that stretches from the Reformation to the witch-hunts, passing through the Council of Trent, is one in which modern states begin to take shape while Christian structures tighten their grip on individual existence. What took place with regard to penance and the confession, at least in Catholic countries, can, I think, be described in the following way. (I leave to one side the problems of Protestant countries; we will come back to them shortly from another angle). First, with the Council of Trent, the sacramental armature of penance is explicitly maintained and renewed, and then, within and around penance in the strict sense, an immense apparatus of discourse and examination, of analysis and control, spreads out. This takes on two aspects. First of all, the domain of the confession is extended and confession tends to be generalized. All, or almost all, of an individual's life, thought, and action must pass through the filter of confession, if not, of course, as sin, at least as an element relevant for an examination or analysis now demanded by the confession. Second, there is an even more pronounced intensification of the power of the confessor corresponding to this formidable extension of the domain of confession. Or rather, the power the priest acquired as master of absolution when penance became a sacrament is flanked by a set of adjacent powers that support and extend it. What could be called the right of examination proliferates around the privilege of absolution. The priest's empirical powers of the eye, the gaze, the ear, and hearing are developed in support of his sacramental power of the keys. Hence the formidable development of the pastoral, that is to say, of the technique offered to the priest for the government of souls. At a time when states were posing the technical problem of the power to be exercised on bodies and the means by which power over bodies could effectively be put to work, the Church was elaborating a technique for the government of souls, the pastoral, which was defined by the Council of Trent[19] and later taken up and developed by Carlo Borromeo.[20]

Penance had, of course, a major and I would even say almost exclusive importance within this pastoral as a technique for the government of souls.[21] A literature develops at this point that is partly double-sided: a literature intended for confessors and a literature intended for the penitent. However, the literature for penitents, the small confession manuals put in their hands, is basically only the other side of the literature for confessors, the major treatises on cases of conscience or confession that the priest must possess, know, and consult when necessary. The fundamental and dominant element seems to me to be this literature for confessors. We find in this literature the analysis of the procedure of examination that is now at the priest's discretion and initiative and that gradually occupies the whole space of penance and even extends far beyond it.

What is this technique of penance that the priest must now know, possess, and impose on the penitent? In the first place, the confessor must himself be qualified. The confessor must possess a number of specific virtues. First, he must have authority: He must be an ordained priest and the bishop must have authorized him to hear confessions. Second, he must also have the virtue of zeal, that is to say, "love" or "desire." (I am following a treatise on the practice of penance written by Habert at the end of the seventeenth century. No doubt it represents a rigorist tendency, but at the same time it is certainly one of the finest elaborations of the technique of penance.)[22] This love or desire that characterizes the priest as confessor is not the love of "concupiscence" but a "benevolent love," a love that "attaches the confessor to the interests of others." It is a love that combats those, whether Christian or non-Christian, who "resist" God. Finally, it is a love that "warms" those who are willing to serve God. This love, then, this desire or zeal must be present in the confession, in the sacrament of penance.[23] Third, the priest must be holy, that is to say, he must not be in a state of "mortal sin," although this is not a canonical ban.[24] After ordination, absolutions will continue to be valid even if one is in the state of mortal sin.[25] What is to be understood by the priest's holiness is that he must be "confirmed in the practice of virtue" precisely because of the "temptations" to which he will be exposed ministering the penance. The confessional, Habert says, is like the "sick room" in which a certain "bad air" prevails arising from the penitent's sins and which risks contaminating the priest himself.[26] Thus the confessor needs holiness as a kind of armor and protection against the sin being passed on to him at the very moment of its utterance. There must be verbal communication, but no real transmission; communication at the level of the utterance must not be transmission at the level of culpability. The desire displayed by the penitent must not be turned into the confessor's desire; hence the principle of holiness.[27] Finally, the priest who hears confessions must have a holy dread of venial sins. This is not simply a dread of others' sins, but also of his own. For if the priest is not moved by a dread of venial sins on his own behalf, then his charity will be extinguished as fire is extinguished by ashes. Venial sins, in fact, tie one to the flesh and blind the spirit.[28] Consequently, this double process of a zealous and benevolent love that brings the confessor near the penitent and its correction by a holiness that annuls the evil of the sin at the very moment of its communication would not be able to function if the confessor was too linked to his own sins, even to his venial sins.[29]

The confessor must be zealous and holy, and he must be learned (*savant*). He must be learned in three capacities (still following Habert's treatise). He must be learned "as a judge," for "he must know what is permitted and what is forbidden"; he must know the law, both the "divine laws" and "human laws," as well as "ecclesiastical" and "civil" laws. He must be learned "as a doctor," for he must recognize in sin not only the act committed that breaks the law, but also the kind of illness that is the sin's raison d'être. He must know the "spiritual maladies" and their "causes" and "remedies." He must recognize these maladies according to their "number" and "nature." He must distinguish the genuine spiritual malady from mere "imperfection." Finally, he must recognize those maladies that lead to "venial sin" and those that lead to "mortal sin." He must, then, be learned as judge[30] and as doctor,[31] and he must also be learned "as a guide",[32] for he must "govern the conscience of his penitents." He must "remind them of their errors and follies" and he must "make them avoid the dangers" facing them.[33]

Lastly, the confessor must not only be zealous, holy, and learned, he must also be prudent. The confessor must have prudence, that is, the art of adapting this science, zeal, and holiness to particular circumstances. According to Habert, the confessor's prudence consists in this: "Observe all the circumstances, compare them with each other, discover what is hidden behind what appears, and foresee what might happen."[34]

A number of things follow from this characterization of the qualities needed by the confessor, which are, as you can see, very different from what was required in the Middle Ages. In the Middle Ages it was essential and sufficient that the priest be ordained, hear the sin, and decide whether to apply a penalty according to an obligatory tariff or one chosen arbitrarily by himself. A series of supplementary conditions are now added to these simple requirements that qualify the priest as someone intervening as such, not so much in the sacrament of penance as in the general operation of the examination, analysis, correction, and guidance of the penitent. In fact, the priest will have to undertake a large number of tasks on this basis. It is no longer just a question of giving absolution. First of all, he must promote and encourage the right mood in the penitent. That is to say, when the penitent arrives to make his confession, the priest must be welcoming, show that he is available and open to the confession he is going to hear. According to Carlo Borromeo, the priest must, with "promptitude and ease," receive "those who present themselves": he must never "put them off by abhorring this work." The second rule is that of benevolent attention, or rather, of not showing the absence of benevolent expectation: Never "show" penitents, "by word or gesture," that one does not listen to them "willingly." The final rule is what could be called the double consolation of the penalty. When sinners present themselves to the confessor, they must be consoled by the fact that the confessor himself takes "a noticeable consolation and a particular pleasure in the pains they take for the good and the solace of their souls." There is an economy of pain and pleasure: pain of the penitent who does not like to confess his transgressions, his consolation in seeing that the confessor suffers pain in listening to his sins, but who also consoles himself for the pain he thus gives himself by securing through confession solace for the penitent's soul.[35] It is this double investment of pain, pleasure, and solace on the part of both penitent and confessor that will ensure a good confession.

All this may seem theoretical and subtle. In actual fact, it was crystallized within an institution, or rather within a little object, a small piece of furniture with which you are quite familiar—the confessional: an open, anonymous, and public place within the church where the faithful can present themselves and will always find a priest available who will hear them, remaining close beside them, but from whom they are separated by a small curtain or screen.[36] This is, as it were, the material crystallization of all the rules that characterize both the qualification and power of the confessor. It seems that the first reference to a confessional is in 1516, one year after the battle of Marignan.[37] There were no confessionals before the sixteenth century.[38]

After welcoming the penitent, the priest must look for signs of contrition. He needs to know if the penitent is in an appropriate state of contrition for the effective remission of sins.[39] He then has to submit the penitent to an examination that is partly verbal and partly silent.[40] Then he must question him about the preparation of his confession and about when he last confessed.[41] He must also ask him if he has changed his confessor and if so why. Is he looking for a more indulgent confessor, which would mean that his contrition is not genuine or deep?[42] Without saying anything, he must also observe his comportment, his clothes, gestures, demeanor, and the sound of his voice, sending away, of course, women who arrive with their "hair curled, made up, and prettified."[43]

After this assessment of the penitent's contrition, the priest must proceed to the examination of conscience itself. If it is a general confession, the penitent must be exhorted to "picture to himself his whole life" and to do so according to a schedule. (I refer here to a number of rules published in dioceses after the Council of Trent according to pastoral rules given by Carlo Borromeo in Milan.[44]) First, he must go through the important periods of life followed by the different conditions of life: bachelor, married, posts held; then he must take up the different tests of his fortune and misfortune; then he must list and examine the different countries, places, and houses he has frequented.[45] The penitent must be questioned on his previous confessions.[46] Then he must be questioned according to an order that starts by going through "God's commandments," then the "seven deadly sins," then the "five senses of man," then the "commandments of the Church," then the list of "charitable works,"[47] then the three cardinal virtues, and then the three ordinal virtues.[48] Finally, after this examination, the "satisfaction" can be imposed.[49] In the satisfaction, the confessor must take into account two aspects of the penance itself: the penalty, the penal aspect, the punishment in the strict sense, and the aspect that after the Council of Trent is called the "medicinal" or corrective aspect of the satisfaction, that is to say, the aspect that allows the penitent's future to be protected from relapse.[50] This search for the double-edged satisfaction, penal and medicinal, must also obey a number of rules. The penitent must not only accept the penalty, but he must also recognize its usefulness and indeed its necessity. It is in this spirit that Habart recommends that the confessor ask the penitent to determine his own penance and, if he chooses a penance that is too weak, to convince him that it is not sufficient. A number of remedies must also be imposed according, as it were, to medical rules: to cure opposites with opposites, greed with charity and concupiscence with mortifications, et cetera.[51] Finally, penalties must be found that take account of the gravity of the transgressions and the penitent's own tendencies.[52]

We could continue to enumerate at great length the enormous arsenal of rules that surround this new practice of penance, or rather, this new and formidable extension of mechanisms of discourse, examination, and analysis that are involved in the sacrament of penance. There is not so much an explosion of penance as a formidable inflation of the sacrament of penance that introduces the individual's entire life into what is more a practice of general examination than a practice of absolution. We should add that in the second half of the sixteenth century, and starting from Borromeo's pastoral, we see the development of the practice of spiritual direction (*direction de conscience*), which is not exactly a practice of confession. In the most Christianized and urbanized environments, in seminaries and, to a certain extent, in colleges, we find the rule or at least the strong recommendation of spiritual direction alongside the rule of penance and confession. What is a spiritual director (*directeur de conscience*)? I will quote the definition and obligations given in the seventeenth-century regulations of the Châlons seminary: "In the desire that each must have for his progress in perfection, seminarists will take care that they they see their director from time to time outside of confession." What will they say to this director? What will they make of this director? "They will consider with him those things that concern their advancement in virtue, the way in which they comport themselves with their fellow man and in their external actions. They will also deal with those things that concern their self and their inner being."⁵³ (Olier defined the spiritual director as "the person to whom one communicates one's inner being."⁵⁴) With the spiritual director, then, one must deal with those things that concern the self and one's inner being: the little trials of the spirit, temptations, and bad habits, along with the sources from which they spring and the means to be employed to correct them. Beuvelet, in his *Méditations*, said: "If apprenticeship for the least profession requires one to pass through the hands of masters, if the body's health requires one to consult a doctor ... how much more must we consult those who are experts in the salvation of our soul." Seminarists must therefore consider their director as a "guardian angel." They must speak to him "with open heart, sincerely and faithfully," without "pretense" or "concealment."⁵⁵ You can see that as well as a general commitment to the narration and examination of one's entire life in the confession, the same entire life, including its least details, is also committed to spiritual direction. There is a double fastening, a double discursive filter through which one must pass all behavior, conduct, and relationships with others, as well as every thought, pleasure, and passion (but I will return to this shortly).

In short, the immense development that takes place from the tariffed penance of the Middle Ages to the seventeenth and eighteenth centuries tends to double the operation of penance—which initially was not even a sacrament—with a concerted technique of analyses, reflected choices, and the continual management of souls, conducts, and finally bodies. It is an evolution that inserts the juridical form of the law, of offense and penalty, which was originally the model for penance, within a field of practices that have the nature of correction, guidance, and medicine. Finally, it is an evolution that tends to replace, or at least to back up, the irregular confession of particular transgressions with an immense discursive journey that is the continual passage of a life before a witness, the confessor or director, who must be both its judge and doctor or who, at any rate, defines its punishments and prescriptions. Of course, the evolution I have hastily sketched is peculiar to the Catholic Church. A somewhat similar evolution takes place in Protestant countries, but through very different institutions and with a fundamental fragmentation of both religious theory and forms. At any rate, at the same time as this practice of confession-examination of conscience and spiritual direction is constituted as a constant discursive filter of life, we see the emergence in English Puritan circles of the practice of permanent autobiography in which each individual recounts his own life to himself and to others, to those close to him and the people of his own community, in order to detect the signs of divine election within this life. The establishment of this immense total narration of existence within religious mechanisms is, I believe, the innermost core, as it were, of all the techniques of examination and medicalization that appear later.

Having established this background, I would like to say a few words on the Sixth Commandment, that is to say, on the sin of lust and the position occupied by lust and concupiscence in the establishment of the general procedures of examination. How was the confession of sexuality defined before the Council of Trent, that is to say, in the period of "scholastic" penance between the twelfth and six-teenth centuries? It was essentially organized according to juridical forms. What the penitent was asked about when he was questioned, or what he talked about if he spoke spontaneously, were offenses against a number of sexual rules. Essentially, these offenses were for-nication: acts between people not joined by vows or marriage; adul-tery: acts between married people or between a married and an unmarried person; debauchery (*stupre*): an act with a consenting virgin but whom it is not necessary to marry or provide with a dowry; abduction (*rapt*): kidnap with violence and carnal offense; sensual self-indulgence (*mollesse*): caresses that do not lead to a legitimate sexual act; sodomy: sexual consummation in an unnatural vessel; in-cest: having sex with one's blood relations or someone related to the fourth degree; and finally, bestiality: acts committed with an animal. This filtering of sexual obligations and offenses focuses almost entirely and exclusively on what could be called the relational aspect of sex-uality. The main sins against the Sixth Commandment concern the legal ties between people (adultery, incest, and abduction). They con-cern the status of individuals, depending on whether one is a member of the secular or regular clergy. They concern the form of the sexual act between individuals (sodomy). They concern, of course, those well-known caresses that do not result in a legitimate sexual act (broadly, masturbation), but which figure as one of these sins because it is a way of not performing the sexual act in its legitimate form, that is to say, in the form required at the level of relationships with a partner.

Starting in the sixteenth century this kind of framework—which does not disappear from the texts and is still found for a long time—is gradually swept away and submerged by a triple transformation. First, at the level of the technique of confession, questioning on the Sixth Commandment raises a number of specific problems as much for the confessor, who must not be soiled, as for the penitent, who must never confess less than he has done but must never learn through the con-fession more than he already knows. Confession of the offenses of lust (*luxure*) must thus take place in such a way as to preserve the priest's sacramental purity and the penitent's natural ignorance. This implies a number of rules that I will summarize briefly. The confessor must know only what "is necessary." When the confession is over, he must forget everything that has been said to him. First of all, he must question the penitent on his "thoughts" in order to avoid questioning him on his acts in case the latter have not been committed (thus avoiding the penitent being taught something he does not know). He must never name the kinds of sin (he must not name, for example, sodomy, sensuality (*la mollesse*), adultery, incest, et cetera). However, he will question the penitent by asking what kind of thoughts he has had, what sort of acts he has performed and "with whom," and through this type of questioning he will, Habert says, "draw from the penitent's mouth every kind of lust, without the risk of teaching him any."[56]

The point on which the examination hangs is considerably modified with this technique. From the sixteenth century on, the fundamental change in the confession of the sin of lust is that the relational aspect of sexuality is no longer the important, primary, and fundamental element of penitential confession. It is no longer the relational aspect that is now at the very heart of questioning concerning the Sixth Commandment, but the movements, senses, pleasures, thoughts, and desires of the penitent's body itself, whose intensity and nature is experienced by the penitent himself. The old examination was essentially the inventory of permitted and forbidden relationships. The new examination is a meticulous passage through the body, a sort of anatomy of the pleasures of the flesh (*la volupté*). The body with its different parts and different sensations, and no longer, or much less, the laws of legitimate union, constitutes the organizing principle of the sins of lust. The body and its pleasures, rather than the required form for legitimate union, become, as it were, the code of the carnal.

I would like to take two examples. The first, a model of questioning of the Sixth Commandment at the beginning of the seventeenth century, comes from a book by Milhard that is, so to speak, the common, undeveloped, average, and quite archaic practice of penance.[57] In his *La Grande Guide des curés*, Milhard says that the examination must follow the following order of questions: simple fornication, defloration of a virgin, incest, abduction, adultery, voluntary emissions, sodomy, and bestiality. This is followed by questions concerning immodest looking and touching and the problem of dancing, books, songs, and the use of aphrodisiacs. Then there is the question of whether one has been physically excited by songs and, finally, whether one has dressed and made oneself up ostentatiously.[58] You can see that such an organization of the questioning, however crude, shows that what is essential and at the forefront in the examination are the major transgressions, but major transgressions at the level of relationships with someone else: fornication, defloration of a virgin, incest, abduction, and so on. By contrast, in the second example, a later treatise by Habert written at the end of the seventeenth century, the order of the questions, or rather the point of departure for the questions, is quite different. In fact, Habert starts from the fact that the sins of concupiscence are so numerous, practically infinite, that there is a problem of their classification and of how and in what order the questions should be organized and posed. Habert answers: "As the sin of impurity is committed in infinite ways, by all the senses of the body and by all the powers of the soul, the confessor ... will go through all the senses one after the other. Then he will examine desires. Finally he will examine thoughts."[59] You can see that the body is like the analytic principle of the infinite sins of concupiscence. The confession no longer unfolds in terms of the degree of importance of the laws of relationships that can be broken, but follows instead a sort of cartography of the sinful body.[60]

First, there is the sense of touch: "Have you not performed some improper touching? Which ones? Of what?" If the penitent "says that it was of himself," one will ask him: "For what reason?" "Ah! Was it only out of curiosity (which is very rare), or from sensuality, or in order to excite indecent movements? How many times? Did these movements arrive at *usque ad seminis effusionem?*"[61] You can see that lust no longer begins with that well-known illegitimate relationship, fornication. Lust begins with contact with oneself. In the order of sin, Condillac's statue (Condillac's sexual statue, if you like) does not emerge by becoming the smell of the rose, but by making contact with its own body.[62] The first form of the sin against the flesh is not contact with this or that person to whom one has no right, it is contact with oneself: It is being touched by oneself, masturbation. Second, after touch, there is sight. Looking must be analyzed: "Have you looked at improper objects? What objects? For what purpose? Was your looking accompanied by sensual pleasure? Did this pleasure lead you to desires? What desires?"[63] Reading is analyzed in the chapter on sight and looking. Reading can become sinful, not directly through thought, but first of all through the relationship to the body. It is as pleasure of sight, as concupiscence of looking, that reading may be sinful.[64] Third, is the tongue. Pleasures of the tongue are the pleasures of indecent speech and dirty words. Dirty words give pleasure to the body; nasty speech causes concupiscence or is caused by concupiscence at the level of the body. Has one uttered "dirty words" and "indecent speech" without thinking? Were these words spoken "without being accompanied by improper feelings"? "Were they, rather, accompanied by bad thoughts? And were these thoughts accompanied by bad desires?"[65] In this chapter lewd songs are condemned.[66] The fourth stage concerns the ears. There is the problem of the pleasure of hearing indecent words and smutty talk.[67] Generally, then, the whole of the external body has to be questioned and analyzed. Have you performed "lewd actions"? Was this alone or with others? With whom?[68] Do you "dress" in a way that is not quite decent? Has dressing like this given you pleasure?[69] Have you played immodest "games"?[70] While "dancing," have you experienced "sensual movements when taking someone's hand,[71] or when seeing effeminate postures and steps?" Have you experienced pleasure "hearing the voice, singing and tunes"?[72]

Broadly speaking, we can say that the sins of the flesh are newly focused on the body. Sins are no longer distinguished and ordered in terms of illegitimate relationships but rather by the body itself. It is the body that determines the order of questions. In a word: We are witnessing the flesh being pinned to the body. Previously, the flesh, the sin of the flesh, was above all breaking the rule of union. Now the sin of the flesh dwells within the body itself. One tracks down the sin of the flesh by questioning the body, by questioning its different parts and its different sensory levels. The body and all the pleasurable effects that have their source in the body must now be the focal point of the examination of conscience with regard to the Sixth Commandment. The different breaches of the relational laws concerning partners, the form of the act, and everything from fornication to bestiality will henceforth be no more than the exaggerated development, as it were, of this primary and fundamental level of sin that constitutes the relationship to self and the sensuality of the body itself. We can see, then, how this constitutes the starting point for another very important shift. Henceforth, the essential problem is no longer the distinction between real action and thought that worried the scholastics; it is the problem of desire and pleasure.

In the scholastic tradition it was known that not only actions but also intentions and thoughts had to be judged, because confession was an internal jurisdiction (*for intérieur*) that had to judge the individual himself, rather than an external jurisdiction (*for extérieur*) concerned with the examination of actions. However, the problem of the relationship between action and thought was ultimately only the problem of the relationship between intention and realization. By contrast, when the body and its pleasures are questioned in an examination concerning the Sixth Commandment, the distinction between a sin that is merely desired, a sin that is consented to, and a sin that is carried out is no longer sufficient to cover the field being addressed. Placing the body in the forefront introduces an immense domain and the constitution of what could be called a moral physiology of the flesh. I would like to give you some idea of this domain.

In 1722, in a confession manual from the diocese of Strasbourg, it is recommended that the examination of conscience begin with thoughts rather than actions (and it is a recommendation found in both Habert and Carlo Borromeo). The following order is recommended: "One should go from simple thoughts to lingering (*moroses*) thoughts, that is to say, those thoughts on which one dwells; then from lingering thoughts to desires; then from loose desires to consent;

then from consent to more or less sinful acts, arriving finally at the most criminal acts."[73] Habert, in the treatise to which I have referred several times, explains in the following way the mechanism of concupiscence and, consequently, the guiding thread for analyzing the gravity of a sin. For him, concupiscence begins with an emotion in the body that is a purely mechanical emotion produced by Satan. This bodily emotion causes what he calls a "sensual enticement." This enticement induces a sweet feeling localized in the flesh itself, a feeling of sweetness and delight, or even titillation and inflammation. This titillation or inflammation awakens thinking about pleasures that one begins to examine, compare with each other, and weigh, et cetera. Thinking about pleasures can produce a new pleasure; the pleasure of thought itself. This is the delight of thought. This delight of thought will then present the will with different sensual delights aroused by the first emotion of the body, not as sinful things, but rather as acceptable and worth being embraced. Since the will itself is a blind faculty and cannot in itself distinguish between good and evil, it will let itself be persuaded. As a result, consent is given and this consent, which is not yet intention, or even desire, is the first form of the sin. In most cases consent is the venial base on which the sin subsequently develops. There then follows an immense deduction of the sin itself that I will pass over.

All these subtleties now constitute the space within which the examination of conscience is developed. The guiding thread is no longer the law and breaches of the law, it is no longer the old juridical model proposed by the tariffed penance of former times, but this dialectic of delight, lingering thoughts (*morosité*), pleasure, and desire that at the end of the eighteenth century is simplified by Alphonse de Ligouri, who gives the general and relatively simple formulation followed by the Catholic pastoral of the nineteenth century.[74] In Alphonse de Ligouri there are only four stages: the impulse, which is the first thought to do evil, then the consent (whose genesis according to Habert I have just described), which is followed by delight, which is followed by the pleasure or satisfaction.[75] In effect, delight is pleasure of the present; desire is delight with regard to the future; and satisfaction is delight with regard to the past. In any case, the examination of conscience, and with it the avowal and confession inherent in penance, now spreads out in an entirely new setting. Certainly, the law is present as well as the interdiction linked to the law, and certainly it is still a question of identifying offenses, but the whole process of examination now focuses on this body of pleasure and desire that now constitutes the real partner of the operation and of the sacrament of penance. The reversal is total or, if you prefer, radical: We have gone from the law to the body itself.

Of course, this complex apparatus does not represent the massive and extensive real practice of confession since the sixteenth or seventeenth century. We know that in practice confession was a kind of ritual performed more or less annually by the vast majority of the Catholic population in the seventeenth and the first half of the eighteenth centuries and that it is already beginning to decline in the second half of the eighteenth century. In their rustic character and rapidity, these massive annual confessions carried out by mendicant orders or preachers, or by local priests, clearly had nothing to do with the complex construction I have just been describing. But I think it would be wrong to see this construction as no more than a theoretical edifice. The formulae for complex and complete confession were in fact put to work at an essentially secondary level. They were effectively put to work in the formation of confessors themselves, rather than in the average faithful among the people. In other words, there was a whole didactics of penance to which the rules I have been describing were directed. The practice of penance as I have set it out was developed in the seminaries, that is to say, in those institutions that were imposed—invented, defined, and established—by the Council of Trent, and which were like training schools for the clergy. We can say that the seminaries were the point of departure and often the model for the major educational establishments intended for what we call secondary education. Jesuit and Oratorian colleges extended or imitated these seminaries. So although the subtle technology of the confession was not, to be sure, a mass practice, neither was it a pure dream or utopia. It really formed elites. We only have to see the massive way in which, for example, all the treatises on the passions published in the seventeenth and eighteenth centuries freely borrowed from this landscape of the Christian pastoral to understand that, in the end, the vast majority of the elites of the seventeenth and eighteenth centuries had a deep knowledge of these concepts, notions, methods of analysis, and grids of examination peculiar to the confession.

Generally the history of penance from the sixteenth century to the eighteenth century is usually centered on the problem of casuistry.[76] I do not think that this is the really new element. Casuistry was no doubt important as a stake in the struggle between the different orders and the different social and religious groups. However, in itself casuistry was not something new. Casuistry exists within the very old legalistic tradition of penance as the sanction for offenses and as analysis of the particular circumstances in which an offense was committed. Essentially, casuistry is already rooted in the tariffed penance. However, what is new after the Tridentine pastoral and the sixteenth century is this technology of soul and body, of the soul in the body and of the body as the bearer of pleasure and desire. I think that this technology, with all its procedures for analysis, recognition, guidance, and transformation, is the fundamentally new element of this pastoral. With this new technology there is the formation or development of a series of new objects that pertain to both the soul and the body at the same time: forms and modalities of pleasure. Thus we pass from the old theme that the body was at the origin of every sin to the idea that there is concupiscence in every transgression. This assertion is not merely abstract; it is not just a theoretical postulate: It is necessarily required by this technique of intervention and this new way of exercising power. Beginning in the sixteenth century, around these procedures of penitential confession, there is an identification of the body and the flesh or, if you like, the body is made flesh and flesh is incorporated in a body (*une incarnation du corps et une incorporation de la chair*), which brings to light the original game of desire and pleasure at the point where soul and body meet, in the space of the body and at the very root of consciousness. Concretely, this means that masturbation will be the first confessable form of sexuality, in the sense of sexuality to be confessed. The discourse of confession, the discourse of shame and of the control and correction of sexuality essentially begins with masturbation. Even more concretely, this huge technical apparatus of penance had, it is true, little effect except in the seminaries and colleges, where the only form of sexuality to be controlled was, of course, masturbation.

There is a circular process that is very typical of these technologies of knowledge and power. The finest subdivisions of the new Christianization that began in the sixteenth century brought about institutions of power and specializations of knowledge that developed in the seminaries and colleges, that is, in institutions in which it was not sexual relationships between individuals, or legitimate and illegitimate sexual relationships, that were singled out for special attention, but rather the solitary desiring body. It is the adolescent masturbator who becomes the not yet scandalous but already disturbing figure who, through these spreading and multiplying seminaries and colleges, increasingly obsesses spiritual direction and the confession of sin. All the new procedures and rules of confession developed after the Council of Trent, this great internalization of the entire life of individuals in the discourse of penance, are actually secretly focused on the body and masturbation.

I will close by saying that at the same time, that is, in the sixteenth and seventeenth centuries, in the army, colleges workshops, and schools we see the development of a training of the body as a useful body. New procedures of surveillance, control, spatial distribution, and notation, et cetera are perfected. The body is invested by mechanisms of power that seek to render it both docile and useful. There is a political anatomy of the body. However, if instead of the army, workshops, and primary schools et cetera, we consider these techniques of penance and practices in the seminaries and colleges that derive from them, then we see an investment of the body at the level of desire and decency rather than an investment of the useful body at the level of aptitudes. Facing the political anatomy of the body there is a moral physiology of the flesh.[77]

Next week I want to show how this moral physiology of the flesh, or of the body made flesh (*incarné*) or embodied (*incorporée*) flesh, came together with the problems of the discipline of the useful body at the end of the eighteenth century. And I want to show how what could be called a pedagogical medicine of masturbation was constituted and extended the problem of desire to the problem of instinct that is the central element in the organization of abnormality. It is, then, this masturbation singled out by penitential confession in the seventeenth century, this masturbation that becomes a pedagogical and medical problem, that brings sexuality into the field of abnormality.

1. On the theory of heredity, cf. P. Lucas, *Traité philosophique et physiologique de l'hérédité naturelle dans les états de santé et de maladie du système nerveux, avec l'application méthodique de lois de la procréation au traitement génerale des affections dont elle est le principe*, vols. 1 - 2 (Paris, 1847-1850); on the theory of degeneration, see the lecture of February 5 in this volume.

2. The case of Roch-François Ferré, with the expert opinions of A. Brierre de Boismont, G. M. A. Ferrus, and A. L. Foville, is set out in *Annales médico-psychologiques*, 1 (1843), pp. 289-299.

3. C.-F. Michéa, "Des déviations maladives de l'appétit vénérien," *L'Union médicale* 3/85 (17 July 1849), pp. 338c-339c.

4. J. G. F. Baillarger, "Cas remarquable de maladie mentale. Observation receuillie au dépôt provisoire des aliénés de l'Hôtel-Dieu de Troyes, par le docteur Bédor," *Annales médico-psychologiques* 4 (1858), pp. 132-137.

5. The definitive version of "Aberrations du sens génésique" can be read in P. Moreau de Tours, *Des aberrations du sens génésique*, (1880; reprint, Paris, 1883)³.

6. R. Krafft-Ebing, *Psychopatha sexualis. Eine klinische-forensische Studie* (Stuttgart, 1886). English translation: *Psychopatha sexualis, with Especial Reference to Antipathic Instinct*, authorized translation, tenth German edition translated by Francis J Rebman (London, 1899). The study of the "antipathic sexual instinct" is developed in the second edition (*Psychopathia sexualis, mit besonderer Berücksichtigung der conträren Sexualempfindung*, [Stuttgart, 1887]). The first French translation is from the eighth German edition: *Étude médico-légale. Psychopathia sexualis, avec recherches spéciales sur l'inversion sexuelle* (Paris, 1895). The edition currently in circulation reproduces the edition edited by A. Moll (1923): *Psychopathia sexualis. Étude médico-légale à l'usage des medicines et des juristes*, (Paris: s.l., 1950).

7. J. C. Westphal, "Die conträre Sexualempfindung, Symptome eines nevropathischen (psychopathischen) Zustand," *Archiv für Psychiatrie und Nervenkrankheiten*, 2 (1870), pp. 73-108. Cf. V. Magnan, *Des anomalies, des aberrations et des perversions sexuelles* (Paris, 1885), p. 14: "The tendency may ... be connected to a profound abnormality and have the same sex as its object. This is what Westphal calls *contrary sexual sense* and that we, with Charcot, have designated as *inversion of the genital sense*" (emphasis in the original). On the French debate, see J. M. Charcot and V. Magnan, "*Inversion du sens genital*," *Archives de neurologie*, 3 (1882), pp. 53-60; *Archives de neurologie*, 4 (1882), pp. 296-322; V. Magnan, "Des anomalies, des aberrations et des perversions sexuelles," *Annales médico-psychologiques* 1 (1885), pp. 447-472.

8. The French debate can be followed in P. Garnier's collection, *Les Fétichistes: pervertis et invertis sexuels. Observations médico-légales* (Paris, 1896.) This is a species of response to the publication of A. Moll, *Die conträre Sexualempfindung* (Berlin, 1891); French translation: *La Perversion de l'instinct génital* (Paris, 1893).

9. Foucault develops this argument in *La Volonté de Savoir*, pp. 25-49; see chapter two: "L'incitation à discours," section 1: "L'hypothèse repressive." English translation: *The History of Sexuality* vol. I: *An Introduction*, translated by Robert Hurley (London: Allen Lane, 1979), pp. 17-35. See also part two, chapter two: "The incitement to discourse."

10. Cf. *La Volonté de Savoir*, p. 9; *The History of Sexuality* vol. I: *An Introduction*, p. 3.

11. In this lecture Foucault basically relies upon the three volumes of H. C. Lea, *A History of Auricular Confession and Indulgences in the Latin Church* (Philadelphia, 1896).

12. See the previously cited course at the Collège de France, *Théories et Institutions pénales*.

13. F. Albinus seu Alcuinus, *Opera omnia*, vol. 1: (*Patrologiae cursus completus*, second series, tome 100) (Paris, 1851), col. 337.

14. Ibid., col. 338-339: "Erubescis homini in salutem tuam ostendere, quod non erubescis cum nomine in perditionem tuam perpetrare? ... Quae sunt nostrae victimae pro peccatis, a nobis commissis, nisi confessio peccatorum nostrorum? Quam pure deo per sacerdotem offerre debemus; quatenus orationibus illius, nostrae confessionis oblatio deo

acceptabilis fiat, et remissionem ab eo accipiamus, cui est sacrificium spiritus contribulatus, et cor contritum et humuliatum non spernit."

15. Ibid., col. 337: "Dicitur vero neminem vero ex laicis suam velle confessionem sacerdotibus dare, quos a deo Christo cum sanctis apostolis ligandi solvendique potestatem accepisse credimus. Quid solvit sacerdotalis potestas, si vincula non considerat ligati? Cessabunt opera medici, si vulnera non ostendunt aegroti. Si vulnera corporis carnalis medici manus expectant, quanto magis vulnera animae spiritualis medici solatia deposcunt?"

16. On the canonical legislation of 1215, cf., R. Foreville, *Latran 1, 2, 3, and 4* (Paris: s.l., 1965), pp. 287-306. See also the sixth volume of the series *Histoire des conciles œcuméniques*, edited by G. Dumeige, where one can also find the French translation of the conciliar decree of 30 November 1215, *De la confession, du secret de la confession, de l'obligation de la communion pascale,* pp. 357-358. Especially note: "Each and every faithful of both sexes must faithfully confess their sins to their priest at least once a year, perform with care as far as they are able the penance imposed on them, receive with respect, at Easter at least, the Eucharist sacrament, unless, on the advice of the priest, for a valid reason, they think they should abstain from it temporarily. If they do not they will be forbidden *ab ingressu ecclesiae* while alive and deprived of a Christian burial after death. This salutary decree will be published in the churches so that no-one can hide his blindness with a veil of ignorance". Cf. the Latin original in *Conciliorum oecumenicorum decreta* (Freiburg: s.l., 1962), pp. 206-243.

17. Gratianus, *Decretum, emandatum et variis electionibus simul et notationibus illustratum, Gregorii XIII pontificis maximi iussu editum,* (Paris, 1855), pp. 1519-1656 (*Patrologia latina,* tome 187). The decree was promulgated in 1130.

18. See especially, "Christianisation" and "Dechristianisation" in J. Delumeau, *Le Catholicisme entre Luther et Voltaire* (Paris: s.l., 1971), pp. 256-292. English translation: *Catholicism between Luther and Voltaire, a New View of the Counter-Reformation* translated by J. Moiser (London: s.l., 1977).

19. The pastoral of the confession was established in the fourteenth session (November 25, 1551). The proceedings are published in *Canones et decreta concilii tridentini* edited by Æ. L. Richter (Leipzig, 1853), pp. 75-81 (*repetitio* of the edition published in Rome, 1834).

20. C. Borromeus [Carlo Borromeo/St. Charles Borromeo], *Pastorum instructiones ad concionandum, confessionisque et eucharistiae sacramenta ministrandum utilissimae* (Antwerp, 1586).

21. The twenty-third session (*De reformatione*) of the Council of Trent requires careful attention to the preparation of the clergy in the sacrament of penance: "Sacramentorum tradendorum, maxime quae ad confessiones audiendas videbuntur opportuna, et rituum ac caeremoniarum formas ediscent" (*Canones et decreta,* p. 209).

22. L. Habert, *Pratique du sacrement de penitence ou méthode pour l'administrer utilement* (Paris, 1748), especially for the description of the confessor's virtues, pp. 2-9, 40-87 (but the entire treatise is devoted to his qualities, pp. 1-184). On Habert's rigorism and its consequences for French religious history between the end of the seventeenth and the beginning of the eighteenth century, see the biographical note by A. Humbert in *Dictionnaire de théologie catholique* vol. 6 (Paris, s.l., 1920), col. 2013-2016.

23. L. Habert, *Pratique du sacrament de penitence,* pp. 40-41.

24. Ibid., p. 12.

25. The restriction is not Habert's, who writes in *Pratique du sacrament de penitence*: "Although the effect of the sacraments is in no way dependent upon the holiness of the minister but only on the merits of Jesus Christ, nonetheless it is a great disgrace and a horrible sacrilege for someone who has rejected pardon to undertake to give it to others."

26. Ibid., p. 13: "He must be well confirmed in the practice of virtue due to the great temptations to which this ministry exposes him. For the bad air of the sick room does not have a greater effect on the body than the recounting of certain sins has on the mind. If, then, it is only those with a good constitution who can treat the sick, dress their wounds, and remain by their side without their own health being upset, we should

necessarily acknowledge that only those who have taken care to fortify themselves in virtue by a lengthy practice of good works can govern gangrenous consciences without danger to their health."

27. Ibid., p. 14: "However, of all the sins, none is more contagious and more easily transmitted than the sin that is contrary to chastity."

28. Ibid., "The holiness necessary to a confessor must give him a holy dread of all venial sins.... And although they [the venial sins] do not extinguish habitual charity, nonetheless their effect is like that of ash, that covers the flame and prevents it from lighting and warming the room in which it is kept."

29. Ibid., pp. 16-40. The second part of chapter two develops the three following points synthesized by Foucault: (1) "the blindness of a man who has not taken care to avoid venial sins"; (2) "his insensitivity with regard to those who are accustomed to them"; (3) "the ineffectiveness of the measures he might take to free them from them."

30. Ibid., p. 88: "As a judge, he must know what is permitted and what is forbidden to those who come before his court. But how could he know this except through the law? But which persons and in what matters must he judge? All kinds of persons and all kinds of things, since all the faithful, whatever their condition, are obliged to confess. Thus he must know the duty of each, the divine and human laws, ecclesiastical and civil laws, what they permit and what they forbid to each profession. For a judge would only pronounce randomly and expose himself to great injustices if, in ignorance of the law, he condemned some and upheld others. The law is the necessary balance in which the confessor must examine the actions and omissions of his penitents: the rule and the measure without which he is unable to judge whether they have fulfilled or neglected their duties. Much insight is needed therefore in his capacity as judge."

31. Ibid., pp. 88-89: "As a doctor he must be familiar with spiritual maladies, their causes and remedies. These maladies are sins whose nature ... number ... and difference he must know." Knowing the nature of the sin means distinguishing "the circumstances that change the kind; those which, without changing the kind, significantly diminish or augment the nature of the sin." Knowing the number means knowing "when several repeated actions or words or thoughts are morally only one sin, or when they multiply it and one must express their number in the confession." Knowing the difference enables one to separate a sin from an imperfection: "For sin alone is the subject of the sacrament of penance and one cannot give absolution to those who only accuse themselves of mere imperfections as sometimes happens with devout persons."

32. Ibid., p. 89: "The confessor is the judge, the doctor and the guide of penitents."

33. Ibid. : "As a guide, the confessor must govern his penitents' conscience, remind them of their errors and their follies and make them avoid the dangers encountered in each profession, which is like the path by which he must lead them to eternal beatitude."

34. Ibid., p. 101: "Prudence does not exclude science but necessarily presupposes it. It does not make up for the lack of study but calls for a great purity of heart and honesty of intention, much strength and greatness of mind in order to observe all the circumstances, compare them with each other, discover what is hidden through what appears and foresee what might happen through what is already present."

35. C. Boromée [Borromeo], *Instructions aux confesseurs de sa ville et de son diocèse. Ensemble: la manière d'administrer le sacrement de pénitence, avec les canons pénitentiaux, suivant l'ordre du Décalogue. Et l'ordonnance du même saint sur l'obligation des paroissieurs d'assister à leurs paroisses,* (1648; reprint, Paris, 1665), pp. 8-9. The instructions were "printed by order of the assembly of the clergy of France at Vitré."

36. Ibid., p. 12: "Confessionals must be placed in an open spot in the church that can be seen from everywhere, and it would also be a good idea if they were in a spot provided with some way of preventing others coming too close while someone is confessing."

37. We have not been able to trace this information given by Foucault.

38. H. C. Lea, *A History of Auricular Confession,* vol. 1, p. 395: "The first allusion I have met to this contrivance is in the council of Valencia in 1565, where it is ordered to be erected

in churches for the hearing of confession, especially of women." In the same year Carlo Borromeo prescribes the "use of a rudimentary form of confessional—a set with a partition (*tabella*) to separate the priest from the penitent."

39. C. Boromée [Borromeo], *Instructions aux confesseurs*, pp. 21-22.

40. Ibid., p. 24: "At the start . . . the confessor must make some inquiries in order to know how best to conduct the subsequent confession," pp. 24-25.

41. Ibid., pp. 21-22, 24-25.

42. Ibid., pp. 24-25 ("Questions that must be posed at the beginning of the confession").

43. Ibid., p. 19. However, "the same thing should be observed with regard to men," ibid., p. 20.

44. C. Borromeus [Borromeo], *Acta ecclesiae mediolanensis*, (Mediolani, 1583) (the *in-folio* in Latin for France was published in Paris in 1643). Cf. C. Boromée [Borromeo], *Instructions aux confesseurs* and; *Règlements pour l'instruction du clergé, tirés des constitutions et décrets synodaux de saint Charles Borromée* (Paris, 1663).

45. C. Boromée [Borromeo], *Instructions aux confesseurs*, pp. 25-26.

46. Ibid., p. 30.

47. Ibid., pp. 32-33: "He must proceed with these questions in order, starting with God's commandments. Although all the counts upon which one must conduct the inquiry can be referred back [to the Ten Commandments], nonetheless, dealing with someone who rarely takes the sacrament, it will be good to examine the seven cardinal sins, the five senses of man, the commandments of the church, and the works of charity."

48. The list of virtues does not appear in the edition we have used.

49. C. Boromée [Borromeo], *Instructions aux confesseurs*, pp. 56-57.

50. Ibid., pp. 52-62, 65-71; L. Habert, *Pratique du sacrement de pénitence*, p. 403 (third rule). Cf. *Canones et decreta*, pp. 80-81 (session fourteen, chapter eight: "De satisfationis necessitate et fructu").

51. L. Habert, *Pratique du sacrement de pénitence*, p. 401 (second rule).

52. Ibid., p. 411 (fourth rule).

53. Foucault here summarizes what F. Vialart says in his *Règlements faits pour la direction spirituelle du séminaire . . . établi dans la ville de Châlons afin d'éprouver et de préparer ceux de son diocèse qui se présentent pour être admis aux saints ordres*, second edition, (Châlons, 1664), p. 133: "They must have a great openness of heart in their dealings with their confessor and have full confidence in him if they wish to benefit from his conduct. This is why they will not be content with opening themselves to him frankly in confession, but will readily see him and consult him about all their difficulties, troubles, and temptations"; pp. 140-141: "In order to reap the most profit, they will have perfect confidence in their director and will give him an account of their exercises with simplicity and obedience of spirit. The means for doing both one and the other is to consider the director as an invisible angel that God has sent to them in order to lead them to heaven if they listen to his voice and follow his advice; it is to persuade themselves that without this trust and openness of heart, retreat is more an amusement of the mind by which it deceives itself, than an exercise of piety and devotion, of working firmly for its salvation and giving itself to God in order to advance in virtue and the perfection of its condition. If they feel reluctant to communicate with him, they will be all the more courageous and faithful in fighting this temptation, so much greater will be the merit of those who defeat it, since if they heed it, it could prevent them seeing the fruit of their retreat."

54. Foucault refers here to J.-J. Olier, *L'Esprit d'un directeur des âmes*, in *Œuvres completes* (Paris, 1856), col. 1183-1240.

55. M. Beuvelet, *Méditations sur les principales vérités chrétiennes et ecclésiastiques pour tous les dimanches, fetes et autres jours de l'année*, vol. 1 (Paris, 1664), p. 209. The passage cited by Foucault is from the meditation seventy-one entitled "Quatrième moyen pour faire progrès en la vertu. De la nécessité d'un directeur." English translation: "Fourth Means of Making Progress in Virtue. The Need for a Director."

56. L. Habert, *Pratique du sacrement de pénitence*, pp. 288-290.

57. P. Milhard, *La Grand Guide des curés, vicaires et confesseurs* (Lyon, 1617). The first edition,

known under the title *Le Vrai Guide des curés*, is from 1604. Made obligatory within his jurisdiction by the Archbishop of Bordeaux, it was withdrawn from circulation in 1619 following condemnation by the Sorbonne.

58. P. Milhard, *La Grand Guide*, pp. 366-373.

59. L. Habert, *Pratique du sacrement de pénitence*, pp. 293-294.

60. Ibid., pp. 294-300.

61. Ibid., p. 294.

62. E. Bonnot de Condillac, *Traite des sensations* (Paris, 1754), I, 1,2; English translation: *Condillac's Treatise on the sensations* translated by Geraldine Carr (London: s.l., 1930): "If we give the statue a rose to smell, to us it is a statue smelling a rose, to itself it is smell of rose. The statue therefore will be rose smell, pink smell, jasmine smell, violet smell, according to the flower which stimulates its sense organ." p. 3.

63. L. Habert, *Pratique du sacrement de pénitence*, p. 295.

64. Ibid., p. 296.

65. Ibid.

66. Ibid., p. 297.

67. Ibid.: "Beyond discussions in which one says and hears improper words, one can also sin by hearing speech in which one does not participate. It is to explain these kinds of sin that the following questions are put forward (as for the first, they have been sufficiently clarified in the previous article)."

68. Ibid., pp. 297-298: "Have you performed lewd actions? For what purpose? How many times? Was anyone present? Which persons? How many persons? How many times?"

69. Ibid., p. 298: "Have you dressed up to give pleasure? To whom? For what purpose? How many times? Is there anything lewd in your dress, for example, leaving your breast uncovered?"

70. Ibid. (Foucault has omitted the words "with someone of the opposite sex" from the end of the sentence.)

71. Ibid., p. 297. (Foucault has omitted "of the opposite sex".)

72. Ibid., pp. 297-298.

73. We have not been able to consult chapter two, section 3, of *Monita generalia de officiis confessarii olim ad usum diocesis argentinensis* (Strasburg, 1722). The passage quoted by Foucault ("sensim a cogitationibus simplicibus ad morosas, a morosis ad desideria, a desideriis levibus ad consensum, a consensus ad actus minus peccaminosos, et si illos fatentur ad magis criminosos ascendendo") is taken from H. C. Lea, *A History of Auricular Confession*, vol. 1, p. 377.

74. A. de Ligouri, *Praxis confessarii ou Conduite du confesseur* (Lyon, 1854); A.-M. de Ligoury [de Ligouri], *Le Conservateur des jeunes gens ou Remède contre les tentations déshonnètes* (Clermont-Ferrand, 1835).

75. A. de Ligorius [de Ligouri], *Homo apostolicus instructus in sua vocatione ad audiendas confessiones sive praxis et instructio confessariorum*, fifth edition, vol. 1, (Bassani, 1782) pp. 41-43 (treatise 3, chapter 2, section 2: "De peccatis in particulari, de desiderio, compiacentia et delectatione morose"). Cf. A. de Ligouri, *Praxis, confessarii*, pp. 72-73 (article 39); A.-M. de Liguory [de Ligouri], *Le Conservateur des jeunes gens*, pp. 5-14.

76. Foucault no doubt refers here to developments of chapter 2 ("Probabilism and casuistry") of H. C. Lea's *A History of Auricular Confession*, vol. 2, pp. 284-411.

77. See the course entitled *La Societé punitive* (lectures of March 14 and 21, 1973) and M. Foucault, *Surveiller et punir*, pp. 137-161; English translation: *Discipline and Punish*.

eight

26 February 1975

A new procedure of examination: the body discredited as flesh and the body blamed through the flesh. ~ Spiritual direction, the development of Catholic mysticism, and the phenomenon of possession. ~ Distinction between possession and witchcraft. ~ The possessions of Loudon. ~ Convulsion as the plastic and visible form of the struggle in the body of the possessed. ~ The problem of the possessed and their convulsions does not belong to the history of illness. ~ The anti-convulsives: stylistic modulation of the confession and spiritual direction; appeal to medicine; recourse to disciplinary and educational systems of the seventeenth century. ~ Convulsion as neurological model of mental illness.

LAST WEEK I TRIED to show how the body of pleasure and desire appeared at the heart of the practices of penance and the technique of spiritual direction that we see, if not fully formed, at least developing from the sixteenth century. In a word, we can say carnal disorder corresponds to spiritual direction, that is to say, carnal disorder as a discursive domain, field of intervention, and object of knowledge for this spiritual direction. The complex and floating domain of the flesh as a domain of the exercise of power and objectification begins to stand out from the body, from the corporeal materiality that the penitential theology and practice of Middle Ages merely identified as the origin of sin. The body is now a body in which there exists a series of mechanisms called "ticklings," "titillations," and so on, a body that is the seat of multiple intensities of pleasure and delight, and a body that is driven, sustained, and possibly held back by a will that does or does not consent, that takes pleasure or refuses to take pleasure. In short, it is the sensitive and complex body of concupiscence. This, I believe, is the correlate of this new technique of power. What I wanted to show was that this description of the body as flesh at the same time discredits the body as flesh; that making the body guilty through the flesh makes possible an analytic discourse and investigation of the body; and that both assigning fault to the body and, at the same time, the possibility of objectifying this body as flesh, are correlative to what can be called a new procedure of examination.

I tried to show that this examination obeyed two rules. First of all, examination should be as far as possible coextensive with the whole of an individual's life: Whether examination takes place in the confession or is undertaken with a spiritual director, the whole of one's life should be passed through the filter of examination, analysis, and discourse. Everything one says and does must pass through this discursive grid. Second, the examination exists within a relationship of authority, a power relation, which is both very strict and very exclusive. It is true that everything must be said to the director or to the confessor, but it must be said only to him. Thus the examination that characterizes these new techniques of spiritual direction obeys the rules of both exhaustiveness and exclusivity. As a result, when the flesh becomes the object of an unlimited analytical discourse and constant surveillance, it is linked both to a procedure of complete examination and the establishment of a closely related rule of silence. One must say everything, but one must only say it here and to this person. One must only say it in the confessional as part of the act of penance, or within the practice of spiritual direction. Speaking only here and to this particular person is not, of course, a fundamental and original rule of silence on which the necessity for a confession is then superimposed as a corrective in particular cases. Actually, we have a complex element in which silence, the rule of silence or of not-saying, is correlative to another mechanism that is a mechanism of enunciation: You must say everything, but you must do so only under certain conditions, within a particular ritual, and to a particular person. In other words, we are not entering an age in which the flesh is reduced to silence, but rather one in which the flesh appears as the correlate of a system or mechanism of power that comprises an exhaustive discursiveness and a surrounding silence installed around this obligatory and permanent confession. The power exercised in spiritual direction does not therefore prescribe silence and not-saying as a fundamental rule; it posits it simply as the necessary auxiliary or condition of functioning of the wholly positive rule of enunciation. One names the flesh, talks about it, and expresses it. In the seventeenth century, and still in the eighteenth and nineteenth centuries, sexuality is essentially not what one does but what one confesses: It is so that one can confess in good conditions that one must stay silent in all others.

Last week I tried roughly to reconstruct the history of this type of apparatus of confession-silence. Obviously, this apparatus, this technique of spiritual direction, which makes the flesh appear as its object or as the object of an exclusive discourse, does not concern the entire Christian population. This difficult and subtle apparatus of control and the body of pleasure and desire that is born in correlation with it obviously only concerns that thin strata of the population that could be reached by these complex and subtle forms of Christianization: the highest strata of the population, seminaries and monasteries. It is clear that almost nothing of these relatively subtle mechanisms is found in the immense confusion of the annual penance that most of the rural and urban population took part in during the seventeenth and eighteenth centuries (confession for Easter communion). Nonetheless, I think they are important for at least two reasons. I will pass over the first quickly, but I will dwell at greater length on the second.

The first reason is that Catholic mysticism, in which the theme of the flesh was very important, no doubt developed on the basis of this technique in the second half of the sixteenth century and, especially in France, in the seventeenth century. In France, if we consider all that happened and all that was said between the time of Father Surin and the time of Madame Guyon,[1] it is clear that these themes, these new objects, and this new form of discourse were linked to the new techniques of spiritual direction. However, I think that we see this body of desire and concupiscence appear more broadly, or at least more profoundly, in certain more extensive strata of the population in which a number of processes were put to work that were more profound than Madame Guyon's unsophisticated discourse of mysticism. I am talking about what could be called the front of in-depth Christianization.

At the summit, then, the apparatus of spiritual direction brings out these forms of mysticism. And then, below, it brings out another phenomenon that is linked to and corresponds to mysticism and which finds in mysticism a series of supporting mechanisms, but whose destiny is ultimately very different: the phenomenon of possession. As a typical phenomenon of the installation of a new apparatus of control and power in the Church, possession should, I believe, be distinguished from witchcraft, from which it differs radically. To be sure, the witchcraft of the fifteenth and sixteenth centuries and the possessions of the sixteenth and seventeenth centuries emerge within a kind of historical continuity. We can say that witchcraft, or the great epidemics of witchcraft that took place from the fifteenth century until the beginning of the seventeenth century, and then the great wave of possessions that took place from the end of the sixteenth century until the beginning of the eighteenth century, should both be situated as general effects of the Christianization I have been talking about. However, they are two completely different series of effects resting on quite distinct mechanisms.

According to historians currently studying the problem, witchcraft reflected the struggle ushered in by the new wave of Christianization at the end of the fifteenth century and the beginning of the sixteenth that was organized around and against a number of religious forms that the first and very slow waves of Christianization in the Middle Ages had left, if not completely intact, at least still very much alive. Witchcraft was very likely a peripheral problem. In places where Christianization had not yet taken hold, where cult forms had persisted for centuries, or even perhaps for millennia, the Christianization of the fifteenth and sixteenth centuries came up against obstacles that it sought to encircle and counter with a form of both manifestation and opposition. Witchcraft is then codified, captured, judged, repressed, burned, and destroyed by the mechanisms of the Inquisition. Witchcraft, then, is caught up within the process of Christianization, but it is a phenomenon situated on the outer fringes of this process. It is a peripheral phenomenon that consequently belongs more to the country and to coastal and mountainous regions where the towns, the major traditional centers of Christianization since the Middle Ages, had not penetrated.

Possession, although inscribed within this Christianization that gets under way at the end of the fifteenth century, is an internal, rather than an external, effect. It appears to be the aftereffect of a religious and detailed investment of the body and, through the double mechanism that I have just been talking about, of an exhaustive discourse and exclusive authority, rather than of the penetration of new regions and new geographical or social domains. Moreover, this is immediately indicated by the fact that witchcraft is after all essentially something denounced from outside by the authorities or by notables. The witch is the woman on the outskirts of the village and at the edge of the forest. The witch is the bad Christian. But in the sixteenth century and especially in the seventeenth and the beginning of the eighteenth century, who is it that is possessed? Rather than someone who is denounced by another person, she is someone who confesses, and who does so spontaneously. She is not, moreover, a woman of the country but a woman of the town. From Loudon to the Saint-Médard cemetery in Paris, the theater of possession is the small or big town.[2] Better still, she is not just any woman in the town; she is the nun and it is to the superior or the prioress within the convent that she speaks. This new personage who appears at the very heart of the Christian institution, at the very heart of the mechanisms of spiritual direction and the new penance, is no longer marginal but absolutely central in the new technology of Catholicism. Witchcraft appears at the outer limits of Christianity. Possession appears at its inner core, where Christianity seeks to sink its mechanisms of power and control and its discursive obligations in the bodies of individuals. Possession appears when Christianity seeks to put to work its mechanisms of control and obligatory, individualizing discourse.

This is reflected in the fact that the scene of possession, with its principal elements, is quite different and distinct from the scene of witchcraft. The central character in phenomena of possession is the confessor, director, or guide. He is found in the major possession cases of the seventeenth century: Gaufridi in Aix[3] and Grandier in Loudon.[4] There is a really important figure in the Saint-Médard case at the beginning of the eighteenth century, the deacon Pâris, although he has already disappeared when the possession unfolds.[5] So, at the center of the scene of possession and the mechanisms of possession is the holy figure with the powers of the priest (and so the powers of direction, authority, and discursive constraint). Whereas with witchcraft there is a form of duel, with the devil on one side and the witch on the other, in possession there is a triangular or even more complex system of relationships. There is a matrix of three terms: the devil, of course, the possessed nun at the other extreme, and between them, triangulating the relationship, there is the confessor. Now the confessor or director is already a very complex figure who immediately splits. There is the confessor who was initially the good confessor or director but who, at a certain point, becomes the bad one and switches sides. Or there are two groups of confessors or directors confronting each other. This is very clear in the Loudon case, for example, where there is a representative of the secular clergy (Grandier, the priest) and opposite him other confessors or directors who intervene as representatives of the regular clergy. This is the first duality. Then there is a new conflict, a new split within the regular clergy between those who are authorized exorcists and those who will play the role of both directors and healers. There is conflict and rivalry, a joust and competition between the Capuchins, on the one hand, and the Jesuits, on the other, and so on. In any case, the central figure of the confessor or director is multiplied and split depending on particular conflicts within the ecclesiastical institution itself.[6] As for the person possessed, the third term in the triangle, she, too, is split in the sense that she is not the support or docile servant of the devil as in witchcraft. Things are more complicated. Naturally, the person possessed is someone who is under the devil's power. However, as soon as this power has settled into, penetrated, and entered the body of the possessed it encounters resistance. The possessed is someone who resists the devil's power at the very moment she becomes his receptacle. As a result, a duality immediately appears within her: What is due to the devil and is no longer the possessed herself becomes simply diabolical machinery; and then, at another level, there is the possessed herself, a resistant receptacle, who advances her own forces against the devil or seeks the support of the director or confessor and the Church. The evil effects of the devil within her come up against the beneficial effects of the divine or priestly protection to which she appeals. We can say that the possessed endlessly fragments and divides the witch's body. Previously, taking the schema of witchcraft in its simple form, the witch's body was a somatic singularity for which the problem of division did not arise. The witch's body was simply a servant of the devil or was surrounded by a number of powers. The body of the possessed is a multiple body that is somehow volatized and pulverized into a multiplicity of powers that confront each other, a multiplicity of forces and sensations that beset it and pass through it. This indefinite multiplicity, rather than the great duel between good and evil, generally characterizes the phenomenon of possession.

One could even say that in the great witch trials perfected by the Inquisition, the witch's body was a single body that was simply in the service of, or penetrated by, the countless armies of Satan, Asmodeus, Beelzebub, Mephistopheles, and so on. Sprenger counted thousand and thousands of devils running around the world (I no longer recall if he counted 300,000 of them, it is not important).[7] Now the body of the possessed is the seat of an indefinite multiplicity of movements, jolts, sensations, tremors, pains, and pleasures. From this you can see how and why the pact, one of the fundamental elements of witchcraft, disappeared in possession. Witchcraft usually took the form of an exchange: "Give me your soul," Satan said to the witch, "and I will give you some of my power"; or Satan said, "I possess you carnally, and I will possess you carnally whenever I like. As a reward, or in exchange, you will be able to call upon my supernatural presence whenever you need it"; "I give you pleasure," Satan said, "but you will be able to do as much evil as you like. I will transport you to the Sabbath, but you will be able to summon me when you like, and I will be wherever you want." There is a principle of exchange indicated by the pact that sanctions a transgressive sexual act: the visit of the incubus, the kiss of the goat's anus.[8]

In possession, however, rather than a pact sealed by an action, there is an invasion; the devil's insidious and invincible penetration of the body. The possessed is not bound to the devil by a contract; rather, the link is of the order of a habitat, residence, and impregnation. The figure of the great black devil appearing at the foot of the witch's bed proudly brandishing his sex is transformed and replaced by something else. Consider, for example, the following scene which more or less inaugurated the Loudon possessions: "The prioress being in bed, her candle lit . . . she felt without seeing [hence disappearance of the image and of that great black form; M.F.] a hand that closed on hers and put in her hand three thorns. . . . After receiving these thorns, the prioress, and other nuns, felt strange changes in their bodies . . . of such a kind that they sometimes lost all judgment and were shaken by great convulsions that seemed to be due to extraordinary causes."[9] The devil's form has disappeared and the presence of his clearly delineated image has been effaced. There are sensations, the handing over of an object, and various strange changes in the body. There is no longer sexual possession but merely this insidious penetration of the body by strange sensations. Or consider this, also in the dossier of the Loudon affair that can be found in Michel de Certeau's book *La Possession de Loudon*: "The same day that sister Agnès, an Ursuline novice, took her vows, she was possessed by the devil." This is how the possession was carried out.

The charm was a bunch of musk roses found on a dormitory step. The Mother Prioress having picked it up, smelled it, as did others after her, who were all immediately possessed. They began to cry out and summon Grandier, by whom they were so enchanted that neither the other nuns nor anyone else could hold them back [I will return to this shortly; M.F.]. They wished to find him and in order to do so they climbed onto and ran over the convent roofs in their nightgowns and onto the trees, staying at the ends of the branches. There, after dreadful screams, they endured hail, frost and rain, remaining for four or five days without eating.[10]

This, then, is a completely different system of possession, a completely different diabolical initiation. There is neither the sexual act nor the great sulfurous vision, but a slow penetration of the body. The system of exchange also disappears. In its place there is an infinite game of substitution: The devil's body is substituted for the nun's body. As soon as the nun, seeking help from outside, opens her mouth to receive the host, the devil, or one of them, Beelzebub, suddenly takes her place. Beelzebub spits out the host from the nun's open mouth. In the same way, the devil's discourse even takes the place of the words of prayer and oration. When the nun wishes to recite the Lord's Prayer, the devil answers in her place in his own words: "I curse him."[11] However, these substitutions do not take place without battles, conflicts, interactions, and resistance. When the nun is about to receive the host that she spits out, she puts her hand to her throat in an attempt to drive out the devil who is about to spit out the host that she is swallowing. Or again, when the exorcist wishes to make the devil confess his name, that is to say, to identify him, the demon replies: "I have forgotten my name. . . . I lost it in the wash."[12] It is this game of substitutions, disappearances, and struggles that characterize the scene, the plastic form of possession, which is consequently very different from all the games of illusion peculiar to witchcraft. You can see that at the heart of all this the game of consent, the consent of the subject possessed, is much more complex than the game of consent in witchcraft.

In witchcraft, the witch's will is really a juridical type of will. The witch agrees to an offered exchange: You offer me pleasure and power and I give you my body and soul. The witch goes along with the exchange and signs the pact: In the end she is a legal subject and it as such that she can be punished. From all the elements and details I have described, you can guess that in possession the will is charged with all the ambiguities of desire. The will does and does not desire. Thus, in the Loudon case, in the story of Mother Jean des Anges, the subtle play of the will on itself, both asserting itself and immediately giving way, can be seen very clearly.[13] The exorcists said to Mother Jean des Anges that the demon produced sensations in her such that she was unable to see that it was the demon at work.[14] Mother Jean des Anges, however, knew perfectly well that when the exorcists told her this they did not speak the truth even so and had not plumbed the depths of her heart. She knew that it was not as simple as this and that if the demon was able to produce in her these sensation behind which he hid, then this was because she had allowed him to do so. The sensations are introduced through a game of little pleasures, imperceptible sensations, tiny consents, and a sort of permanent slight connivance in which will and pleasure are entwined, somehow twist around each other and produce a deception: a deception for Mother Jean des Anges, who only saw the pleasure and not the evil, and deception for the exorcists as well, since they thought it was the devil. As she said in her confession: "The devil often deceived me with a little pleasure I took in the excitations and other extraordinary things he produced in my body."[15] Or again: "To my great confusion it happened that in the first days after Father Lactance was assigned to me as director and exorcist, I disapproved of many little things in his way of acting, however good they were, but it was because I was wicked."[16] Thus, when Father Lactance offers to give the nuns communion through the grille, Mother Jean des Anges is annoyed and begins to murmur in her heart: "I thought to myself that it would be [much] better to follow the method of other priests. As I negligently lingered on this thought it came to my mind that in order to humiliate the Father the demon had done something irreverent to the very holy Sacrament. I was so wretched that I could not resist this thought with sufficient determination. When I presented myself at the communion [grille; M.F.], the devil seized hold of my head and, after I had received and half moistened the sacred host, the devil spat it in the priest's face. I am aware that I did not do this freely, but to my great shame I am sure that I allowed the devil to do it, and that he would not have had that power if I was not in some way linked with him."[17] We find again here the theme of the bond that was the very basis of witchcraft, the bond with the devil. But we can see that in this game of pleasure, consent, nonrefusal, and petty connivance we are very far from the great juridical bloc of heartfelt consent given once and for all by the witch when she signs the pact with the devil.

There are two kinds of consent, but there are also two kinds of body. As you know, two features essentially characterize the bewitched body. First, the witch's body is a body completely surrounded by or in some way the beneficiary of a number of magical powers. Some considered these to be real and others illusory, but this is not important. The witch's body can transport itself or be transported; it is capable of appearing and disappearing; it becomes invisible and in some cases it is also invincible. In short, it is affected by a sort of transmateriality. Second, the bewitched body is also characterized by the fact that it always carries signs, spots, or zones of insensitivity that are the demon's signatures. This is the means by which the demon can recognize his own and, conversely, it is also the means by which inquisitors, men of the Church, and judges can recognize someone as a witch. In short, the witch's body benefits from the magical powers that enable it to take advantage of diabolical powers and so enable it to escape those who pursue it. However, at the same time the witch's body is marked, and this mark links the witch both to the demon and to the priest or judge who hunts down the demon. She is tied down by her marks at the same time as she is raised up by her spells.

The body of someone possessed is completely different. It is a theatrical stage rather than a body enveloped by magical powers. Different powers and their confrontations manifest themselves within the body. It is not a body transported but a body penetrated in depth. It is the body of investments and counterinvestments. Ultimately, it is a fortress body that is surrounded and besieged. It is a citadel body, the stake in a battle between the demon and the possessed body that resists, between the part of the person possessed that resists and the part of herself that gives way and betrays her. It is a battle between demons and exorcists and directors and the possessed person herself who sometimes helps them and sometimes betrays them, who is sometimes led by the game of pleasure to take the demon's side and at others, adopting the standpoint of resistance, to take the side of the directors and inquisitors. All this constitutes the somatic theater of possession. For example: "What was truly impressive was that having ordered [the devil; M.F.] in Latin to let [Jeanne des Anges; M.F.] join her hands, we observed a forced obedience and her hands came together, shaking all the time. When the holy sacrament was in her mouth, the devil wanted to reject it, exhaling and roaring like a lion. Ordered not to commit any more irreverence, we saw [the devil; M.F.] stop, the holy sacrament descending to her stomach. We saw him heaving so as to vomit, but forbidden to do so he yielded."[18] The witch's body could be transported and made invisible, but we now see a new detailed body taking the place of or arising from that body, a constantly agitated and shaking body in which one can follow the different episodes of the battle: a body that swallows and spits out and that absorbs and rejects in this kind of physiological-theological theater that constitutes the body of the possessed. I think it is this that distinguishes it quite clearly from the witch's body. Furthermore, while this struggle no doubt has the devil's signature, this is not any kind of identifying mark like that found on witches. The mark or signature of possession is not the spot, for example, that was found on the witch's body. It is something very different, an element that will have a fundamental importance in Western medical and religious history: the convulsion.

What is the convulsion? The convulsion is the plastic and visible form of the struggle taking place in the body of the possessed. The demon's all-powerfulness, his physical achievement, is found in that aspect of the phenomena of convulsion that constitutes rigidity, the circle's arc, insensitivity to blows. There are also always shakes and tremors in the phenomenon of convulsion, which are purely mechanical effects of the struggle, of the shock of forces confronting each other, as it were. There is also a series of involuntary but meaningful actions: struggling, spitting, adopting negative attitudes, and uttering obscene, irreligious, blasphemous words, but always automatically. All of these things constitute the successive episodes of the battle, the attacks, and counterattacks, the victory of one side or the other. Finally, choking, breathlessness, and fainting indicate the point when the body is destroyed in the struggle by the very excess of the opposing forces. The extreme valorization of the convulsive element appeared here for the first time so clearly. Convulsion is this immense spidery notion that extends its web over both religion and mysticism on one side and medicine and psychiatry on the other. This convulsion will be the stake in an important battle between medicine and Catholicism for 250 years.

However, before returning to this battle, I would like to show you that when the flesh brought to light by the spiritual practices of the sixteenth and seventeenth centuries is pushed to a certain point, it becomes the convulsive flesh. In the field of the new practice of spiritual direction, the convulsive flesh appears as the endpoint, the abutment of the new investment of the body established by the government of souls after the Council of Trent. The convulsive flesh is the body penetrated by the right of examination and subject to the obligation of exhaustive confession and the body that bristles against this right and against this obligation. It is the body that opposes silence or the scream to the rule of complete discourse, the body that counters the rule of obedient direction with intense shocks of involuntary revolt or little betrayals of secret connivance. The convulsive flesh is at once the ultimate effect and the point of reversal of the mechanisms of corporeal investment that the new wave of Christianization organized in the sixteenth century. The convulsive flesh is the resistance effect of Christianization at the level of individual bodies.

Broadly speaking, we can say that just as witchcraft was no doubt simultaneously the effect, point of reversal, and center of resistance to this wave of Christianization and its instruments—the Inquisition and its courts—so possession was similarly the effect and point of reversal of this other technique of Christianization, namely the confessional and spiritual direction. What witchcraft was to the court of Inquisition, possession was to the confessional. The problem of the possessed and their convulsions, therefore, should not be seen as forming part of the history of illness. A history of Western physical and mental illness does not enable us to understand the appearance of the possessed and their convulsions. Nor does a history of superstitions or mentalities enable us to understand this phenomenon: Convulsions and possessions do not appear because of belief in the devil. In order to understand how and why the new phenomena of possession appeared at this time, taking over from the earlier phenomena of witchcraft, I think we need a history of the relations between the body and the mechanisms of power that invest it. The appearance, development, and supporting mechanisms of possession form part of the political history of the body.

You will say to me that by making such a clear distinction between witchcraft and possession, as I have just tried to do, I am in danger of failing to grasp a number of fairly obvious phenomena, such as the interpenetration of witchcraft and possession at the end of the sixteenth and the beginning of the seventeenth centuries. At any rate, when witchcraft emerged at the end of the fifteenth century it always included in its margins a number of elements that are due to possession. Conversely, in the principal cases of possession, especially those at the beginning of the seventeenth century, the action or presence of the witch is quite explicit and marked. The Loudon affair, which dates from 1632, is an example of this interpenetration. There are many elements of witchcraft: the court of Inquisition, torture, and ultimately the sanction of the stake for the person identified as the witch in the affair, that is to say, Urbain Grandier. There is then the whole panorama of witchcraft. And then, also, alongside this and mixed up in it, there is the panorama of possession. There is no longer the court of Inquisition with its torture and the stake, but the chapel, the convent parlor, the confessional, the convent grille, and so forth. The double apparatus of possession and witchcraft is very clear in this case from 1632.

However, I think we can say that possession was no more than an aspect of witchcraft until the sixteenth century, but that starting in the seventeenth century (in all likelihood from the years 1630-1640) the tendency, in France at least, was for the relationship to be reversed and for witchcraft to become no more than a dimension of possession, and a dimension that is not always present. If the Loudon case was so scandalous, if it stood out and still marks the memory of this history, it is because it represented the most systematic and the most desperate attempt, doomed to failure, to retranscribe the phenomenon of possession, absolutely typical of the Church's new mechanisms of power, in the old liturgy of the witch-hunt. It seems to me that the Loudon affair is typically one of possession, at least to start with. In fact, all the characters who figure in the 1632 affair are characters internal to the Church: nuns, priests, monks, Carmelites, Jesuits, and so on. The external characters, judges or representatives of the central power, only enter secondarily. At the start it was an internal Church affair. There are none of those marginal, barely Christianized characters that we find in cases of witchcraft. The landscape of the affair is entirely defined not only within the Church but also within a precise and determinate convent. It is a landscape of dormitories, oratories, and convents. As for the elements that are brought into play, they are, as I have just said, sensations, the perfume of a rose, almost like that in Condillac, that invades the nostrils of the nuns.[19] They are convulsions and contractions. In short, it is a case of carnal disorder.

What I think happened in this affair, and we could no doubt find the same mechanism in the Aix and other cases, is that when the Church was confronted with these phenomena that both followed the trajectory of its new techniques of power and were, at the same time, the moment or point at which these techniques came up against their limits and point of reversal, it sought to control them. It sought to liquidate these conflicts arising from the very technique it used to exercise power. Then, since it lacked the means to control these effects of the new mechanism of power it had installed, it reinscribed the phenomenon that it was forced to observe in the old procedures of control typical of the witch-hunts, and it could only dominate it by retranscribing it in terms of witchcraft. That is why, when it was faced with these phenomena of possession spreading in the Ursuline convent of Loudon, it had to find the witch at any cost. In the event the only person who could play the role of witch was precisely someone who belonged to the Church, since everyone involved at the start was ecclesiastical. The result was that the Church was obliged to cut itself off from one of its members and designate a priest as the witch. Urbain Grandier, the priest of Loudon, was required to play the role of the witch; he was inevitably assigned this role in what was a typical case of possession. Consequently, procedures that had already begun to disappear, the procedures of witch trials and Inquisition trials, were reactivated or continued. They were reinstated and reutilized in order to succeed in controlling and mastering phenomena that were in fact due to something quite different. The Church tried to refer all the carnal disorders of possession in the Loudon affair to the traditional, legally known form of the diabolical pact of witchcraft. In this way Grandier was at the same time consecrated witch and sacrificed as such.

This sort of operation was, of course, very costly. It was costly first of all because of the self-mutilation to which the Church was constrained, and to which it would certainly be constrained again in every other case of this kind if it put the old practices of the witch-hunt to work. It was also costly because of the reactivation of forms of intervention that were completely archaic with regard to the new forms of ecclesiastical power. How could a court like that of the Inquisition function coherently in the age of spiritual direction? Finally, it was a very costly operation because it had to call upon a type of jurisdiction that the civil power of the monarchy was finding increasingly difficult to tolerate. As a result, in Loudon we see the Church come up against the climactic effects of its new mechanisms of government and its new individualizing technology of power, and we see it failing in its regressive and archaic recourse to Inquisitorial methods of control. In the Loudon affair I think we see for the first time the clear formulation of what becomes one of the major problems of the Catholic Church from the middle of the seventeenth century. We can state this problem in the following way: How can one maintain and develop the technologies for the government of souls and bodies that were established by the Council of Trent? How can one pursue this great discursive subdivision and examination of the flesh while avoiding the consequences that are its aftereffects: those resistance effects whose most visible climactic and theatrical forms are the convulsions of the possessed? In other words, how can we govern souls according to the Tridentine formula without, at a certain point, coming up against the convulsion of bodies? Starting in the seventeenth century, the great problem for the Church, and its great debate with itself with regard to sexuality, the body, and the flesh, was, I believe, how to govern the flesh without being caught in the trap of convulsions. Its problem was to penetrate the body, to pass it through the filter of exhaustive discourse and permanent examination; it was to submit it, consequently, in detail, to an exclusive power and thereby always maintain the precise direction of the flesh, always master it at the level of direction, while avoiding at any cost its withdrawal, evasion, flight, and counterpower of possession. How can one have direction of the flesh without the body objecting to this direction in the phenomena of resistance that constitute possession?

To resolve this problem the Church established a number of mechanisms that I will call the great anticonvulsives. I will put them in three groups.

First, an internal moderator. An additional rule of discretion is imposed within the practices of the confession and spiritual direction. One still has to say everything in spiritual direction and one still has to confess everything in the practice of penance, but one cannot do this in whatever way one chooses. A rule of style or rhetorical imperatives is imposed within the general rule of exhaustive confession. This is what I mean more precisely. In a confession manual from the first half of the seventeenth century drawn up by Tamburini, *Methodus expeditae confessionis* (so, if I am not mistaken, a method for rapid, fast confession), we find the details of what could or should be a good confession concerning the Sixth Commandment (the sin of lust) prior to the introduction of a stylistic moderator.[20] Here are some examples of what had to be said or questions that had to be put by the confessor in the course of this kind of penance. With regard to the sin of *mollities*, that is to say, voluntary pollution without the conjunction of bodies,[21] if the penitent had committed this sin he had to say exactly what he had been thinking about while he was engaged in this activity, since the kind of sin changed according to his thoughts. Thinking about incest was obviously a more serious sin than thinking about pure and simple fornication, even if it resulted in a voluntary pollution without the conjunction of bodies.[22] The confessor had to ask, or at least he had to learn from the penitent's mouth, whether he had used an instrument,[23] or if he had used another person's hand[24] or a part of their body. The penitent had to say what part of another person's body he had used.[25] He had to say if he had made use of this part of the body solely for functional purposes or if he had been driven by an *affectus particularis*, by a particular desire.[26] Again, a number of questions had to be put and a number of things said when the sin of sodomy was broached.[27] If it involved two men who reached orgasm, they had to be asked if it had been by combining and exciting their bodies, which would constitute perfect sodomy.[28] In the case of two women, however, if pollution was due to the simple need for the discharge of libido (*explenda libido* the text says), then the sin is not very serious but only one of *mollities*.[29] However, if pollution is due to affection for the same sex (which is the undue sex since it is a woman), then it is a case of imperfect sodomy.[30] As for sodomy between a man and a woman, if it is due to a desire for the female sex in general, then it is only *copulatio fornicaria*.[31] But if sodomy between a man and a woman is due to a particular taste for the rear parts, then this is imperfect sodomy because the desired part is not natural; the category is still that of sodomy, but since it is not with the undue sex—since it involves a woman with a man—then the sodomy is not perfect but only imperfect.[32]

This is the kind of information that, by statute, had to be gathered in a confession (which was nonetheless an *expedita confessio*, a rapid confession). In order to block the inductive effects of the rule of exhaustive discourse, a number of attenuating principles were formulated. Some of these attenuations concerned the material staging of the confession: the need for darkness, the appearance of the grille in the little confessional box, and the rule that the confessor must not look the penitent in the eye if the penitent is a woman or a young man (this rule was formulated by Angiolo de Chivasso).[33] Other rules concerned the discourse of confession, such as one, for example, that consists in advice given to the confessor: "Only insist on a confession of sins in their details during the first confession, and then in subsequent confessions refer to the sins named in the first confession (but without describing them and without going into details). Have you done what you confessed to having done in the course of your first confession, or have you done what you did not confess to having done in the course of the first confession?"[34] In this way one avoids having to use directly the discourse of confession in the strict sense. However, more important and serious is the rhetoric perfected by the Jesuits: the method of insinuation.

Insinuation is part of the famous laxity with which the Jesuits are accused and which we should not forget always has two aspects. There is no doubt laxity at the level of penance, that is to say, light satisfaction for sins, at least when one can find circumstances for them that allow their seriousness to be lessened. However, there is also laxity at the level of enunciation. The laxity of the Jesuits allows the penitent not to say everything, or at least it allows him not to be specific. The permissive principle is that it is better for the confessor to absolve a sin he believes to be venial but is in fact mortal than it is for him to induce new temptations in the penitent's mind, body, and flesh through the confession. This was how the Council of Rome in 1725[35] explicitly advised confessors to be prudent toward their penitents, especially young people and above all children. Thus we arrive at the paradoxical situation in which there are two rules at work within the structure of confession: One is the rule of exhaustive and exclusive discourse, and the other is the new rule of reserved enunciation. One must say everything and as little as possible. Or, saying as little as possible is the tactical principle in a general strategy for everything to be said.

Thus, at the end of eighteenth century and the beginning of the nineteenth century, Alfonso de Liguori gives a series of rules that characterize the modern confession and the forms of confession in modern and contemporary penance.[36] Alfonso de Liguori, while maintaining the principle of exhaustive confession, says in his instruction on the sixth precept (translated into French as *Le Conservateur des jeunes gens*): "In confession, not only must one uncover every consummated act, but also all sensual touching, all impure looks, and all obscene intentions, especially if they have given pleasure.... One will also take into account all indecent thoughts."[37] However, in another text, *La Conduite du confesseur*, he says that the greatest reserve should be observed when one broaches the Sixth Commandment, especially when one is confessing children. One should start "with some rather vague and roundabout questions"; one should simply ask them "if they have spoken any bad words, if they have played with other little boys or girls and if it was in secret." Then one asks them "if they have done anything unseemly or naughty. Children often answer in the negative. It is then useful to ask them questions that lead them into replying, for example: 'How many times have you done that? Is it ten or fifteen times?'" One must ask them "who they sleep with and if they have had fun with their hands in bed." One will ask little girls if they have had a friendship for someone, if there were bad thoughts and words or bad games. And one proceeds further depending on their answer. But one always keeps from "asking them," the little girls as well as "the little boys, *an adfuerit seminis effusio* [I do not need to translate; M.F.]. With them it is much better for the confession to lack material completeness than to be the cause of their learning the evil they do not know or to inspire in them the desire to know it." One will ask them simply "if they have taken presents, run errands for men and women. One will ask little girls if they have received presents from suspicious people," and from priests and members of religious orders in particular![38] You can see that a completely different mechanism of confession is established on a rule that remains the same: the need to establish a series of stylistic and rhetorical procedures that enable things to be said without ever naming them. The prudish codification of sexuality, of which there was still no trace in Tamburini's text in the middle of the seventeenth century, is at this point introduced into a practice of confession. This, then, is the first anticonvulsive employed by the Church: the stylistic modulation of the confession and spiritual direction.

The second method or procedure employed by the Church is external transfer: expulsion of the convulsive. I think that what the Church wanted (and relatively soon, from the second half of the seventeenth century), was to establish a line of demarcation between the uncertain, sinful flesh on the one hand, which spiritual direction must control and scour with its infinite and meticulous discourse, and the famous convulsion on the other, which spiritual direction came up against as both its last effect and most visible resistance and that the Church will try to get rid of and relinquish in order to avoid the whole mechanism of direction being ensnared by it. The convulsive, that is to say, the paroxysms of possession, must be shifted to a new level of discourse (which is no longer that of penance and spiritual direction) and to a different mechanism of control at the same time. It is at this point that the major and famous transfer of power to medicine begins.

Schematically, we can say that there was an appeal to medicine and doctors during the major episodes of witch trials, but doctors were called in precisely against ecclesiastical power and the abuses of the Inquisition.[39] It was generally the civil power, or even the organization of the magistracy, that tried to introduce medical questions into matters concerning witchcraft, but as an external moderation of Church power.[40] Now ecclesiastical power itself appeals to medicine in order to rid itself of this problem, of this question and trap that possession raises against the spiritual direction established in the sixteenth century.[41] It is a fearful, contradictory, and reticent appeal to be sure, since by bringing doctors into cases of possession, medicine will be brought into theology, doctors into the convents and, more generally, the jurisdiction of medical knowledge into the order of the flesh that the new ecclesiastical pastoral had constituted as its domain. The flesh, through which the Church secured its control over bodies, now risks being taken over by another mode of analysis and management of the body, by a different, secular, and medical power. Hence the mistrust with regard to medicine and the reticence that the Church itself sets against its own need to resort to medicine. For this recourse to medicine cannot be set aside. In terms of spiritual direction, it became necessary that convulsion cease being the means by which those being directed rose up bodily and carnally against their directors, to the point of trapping them and, as it were, counterpossessing them. The mechanism by which spiritual direction is overturned and in which it is trapped must be broken. For that reason, a radical break is needed that turns convulsion into an autonomous and foreign phenomenon completely different in kind from what may take place within the mechanism of spiritual direction. And, of course, the need becomes more urgent the more possession is connected directly with religious or political resistance. Medical codification immediately becomes absolutely imperative when convulsions are no longer confined to Ursuline convents but are also found, for example, in the convulsive mystics of Saint-Médard (that is, in a relatively low social strata of the population), or even in the Protestants of Les Cévennes. Between Loudon (1632) and the convulsive mystics of Saint-Médard or those of Les Cévennes (at the beginning of the eighteenth century) a history gets under way: the history of convulsion as the instrument and stake in a battle of religion with itself and between religion and medicine.[42] This history gives rise to two series of phenomena.

First, starting in the eighteenth century, convulsion becomes a privileged object for medicine. From the eighteenth century the convulsion, or all the phenomena related to the convulsion, constitutes that extensive domain that is so important and fruitful for doctors: nervous illnesses, the vapors, crises. What the Christian pastoral organized as the flesh becomes a medical object in the eighteenth century. Medicine establishes itself in the order of sexuality for the first time by annexing the flesh offered to it by the Church itself through the phenomenon of convulsion. In other words, medicine did not discover the domain of illnesses with a sexual connotation, origin, or support by extending the traditional considerations of Greek and medieval medicine on the uterus or the humors. Medicine began to become an institution claiming scientific status for its hygienic control of sexuality only inasmuch as it inherited the domain of the flesh demarcated and organized by ecclesiastical power, only to the extent that it inherited or partly inherited this domain at the request of the Church itself. The importance of what was called the "nervous system" in eighteenth-century pathology is due precisely to the fact that it served as the first major anatomical and medical codification of the domain of the flesh that the Christian art of penance had until then explored merely with the help of notions such as "movements," "tickling," "titillation," et cetera. The analysis of the nervous system and the fantastic mechanics attributed to it during the eighteenth century were a way of medically recodifying the domain of objects that had been isolated and constituted by the practice of penance since the sixteenth century. Concupiscence was the sinful soul of the flesh. Since the eighteenth century, the nervous type is the rational and scientific body of this same flesh. The nervous system takes the place of concupiscence by right. It is the material and anatomical version of the old concupiscence.

Thus we can see why the study of the convulsion as the climactic form of action of the nervous system is the first major form of neuropathology. I do not think we can underestimate the historical importance of convulsion in the history of mental illness, because, if you recall what I said in earlier sessions, psychiatry is finally "disalienized" around 1850. It ceased being the analysis of error, delirium, and illusion in order to become the analysis of all the disturbances of instinct. Psychiatry takes instinct and its disorders, all the confusions of the voluntary and the involuntary, as its own domain. This convulsion, that is to say, this paroxysmal agitation of the nervous system that was eighteenth-century medicine's way of recodifying the old convulsion and the effect of the concupiscence of the Christian heritage, now appears as the involuntary release of automatisms and so quite naturally constitutes the neurological model of mental illness. Psychiatry, as I have described it, goes from the analysis of mental illness as delirium to the analysis of abnormality as instinctual disorder. Over the same period, or even before, from the eighteenth century, another connection was forged that had a quite different origin since it was a question of this famous Christian flesh. The flesh of concupiscence, recodified within the nervous system by way of the convulsion, provides a model for the conceptualization and analysis of instinctual disorder. This model is convulsion as the automatic and violent release of basic and instinctual mechanisms of the human organism: Convulsion becomes the prototype of madness. You can see how, in the middle of the nineteenth century, psychiatry was able to construct hystero-epilepsy, which for us is a heterogeneous and heteroclite monument. Hystero-epilepsy, which reigned from around 1850 until its demolition by Charcot around the years 1875-1880, was the way of analyzing, as nervous convulsion, the disturbance of instinct that the analysis of mental illness and especially of monstrosities had opened up.[43] Thus we see the long history of Christian confession and of the monstrous crime come together and converge in the analysis and notion of hystero-epilepsy that is so typical of the psychiatry of this time.

This convergence initiates an always deeper and more marked penetration of convulsion into medical discourse and practice. Expelled from the field of spiritual direction, convulsion serves the medicine that inherits it as an analytical model for the phenomena of madness. However, while convulsion was increasingly penetrating medicine, the Catholic church, for its part, increasingly sought to rid itself of this embarrassment, to relieve the flesh it controlled of this danger, and all the more so because medicine was at the same time using convulsion in its struggle against the Church. When doctors analyzed convulsion they were at the same time trying to show the extent to which the phenomena of witchcraft, or even those of possession, were in actual fact only pathological phenomena. The more medicine took hold of convulsions, the more it used them as an argument against a range of beliefs or ecclesiastical rituals, the more quickly and radically the Church sought to get rid of these famous convulsions. The result is that convulsion is increasingly discredited by Christian piety in the new wave of nineteenth-century Christianization. Convulsion is increasingly discredited, and something else—the vision—takes its place. The Church discredits convulsion or leaves medicine to discredit it. It no longer wants to hear anything that reminds it of that insidious invasion of the director's body in the nun's flesh. However, it promotes the vision, which is no longer the vision of the devil or that insidious sensation experienced by nuns in the seventeenth century. The vision is the vision of the Virgin: It is a vision at a distance, both near and far, ready to hand in one sense and yet inaccessible. In any case, the visions of the nineteenth century, and those of La Salette and Lourdes are typical, absolutely exclude physical struggle. One of the fundamental rules in the system of visions established in the nineteenth century is that there should be no contact, no physical struggle, and no mixing of the Virgin's spiritual body with the material body of the person who is miraculously cured. It is a vision then, of the Virgin herself at a distance and without physical contact, and the subject who has the vision is not the sexually hungry cloistered nun who is such a trap for spiritual direction. The subject is now the child, the innocent child who has scarcely begun the dangerous practice of spiritual direction. In the angelic gaze of the child, before the child's gaze, in front of the child's face, appears the weeping face at La Salette, or the whispering of the one who cures at Lourdes. Lourdes corresponds to Loudon or is in any case another striking episode in this long history of the flesh.

Roughly speaking, around the years 1870-1890 there is a kind of face off between Lourdes and La Salette on one side, and Salpêtrière on the other, and behind them all is the focal and historical point of Loudon making up the triangle. On one side there is Lourdes saying: "Actually, the devilry at Loudon was perhaps hysteria, like that found at Salpêtrière. We will leave the Loudon devilry to Salpêtrière. But this does not affect us at all, since we are only concerned with visions and little children." Salpêtrière replies: "We, too, can do what Loudon and Lourdes have done. We, too, can produce visions as well as convulsions." Lourdes retorts: "Cure as much as you like. There are a number of cures that you will not be able to perform and that we do." Thus, still within the great dynasty of the history of convulsions, we see this entanglement and battle between ecclesiastical power and medical power. From Loudon to Lourdes, La Salette or Lisieux,[44] a complete shift took place, a complete redistribution of medical and religious investments of the body, a kind of relocation of the flesh, a reciprocal displacement of convulsions and visions. These phenomena are, I think, very important for the emergence of sexuality within the field of medicine, and they cannot be understood in terms of science or ideology, or in terms of the history of mentalities, or in terms of a sociological history of illness, but simply through a historical study of technologies of power.

Finally, there remains a third anticonvulsive. The first was the transition from the rule of exhaustive discourse to a reserved stylization of discourse. The second was the handing over of convulsion itself to medical power. The third anticonvulsive, about which I will talk next week, is the support sought by ecclesiastical power from disciplinary and educational systems. In order to control, block, and definitively remove all the phenomena of possession that trapped the new mechanism of ecclesiastical power, there was an attempt to get spiritual direction and confession, all the new forms of religious experience, to function within the disciplinary mechanisms that were being established in barracks, schools, hospitals, and so forth at the same time. I will take just one example of this insertion of the spiritual techniques of Tridentine Catholicism into the new disciplinary apparatus that is taking shape and being constructed in the seventeenth century. (I will start again from this point next week.) The example is that of M. Olier: When he founded the Saint-Sulpice seminary, he decided to construct a suitable building for the task he had undertaken. Olier envisaged the Saint-Sulpice seminary putting to work in all their details precisely those techniques of spiritual control, self-examination, and confession that are typical of Tridentine piety. He needed a building suited to its purpose. M. Olier did not know how to construct this seminary. He went therefore to Notre-Dame and asked the Virgin to tell him how to build his seminary. The Virgin actually appeared to him and she had in her hand a plan, which is the plan of the Saint-Sulpice seminary. However, what struck Olier straightaway was that there were separated rooms rather than dormitories. This, not the placing of the chapel or the size of the oratory, is the principal feature of the Virgin's proffered plan of construction. Because the Virgin was not deceived. She knew perfectly well that the snares set at the conclusion, end, or limit of these techniques of spiritual direction were fomented precisely at night and in bed. That is to say, it is the bed, the night, and bodies considered in their detail and in the course of their potential sexual activities, which is the cause of all those traps into which spiritual directors insufficiently apprized of the real nature of the flesh had fallen some years previously. It was necessary to determine exactly the process of constitution, the origin, and the functional mechanisms of this rich, complex flesh run through with sensations and shaken by convulsions, the flesh with which spiritual directors had to deal. By dividing the body up precisely and by placing bodies in a meticulous analytical space, the disciplinary apparatuses (colleges, seminaries, et cetara) can replace the complex and somewhat unreal theology of the flesh with the precise observation of sexuality in its periodic and real unfolding. It is, then, a question of the body, the night, the toilet, the nightclothes, and the bed: The mechanisms at the origin of all those disorders of the flesh that the Tridentine pastoral had brought to light, that it had wished to control, and by which it finally became ensnared, must be found between the sheets.[45]

Thus, at the heart, the core, the very center of all these carnal disorders linked to the new spiritual direction, we find the body: the supervised body of the adolescent, the body of the masturbator. I will talk about this next week.

1. To know "everything that was said in the period between" J.-J. Surin (1600-1665) and Madame Guyon (1648-1717), cf. H. Bremond, *Histoire littéraire du sentiment religieux en France depuis la fin des guerres de Religion* (Paris, 1915-1933), vols. 1-11.

2. The documentation concerning the episodes of possession indicated by Foucault is vast. For the first case we confine ourselves to indicating *La Possession de Loudon* presented by M. de Certeau, (1970; reprint, Paris, 1980) and referring to M. Foucault, *Folie et Déraison. Histoire de la folie à la âge classique*, as "fundamental for understanding the epistemological problem at the center of the Loudon affair" (p. 330). For the second case, see P. F. Mathieu, *Histoire des miraculés et des convulsionnaires de Saint-Médard* (Paris, 1864).

3. On L. Gaufridi, cf. J. Fontaine, *Des marques des sorciers et de la réelle possession que le diable prend sur le corps des hommes. Sur le sujet du procès de l'abominable et détestable sorcier Louys Gaufridy, prêtre bénéficié en l'église paroissiale des Accoules de Marseille, qui naguère a été exécuté à Aix par l'arrêt de la cour de parlement de Provence* (Paris, 1611; reprint, Arras, 1865).

4. On U. Grandier, cf. *Arrêt de la condamnation de mort contre Urbain Grandier, prêtre, curé de l'église Saint-Pierre-du-Marché de Loudon, et l'un de chanoines de l'église Sainte-Croix dudit lieu, atteint et convaincu du crime de magie et autres cas mentionnés au procès* (Paris, 1634); M. de Certeau, *La Possession de Loudon*, pp. 81-96.

5. The Jansenist deacon François de Pâris is the first protagonist of the phenomenon of convulsion of Saint-Médard. Attributed to him is *La Science du vrai qui contient les principaux mystères de la foi* (Paris, 1733). Principal source: L.-B. Carré de Montgeron, *La Vérité des miracles opérés par l'intercession de M[édard] de Paris et autres appelants*, vol. 1-3 (Cologne, 1745-1747).

6. On this question, see J. Viard, "Le procès d'Urbain Grandier. Note critique sur la procédure et sur la culpabilité," in *Quelques procès criminels des XVIIe et XVIIIe siècles*, edited by J. Imbert (Paris, 1964), pp. 45-75.

7. H. Institoris and I. Sprengerus, *Malleus maleficarum*, (Strasbourg, 1488); French translation: *Le Marteau des sorcières* (Paris: s.l., 1973).

8. M. Foucault, "Les déviations religieuses et le savoir médical" (1968), in *Dits et écrits*, vol. 1, pp. 624-635.

9. More exactly: "The prioress being in bed, her candle lit...she felt a hand, without seeing anything, which, closing over hers, left there three thorns...The prioress and other nuns, after receiving the three thorns, felt strange changes in their bodies...of such a kind that they lost all judgment and were shaken by great convulsions that seemed to arise from extraordinary causes." M. de Certeau, *La Possession de Loudon*, p. 28. [Foucault's quotation in the lecture differs very slightly from the original.]

10. Ibid., p. 50.

11. Ibid., p. 157. In reality: "And when, returning to her, the creature was commanded to sing the verse *Memento salutis* and desired to deliver *Maria mater gratiae*, a horrible voice was suddenly heard coming from her mouth saying: 'I deny God. I curse her [the Virgin].'"

12. Ibid., p. 68.

13. Jeanne des Anges, *Autobiographie*, preface by J. M. Charcot (Paris, 1886). This text, which appeared in the issues of the *Progrès médical*, in the collection "Bibliothèque diabolique" edited by D. M. Bourneville, was republished in Grenoble in 1990 with a previously published essay by M. de Certeau as an appendix to *Correspondance de J.-J. Surin* (Paris: s.l., 1966), pp. 1721-1748.

14. Cf. the account of J.-J. Surin, *Triomphe de l'amour divin sur les puissances de l'enfer en la posesion de la mère prieure des Ursulines de Loudon et Science expérimentale des choses de l'autre vie* (Avignon, 1828; Grenoble, 1990).

15. M. de Certeau, *La Possession de Loudon*, p. 47. Cf. Jeanne des Anges, *Autobiographie*, p. 83.

16. M. de Certeau, *La Possession de Loudon*, p. 48. Cf. Jeanne des Anges, *Autobiographie*, p. 85.

17. M. de Certeau, *La Possession de Loudon*, p. 49. Cf. Jeanne des Anges, *Autobiographie*.

18. M. de Certeau, *La Possession de Loudon*, p. 70.

19. See the lecture of February 19, in this volume.

20. T. Tamburinus [Tamburini], *Methodus expeditae confessionis tum pro confessariis tum pro poen-titentibus* (Rome, 1645). We have used: *Methodi expeditae confessionis libr quattuor*, in *Opera omnia*, vol. 2: *Expedita moralis explicatio* (Venice, 1694), pp. 373–414.

21. Ibid., p. 392: "Mollities est pollutio volontaria sine coniunctione corporum seu ... est peccatum contra naturam per quod voluntaria pollutio procuratur, extra concubitum, causa explendae delectationis venereae" (Article 62).

22. Ibid.: "Si quis tamen, dum se polluit, consentiat vel cogitet morose in aliquam aliam speciem - verbi gratia: in adulterium, incestum—contrahit eandem malitiam, quam cog-itat, adeoque confitendam" (Article 62).

23. Ibid.: "Inanimatum instrumentum quo quis se polluat non facit mutationem speciei" (Article 63).

24. Ibid.: "Dixi inanimato [instrumento], nam si animato, ut si manibus alterius fiat, iam nunc subdo" (Article 63).

25. Ibid.: "Si quis se pollueret inter brachia, coxendices, os feminae vel viri, cum id regu-lariter procedat ex affectu personae seu concubitus cum illa, est sine dubio specialiter explicandum, quia non est mera pollutio, sed copula inchoata" (Article 64).

26. Ibid.: "Non tamen credo necessarium esse explicandas peculiares partes corporis, nisi sit affectus aliquis particularis—verbis gratia: ad partes praepostera, ob sodomiam.... Illa maior delectatio quae in una ex partibus quaeritur non trascendit speciem malitiae quae est in alia" (Article 64).

27. Ibid.: "Sodomia — et quidem perfecta—est concubitus ad sexum non debitum, ut vir cum viro, femina cum femina" (Article 67); "Concubitus viri cum femina in vase pre-posero est sodomia imperfecta" (Article 67); "Concubitus est copula carnalis carnalis consumata: naturalis si sit in vase debito; innaturalis si sit in loco seu vase non debito" (Article 67); "Sed hic est quaestio: quando mutua procuratio pollutionis inter mares vel inter feminas debeat dici mollities, quando sodomia" (Article 68); "Respondeo: quando ex affectu ad personam adest concubitus, si sit inter indebitum sexum, hoc est inter virum et virum, feminam et feminam, tunc est sodomia" (Article 68); "Quando vero est mutua pollutio absque concubitu, sed solum ad explendam libidinem est mollities" (Article 68).

28. Ibid.: "Hic si duo mares commisceant corpora et moveantur ad procurandam polluti-onem, vel quandocunque se tangant impudice, ex affectu indebiti sexus, ita ut effusio seminis vel sit intra vas praeposterum, vel vetiam extra, puto esse sodomiam" (Article 69).

29. Ibid.: "Sed si ipsae feminae commisceant corpora ex affectu solum se polluendi—id est explendae libidinis—est mollities" (Article 69).

30. Ibid.: "Si [ipsae feminae commisceant corpora] ex affectu ad indebitum sexum est so-domia" (Article 69).

31. Ibid.: "Sed quid dicendum si quis se polluat inter caeteras partes feminae (coxendices, brachia)? Respondeo: Si primo sit concubitus ex affectu ad personam ipsam, sexumque femineum, est copula fornicaria, sive adulterina, sive incestuosa, iuxta conditionem per-sonae, atque adeo est aperiendus. Si secondo sit concubitus ex affectu ad praeposteras partes est sodomia imperfecta ... ac similiter aperiendus. Si tertio denique sit sine con-cubitu, sed mere ad explendam libidinem, est mollities" (Article 74).

32. It is perfect in the first case ("effusio intra vas praeposterum") and imperfect in the second ("effusio extra vas praeposterum"): "Quia, quamvis tunc non sit copula, tamen per illum concubitum est affectus venereus ad indebitum sexum, qui proprie constituit sodomiam. Nam coeterum, sive semen effundatur intra, sive extra, semper aeque in loco non suo dispergitur. Locus enim praeposterus videtur materialiter se habere in sodomia. Sed formaliter eius essentia sumitur ex motivo, scilicet ex concubitu cum affectu ad indebitum sexum. Confirmo [the previous thesis] quia femina cum femina non alio modo commiscetur nisi per dictum concubitum cum effusione seminis et non intra vas prae-

posterum. Inter illas enim non potest esse copula proprie" (ibid., Article 69); "Sodomiam imperfectam, quam alii vocant innnaturalem concumbendi modum, est peccatum contra naturam, per quod vir cum femina concumbit extra vas naturale. Est specie distinta a sodomia perfecta. Adeoque speciatim in confessione exprimenda. Perfecta enim procedit ex affectu ad indebitum sexum. Haec vero procedit non ex affectu ad indebitum sexum, sed licet ad indebitum tamen ad partem innaturalem" (ibid., Article 74).

33. It was a rule common to several canonists in the Middle Ages. According to the *Interrogationes in confessione* of A. de Clavasio, *Summa angelica de casibus conscientiae*, with additional material by I. Ungarelli, (Venice, 1582), p. 678: "Quod stet [the penitent] facie versa lateri confessoris (si est mulier vel iuvenis) et non permittas quod aspiciat in faciem tuam, quia multi propter hoc corruerunt." Cf. H. C. Lea, *A History of Auricular Confession*, vol. 1, p. 379.

34. Th. Tamburinus, *Metodi expeditae confessionis*, p. 392, which develops his discourse on discretion based on the notion of *prudentia* in V. Filliucius, *Moralium quaestionum de christianis officiis et casibus conscientiae ad formam cursus qui praelegi solet in collegio romano societatis Iesu tomus primus*, (Lyon, 1626), pp. 221-222.

35. By the *Concilium romanum* or *Concilium lateranense* of 1725 it should be understood this refers to the provincial synod of Italian bishops convoked by Benoît XIII. Cf. L. von Pastor, *Geschichte der Päpste*, XV, (Freiburg: s.1., 1930), pp. 507-508.

36. Cf. J. Guerber, *La Ralliement du clergé français à la morale liguorienne* (Rome, 1973).

37. A. M. de Liguori, *Le Conservateur des jeunes gens*, p. 5.

38. A. M. de Liguori, *Praxis confessarii*, pp. 140-141, Article 89.

39. The schema used here by Foucault was formulated by the chief physician, I. Wierus, in the dedication to his lord, Guillaume, duke of Jülich-Kleve. I. Wierus, *De praestigiis daemonum et incantationibus ac veneficiis libri quinque* (Basel, 1563). The problem was considered by Foucault in "Médecins, juges et sorciers au XVIIᵉ siècle" (1969), *Dits et Écrits*, vol. 1, pp. 753-767.

40. R. Mandrou, *Magistrats et Sorcières en France au XVIIᵉ siècle. Une analyse de psychologie historique* (Paris: s.1., 1968).

41. Cf. P. Zacchia, *Quaestiones medico-legales*, vol. 2, (Avignon, 1660), pp. 45-48 (especially the article "De daemoniacis," the chapter "De dementia et rationis laesione et morbis omnibus qui rationem laedunt").

42. Principal source: [M. Misson], *Le Théâtre sacré des Cévennes ou Récit des diverses merveilles opérées dans cette partie de la province de Languedoc* (London, 1707) (reprinted with the title: *Les Prophètes protestants* [Paris, 1847]).

43. Cf. J. M. Charcot, *Leçons sur les maladies du systéme nerveux faites à la Salpêtrière* (Paris, 1874); English translation: *Lectures on the Diseases of the nervous system*, translated by G. Sigerson (London, 1877-89). In the section *Clinique nerveuse* of the *Archives de neurology*, 3 (1882), pp. 160-175, 281-309, C. Féré published the first *Notes pour servir à l'histoire de l'hystéro-épilepsie*, at the same time as Charcot's description was becoming known. These points are taken up by Foucault in the lecture *Le Pouvoir psychiatrique* of February 6, 1974. English translation: *Psychiatric power*.

44. See the sections "Apparitions et pèlerinages" from the articles "La Salette" and "Lourdes" in *La Grande Encyclopédie*, vol. 22, (Paris, no date), pp. 678-679; vol. 23, pp. 345-346. For Lisieux, the reference is to Carmel, where Thérèse Martin (alias Thérèse de l'Enfant Jésus) lived.

45. Foucault relies on the *Vie*, the *Mémoires* and *L'Esprit d'un directeur des âmes*, published in J.-J. Olier, *Œuvres complètes* (Paris, 1865), col. 9-59, 1082-1183, 1183-1239. See also his many *Lettres* (Paris, 1885).

nine

5 MARCH 1975

The problem of masturbation between the Christian discourse of
the flesh and sexual psychopathology. ~ Three forms of the
somatization of masturbation. ~ The pathological responsibility of
childhood. ~ Prepubescent masturbation and adult seduction; the
offense comes from outside. ~ A new organization of family space
and control: the elimination of intermediaries and the direct
application of the parent's body to the child's body. ~ Cultural
involution of the family. ~ The medicalization of the new family
and the child's confession to the doctor, heir to the Christian
techniques of the confession. ~ The medical persecution of
childhood by means of the restraint of masturbation. ~
The constitution of the cellular family that takes responsibility
for the body and life of the child. ~ Natural education
and State education.

LAST WEEK I TRIED to show how the body of pleasure and desire
seems to have appeared in correlation with the new wave of Christianization that developed in the sixteenth and seventeenth centuries.
In any case, it seems to me that it is this body that unfolds in a
garrulous and complaisant way in all the techniques of the government of souls, spiritual direction, and detailed confession that we
could call, in short, analytical penance. I also tried to show how this
same body of pleasure and desire invested these mechanisms of power
in return, and how, through the play of resistance, complicity, and

counterpower, it took up these mechanisms that sought to divide it and control it in order to surround them and turn them back against themselves. It did this in the exacerbated form of the convulsion. Finally, I tried to show how, in teaching establishments such as seminaries, boarding schools, schools, and colleges, et cetera, various attempts were made within the Christian technique of the government of individuals to control the effects of this convulsive flesh, of this body of movement, agitation, and pleasure.

I would now like to try to describe the evolution of this control of sexuality in establishments of Christian and especially Catholic school education in the eighteenth and nineteenth centuries. First of all, there is an increasingly clear tendency to reduce that kind of garrulous indiscretion and discursive insistence on the body of pleasure that marked seventeenth-century techniques for the direction of souls. There is an attempt to extinguish, as it were, all those verbal blazes that flare up in the analysis of desire and pleasure, and in the analysis of the body. Things are glossed over, veiled, expressed metaphorically, and a stylistics of discretion is invented in the confession and in spiritual direction. This was the work of Alfonso de Ligouri.[1] However, at the same time as this glossing over, veiling, and use of metaphorical language, at the same time as one tries to introduce a rule if not of silence then at least of *discretio maxima*, the architecture of educational establishments, the arrangements of sites and things, the way in which dormitories are laid out, surveillance is institutionalized, and even tables and benches are constructed and set out in a classroom, the way in which the entire space of visibility is carefully organized (the shape and layout of the latrines, the height of doors, the getting rid of dark corners), all this replaces—and so as to make it fall silent—the indiscreet discourse of the flesh in spiritual direction. In other words, the incandescent chattering that the post-Tridentine Christian technique had established in the sixteenth and seventeenth centuries must be rendered pointless by material apparatuses. The direction of souls will be able to become all the more allusive, and consequently all the more silent, as the spatial partitioning and control of bodies becomes tighter. In a word, while in colleges, seminaries, and schools one speaks of the body of pleasure as little as possible, everything in the arrangement of their sites and things designates its dangers. One says as little as possible about it; but everything speaks of it.

Suddenly, in the midst of this great silencing, in the midst of this transfer of the task of controlling souls, bodies, and desires to things and space, a loud fanfare blares out and a sudden and noisy chattering starts up that does not stop for more than a century (that is, until the end of the nineteenth century) and which continues, in a modified form no doubt, down to the present. Around 1720-1725 (I no longer remember exactly) a book appears in England called *Onania* that is attributed to Bekker;[2] in the middle of the eighteenth century Tissot's famous book appears;[3] around 1770-1780 Basedow,[4] Salzmann,[5] and others in Germany take up this discourse on masturbation. Bekker in England, Tissot in Geneva, and Basedow in Germany: You can see that we are in Protestant lands. It is not at all surprising that this discourse on masturbation should emerge in countries in which neither the Tridentine and Catholic form of spiritual direction nor the big educational establishments existed. The blocking of the problem by the existence of these educational establishments and by the techniques for spiritual direction explains why the problem is posed a bit later in Catholic countries and why it emerges in a burst. However, it is only a matter of an interval of a few years. Soon after the publication of Tissot's book in France, the problem, the discourse, the immense jabbering about masturbation starts up and does not stop for a whole century.[6]

So, in the middle of the eighteenth century, a rash of texts, of books, but also leaflets and tracts, suddenly appears, about which two comments must be made. First of all, this discourse about masturbation is completely different from the Christian discourse on the flesh (the genealogy of which I tried to outline last week). It is also very different from the future *psychopathia sexualis*, sexual psychopathology, the first text of which, by Heinrich Kaan, appears a century later in 1840 [*rectius:* 1844].[7] This very particular discourse on masturbation appears, therefore, between the Christian discourse on the flesh and the discourse of sexual psychopathology. It is not at all the Christian discourse on the flesh for a very simple reason that is immediately apparent: The words, the very terms of desire and pleasure, never appear. For a number of months I have gone through this literature with some curiosity, but also with some boredom, and in all I found just this one comment: "Why do adolescents masturbate?" and, around 1830-1840, a doctor suddenly had the idea: "But it must be because it gives them pleasure!"[8] This is the only time. So, in contrast with the earlier Christian literature, it is a discourse from which desire and pleasure are totally absent.

On the other hand, what is equally interesting is that nor is it the later sexual psychology or the sexual psychopathology of Kaan, Krafft-Ebing,[9] or Havelock Ellis,[10] inasmuch as sexuality is almost absent from it. It is referred to, of course. There is allusion to the general theory of sexuality as conceptualized at that time within a climate of the philosophy of nature. It is very interesting to note, however, that adult sexuality hardly ever comes into these texts on masturbation. Furthermore, the child's sexuality does not appear, either. The texts are about masturbation and masturbation itself, with practically no connection with either normal or abnormal sexual behavior. I have found only two very discreet allusions to the fact that excessive infantile masturbation could lead some subjects to forms of desire with a homosexual tendency.[11] However, even in these two cases, impotence much more than homosexuality was the sanction of excessive masturbation. The target of this literature, then, is masturbation itself in its specificity and somehow detached from, although not completely shorn of, its sexual context. Moreover, there are texts that say there is a real difference between the nature of masturbation and that of normal, relational sexuality, and that the mechanisms that lead one to masturbate and those that lead one to desire someone are not at all the same.[12] The first thing to be noted, then, is that if this discourse does not occupy an intermediate region between the discourse of the flesh and the discourse of sexual psychopathology, it does occupy a region that is completely different from these two discourses.

The second point I would like to emphasize is that the discourse on masturbation takes the form of a veritable campaign more than one of scientific analysis (although there is a strong reference to scientific discourse to which I will return): It takes the form of exhortations, advice, and injunctions. It is a literature of manuals, some of which are intended for parents. Around 1860, for example, we find handbooks for fathers on how to prevent children from masturbating.[13] But there are also tracts intended for children, for the adolescents themselves. The most famous is the *Livre sans titre*, which does not have a title but includes illustrations; all the disastrous consequences of masturbation are analyzed on one side and on the facing page there are depictions of the increasingly decomposed, ravaged, skeletal and diaphanous physiognomy of the exhausted young masturbator.[14] This campaign also includes institutions for the cure or care of masturbators, tracts for remedies and appeals from doctors that promise families they will cure their children of this vice. One institution, like Salzmann's in Germany for example, claimed that it was the only institution in the whole of Europe where children never masturbated.[15] You find formulae, prospectuses for remedies, and apparatuses and bindings to which we will return. I will end this very rapid survey of this campaigning, crusading antimasturbation literature with a little fact. It seems that under the Empire in France (anyway, in the last years of the eighteenth century and at the start of the nineteenth century) there was a wax museum to which parents were invited, accompanied by their children if these had shown any signs of masturbation. In this museum, all the health problems someone could suffer if they masturbated were exactly represented by means of wax statues. The museum, both the Grévin museum and the Dupuytren museum of masturbation, seems to have disappeared from Paris around 1820, but there is a trace of it in Marseille in 1825 (and many Paris doctors complained about not having this little theater available to them).[16] I do not know if it still exists in Marseille!

There is a problem then. How was it that such an extensive and indiscreet crusade broke out so suddenly in the middle of the eighteenth century? The phenomenon is well known and I have not invented it (at least, not entirely!). It has given rise to a number of commentaries, and Van Ussel's *Histoire de la répression sexuelle*, published fairly recently, gives considerable and, I think, just attention to the appearance of masturbation as a problem in the eighteenth century. Broadly speaking, Van Ussel's explanatory schema is hastily drawn from Marcuse.[17] It consists in saying that with the development of capitalist society, the body, which until then Van Ussel says was an "organ of pleasure," becomes and must become an "instrument of performance," of the performance necessary for the requirements of production. Hence there is a split, a caesura in the body, which is repressed as an organ of pleasure and is codified and trained instead as an instrument of production and performance. Such an analysis is not false and it cannot be false because it is so general. However, I do not think it gets us very far in explaining the fine details of this campaign and crusade. In analyses like this I am generally a little uncomfortable with the use of a series of concepts that are both psychological and negative: putting notions such as "suppression" or "repression" at the center of the analysis, for example, or using notions such as "organ of pleasure" and "instrument of performance." All this seems to me both psychological and negative. Although such notions may be valid in psychological or psychoanalytic analysis, they cannot, in my view, account for the mechanisms of a historical process. Moreover, such concepts are negative in the sense that they do not reveal the number of positive and constitutive effects produced in the history of society by campaigns like the crusade against masturbation.

Then again, there are two things that I find awkward in this history. If it is true that the eighteenth-century campaign against masturbation is part of the process of repression of the body of pleasure and the celebration of the performing or productive body, it nonetheless fails to account for two things. The first is why it is a question precisely of masturbation and not of sexual activity in general? If one really wanted to suppress or repress the body of pleasure, why is it that it was only masturbation that one got agitated about and stressed, rather than calling into question sexuality in its more general form? It is only after 1850 that sexuality in general is brought into question from a medical and disciplinary point of view. Second, the crusade essentially concerns children and adolescents from a bourgeois milieu. It is only within this bourgeois milieu, in educational establishments intended for these children or as instructions given to bourgeois families, that the struggle against masturbation becomes the order of the day. If it really was purely and simply a question of repressing the body of pleasure and celebrating the productive body, then one would normally expect to see a repression of sexuality in general and, more precisely, of the sexuality of the adult in work or, if you like, of the adult worker's sexuality. However, we are dealing with something different, not with the questioning of sexuality but of masturbation, and of the masturbation of bourgeois children and adolescents. I think that we must try to account for this phenomenon by a somewhat more detailed analysis than that given by Van Ussel.

I cannot guarantee that I will provide a solution to the problem. I can even say that in all likelihood I will only provide a very imperfect sketch of a solution. But we must try to make some progress. To account for this phenomenon we should examine the tactics rather than the themes of this campaign, or the crusade's themes as indicators of its tactics. Initially, and subject to a more precise examination, what is striking is, of course, what could be called "blaming the children." Actually, on closer inspection we can see that children are not really blamed in this campaign. On the contrary, it is surprising that there is very little moralizing in this discourse against masturbation. For example, there is very little about the different forms of sexual or other vices to which masturbation could give rise. Immorality is not derived from masturbation in any significant way. When one forbids children to masturbate one threatens them with an adult life crippled by illness, rather than an adult life lost in debauchery and vice. That is to say, there is not so much a moralization as a somatization and pathologization of masturbation. This somatization develops in three different forms.

First of all, there is what could be called the fiction of total illness. In these crusading texts you regularly come across the fabulous description of a sort of polymorphous, absolute illness without remission that accumulates every symptom of every possible illness or, at least, a considerable number of symptoms. All the signs of illness are superimposed in the masturbator's emaciated and ravaged body. Without resorting to the more dubious or marginal texts of the crusade, we can cite this example taken from a scientific text, an article by Serrurier in the *Dictionnaire des sciences médicales*, the bible of serious medicine at the beginning of the nineteenth century: "This young man suffered from the most complete apathy; to sight, he was entirely lifeless. He satisfied the call of nature wherever he happened to be. His body gave off a particularly nauseating odor. His skin was ashen, his tongue lolled, his eyes were sunken, all his teeth were loose, and his gums were covered with ulcers that foretold a scorbutic degeneration. Death for him could only be a happy release from his lengthy suffering."[18] We recognize here the portrait of the young masturbator with its fundamental characteristics: exhaustion, loss of substance, an inert, diaphanous, and dull body, a constant discharge, a disgusting oozing from within the body, the infection of those around him and the consequent impossibility of their approaching him, polymorphous symptoms. The entire body is covered and invaded with not a square inch left unaffected. Finally, there is the presence of death, since the skeleton can already be seen in the loose teeth and cavernous eyes. I was going to say that we are in the world of science fiction, but to distinguish the genres let us say scientific fabulation, concocted and transmitted on the periphery of medical discourse. I say on the periphery, but I have quoted the *Dictionnaire des sciences médicales* precisely so as not to quote one of the many little writings published in the name of doctors, or even sometimes by doctors, but lacking any scientific status.

[In the second form of somatization] what is more interesting is that this campaign, which takes the form of a scientific fabulation of total illness, is also found in the more regular literature, the literature more in keeping with the scientific norms of medical discourse of the time (or at least we find the effects and guarantors of this campaign, along with some of its elements). If we consider the various books written on different illnesses by the most accredited doctors of the time, rather than those devoted to masturbation, we no longer find masturbation at the origin of this kind of fabulous and total illness, but rather as the possible cause of every possible kind of illness. Masturbation constantly appears in the etiological table of different illnesses. According to Serres, in his *Anatomie comparée du cerveau*, it is the cause of meningitis.[19] According to Payen, in his *Essai sur l'encéphalite*,[20] it is the cause of encephalitis and phlegmasia of the meninges. In an article in *La Lancette française* in 1833,[21] Dupuytren says that it is the cause of myelitis and various symptoms of the spinal cord. It causes bone disease and degeneration of the bone tissues, according to Boyer in *Leçons sur les maladies des os* in 1803.[22] It causes diseases of the eyes and particularly amaurosis, according to Sanson in the article "Amaurose" in the *Dictionnaire des sciences médicales* [*rectius: Dictionnaire de médecine et de chirurgie pratiques*][23] and Scarpa in his *Traité de maladies des yeux*.[24] In an article in the *Revue médicale*, from 1833, Blaud explains that it is frequently, if not constantly, involved in the etiology of all heart diseases.[25] It is of course found at the origin of phthisis and tuberculosis, as Portal claims in his *Observations sur la nature et le traitement du rachitisme* as early as 1797.[26] This thesis of the link between phthisis and masturbation is found throughout the nineteenth century. The highly developed and quite ambiguous character of the young consumptive must be explained in part by the fact that the consumptive always harbors a hideous secret. Finally, of course, alienists regularly cite it as the cause of madness.[27] In this literature, masturbation sometimes appears as the cause of that kind of fabulous and total illness and sometimes it is carefully distributed in the etiology of different illnesses.[28]

Finally, there is the third form in which the principle of somatization can be found. The doctors of this time, for reasons I will try to explain shortly, appealed to and incited a kind of delirious hypochondria in young people, in their patients, through which they sought to get them to attach every symptom they might experience to this primary and greatest fault of masturbation. In medical treatises, and in the tracts and leaflets, we find a literary genre of the "patient's letter." Was the patient's letter written or invented by doctors? Tissot certainly composed the ones he published, but others are surely authentic. It is a complete literary genre. It comprises a little biography of the masturbator focused entirely on the history of the body and its illnesses, sensations and various disorders that are listed in detail from childhood, or from adolescence at least, until the time they are confessed.[29] I will give just one example of this, taken from a book by Rozier entitled *Les Habitudes secrètes chez les femmes* (written by a man, but it does not matter): "This habit placed me in the most dreadful situation. I had not the slightest hope of hanging on to life for a few years. Every day I was alarmed. I saw death advancing with great strides.... From the time [I began my bad habit; M.F.] I have suffered from an ever-increasing weakness. In the morning, when I got up ... I had dizzy spells. All the joints in my limbs made a noise like a shaken skeleton. Some months later ... when I left my bed in the mornings, I always spat and coughed up blood that was sometimes red and sometimes black. I felt the onset of nervous attacks that prevented me from moving my arms. I have had fainting fits and from time to time heart pains. The amount of blood I lose ... is always increasing [and what's more I've got a bit of a cold! M.F.]."[30]

So, first of all there is the scientific fabulation of total illness; then the etiological codification of masturbation in the best established nosographical categories; and finally, under the leadership and direction of the doctors themselves, the organization of a kind of thematic of hypochondria, of somatization of the effects of masturbation, in the discourse, life, sensations, and body of the patient.[31] I would not say that masturbation was transferred to or placed on the moral level of fault. Rather, I would say that we see in this campaign a somatization of masturbation that is, on the order of the doctors, directly linked to the body (or at any rate whose effects are directly linked to the body) even in the discourse and experience of the subjects. What could be called the inexhaustible causal power of infantile sexuality, or at any rate of masturbation, emerges through this undertaking, this scientific fabulation firmly anchored in medical discourse and practice. Broadly speaking, it seems to me that, through the action and injunctions of doctors, masturbation is established as a sort of diffuse, general, and polymorphous etiology that enables the whole of the pathological field, including death, to be connected to it, that is to say, to be connected to a certain sexual prohibition. We could find many confirmations of this in the fact that we constantly find in this literature the idea that, for example, although masturbation has no specific symptomatology, any illness whatsoever can derive from it. We also find the idea that the time it takes to produce its effects is absolutely random: An illness of old age may well be due to childhood masturbation. If it comes to it, someone who dies of old age dies of his childhood masturbation and from a kind of premature exhaustion of his organism. Masturbation becomes the cause, the universal causality of every illness.[32] Unable to calculate the consequences, even if he is relatively old and aware, the child fundamentally puts his entire life at risk once and for all when he puts his hand on his sex. In other words, at the end the eighteenth and the beginning of the nineteenth centuries, when pathological anatomy was identifying a causality of lesions in the body that founds nineteenth-century clinical and positive medicine, a campaign against masturbation brought to light around sexuality, or more precisely around autoeroticism and masturbation, a different medical causality, a different pathogenic causality, that plays both a supplementary and conditional role with regard to the organic causality being identified by the great clinicians and pathological anatomists of the nineteenth century.[33] Sexuality enables everything that is otherwise inexplicable to be explained. It is also an additional causality since it superimposes on the visible causes that can be localized in the body a sort of historical etiology in which the patient is responsible for his own illness: If you are ill, it is because you willed it; if your body is afflicted by illness, it is because you touched it.

Of course, this kind of pathological responsibility of the subject for his own illness is not a discovery, but I think that it underwent a double transformation at this moment. In fact, it is well known that in traditional medicine, in the medicine still dominant at the end of the eighteenth century, doctors always sought to assign patients a degree of responsibility for their own symptoms and illnesses by referring to their diet. It was excess, abuse, or carelessness in a diet that made the patient responsible for the illness he was suffering. This general causality is now concentrated around sexuality, or rather around masturbation itself. The question: "What have you done with your hand?" begins to replace the old question: "What have you done with your body?" From another angle, at the same time as the patient's responsibility for his illness moves from diet in general to masturbation in particular, sexual responsibility, which in eighteenth-century medicine was only recognized and assigned in cases of venereal diseases, is now extended to every illness. The discovery of autoeroticism and the attribution of pathological responsibility interpenetrate in an autopathologization. In short, childhood is assigned pathological responsibility—something that will not be forgotten by the nineteenth century.

From this kind of general etiology, this causal power attributed to masturbation, we get the child who is responsible for the whole of his life, illnesses and death. He is responsible, but is he culpable? This is the second point I want to stress. Actually, it seems to me that precisely those people who conducted this crusade frequently insisted that the child could not really be considered guilty of his masturbation. Why? Quite simply because, according to them, masturbation did not have an endogenous causality. To be sure, the warming up of the humors with puberty, the development of the sexual organs, the accumulation of liquids, the tension of the walls, and the general irritability of the nervous system could all explain why the child masturbates, but the child's natural development must be exonerated of masturbation. Besides, Rousseau had said that it was not a question of nature, but of example.[34] That is why when the doctors of the time raise the question of masturbation they insist on the fact that masturbation is not linked to natural development, to the natural thrust of puberty, and that the best proof of this is that it occurs before puberty. Starting in the end of the eighteenth century, we regularly find observations on masturbation in prepubescent children, and even in very young children. Moreau de la Sarthe observed two little girls who were masturbating at seven years.[35] In 1812, at the children's hospice on rue de Sèvres, Rozier observed a seven-year-old imbecile who masturbated.[36] Sabatier took statements from young girls who confessed that they had masturbated before they were six years old.[37] In 1836, Cerise, in his *Médecin des salles d'asile*, says: "In a ward, and elsewhere, we have seen children two and three years old carried away by completely automatic actions that would seem to suggest a special sensibility."[38] Finally, in 1860 in his *Mémento du père de famille*, De Bourge writes: "Children should be supervised from the cradle."[39]

The importance attached to prepubescent masturbation is due precisely to the desire to exonerate the child somehow, or at least the child's nature, from this phenomenon of masturbation that nonetheless makes him responsible, in a sense, for everything that will happen to him. Who, then, is the guilty party? Guilt lays with external accidents, that is to say, chance. In 1827, a doctor Simon says in his *Traité d'hygiène appliquée à la jeunesse*: "From the youngest age, around four or five years, sometimes earlier, children following a sedentary life are often led, at first by chance or attracted by an itch, to put their hands on their sexual parts, and the excitation that results from a slight rubbing brings blood to that spot, causes a nervous emotion and an instantaneous change in the form of the organ, which arouses curiosity."[40] As you can see, there are chance, random, and purely mechanical gestures in which pleasure is not involved. The only point at which the psyche enters is as curiosity. However, if chance is invoked, most frequently this is not the case. Seduction by an adult is the most frequent cause of masturbation invoked by the crusade: The fault comes from outside. In *Le Tissot moderne*, Malo says: "Can we convince ourselves that without the influence of a masturbator we can become criminal by ourselves? No, it is the advice, the hints, secrets, and examples that awaken the idea of this kind of libertinism. One would have to possess a really corrupt heart to conceive an idea from birth of an abuse against nature the full monstrosity of which we are scarcely able to define ourselves."[41] That is to say, nature does not come into it. What about examples? It may be the example willingly given by an elder child, but more often it is the involuntary and imprudent encouragement given by parents and educators while washing the child with those "careless and tickling hands," as one text puts it.[42] Or it may be a deliberate stimulation, more perverse than careless, by nurses, for example, who want to get children to sleep. It may be pure and simple seduction by servants, private tutors, and teachers. The whole campaign against masturbation is very quickly directed, we can say from the start, against the sexual seduction of children by adults, and not just by adults, but by those belonging to the child's immediate circle, that is to say, by all those who at this time were statutory figures of the household. Servants, governesses, private tutors, uncles, aunts, and cousins will all come between the parents' virtue and the child's natural innocence and introduce a dimension of perversion. In 1835 Deslandes says: "We are especially suspicious of female domestics; since we confide young children to their care, they often seek in them compensation for their forced celibacy."[43] At the origin of masturbation is adult desire toward children. Andrieux gives an example that you will allow me to read because it was repeated in all the literature of the time. In a paroxysmal, if not fantastic, account, he homes in on this basic mistrust, or rather, he clearly points to domestic staff, in the broadest sense, as the target of the campaign. He has the intermediary figures in the family space in his sights. A little girl entrusted to her wet nurse was wasting away. The parents were concerned. One day they entered the wet nurse's room, and how angry they must have been "when they found this wretched girl [the wet nurse; M.F.], exhausted and immobile, with her suckling who was still seeking, in a horrible and inevitably fruitless sucking, the nourishment that only breasts could have provided!"[44] We are right in the middle of a domestic obsession. The devil is there beside the child in the form of the adult, and essentially in the form of the adult intermediary.

Consequently, it is the average and unhealthy household that is blamed more than the child. However, the parents are ultimately guilty since these problems occur because they do not want to take direct responsibility for their children. It is their lack of care, their inattention, their laziness, and their desire for tranquillity that is ultimately in question in children's masturbation. After all, they only needed to be present and to open their eyes. For that reason, and quite naturally, it is the parents and their relationship with their children within the family space that is called into question. This is the third important point in the campaign against masturbation. Parents are exhorted or even challenged in the campaign directed against childhood masturbation: "Such facts," Malo says, "which are infinitely multiplied, necessarily tend to make fathers and mothers more wary."[45] The crusade puts the guilt of the parents into the mouths of the children themselves, into the mouths of all those exhausted little masturbators on the edge of the grave who, as they are dying, turn to their parents for the last time and say to them, as one of them did, it seems, in a letter reproduced by Doussin-Dubreuil: "How cruel are . . . the parents, teachers, and friends who did not warn me of the danger to which this vice leads." Rozier writes: "Parents . . . who, through a blameworthy lack of concern, allow their children to fall into a vice that will lead to their ruin, expose themselves to the risk of hearing one day the cry of despair from a child who is dying while committing a final offense: 'Woe to who has caused my ruin!' "[46]

What is required—and this is the third important point of this campaign—is essentially a new organization, a new physics of the family space: the elimination of all intermediaries and the suppression, if possible, of domestics, or at least a very close supervision of domestics, the ideal solution being the infant alone in a sexually aseptic family space. "We would do well to give a little girl no other company than her doll," Deslandes says, "and to a little boy his horse, soldiers, and drums. This state of isolation could only be to their great advantage."[47] The ideal situation, if you like, is the child alone with her doll or his drum. It is ideal but unrealizable. Actually, the family space must be a space of continual surveillance. Children must be watched over when they are washing, going to bed, getting up, and while they sleep. Parents must keep a lookout all around their children, over their clothes and bodies. The child's body must be the object of their permanent attention. This is the adult's primary concern. Parents must read their child's body like a blazon or as the field of possible signs of masturbation. If the child has a pale complexion, if his face is wan, if his eyelids are bluish or purplish, if he has a certain languid look and has a tired or listless air about him when he leaves his bed, the reason is clear: masturbation. If it is difficult to get him out of bed in the morning: masturbation. Hence it is necessary to be present at the important and dangerous moments of going to bed and getting up. Parents must also organize a series of traps that will enable them to catch the child at the very moment he is committing what is not so much a fault as the cause of all his illnesses. Deslandes gives this advice to parents:

> Keep your eye on a child who seeks out the dark and solitude, who remains alone for a long time without being able to give good reasons for his isolation. Direct your vigilance principally to the moments following going to bed and just before getting up; it is then above all that the masturbator can be caught in the act. His hands are never outside the bed and generally he likes to hide his head under the blankets. Scarcely has he lain down than he seems to be plunged into a deep sleep: this circumstance, always mistrusted by an experienced man, is one that contributes most to cause or nourish the parents' security. . . . When one uncovers the young man one suddenly finds his hands, if he has not had time to move them, on or nearby the organs he abuses. One may also find the penis erect or even traces of a recent emission: The latter may even be recognized by the special odor coming from the bed or with which his fingers are impregnated. Generally mistrust young people who, when they are in bed or while they sleep, often have their hands in the position I have just described. . . . There are grounds for considering traces of sperm as certain proof of onanism in subjects not yet pubescent, and as the most probable signs of this habit in those who are a bit older."[48]

Forgive me for quoting all these details (and under Bergson's portrait!),[49] but I think that we see here the establishment of a whole family drama with which we are quite familiar and which is the great family drama of the nineteenth and twentieth centuries: the little theater of the family comedy and tragedy with its beds, its sheets, the night, the lamps, with its stealthy approaches, its odors, and the carefully inspected stains on the sheets; the little drama that brings the adult's curiosity ever closer to the child's body. A tiny symptomatology of pleasure. In the adult's always closer approach toward the child's body, at the moment when the child's body is in a state of pleasure, one comes across the instruction, symmetrical to the instruction of solitude I referred to a moment ago, of the immediate physical presence of the adult beside, alongside, almost on the child. If need be, say doctors such as Deslandes, one should sleep beside the young masturbator, in the same room and possibly in the same bed, in order to prevent him from masturbating.[50]

There are a series of techniques for more effectively linking the parent's body to the child's body in a state of pleasure, or to the child's body that must be prevented from arriving at the state of pleasure. Children are made to sleep with their hands tied and attached by cords to the parent's hands, so that the adult will be awakened if the child moves his hands. There is the story, for example, of an adolescent who, of his own free will, was tied to a chair in the room of his elder brother. There were little bells on the chair and he slept like that. Whenever he moved during the night, wanting to masturbate, the bells rang and his brother woke up.[51] Rozier tells another story of a young boarder whose superior noticed that she had a "secret habit." The superior immediately "shuddered." "From that moment" she decides to "share her bed at night with the young patient. During the day she did not let her out of her sight for an instant." Thus, "some months after," the superior (of the convent or boarding school) was able to take the young boarder back to her parents who were then proud to present to the world a young woman full of "spirit, health and reason; in sum, a very attractive woman"![52]

Beneath these puerilities there is, I think, a very important theme. This is the instruction for the direct, immediate, and constant application of the parents' bodies to the bodies of their children. Intermediaries disappear, but positively this means that from now on children's bodies will have to be watched over by the parents' bodies in a sort of physical clinch. There is extreme closeness, contact, almost mixing; the urgent folding of the parents' bodies over their children's bodies; the insistent obligation of the gaze, of presence, contiguity, and touch. This is what Rozier says about the example I have just given: "The mother of such a patient is, so to speak, like the wrapping or the shadow of her daughter. When danger threatens the young of the possum [a kind of kangaroo, I think; M.F.], the mother does not confine herself to fearing for them, she puts them in her flesh."[53] The parent's body envelops the child's and at this point the central objective of the maneuver or crusade is revealed: the constitution of a new family body.

Until the middle of the eighteenth century the aristocratic or bourgeois family (since the campaign is limited to these forms of the family) was above all a sort of relational system. It was a bundle of relations of ancestry, descent, collateral relations, cousinhood, primogeniture, and alliances corresponding to schemas for the transmission of kinship and the division and distribution of goods and social status. Sexual prohibitions effectively focused on these kinds of relations. What is now being constituted is a sort of restricted, close-knit, substantial, compact, corporeal, and affective family core: the cell family in place of the relational family; the cell family with its corporeal, affective, and sexual space entirely saturated by direct parent-child relationships. In other words, I am not inclined to say that the child's sexuality that is tracked down and prohibited is in some way the consequence of the formation of the nuclear family, let us say of the conjugal or parental family of the nineteenth century. Rather, I would say that this sexuality is one of the constitutive elements of this family. By highlighting the child's sexuality, or more exactly the child's masturbatory activity, and by highlighting the body of the child in sexual danger, parents were urgently enjoined to reduce the large polymorphous and dangerous space of the household and to do no more than forge with their children, their progeny, a sort of single body bound together through a concern about infantile sexuality, about infantile autoeroticism and masturbation: Parents! Keep watch over your excited daughters and the erections of your sons because this is how you will become fully and truly parents! Do not forget the image of the possum given by Rozier. It is a matter of constituting a kangaroo family: the child's body as the nuclear element of the family body. The little family solidifies around the adolescent's warm and suspect bed. The emphasis placed on the child's sexualized body, on the child's autoeroticized body, was the instrument, element, or vector for constituting what could be called the great or, if you prefer, the little cultural involution of the family around the parent-child relationship. The child's nonrelational, autoerotic sexuality was the point to which the parents' duties, guilt, power, concern, and physical presence were hitched up and anchored and was one of the factors in the constitution of a close-knit and interdependent family, of a physical and affective family, of a small family that developed, of course, within the network family, but that also developed at the cost of this larger family and constituted the cell family with its body and physico-affective and physico-sexual substance. It may very well be, I suppose, that the big relational family made up of permitted and prohibited relationships was constituted historically on the basis of the prohibition of incest. However, I would say that the small, affective, close-knit and substantial family that is characteristic of our society and that arose at the end of the eighteenth century was constituted on the basis of the caressing incest of looks and gestures around the child's body. It is this incest, this epistemophilic incest of touch, gaze, and surveillance that was the basis of the modern family.

Of course, the direct parent-child contact so urgently prescribed in this familial cell gives absolute power to parents over the child. All power? Yes and no. In fact, at the very moment when the crusade enjoins parents to take responsibility for the meticulous, detailed, and almost shameful surveillance of their children's bodies, at that moment and by virtue of this injunction itself, parents are essentially connected to a completely different type of relations and control. I mean that when parents are told to be careful to know what is happening to their children's bodies and in their children's beds, when masturbation becomes the object of the moral order of the day, almost the first order of the new ethic of the new family, you will recall that it is not registered at the level of immorality but of illness. It is made into a sort of universal practice, a sort of dangerous, inhuman, and monstrous X from which any illness may derive. So that the internal parental control that fathers and mothers are required to exercise is necessarily plugged in to an external medical control. Internal parental control must model its forms, criteria, interventions, and decisions on medical reasons and knowledge. Parents are told that they must watch over their children because they will become ill, because this or that physiological, functional, and potentially even lesional problem will occur that doctors are familiar with. The parents-children relationship that is solidifying into a sort of physical-sexual unit must therefore be consistent with the doctor-patient relationship; it must extend the doctor-patient relationship. The father or mother who is so close to the children's bodies, the father or mother who literally covers the child's body with their own, must at the same time be a father and a mother who are diagnosticians, therapists, and agents of health. But this also means that their control is subordinate, that it must be open to medical and hygienic intervention, and that they must call upon the external and scientific authority of the doctor at the first warning signs. In other words, at the very moment that the cellular family is enclosed in a dense, affective space, it is endowed with a rationality that, in the name of illness, plugs it into a technology, into an external medical power and knowledge. The new substantial, affective, and sexual family is at the same time a medicalized family.

I will give just two examples of this process of the closure of the family and the endowment of its new space with a medical rationality. The first is the problem of confession. Parents must watch over their children, spy on them, creep up on them, peer beneath their blankets, and sleep beside them. However, as soon as the sickness is discovered they must call in the doctor to cure it. It will only be a genuine and effective cure if the patient accepts it and participates in it. The patient must acknowledge his illness, understand its consequences, and accept the treatment. In short, he must confess. As all the texts of the crusade say, the child cannot and must not confess to his parents. He can only confess to the doctor. "Of all the proofs," says Deslandes, "the most important to acquire is a confession," because confession removes "any kind of doubt." It makes the doctor's actions "more frank" and "more effective." It prevents the subject from refusing treatment. It puts the doctor and "everyone in authority . . . in a position that enables them to get straight to the point and thereby achieve their aim."[54] Likewise, in the English author La Mert there is a very interesting discussion about whether confession should be made to the family doctor or to a specialist doctor. He concludes that confession should not be to the family doctor because he is still too close to the family.[55] The family doctor must acquire only collective secrets; individual secrets must be confided to a specialist. There is a long series of examples of cures in this literature that were obtained thanks to confessions to the doctor. The result is a childhood sexuality or masturbation that is subject to continuous parental surveillance, acknowledgment, and control. At the same time, this sexuality becomes the object of confession and discourse, but externally, to the doctor. There is an internal medicalization of the family and of the relationships between parents and children, but an external discursivity in the relationship with the doctor. Sexuality is silent within the family in which nonetheless it appears quite clearly through the system of surveillance, but where it must not speak. However, beyond the borders of this family space it must be put into words, to the doctor. Consequently, infantile sexuality is established at the very heart of the family bond, within the mechanism of familial power, but the enunciation of this sexuality is shifted to the medical institution and authority. Sexuality is one of those things that can be spoken about only to the doctor. To the physical intensity of sexuality within the family corresponds a discursive extension of sexuality outside the family and within the medical field. Medicine is able to put sexuality into words and make it speak at the very moment that the family makes it visible because it is watching over it.[56]

The problem of instruments for preventing masturbation also shows how familial power is connected with medical power. To prevent masturbation the family must become an agency for transmitting medical knowledge. Essentially, the family must function merely as a relay or transmission belt between the child's body and the doctor's technique. Hence the remedies that doctors prescribe for the child and that the family must apply. There is a whole range of them in the prospectuses and medical texts I referred to a moment ago. There are the famous nightshirts, which you may even have seen, with low drawstring hems and corsets and bindings. There is the famous Jalade-Laffont belt that was in use for dozens of years. It comprised a sort of metal corselet that was attached to the pelvic area with, for boys, a little metal tube lined with velvet and with a number of holes pierced at the end through which he could urinate. The device was closed, padlocked and opened only once a week in the presence of the parents so the child could be cleaned. This belt was the one most often used in France at the beginning of the nineteenth century.[57] There are mechanical devices like Wender's cane, invented in 1811. It consisted in a little cane that was split up to a certain point, hollowed out, placed on the boy's penis and tied up. This, as Wender said, is enough to keep voluptuous sensations at bay.[58] A surgeon, Lallemand, proposed inserting a permanent probe in the urethra. At the very beginning of the nineteenth century it seems that Lallemand used acupuncture against masturbation, or anyway the insertion of needles in the genital area.[59] Then there are chemical methods like the opiates used by Davila, for example, and bathing and washing with different solutions.[60] Napoleon's surgeon, Larrey, invented a remedy that seems somewhat drastic. He proposed injecting a solution of what he called subcarbonate of soda in a boy's urethra (I do not know what this solution might be; is it bicarbonate of soda?). However, beforehand one took the precaution of tying the boy's penis firmly at the base so that the solution did not enter the bladder and remained permanently in the urethra. It seems that this caused lesions that took several days or weeks to heal during which time the boy did not masturbate.[61] There was cauterization of the urethra and, for girls, cauterization and removal of the clitoris.[62] It appears to have been Antoine Dubois who, at the beginning of the nineteenth century, removed the clitoris of a girl after other cures had failed. After tying her arms and legs together, her clitoris was removed "with a single slice of the lancet," says Antoine Dubois, and the stump was cauterized "with a flaming bud." Success was "complete."[63] Graefe practiced removal of the clitoris after the failure of a previous cure (he had cauterized the girl's head, that is to say, he produced a burn on her head that he injected with tartar to prevent the wound from healing, but, in spite of everything, she continued to masturbate). The patient's "intelligence"— that had collapsed or even never developed (she was a young imbecile)—"somehow held back until then, now took flight."[64]

The legitimacy of castrations or semicastrations was, of course, discussed in the nineteenth century. However, in 1835 the great theorist of masturbation, Deslandes, said that "far from wounding the moral sense, such a decision is in keeping with the strictest requirements. We act as we do on other occasions when we amputate a limb; we sacrifice the secondary for the principal, the part for the whole." And anyway, he says, what disadvantage does a woman suffer if we remove her clitoris? "The greatest disadvantage" is to place this woman in "the already very large category" of women who are "insensitive" to the pleasures of love, "which does not prevent them from becoming good mothers and devoted wives."[65] In 1883, a surgeon, Garnier, was still practicing removal of the clitoris from girls who gave themselves up to masturbation.[66]

In any case, a sort of interaction and continuity is established between medicine and patient through what could be described as a widespread physical persecution of childhood and masturbation in the nineteenth century that, without having the same consequences, was almost as extensive as the persecution of witches in sixteenth and seventeenth centuries. Medicine and sexuality were brought into contact through the family: by calling upon the doctor and by receiving, accepting, and when necessary applying the remedies he prescribed, the family linked sexuality with a medicine that previously had in practice related to sexuality only in a very distant and indirect way. The family itself became an agent of the medicalization of sexuality within its own space. Thus we see the emergence of complex relations with a sort of division between the mute surveillance and nondiscursive encirclement of the child's body by its parents on one side and, on the other, the extra-familial, scientific discourse, or discourse of confession, localized in medical practice, which thus becomes heir to the techniques of Christian confession. Alongside this division there is a continuity of the medicine-patient relationship that gives birth, with and within the family, to a constant advance of sexual medicine, of a sort of medicalization of sexuality, which is ever more insistent and which introduces medical techniques and forms of intervention into the family space. In short, there is an exchange in which medicine operates as a means of ethical, physical, and sexual control within family morality and in return makes the internal problems of the family body, focused on the child's body, appear as medical need. The child's vices and the parents' guilt call on medicine to medicalize the problem of masturbation, the problem of sexuality, and of the child's body in general. A medico-familial mesh organizes a field that is both ethical and pathological in which sexual conduct becomes an object of control, coercion, examination, judgment, and intervention. In short, the medicalized family functions as a source of normalization. All immediate power over the child's body, without any intermediary, is given to this medicalized family that is, however, controlled externally by medical knowledge and techniques. It is this family that reveals, and which from the first decades of the nineteenth century can reveal, the normal and the abnormal in the sexual domain. The family becomes not only the basis for the determination and distinction of sexuality but also for the rectification of the abnormal.

There is a question that requires an answer: Where did this campaign come from and what does it signify? What made masturbation emerge in this way as the major, or at least one of the major problems, in the relationship between parents and children? The campaign should, I think, be situated within the general process of the constitution of the cellular family that I have been referring to, which, notwithstanding its apparent closure, extends a power over individuals, bodies, and gestures that takes the form of medical control. Essentially, at the end of the eighteenth century the nuclear family, the cell family, the physical and substantial family was called upon to take responsibility for the child's body that was becoming an important stake under two headings. First, the nuclear family was required to care of the child's body quite simply because it was living and should not die. Certainly, one of the reasons it was desirable to replace the loose, polymorphous, and complex apparatus of the large relational family with the limited, intense, and constant apparatus of the parental surveillance of children was the discovery of a political and economic interest in the child's survival. Parents must be concerned with their children; they must take care of them in the fullest sense: They must prevent them from dying, watch over them, and at the same time train them. The future lives of children lie in the hands of their parents. The State demands from parents, and the new forms or relations of production require, that the costs entailed by the very existence of the family, by the parents and recently born children, are not squandered by the early death of children. The family must therefore take responsibility for the child's body and life and this is certainly one of the reasons why parents are called upon to focus continuous and intense attention on the bodies of their children.

This, I think, is the context in which we should set the crusade against masturbation. Really, it is only a chapter of a broader, well-known crusade for the natural education of children. What exactly is this idea of natural education that was developed in the second half of the nineteenth [*rectius:* eighteenth] century? It is the idea of an education that is first and foremost entrusted entirely, or in its essentials, to parents themselves as the natural educators of their children. Everyone else, domestics, private tutors, governors and governesses, et cetera, are at best only the most faithful relay of this natural relationship between parents and children. Ideally, however, all these intermediaries should disappear and parents should be effectively left in direct charge of their children. Natural education also means an education that conforms to a certain schema of rationality, to a number of rules for securing the survival of the children on the one hand and their training and normalized development on the other. These rules and their rationality, like pedagogical and medical knowledge, belong to authorities like educators and doctors. In short, a series of technical authorities supervise and dominate the family itself. The call for natural education at the end of the eighteenth century is a call for an immediate contact between parents and children, for substance to be given to the small family around the child's body and, at the same time, for the rationalization of parent-child relationships or their opening up to pedagogical or medical rationality and discipline. Restricting the family in this way, and giving it such a compact and close-knit look, effectively opens it up to political and moral criteria; opens it up to a type of power and to a technique of power relayed by medicine and doctors together with families.

Now, and it is at this point that sexuality is encountered, what happens, at least at the level of the aristocracy and bourgeoisie, when parents are enjoined to take serious and direct responsibility for the physical existence of their children, for their very bodies, that is to say, for their lives, their survival, and the possibility of their training? Parents are not only asked to train their children so that they will be useful to the State, but at the same time they are asked to cede back their children to the State and entrust, if not their basic education, then at least their instruction and technical training to an education directly or indirectly controlled by the State. The widespread demand for a State education, or for an education controlled by the State, is found precisely when the campaign against masturbation begins in France and Germany, that is to say, around 1760-1780. La Chalotois, in *Essai sur l'éducation nationale*, develops the theme that the State must ensure education.[67] In the same period, Basedow, in his *Philantropinum*, advances the idea that education for the more fortunate classes in society should take place in a State-controlled space of specialized institutions, rather than in the dubious space of the family.[68] Beyond these projects and exemplary sites and models, such as Basedow's *Philantropinum*, this is a period of the development of large educational establishments and schools throughout Europe: We need your children, it is said. Give them to us. We, like you, need these children to be normally formed. So entrust them to us so that we may form them according to certain norms. As a result, precisely when families are called upon to take responsibility for their children's bodies and for securing their lives and survival, they are also asked to give up these same children, to relinquish their own real presence and the power they can exercise over them. Naturally, the age of children when parents are required to be concerned with them is not the same as when parents are called upon to let go of their children's bodies. Nonetheless, a process of exchange is called for: Take good care of your children's lives and health for us, of their physical strength, obedience, and ability, so that we can put them through the machine of the system of State education, instruction, and training over which you have no control. I think that in this double request—"Concern yourselves with your children" and "Let go of these children later"—the child's sexual body serves as the unit, so to speak, of exchange. Parents are told: There is something in the child's body that belongs imprescriptibly to you and that you will never have to give up because it will never abandon you: their sexuality. The child's sexual body belongs, and will always belong, to the family space, and no one else will ever have any power over or claim on this body. However, when we create for you this field of power so total and complete, we ask you to give us in return your children's bodies, or, if your prefer, their abilities. We ask you to give us these children so that we can make of them something that we really need. The bait can easily be seen in this exchange, since parents are given the task precisely of taking possession of their children's bodies, of covering them and watching over them so exhaustively that they can never masturbate. However, not only have parents never been able to prevent their children from masturbating, but the doctors of the time admit this quite bluntly and cynically: All children masturbate. In the end, parents are committed to the infinite task of possessing and controlling an infantile sexuality that will in any case elude them. Thanks to their possession of the sexual body, however, parents will give up the child's other body of performance or ability.

The child's sexuality is the trick by which the close-knit, affective, substantial, and cellular family was constituted and from whose shelter the child was extracted. The sexuality of children was a trap into which parents fell. It is an evident trap; I mean, it is a real trap, but intended for the parents. It was one of the vectors of the constitution of the close-knit family. It was one of the instruments of exchange that allowed the child to be shifted from his family milieu to the institutionalized and normalized space of education. This worthless fictional element, this worthless money, was left in the parents' possession; worthless money to which, as you know, parents are enormously attached, since even in 1974, when the question arises of sexual education at school, parents who knew their history would have been be justified in saying: We have been deceived for two centuries! For two centuries we have been told: Give us your children and you can take care of their sexuality; give us your children, but you will guarantee that their sexuality will develop in a family space controlled by you. Give us your children, and your power over your children's sexual body, over their body of pleasure, will be maintained. And now the psychoanalysts are saying: It's ours, the body of pleasure is ours! And the State, psychologists, psychopathologists, and others say: It's ours, this education is ours! This is the great deception in which parental power has been caught. It is a fictional power whose fictional organization enabled the real constitution of this space to which one was so attached for the reasons I have just given, the constitution of this substantial space around which the extended relational family has been contracted and restricted and within which the child's life, the child's body, has been both watched over but also developed and treated as sacred. In my view, the sexuality of children concerns parents more than children. In any case, it is around this suspect bed that the sexually irradiated and saturated and medically anxious modern family was born.

In the middle of the nineteenth century this besieged sexuality established within the family will be taken up again by doctors—who already had control over it at the end of the eighteenth century—and, in conjunction with the instinct I spoke about in previous sessions, will constitute the broad domain of abnormalities.

1. A. de Ligouri, *Praxis confessarii*, pp. 72-73, Article 39; pp. 140-141, Article 89; A.-M. de Ligoury [de Ligouri], *Le Conservateur des jeunes gens*, pp. 5-14.

2. *Onania or the Heinous Sin of Self-Pollution and All its Frightful Consequences in Both Sexes Considered, with spiritual and physical advice to those who have already injured themselves by this abominable practice*, fourth edition (London, 1718). There are no known copies of the first three editions. The attribution of the pamphlet to an individual names Bekker derives from Tissot's *Onanisme* (see the following note and note 6) but this has never been confirmed.

3. S. A. A-D. Tissot's book, cited by Foucault, was written in Latin (*Tentamen de morbis ex manu stupratione*) and was included in the *Dissertatio de febribus biliosis seu historia epidemiae biliosae lausannensis* (Lausanne, 1758), pp. 177-264. Although this edition was greeted favorably by specialists, it received almost no notice.

4. J. B. Basedow, *Das Methodenbuch für Väter und Mütter der Familien and Völker*, (Altona-Bremen, 1770): French translation: *Nouvelle Méthode d'éducation*, (Frankfurt-Leipzig, 1772). *Das Elementarwerk*, second edition (Leipzig, 1785); French translation: *Manuel élementaire d'éducation* (Berlin-Dessau, 1774). We have not been able to find the *Petit Livre pour les enfants de toutes les classes* (1771), nor the *Petit Livre pour les parents et éducateurs de toutes les classes* (1771).

5. C. G. Salzmann, *Ists recht, über die eimichen Sünden der Jugend, öffentlich zu schreiben* (Schnepfenthal, 1785); *Carl von Carlsberg oder über das menschliche Elend* (Leipzig, 1783); *Über die heimlichen Sünden der Jugend* (Leipzig, 1785); French translation: *L'Ange protecteur de la jeunesse ou Histoires amusantes et instructives destinées à faire connaître aux jeunes gens les dangers que l'étourderie et l'inexpérience leur font courir* (Paris, 1825).

6. The circulation of the first French edition of S. A. A. D. Tissot, *L'Onanisme ou Dissertation physique sur les maladies produites par la masturbation* (Lausanne, 1760), was restricted to medical circles. See also the English translation by A. Hume, *Onanism: or, a treatise upon the disorders produced by masturbation: or, the dangerous effects of secret and excessive venery* (London, 1761). The jabbering to which Foucault refers begins with the third, considerably augmented edition of 1764, followed by sixty-four reprints (until 1905), including those published with the commentaries of other doctors who are attributed with certain experience in the struggle against masturbation (for example, C. T. Morel in 1830, E. Clément in 1875, and X. André in 1886).

7. H. Kaan, *Psychopathia sexualis* (Leipzig, 1844).

8. We have been unable to identify the source for this.

9. R. Krafft-Ebing, *Psychopathia sexualis*.

10. H. Havelock Ellis, *Studies in the Psychology of Sex* (Philadelphia: s.1., 1905-1928); French translation: *Études de psychologie sexuelle* translated by A Van Gennep (Paris: s.1., 1964-1965).

11. Foucault is no doubt alluding to texts such as J.-L. Alibert, *Nouveaux Éléments de thérapeutique*, vol. 2 (Paris, 1827), p. 147, or L. Bourgeois, *Les Passions dans leurs rapports avec la santé et les maladies*, vol. 2 (Paris, 1861), p. 131.

12. We have not been able to identify such passages.

13. For example, J. B. de Bourge, *Le Mémento du père de famille et de l'éducateur de l'enfance, ou les Conseils intimes sur les dangers de la masturbation* (Mirecourt, 1860).

14. The work was actually published with this title: *Le Livre sans titre* (Paris, 1830).

15. In the Preface to C. G. Salzmann's *Über die heimlichen Sünden der Jugend* (not included in the French edition) we read: "Germany has been roused from its slumber, as Germans have had their attention drawn to an evil that was eating away the roots of humanity. Thousands of young Germans who were at risk of ending their lives wasting away in hospitals have been saved, and today devote their recovered strength to the good of humanity and especially German humanity. Thousands of other children have been prevented from being bitten by this poisonous snake."

16. See the *Précis historique, physiologique et moral des principaux objets en cire préparée et colorée d'après nature, qui composent le museum de J. F. Bertrand-Rival* (Paris, 1801). On the visits to the Dupuytren museum, cf., J.-L. Doussin-Dubreuil, *Nouveau Manuel sur les dangers de l'onanisme, et Conseils relatifs au traitement des maladies qui en résultent. Ouvrage nécessaire aux pères de famille et aux instituteurs* (Paris, 1839), p. 85. There are traces of another museum at the end of the century in P. Bonnetain, *Charlot s'amuse*, second edition (Brussels, 1883), p. 268.

17. *Histoire de la répression sexuelle* by Jos Van Ussel is essentially inspired by H. Marcuse, *Eros and Civilization: A Philosophical Inquiry into Freud* (Boston: Beacon Press, 1955); French translation: *Éros et Civilisation* (Paris: s.l., 1971); and *One-Dimensional Man: Studies in the Ideology of Advanced Industrial Society* (Boston: Beacon Press, 1964); French translation: *L'Homme unidimensionnel* (Paris: s.l., 1970).

18. J.-B.-T. Serrurier, "Pollution," in *Dictionnaire des sciences médicales* 44 (Paris, 1820), p. 114. Cf. "Masturbation," ibid., 31 (1819), pp. 100-135.

19. E.-R.-A. Serres, *Anatomie comparée du cerveau*, vol. 2, (Paris, 1826), pp. 600-613 ("De l'action du cervelet sur les organes génitaux").

20. L. Deslandes (*De l'onanisme et des autres abus vénériens considérés dans leurs rapports avec la santé* [Paris, 1835], p. 159), refers to the thesis of J.-L.-N. Payen, *Essai sur l'encéphalite ou inflammation du cerveau, considérée spécialement dans l'enfance* (Paris, 1826), p. 25.

21. G. Dupuytren, "Atrophie des branches antérieures de la moelle épinière; paralysie générale du mouvement, mais non de la sensibilité; traitement; considérations pratiques. Hémiplégie guérie par une forte commotion électrique," *La Lancette française* 114 (September 14, 1833), pp. 339-340.

22. A. Boyer, *Leçons sur les maladies des os, rédigées en un traité complet de ces maladies*, 1, 9 [1802-1803], p. 344.

23. L.-J. Sanson, "Amaurose," in *Dictionnaire de médecine et de chirurgie pratiques*, vol. 2 (Paris, 1829), pp. 85-119.

24. A. Scarpa, *Saggio di osservazione e di esperienze sulle principali malattie degli occhi*, (Pavia, 1801); French translation: *Traité pratique de maladies des yeux, ou Expériences et Observations sur les maladies qui affectent ces organes*, vol. 2 (Paris, 1802), pp. 242-243; English translation: *A treatise on the principal diseases of the eyes* translated by J. Briggs (London, 1818).

25. P. Blaud, "Mémoire sur les concretions fibrineuses polypiformes dans les cavités du cœur," *Revue médicale française et étrangère. Journal de clinique*, 4 (1833), pp. 175-188, 331-352.

26. A. Portal, *Observations sur la nature et sur le traitement du rachitisme* (Paris, 1797), p. 224.

27. Lisle, "Des pertes séminales et de leur influence sur la production de la folie," *Annales médico-psychologiques*, vol. 3 (1851), p. 333.

28. On the literature cited, see L. Deslandes, *De l'onanisme*, pp. 152-153, 159, 162-163, 189, 198, 220, 221, 223, 243-244, 254-255.

29. To the letters of *Onania* and those published by Tissot, we can add the collection of J.-L. Doussin-Dubreuil, *Lettres sur les dangers de l'onanisme, et Conseils relatifs au traitement des maladies qui en résultent. Ouvrage utile aux pères de famille et aux instituteurs* (Paris, 1806), and *Nouveau Manuel sur les dangers de l'onanisme* (revised edition, corrected with additions by J. Morin).

30. Foucault uses the third edition: Rozier, *Des habitudes secrètes ou des maladies produites par l'onanisme chez les femmes* (Paris, 1830), pp. 81-82. (The first two editions have different titles but the same contents: *Lettres médicales et morales* (Paris, 1806), and *Des habitudes secrètes ou de l'onanisme chez les femmes. Lettres médicales, anecdotiques et morales à une jeune malade et à une mère, dédiées aux mères de famille et aux maîtresses de pensions* (Paris, 1825).

31. Rozier, *Des habitudes secrètes*, p. 82: "I am neither tall nor sturdy. I am thin and unable to think. In the mornings especially, it seems that I rise from the underground. I get no sustenance from food. Sometimes I feel hollow to the pit of my stomach, pierced between my shoulders, and I begin to breathe with difficulty. For some months I have had a continual agitation in my limbs when the circulation of my blood increases. The smallest ascent, the shortest walk tires me. I shake all over, especially in the mornings."

32. Cf. H. Fournier and Bégin, "Masturbation," in *Dictionnaire des sciences médicales* 31 (Paris, 1819), p. 108.

33. Cf. M. Foucault, *Naissance de la clinique*, pp. 125-176. English translation: *Birth of the Clinic*, pp. 124-173.

34. See Rousseau's observations in the *Confessions* and in *Émile*, J. J. Rousseau, *Oeuvres complètes* edited under the direction of B. Ganebin and M. Raymond, vol. 1 (Paris: s.1., 1959) pp. 66-67 and vol. 4 (Paris: s.1., 1969) p. 663. English translations: *Confessions*, translated by Angela Scholar (Oxford: s.1., 2000), and *Emile, or On Education*, translated by Alan Bloom (Harmondsworth: Penguin, 1991).

35. Rozier, *Des habitudes secrètes*, pp. 192-193: "Professor Moreau de la Sarthe reports that he had the opportunity to observe two little girls, seven years of age, who through culpable negligence had been allowed to give themselves up to this excitement, the frequency and excess of which will subsequently lead to exhaustion and consumption."

36. Ibid., p. 193: "Finally, I myself have also seen at the Children's Hospice in the rue de Sèvres, Paris, in 1812, a young person of seven years old who was already affected to the highest degree by this inclination. She was deprived of almost all her intellectual faculties."

37. Sabatier's observation is reported in ibid., p. 192: "The most terrible and frequent results of this vice that I have seen are nodes in the spine. In view of the youth of those affected, my opinion has always been regarded as without foundation. However, I have been informed by recent confessions that several were rendered vulnerable to this before the sixth year of their lives."

38. L. A. P. Cerise, *Le Médecin des salles d'asile, ou Manuel d'hygiène et d'éducation physique de l'enfance, destiné aux médecins et aux directeurs de ces établissements et pouvant servir aux mères de famille*, Paris, 1836, p. 72.

39. J. B. de Bourge, *Le Mémento du père de famille*, pp. 5-14.

40. [F.] Simon [de Metz], *Traité d'hygiène appliquée à la jeunesse* (Paris, 1827), p. 153.

41. C. Malo, *Le Tissot moderne, ou Réflexions morales et nouvelles sur l'onanisme, suivies des moyens de le prévenir chez deux sexes* (Paris, 1815), pp. 11-12.

42. This could refer to A. E. Jozan, *D'une cause fréquente et peu connue d'épuisement prématuré* (Paris, 1858), p. 22: "Children in the hands of nurses are not sheltered from danger."

43. L. Deslandes, *De l'onanisme*, p. 516. Deslandes takes up the question in his *Manuel d'hygiène publique et privée, ou Précis élémentaire des connaissances relatives à la conservation de la santé et au perfectionnement physique et moral des hommes* (Paris, 1827), pp. 499-503, 513-519.

44. The fact, whose authenticity is guaranteed by J. Andrieux, editor of the *Annales d'obstétrique, des maladies des femmes et des enfants* (1842-1844) and of the *Enseignement élémentaire universel, ou Encyclopédie de la jeunesse* (Paris, 1844), is pointed out by L. Deslandes, *De l'onanisme*, pp. 516-517.

45. C. Malo, *Le Tissot moderne*, p. 11.

46. The letter is quoted by Foucault from Rozier, *Des habitudes secrètes*, pp. 194-195.

47. We have been unable to identify the source for this.

48. L. Deslandes, *De l'onanisme*, pp. 369-372.

49. Foucault's course was held in a lecture theater in which there was a portrait of Henri Bergson, who was himself a professor of the Collège de France.

50. L. Deslandes, *De l'onanisme*, p. 533.

51. We have been unable to identify the source for this.

52. Rozier, *Des habitudes secrètes*, pp. 229-230.

53. Ibid., p. 230.

54. L. Deslandes, *De l'onanisme*, pp. 375-376.

55. S. La Mert, *La Préservation personelle. Traité médical sur les maladies des organes de la génération résultant des habitudes cachées, des excès de jeunesse ou de la contagion; avec des observations pratiques sur l'impuissance prématurée* (Paris, 1847), pp. 50-51; English translation: *Self Preservation. A Popular Inquiry into the Concealed Causes of Those Obscure and Neglected Disorders of the Generative System*, (Manchester, 1841), pp. 50-51: "It is however the wish of the author that this publication may become extensively familiar to superintendents of our schools

and collegiate educational institutions, to the clergy, to parents and guardians, and to all whom is entrusted the formation of youthful character. It will be useful without admixture or diminution, in enabling them to make timely discovery of this hateful practice among those committed to their care, and it may put them upon their guard so as to enable them to take such precautions as may be most fitting to avert the consequences. There are few of those who have devoted themselves exclusively to the treatment of sexual diseases who are not deeply impressed with the general prevalence of self-pollution. Is it doubted by the more routine practitioner, is it denied? He, of all men, is least likely to be able to form an accurate conception. He is precisely the last man to be consulted or confided in with the secret. The family physician may be in possession of *family secrets*, he may know the hereditary tendencies common to them all, but it is quite another thing to become entrusted with *individual secrets*, the confession that the solitary victim will not and cannot make to *a mother, a brother, or a sister*. The common medical attendant, never consulted, and very wisely so, is just as ignorant of the extent and prevalence of these pernicious practices as he is of the best mode for their detection and cure."

56. M. Foucault, *La Volonté de Savoir*, pp. 145-147. English translation: *The History of Sexuality*, pp. 120-121.

57. Cf. G. Jalade-Laffont, *Considérations sur la confection des corsets et des ceintures propres à s'opposer à la pernicieuse habitude de l'onanisme* (Paris, 1819). This text was incorporated into *Considérations sur les hernies abdominales, sur les bandages herniaires rénixgrades et sur de nouveaux moyens de s'opposer à l'onanisme*, vol. 1 (Paris, 1821), pp. 441-454. It is here that the doctor-inventor announces the discovery of a corset to keep people of the feminine sex from the dangers of onanism (pp. x-xi).

58. L. Deslandes, *De l'onanisme*, p. 546 which cites A. J. Wender, *Essai sur les pollutions nocturnes produites par la masturbation, chez les hommes, et exposition d'un moyen simple et sûr de les guérir radicalement*, 1811.

59. The methods used by C.-F. Lallemand are mentioned by Deslandes, *De l'onanisme*, p. 543 who probably uses research on the *Maladies des organes génito-urinaires* that we have not been able to consult.

60. According to Deslandes, *De l'onanisme*, pp. 543-545, J. de Madrid-Davila, in *Dissertation sur les pollutions involontaires* (Paris, 1831), also proposes the insertion of a probe in the urethra.

61. This concerns Dominique-Jean Larrey. See his *Mémoires de chirurgie militaire*, vols. 1-4 (Paris, 1812-1817); *Recueil de mémoires de chirurgie* (Paris, 1821); and *Clinique chirurgicale* (Paris, 1829-1836). However, we have not been able to identify the source for this reference. English translation: D. J. Larrey, *Surgical Memoirs* translated by J. C. Mercer (Philadelphia, 1832).

62. Cf. L. Deslandes, *De l'onanisme*, pp. 429-430.

63. The operation carried out by Dubois is reported by L. Deslandes, *De l'onanisme*, p. 422, which refers to A. Richerand, *Nosographie chirurgicale*, second edition, vol. 4 (Paris, 1802), pp. 326-328.

64. L. Deslandes, *De l'onanisme*, p. 425. On E. A G.. Graefe's operation, see "Guérison d'une idiote par l'extirpation du clitoris," *Nouvelle Bibliothèque médicale*, 9 (1825), pp. 256-259.

65. L. Deslandes, *De l'onanisme*, pp. 430-431.

66. P. Garnier, *Onanisme, seul et à deux, sous toutes ses formes et leurs conséquences* (Paris, 1883), pp. 354-355.

67. L.-R. Caradeuc de la Chalotois, *Essai sur l'éducation nationale, ou Plan d'études pour la jeunesse* (Paris, 1763), pp. 354-355; English translation: *Essay on National Education, or, Plan of Studies for the Young*, translated by H. R. Clark (London: s.1., 1934).

68. A. Pinloche, *La Réforme de l'éducation en Allemagne au dix-huitième siècle. Basedow et la Philantropinism*, (Paris, 1889). Cf. M. Foucault, *La Volonté de Savoir*, p. 41. English translation: *The History of Sexuality*, p. 29.

ten

12 MARCH 1975

*What makes the psychoanalytic theory of incest acceptable to the
bourgeois family (danger comes from the child's
desire). ~ Normalization of the urban proletariat and the optimal
distribution of the working class family (danger comes from
fathers and brothers). ~ Two theories of incest. ~ The antecedents
of the abnormal: psychiatric-judicial mesh and psychiatric-familial
mesh. ~ The problematic of sexuality and the analysis of its
irregularities. ~ The twin theory of instinct and sexuality as
epistemologico-political task of psychiatry. ~ The origins of sexual
psychopathology (Heinrich Kaan). ~ Etiology of madness on the
basis of the history of the sexual instinct and imagination. ~ The
case of the soldier Bertrand.*

I WOULD LIKE TO return to a number of things that I did not have
time to deal with last week. It seems to me that the sexuality of the
child and adolescent is posed as a problem in the eighteenth century.
Initially it is posed in a nonrelational form, that is to say, it is the
problem of autoeroticism and masturbation that is posed first of all;
masturbation is hunted down and put forward as the major danger.
From then on, bodies, actions, attitudes, appearance, facial features,
beds, linen, stains, and so forth are brought under surveillance. Parents are required to hunt for odors, traces, and signs. I think that this
represents the installation, the establishment of one of the new forms
of relations between parents and children: a kind of extensive parent

child physical clinch begins that does not seem to me to be characteristic of every family but only of a certain form of the family in the modern period.

It is clear that in this development the Christian flesh is transposed into the family element. It is a transposition in the strict sense in that there is a local and spatial displacement of the confessional: The problem of the flesh has moved to the bed. There is not only transposition but also transformation and above all reduction, inasmuch as all the strictly Christian complexity of spiritual direction, which put into play notions such as incitements, titillations, desires, connivance, delight, voluptuous pleasures, et cetera, is now reduced to a single, very simple problem of the hand's action, of the relation between hand and body, to the simple question: Do they touch themselves? However, at the same time as the Christian flesh is reduced to this extraordinarily simple and, as it were, skeletal problem, there are also three transformations. First of all, there is a transition to somatization: the problem of the flesh tends increasingly to become the problem of the body, of the physical and sick body. Second, there is infantilization in the sense that the problem of the flesh, which was after all the problem of every Christian, even if it was centered with some insistence on adolescence, is now essentially organized around infantile or adolescent sexuality or autoeroticism. Third and finally, there is medicalization, since henceforth the problem is referred to a form of control and rationality that medical knowledge and power is asked to provide. All the ambiguous and proliferating discourse of sin is reduced to the announcement and prognosis of a physical danger and to all the material precautions for avoiding it.

What I tried to show last week is that the hunting down of masturbation does not seem to me to be the result of the constitution of the restricted, cellular, substantial, and conjugal family. Far from being the result of the constitution of this new type of family, it seems to me that the hunting down of masturbation was rather the instrument of this constitution. It was through this crusade that the nuclear and substantial family was gradually constituted. The crusade, with all its practical instructions, was a means of compressing family relationships and closing up the central parent-child rectangle into a substantial, close-knit, and emotionally saturated unit. One way to coagulate the conjugal family was to make parents responsible for their children's bodies, for the life and death of their children, by means of an autoeroticism that had been rendered fantastically dangerous in and by medical discourse.

In short, I would like to reject the linear progression that goes from the constitution of the conjugal family for economic reasons, to the interdiction of sexuality within this family, to the pathological return of this sexuality and neurosis due to the interdiction and finally to the consequent problematization of infantile sexuality. This is the schema that is usually accepted. It seems to me that we should instead consider a series of elements that are linked together in a circular fashion and in which a value is attached to the child's body, his life is given an economic and an affective value, a fear is created around this body, and a fear is installed around sexuality as source of the dangers incurred by the child and his body; the simultaneous blaming and responsibilization of parents and children with regard to this body, setting out an obligatory, statutory closeness between parents and children; the consequent organization of a restricted and close-knit family space; and the infiltration of sexuality throughout this space and its encirclement by medical controls or, at least, by a medical rationality. It seems to me that it was on the basis of these processes and their circular concatenation that the conjugal, nuclear, and quadrangular family of parents and children, characteristic of at least part of our society, ultimately crystallized.

Starting from this, I would like to make two comments.

The first is that if we accept this schema that the problematization of the child's sexuality was originally connected to the contact established between the bodies of parents and children, to the folding of the parents' bodies over the children's bodies, you can see why the theme of incest assumed such intensity at the end of the nineteenth century, that is to say, why it was accepted both with such difficulty and so easily. It was difficult to accept precisely because, since the end of the eighteenth century, it had been said, explained, and profusely portrayed that the child's sexuality was first of all an autoerotic and consequently nonrelational sexuality that could not be superimposed on a sexual relationship between individuals. Moreover, this nonrelational sexuality entirely sealed off in the child's own body could not be superimposed on an adult type of sexuality. It was clearly very difficult to take up this sexuality and insert it in an incestuous relationship with adults and to bring child and adult sexuality back into contact or continuity with each other from the angle of incest, or of child-parent incestuous desire. It was difficult for parents to accept that they were beset and invested by their children's incestuous desire when they had been reassured for one hundred years [by the fact] that children's sexuality was entirely localized, sealed off, and locked up within autoeroticism. However, from another angle, we could say that the crusade against masturbation in which this new fear of incest is inscribed to a certain extent made it easy for parents to accept the idea that their children desire them, and desire them incestuously.

This easiness, alongside or intertwined with the difficulty, can be explained and accounted for fairly easily. From the middle of the eighteenth century, from around 1750-1760, what were parents told? Apply your bodies to the bodies of your children; observe your children; get close to your children; possibly get in bed with your children; slide between their sheets; observe, spy on, and surprise all the signs of your children's desire; come stealthily to their bed at night, lift up their sheets, see what they are doing, and put your hand there, at least to stop them. And now, after having been told this for one hundred years, they are told: This formidable desire you have uncovered—in the material sense of the word—is directed toward you. The most formidable thing about this desire is precisely that it concerns you.

A number of consequences follow from this, three of which are, I think, essential. First, you can see that the relationship of incestuous indiscretion between parents and children that had been organized for more than a century is, as it were, inverted. For more than a century parents had been told to get close to their children: A conduct of incestuous indiscretion had been dictated to them. Now, after a century, they are exonerated of precisely the guilt they may well have felt about actively discovering their children's desiring bodies. They are told: Do not be anxious, it is not you who is incestuous. The incest is not directed from you to them, from your indiscretion or curiosity about their bodies exposed by you. Rather, the incest goes from them to you, since it is they who have desired you from the start. Consequently, precisely at the point at which the incestuous child-parent relation is etiologically saturated, parents are morally exonerated of the incestuous indiscretion, approach, and closeness to which they had been constrained for more than a century. This, then, is the first moral benefit that makes the psychoanalytic theory of incest acceptable.

Second, you can see that parents are given a supplementary guarantee since they are not only told that the sexual body of their children belongs to them by right, that they are to watch over it, supervise it, control it, and surprise it, but they are also told that it belongs to them at an even deeper level since their children's desire is addressed to them. So not only is the child's body in some sense their material possession, but even more they also control the child's desire, which is available to them because it is directed toward them. This supplementary guarantee given to parents may correspond to the family being further dispossessed of the child's body when the extension of schooling and procedures of disciplinary training at the end of the nineteenth century detaches children even more from the family milieu. All this should be examined more closely. However, there was a real reappropriation of the child's sexuality through the assertion that the child's desire is directed toward its parents. It was thereby possible to relax the control of masturbation without children [*rectius:* parents] losing possession of their children's sexuality since infantile desire was directed at them.

The third reason why, despite some difficulties, the theory of incest could, on the whole, be accepted was that by placing such a terrible offense at the very heart of the parent-child relationship, by making the absolute crime of incest the point of origin of every little abnormality, one strengthened the urgency of external intervention, of a kind of mediating element of analysis, control, and correction. In short, one strengthened the chances of medical technology getting a hold on the cluster of relationships within the family; the family was more effectively plugged in to medical power. Broadly speaking, the theory of incest that appeared at the end of the nineteenth century involved a kind of formidable gratification for parents who henceforth knew themselves to be the object of a mad desire and who, at the same time, discovered through this theory that they themselves could be the subject of a rational knowledge concerning their relationships with their children: I no longer have to discover what the child desires by going to his bedroom at night and peering under his sheets like a dubious domestic. I know what he desires from a scientific knowledge that is authentic because it is a medical knowledge. I am therefore both a subject of this knowledge and the object of this mad desire. This enables us to see how—with psychoanalysis, from the beginning of the twentieth century—parents could become (and how willingly!) the zealous, excited, and delighted agents of a new wave in the medical normalization of the family. I think, then, that the functioning of the theme of incest should be situated in the century-old practice of the crusade against masturbation. In the end, it is an episode, or in any case a turning point, in this crusade.

The second comment I want to make is that what I have just said is certainly not valid for society in general or for every type of family. As I pointed out last week, the crusade against masturbation addressed itself almost exclusively to the bourgeois family. Now, at the time when the crusade against masturbation was at its peak a completely different campaign was developing alongside it, but without any direct connection with it. This campaign was addressed to the working-class family or, more precisely, to the family of the urban proletariat that was then being formed. This other crusade, somewhat out of phase with the first (the first began more or less around 1760 and the second at the turn of the century, right at the start of the nineteenth century, blossoming around 1820-1840), is directed at the urban proletarian family and has quite different themes. To start with, its theme is not: Apply your bodies directly to your child's body. Nor, obviously, is it: Get rid of all those servants and usual inter- mediaries who get in the way of, disturb, and upset your relationship with your children. The campaign is quite simply: Get married. Do not have children first only to abandon them later. The whole cam- paign is directed against free unions, against concubinage, and against extra- or parafamilial fluidity.

I do not want to take up the analysis of this, which would no doubt be very difficult and lengthy, but will simply suggest some hypotheses that are currently generally accepted by most historians. Until the eighteenth century, generally speaking, the rule of marriage was strongly respected in the countryside and in the urban popula- tion, even by the poor. There were surprisingly few free unions and natural children. What was the reason for this? No doubt it was due to ecclesiastical control, to a social control, and perhaps to a certain extent also to judicial control. Probably, and more profoundly, it was due to the fact that even among relatively poor people marriage was linked to a system of property exchange. In any case it was linked to the maintenance or transformation of social status. It was also linked to the pressure of communal forms of life in villages, parishes, and so forth. In short, marriage was not just the religious or legal sanction of a sexual relationship. Ultimately, it involved the individual's entire social character along with its ties.

Now it is clear that with the formation and development of an urban proletariat at the beginning of the nineteenth century all these raisons d'être for marriage, all these supports of marriage and the ties and weights that gave it its solidity and necessity, lose their point. A kind of extramatrimonial sexuality develops that is perhaps not so much linked to an explicit revolt against the obligation to marry as to the pure and simple acknowledgment that marriage, with its system of obligations and its institutional and material supports, no longer has a raison d'être when one is part of a floating population waiting or looking for precarious and transitory work in a temporary stopping place. There is, then, the development of free unions in working-class milieus. (There are a number of indications of this and in any case many protests are expressed on the subject in the period 1820-1840.)

Under certain conditions and at certain times the bourgeoisie clearly found advantages in this fragile, episodic, and transitory character of marriage, if only because it supported the mobility of labor. However, the time soon arrived when the stability of the working class became necessary for economic reasons and also for reasons of spatial partitioning and political control to prevent mobility and agitation, et cetera. Hence, for whatever reasons, a broad campaign around marriage got under way in the period 1820-1840. It was conducted by means of pure and simple propaganda (the publication of books, et cetera), by economic pressure and the creation of charitable organizations (which gave aid only to those legitimately married), and through mechanisms like the savings banks, housing policy, and so on. This "matchmaking" campaign for the consolidation of marriage was accompanied and to a certain extent corrected by another campaign that was expressed in these terms: You must be very careful within this close-knit family space that you have been required to establish and within which you must remain in a stable fashion. Do not mix but lay down divisions and create the greatest possible space so that contact between you is reduced to the minimum and family relationships within this space are always clearly specified according to differences between individuals, age, and sex. There is a campaign against shared bedrooms, against parents and children, and children "of a different sex," sharing the same bed. Ultimately, the ideal is one bed per person. The ideal in the workers' cities being planned at this time is the well-known small house with three rooms: a living room for all, a room for the parents and a room for the children, or even a room for the parents and a room for boys and a room for girls.[1] So, there is no close physical contact and no mixing. This campaign is nothing like the campaign against masturbation with its theme: Get close to your children, establish contact with them, observe their bodies closely. Rather, its theme is: Distribute bodies with the greatest possible distance between them. You can see that a different problematization of incest appears in the trajectory of this new campaign. It does not concern the danger formulated by psychoanalysis of incest coming from children. Rather, it concerns the danger of incest between brother and sister and between father and daughter. The essential thing is to prevent the promiscuity between parents and offspring and between the older and younger that could make incest possible.

So, the two campaigns, the two mechanisms, and the two fears of incest that take shape in the nineteenth century are quite different. Of course, it is clear that although the campaign for the constitution of the coagulated and emotionally intense bourgeois family around the child's sexuality and the campaign for the distribution and consolidation of the working-class family do not exactly converge, they do finally arrive at a certain form of family that is exchangeable between, or common to, both. We arrive at what could be called a kind of interclass family model. It is the model of the little cell of parents and children whose elements are differentiated but strongly interdependent and which are both bound together and threatened by incest. However, I think that beneath this common form, which is only the envelope or abstract shell, there are in fact two quite different processes. On one side there is the process I spoke about last week: the process of drawing closer together and coagulation that makes it possible to define a small intense cell grouped around the child's dangerously sexualized body within the network of the large family possessing status and goods. Then, on the other side, there is the different process of the stabilization and distribution of sexual relationships: the establishment of an optimal distance around what is considered to be a dangerous adult sexuality. In one case, the child's sexuality is dangerous and calls for the coagulation of the family; in the other case, adult sexuality is thought to be dangerous and calls instead for the optimal distribution of the family.

Thus we have two processes of formation, two ways of organizing the cellular family around the danger of sexuality, two ways of obtaining the formidable and indispensable sexualization of the family space, two ways of picking out within it the cornerstone of an authoritarian intervention, or rather of an authoritarian intervention that is different in the two cases. The dangerous sexualization of the family based on the child's sexuality evidently calls for a medical form of external intervention, for a medical type of external rationality that must enter the family and arbitrate, control, and correct its internal relationships. Medical intervention and rationality must respond to the dangers of an infantile sexuality on which parents focus their attention. In the other case, the sexuality, or rather, the sexualization of the family based on the dangerous and incestuous appetite of parents or older children, sexualization around a possible incest coming from above, from the older members of the family, also calls for the intervention of an external power of arbitration or rather decision. However, in this case it is a judicial, rather than a medical, type of intervention. It is the judge or the gendarme or all their modern substitutes, the bodies of so-called social control that have developed since the beginning of the twentieth century, social workers and other personnel, who must intervene in the family in order to avoid the danger of incest coming from parents or older members of the family. There are, then, many formal analogies, but the processes are really fundamentally different: In one case there is a necessary appeal to medicine and in the other a necessary appeal to the court, judge, and police, et cetera.

In any case, we should not forget the simultaneous appearance of these two mechanisms or institutional bodies at the end of the nineteenth century. Psychoanalysis appears as the technique for dealing with infantile incest and all its disturbing effects in the family space. Then, appearing at the same time as psychoanalysis but on the basis of the second process I have just described, there are the institutions for the spatial partitioning of working-class families whose essential function is not to manage children's incestuous desires but rather, as we say, to "protect children in danger," that is to say, to protect them from the incestuous desire of the father and mother, and to withdraw them from the family milieu. In the first case, psychoanalysis will place desire within the family (and you know who has shown this better than I),[2] but in the second case, symmetrical with the first and at exactly the same time, there was this other, equally real operation that consisted in withdrawing the child from the family on the basis of the fear of adult incest.

We could perhaps take this identification of two different forms of incest and two corresponding sets of institutions further. We could perhaps say that there are also two radically different theories of incest. One presents incest as the destiny of desire bound up with the child's development and says quietly to parents: Be quite sure that your children are thinking of you when they touch themselves. The other is the sociological, rather than psychoanalytic, theory of incest that describes the prohibition of incest as a social necessity, as the condition of exchanges and goods, and which quietly tells parents: Above all, do not touch your children. You will gain nothing from it and in truth you will lose a great deal—because it is only the structure of exchange that defines and structures the whole of the social body. We could thus amuse ourselves by identifying the play of these two forms of the institutionalization of incest, of the procedures for avoiding it and of ways of theorizing it. In any case, I would like to stress the ultimately abstract and academic nature of any general theory of incest and, in particular, of that kind of ethnopsychoanalytic attempt to connect the prohibition of adult incest with the incestuous desire of children. I would like to show the abstract nature of any theory that amounts to saying that, in the end, it is because children desire their parents too much that we must prohibit parents from touching their children. There have been two types of constitution of the cellular family, two types of definition of incest, two descriptions of the fear of incest, and two clusters of institutions around this fear. I am not saying that there are two sexualities, one bourgeois and the other proletarian (or working class), but I would say that there have been two modes of the sexualization of the family or two modes of the familialization of sexuality, two family spaces of sexuality and sexual prohibition.[3] No theory can validly pass over this duality.

This, then, is how I would have liked to extend last week's lecture. I would like to go back now and try to bring together some comments on sexuality and what I said concerning instinct and the character of the monster, since I think that the character of the abnormal individual, who acquires his full status and scale at the end of the nineteenth century, has in fact two or three antecedents. His genealogy includes the judicial monster whom I have spoken about, the little masturbator, whom I have been talking about in the last sessions, and the third, the undisciplined individual, about whom unhappily I have not been able to talk (but you will see that this is not too important). Anyway, I would like now to try to see how the problematic of the monster and instinct and the problematic of the masturbator and infantile sexuality are brought together.

I will try to show the formation of a meshing together of the psychiatric and the judicial that took place on the basis of the monster, or of the problem of the motiveless criminal. In this meshing together, and on the basis of it, three things appeared that are, I think, important. First, there is the definition of a field common to criminality and madness. It is a confused, complex, and reversible field since it seemed that there might well be something like mad behavior behind every crime and, conversely, that there might well be the risk of crime in all madness. Consequently, it is a field of objects common to crime and madness. Second, on the basis of this common field there appears the need for, if not yet an institution exactly, then at least a medico-judicial authority represented by the psychiatrist who already begins to be an expert in criminal matters. The psychiatrist is in principle the only person who can make the distinction between crime and madness and judge what is dangerous in any madness. Third and finally, as a privileged concept of this field of objects covered by psychiatric power, there appeared the notion of instinct understood as an irresistible drive, as behavior that is either normally integrated or abnormally displaced on the axis of the voluntary and the involuntary: This is Baillarger's principle.[4]

Now what do we see if we take up the other connection or genealogical line that I then tried to follow? Starting with the sins of the flesh, another meshing together appears in the eighteenth century, but of psychiatry and the family rather than of the psychiatric and the judicial. This meshing together is not generated by the great mon-

ster but by the everyday character of the adolescent masturbator rendered fantastically monstrous or, at least, dangerous, to fit the needs
of the cause. What appears in this organization and on the basis of
this mesh? First of all, as I said last week, the essential affinity of
sexuality with illness or, more precisely, of masturbation with the
general etiology of illness. In the field of etiology, in the domain of
the causes of illness, sexuality, at least in the form of masturbation,
appears as both a constant and frequent element. It is a constant
element inasmuch as it is found everywhere, but in actual fact it is
random inasmuch as masturbation may provoke any illness whatsoever. Second, this mesh also reveals the need for recourse to a medical
authority for intervention and rationalization within the family space.
Finally, throughout this common domain of illness and masturbation
delegated to medical knowledge-power there is an element whose
concept is being worked out at this time: This is the notion of a
sexual "tendency" or "instinct," of a sexual instinct that by virtue of
its fragility is destined to escape the heterosexual and exogamous
norm. So, on one side, psychiatry is linked up with judicial power.
Psychiatry owes this interlocking with judicial power to the problematic of the irresistible drive and the appearance of the sphere of instinctive mechanisms as a privileged domain of objects. It owes its
symmetrical interlocking with familial power, which takes place along
a different genealogical line, to the different problematic of sexuality
and its irregularities.

I think two consequences follow from this. The first is, of course,
a tremendous extension of the domain of possible psychiatric intervention. Last year I tried to show how, limited to what was traditionally its specific domain of intervention—mental alienation,
dementia, and delirium—psychiatry* was constituted within the asylum as the government of the mad by putting to work a certain
technology of power.[5] This psychiatry now locks in to a completely
different domain that is no longer the government of the mad but

---

* The French has *madness (folie)*, but the sense of the sentence makes it clear that this should
be *psychiatry*. Trans.

rather control of the family and necessary intervention in the penal domain. This is a tremendous extension: On one side psychiatry has to take responsibility for the whole field of offenses and irregularities with regard to the law, and then, on the other, on the basis of its technology for the government of the mad, it has to take responsibility for irregularities within the family. From the little sovereignty of the family up to the general and solemn form of the law, psychiatry must now appear and function as a technology of the individual that is indispensable to the functioning of the principal mechanisms of power. It becomes one of the internal operational elements found equally or commonly in apparatuses of power as different as the family and the judicial system, in the relationship between parents and children, and in the relationship between the State and the individual, in the management of conflicts within the family as in the control or analysis of breaches of legal constraints. As a general technology of individuals it is eventually found wherever there is power: in the family, school, workshop, court, prison, and so on.

At the same time as its field of intervention is undergoing this tremendous extension, psychiatry is confronted with a completely new task. Psychiatry cannot really perform this general, omnipresent, or polyvalent function unless it can organize a unified field of instinct and sexuality. Now if it really wants to cover this whole domain, whose limits I have tried to show, if it really wants to function within the psychiatric-familial mesh and the psychiatric-judicial mesh, it has to demonstrate the intertwined play of instinct and sexuality. Indeed, it has to show that the sexual instinct is an element in the formation of every mental illness and, even more generally, in the formation of every behavioral disorder, from major offenses that violate the most important laws to tiny irregularities that disturb the little family cell. In short, it must constitute not only a discourse, but also methods of analysis, concepts, and theories such that within psychiatry, and without going outside it, it is possible to pass from infantile autoeroticism to murder, from discreet and caressing incest to the voracity of monstrous cannibals. This is the task facing psychiatry from around 1840-1850 (picking up the thread I left at Baillarger). At the end of the nineteenth century the problem is to constitute an instinct-sexuality, desire-madness, pleasure-crime coupling so that the great monsters who loom up at the limit of the judicial apparatus can be reduced, dispersed, analyzed, rendered commonplace, and given toned-down profiles within family relationships while the little masturbators who warm up in the family nest can become, through geneses, enlargements, and successive slippages, the mad criminals who rape, cut up, and devour their victims. How is this unification brought about? In other words, how is the twin theory of instinct and sexuality developed as the epistemologico-political task of psychiatry from around 1840-1850? This is what I would now like to talk about.

The unification takes place first of all through a decompartmentalization of masturbation with regard to other sexual irregularities. You recall that last week I stressed the fact that masturbation could become the major concern of the family cell essentially because it had been separated from all the other forms of discredited or condemned sexual conduct. I tried to show you how masturbation was always defined as something very separate and singular. It was so singular that it was defined as not arising from the instinct or mechanism found in normal, relational, and heterosexual sexuality (theorists at the end of the eighteenth century insisted that the mechanisms of infantile masturbation were quite different from those of adult sexuality). Also, this sexuality was not linked in its effects to a general immorality or even with sexual immorality or irregularity: Its effects manifested themselves in the field of somatic pathology. It was a physical sanction, a physiological and even an anatomopathological sanction that was ultimately produced by masturbation as the origin of illness. I would say that there was as little sexuality as possible in masturbation as it was defined, analyzed, and hunted down in the eighteenth century. We can no doubt say that this was the highlight of the crusade. Parents were told: Deal with your children's masturbation and be sure that you will not affect their sexuality.

Now when nineteenth-century psychiatry undertakes covering the huge domain that goes from irregularities in the family to breaches of the law, its task is not to isolate masturbation but rather to link together all irregularities, both within and outside the family. Psychiatry has to draw up and set out the genealogical table of every sexual disorder. At this point we find the major nineteenth-century treatises on sexual psychopathology as the first realization of this task, the first being, as you know, Heinrich Kaan's *Psychopathia sexualis* published in Leipzig in 1844. (As far as I am aware it is the first treatise of psychiatry to speak only of sexual psychopathology but the last to speak of sexuality in Latin. Sadly, it has never been translated into French, although, so far as my knowledge of Latin is still up to it, it is a very interesting text.) What do we find in this treatise? In Heinrich Kaan's *Psychopathia sexualis* we find the following theme that places the book very clearly within the theory of sexuality of the time. This theme is the fact that human sexuality, through its mechanisms and general forms, is inscribed within the natural history of a sexuality that can be followed back to plants. It is the assertion of a sexual instinct—*nisus sexualis*, according to the text—that we cannot call the psychic manifestation, but let us say is simply the dynamic manifestation of the functioning of the sexual organs. Just as there is a feeling, an impression, a dynamic of hunger that corresponds to the apparatus of nutrition, so there is a sexual instinct that corresponds to the functioning of the sexual organs. This is both a very marked naturalization of human sexuality and its principle of generalization.

For this instinct, this *nisus sexualis* described by Kaan, copulation, that is to say, the relational, heterosexual sexual act, is both natural and normal. But, Kaan says, it is not enough to determine completely, or rather, canalize completely the force and dynamism of this instinct. The sexual instinct overflows its natural end and it does so naturally. In other words, the instinct is normally excessive and partially marginal with regard to copulation.[6] This overflowing of the force of the sexual instinct with regard to its purpose of copulation is shown and empirically proven by a number of things, essentially by the sexuality of children and principally by the sexuality manifested in their games. Although their sexual organs may still be at a very early stage of development and the sexual *nisus* has not acquired its full force, we notice nonetheless that children's games are in fact very clearly sexually polarized. Girls' games and boys' games are not the same, which proves that the entire behavior of children, including their games, is supported and underpinned by a sexual *nisus,* a sexual instinct, which is already specified even though the organic apparatus it must drive and through which it must pass in order to lead to copulation may still be far from ready. The existence of this sexual *nisus* is also seen in the completely different area of curiosity rather than play. Thus, Kaan says, seven- or eight-year-old children are already not only very curious about their own sexual organs but also about those of other children of both their own and the opposite sex. Anyway, in the functioning of the mind itself, in this desire to know that drives children, and which also makes education possible, there is the presence, the work of the sexual instinct. The liveliness and most dynamic aspect of the sexual instinct thus go far beyond pure and simple copulation: It begins before and goes beyond copulation.[7]

Of course, this sexual instinct is by nature finalized and focused on copulation.[8] But as copulation is only its chronologically final end, so to speak, you can see why this instinct is naturally fragile: It is much too lively, precocious, and wide, and it too easily passes through the whole organism and conduct of individuals to be able really to lodge and take place solely in adult heterosexual copulation. For that reason, Kaan explains, it is susceptible to a series of abnormalities; it is always in danger of deviating from the norm. The set of these both natural and abnormal aberrations constitute the domain of *psychopathia sexualis* and this was how Heinrich Kaan established the dynasty of the different sexual aberrations that, according to him, constitute a unified domain.[9] He lists them: there is *onania* (onanism); there is pederasty, loving prepubescent children; there is what he calls lesbian love, which is the love of a man or woman, it does not matter which, for someone of the same sex; the violation of corpses; bestiality; and then a sixth aberration.[10] In general, in all the treatises on sexual psychopathology there is always a small detail. . . . I think it was Krafft-Ebing who found that one of the worst sexual aberrations was that of men who cut off the pigtails of young girls in the street with a pair of scissors. This, then, is an obsession![11] Some years earlier,

Heinrich Kaan found a sexual aberration that is very important and that greatly worried him. It consists of making love to statues. In any case, this is the first great global dynasty of sexual aberrations. Now, in this general domain of *psychopathia sexualis*, onanism—which, as you can see, figures as one of these aberrations and is therefore only one element in this general class—plays a quite specific role and has a completely privileged place. Where in fact do the other perversions, those that are not onanism, come from? How can such deviations from the natural act arise? Well, the agent of deviation is imagination, what Kaan calls *phantasia*, morbid imagination. This is what creates the desire prematurely, or rather, imagination, driven by premature desires, looks for additional, derivative, or substitute means of satisfaction. As he says in his text, *phantasia*, imagination, prepares the way for all the sexual aberrations. Consequently, sexually abnormal individuals always come from those who used a sexually polarized imagination in onanism and masturbation when they were children.[12]

It seems to me that although to some extent Heinrich Kaan's analysis may seem a bit crude, it nonetheless contains a number of points that are very important in the history of the psychiatric problematization of sexuality. The first is that it is natural for the instinct to be abnormal. Second, this discrepancy between the instinct's naturalness and normality, or even the intrinsic and confused link between the instinct's naturalness and abnormality, appears in a privileged and determining way at the time of childhood. The third important theme is the privileged link that exists between the sexual instinct and *phantasia* or imagination. Whereas instinct was at this time essentially invoked as the support of habitual, irresistible, and automatic actions unaccompanied by thoughts or representations, the sexual instinct actually described by Heinrich Kaan is strictly linked to imagination. It is imagination that opens up to it the space in which it will be able to develop its abnormal nature. The effects of the uncoupling of nature and normality are revealed in the imagination, and it is on this basis that the imagination serves as the intermediary or relay of the causal and pathological effectiveness of the sexual instinct.[13]

Broadly speaking, we can say that psychiatry discovers instinct at the same time, but (remember what I said three or four weeks ago) this instinct is really an alternative to delirium. Where delirium cannot be found, the silent and automatic mechanisms of instinct have to be invoked. However, what Heinrich Kaan discovers through the sexual instinct is an instinct that, although it does not belong to the order of delirium, nonetheless brings with it a particular intense, privileged, and constant relationship with the imagination. It is the reciprocal work of the instinct on the imagination and of the imagination on the instinct, their coupling and interaction, that makes it possible to establish continuity between the mechanism of the instinct and the meaningful unfolding of delirium. In other words, the insertion of the imagination into the instinctual system by way of the sexual instinct is crucial for the analytic fruitfulness of psychiatric notions.

Finally, it should be stressed that Kaan's book also contains what I consider to be a fundamental thesis. This is that, on the basis of this mechanism of the instinct and the imagination, the sexual instinct is at the origin of more than just somatic disorders. In his book, Heinrich Kaan still drags along all the old etiologies I talked about last week, according to which, for example, hemiplegia, general paralysis, and brain tumors may all be the result of excessive masturbation. We still find this in his book, but there is also something that was not found in the crusade against masturbation: Masturbation in itself may entail a series of disorders that are precisely both sexual and psychiatric. A unified field of sexual abnormality is organized within the field of psychiatry. The book was written in 1844, so you can see where it is situated. This is more or less the same time that Prichard writes his famous book on moral madness, which does not exactly put an end to the theory of mental alienation centered on delirium but at least marks a halt in its development: A series of nondelirious behavior disorders enter the psychiatric field.[14] Eighteen forty-four is also more or less the time when Griesinger is laying the foundations of neuropsychiatry in accordance with the general rule that the explanatory and analytical principles of mental illness should be the same as those for neurological disorders.[15] It is also the period in which Baillarger, about whom I have spoken, established the primacy of the voluntary-involuntary axis over the old privilege previously accorded to delirium.[16] Broadly speaking, then, 1844-1845 marks the end of the alienists; it is the beginning of a psychiatry, or of a neuropsychiatry, that is organized around drives, instincts, and automatisms. It is also the date that marks the end of the fable of masturbation or, at least, the emergence of a psychiatry, of an analysis of sexuality that pinpoints a sexual instinct present in all behavior, from masturbation to normal behavior. It is the period in which Heinrich Kaan constitutes a psychiatric genealogy of sexual aberrations. It is the moment when, still with this same book, the primordial and etiological role of the imagination, or rather of the imagination coupled with instinct, is defined. Finally, it is the moment at which the infantile phases of the history of the instincts and the imagination take on a determining value in the etiology of illness, and specifically of mental illness. With Heinrich Kaan's book we have then what could be called the date of birth, or in any case the date of the emergence, of sexuality and sexual aberrations in the psychiatric field.

However, this was, I think, only a first step: decompartmentalization of the masturbation that had been so strongly emphasized and at the same time marginalized by the crusade I talked about last week. Decompartmentalization: Masturbation is linked up with the sexual instinct in general, with the imagination and thereby with the whole field of aberrations and finally with illnesses. However, the second task or maneuver carried out by psychiatry from the middle of the nineteenth century is the definition of a kind of supplementary power that will give the sexual instinct a quite specific role in the genesis of disorders that are not sexual disorders: the constitution of an etiology of madness or mental illness on the basis of the history of the sexual instinct and the imagination linked to it. It becomes necessary to get rid of the old etiology I talked about last week—the etiology of the body's exhaustion, the desiccation of the nervous system, and so forth—and to find the specific mechanism of the sexual instinct and its abnormalities. There are a number of theoretical expressions or assertions of this etiological enhancement or supplementary causality that is attributed to the sexual instinct in an always more pronounced manner. Heinrich Kaan, for example, says: "The sexual instinct controls all mental and physical life." However, I would like for the moment to consider in particular a precise case that shows how the mechanism of the sexual instinct is shifted with respect to the mechanism of all the other instincts so as to get it to play this fundamental etiological role.

It is the story of the soldier Bertrand that took place between 1847 and 1849.[17] Prior to these last weeks I classified this story under the category of cases of monomania, the notorious cases of which were, for example, Henriette Cornier, Léger, Papavoine, and so on. I think I may even have placed it as taking place around 1830,[18] and I apologize if this is the case. The events actually took place in 1847-1849. In any case, whether or not I made a chronological error, I think I have made a historical, epistemological error, as you will see. For this story, at least in many of its vicissitudes, has a quite different configuration from the Cornier case I talked about five or six weeks ago. One day the soldier Bertrand was surprised desecrating graves in the Montparnasse cemetery. He was caught in 1849 but in fact had been committing desecrations in provincial cemeteries or cemeteries in the Paris region since 1847. When these desecrations increased and assumed a very ostentatious character, an ambush was set and one evening, in May 1849, I think, Bertrand was wounded by the gendarmes keeping watch and took refuge in the Val de Grâce hospital (since he was a soldier), where he spontaneously confessed to the doctors. He confessed that from time to time since 1847, at regular or irregular intervals, but not continually, he had been seized by the desire to dig up graves, open the coffins, take out the corpses, cut them up with his bayonet, pull out the intestines and organs, and then spread them around, hanging them from the crosses and cypress branches in a huge garland. While recounting this Bertrand did not draw attention to the fact that there were considerably more female than male corpses among those he desecrated in this way (I think there were only one or two men, all the others, fifteen of them, were the corpses of women and especially of young girls). Attracted and disturbed by this feature of the case, the doctors or examining magistrates called for an examination of the remains. It was noticed that there was evidence that the corpses, which were all, moreover, in a very advanced state of decomposition, had been sexually violated.

What happened at this point? Bertrand himself and his first doctor (a military doctor called Marchal, who provided the expert opinion to the military court that had to judge Betrand) present matters in the following way.[19] They say this (Bertrand speaking in the first person, Marchal in the terminology of an alienist): "What started it all, what came first, was the desire to desecrate the graves; the desire to destroy those corpses that were already destroyed."[20] As Marchal says in his terminology, Bertrand suffers from a "destructive monomania." This destructive monomania was a typical monomania since it was a matter of destroying something that was already in an advanced state of decomposition. This tearing to shreds of bodies already half decomposed was destructive rage in the pure state, so to speak. Once this destructive monomania was established, Marchal explains, the soldier Bertrand was gripped by a second monomania that was somehow grafted onto the first and guaranteed its specifically pathological character. This second monomania is the "erotic monomania" that consists in using corpses, or the remains of corpses, for sexual enjoyment.[21] Marchal makes an interesting comparison with another case from some months or years earlier. This involved a mentally retarded person who was confined in the Troyes hospital and who performed some domestic chores and had access to the morgue. In the morgue he satisfied his sexual needs on the corpses of women.[22] Now, Marchal says, in a case like this there is no erotic monomania because we are dealing with someone who has sexual needs. He cannot satisfy these sexual needs on the live hospital personnel, and no one wants to help or assist him. In the end, there are only the corpses and so the natural and, as it were, rational mechanism of interests leads him quite naturally to violate the corpses. In this sense the mentally retarded individual cannot be regarded as suffering from an erotic monomania. The soldier Bertrand, on the other hand, who began to manifest his pathological condition with a mania for destruction, grafts this other symptom, his erotic monomania, onto the destructive monomania, even though he could very well satisfy his sexual needs quite normally. He is young, he is not deformed, and he has money. Why does he not find a girl in order to satisfy his needs normally? Consequently, using terms taken from Esquirol's analytic terminology, Marchal is able to attribute Bertrand's sexual behavior to monomania, or to the erotic offshoot of a monomania that is fundamentally destructive.

Actually, it is in fact absolutely clear that at the level of the clinical picture the destructive symptoms significantly outnumber the erotic symptoms. Now in 1849, in the journal *L'Union médicale*, a psychiatrist, Michéa, puts forward an opposite analysis in which he undertakes to show that it is the "erotic monomania" that is at the center of Bertrand's pathology, and that the "destructive monomania" is really only a derivative of a monomania or illness of what is called at this time the "generative" instinct.[23] Michéa's analysis is quite interesting. He begins by showing that it is in no way a case of delirium, and he establishes a difference between vampirism and the Bertrand case. What is vampirism? Vampirism, he says, is a delirium in which someone living believes, as in a nightmare ("It is a diurnal variety of nightmare," he says), that the dead, or a particular category of the dead, leave their graves to attack the living.[24] Bertrand is the opposite. First of all, he is not delirious, and furthermore, he is not a vampire at all. He is not absorbed in the delirious theme of the vampire since he is rather a reverse vampire. He is a living being who haunts the dead and, to a certain extent, sucks their blood: consequently there is no trace of delirious belief. We are therefore dealing with a case of madness without delirium. Up to this point, there is agreement. However, in this madness without delirium there are two sets of symptoms: the destructive and the erotic. Despite eroticism having little symptomatological importance, for Michéa eroticism plays the most important role. To be sure, Michéa does not produce a genealogy of symptoms on the basis of eroticism, and no doubt he did not possess the conceptual or analytic framework that would have enabled him to do this. He posits the general principle, however, the general framework of a possible genealogy.[25] He says, the sexual instinct is anyway the most important and "most compelling of the needs that motivate man and the animals."[26] So in purely quantitative terms, in terms of the dynamic or economy of the instincts, whenever there is any instinctual disorder one should look to the sexual instinct as a possible cause because, of all the instincts, it is the most impetuous, the most compelling, and the most wide ranging. Now, he says, this sexual instinct manages to satisfy itself, or at any rate produces pleasure, in more and quite different ways than by just those acts that ensure the propagation of the species.[27] That is to say, for Michéa, there is a lack of fit between pleasure and the act of fertilization that is absolutely essential and natural to the sexual instinct. He sees proof of this in the masturbation of children even before puberty and in the pleasure of women when they are pregnant or after the menopause, that is to say, at a time when they can no longer be fertilized.[28]

So, the instinct is uncoupled from the act of fertilization by the fact that essentially it produces a pleasure that can be actualized anywhere and by countless actions. The act of generation or reproduction is just one of the forms in which pleasure, the economic principle intrinsic to the sexual instinct, is in fact satisfied or produced. For that reason, as producer of a pleasure not intrinsically linked to generation, the sexual instinct can give rise to a series of behaviors that are not governed by generation. Michéa lists "Greek love," "bestiality," "attraction to a naturally insensitive object," "attraction to the human corpse" (the attraction of destruction, of someone's death, et cetera), as producers of "pleasure."[29] Thus the strength of the sexual instinct makes it the most important and consequently dominant instinct in the general economy of the instincts. However, as a pleasure-producing principle (producing pleasure no matter where, when, or in what circumstances), it grafts itself onto the other instincts and the pleasure one experiences satisfying an instinct must be referred both to the instinct itself and to the sexual instinct that is, as it were, the universal producer of universal pleasure. I think that Michéa's analysis introduces into psychiatry a new object or concept that had previously never had a place, except perhaps glimpsed, emerging sometimes in some of Leuret's analyses (I spoke about this last year): This is the role of pleasure.[30] Pleasure now becomes a psychiatric object, or an object that can be psychiatrized. The uncoupling of the sexual instinct from reproduction is secured by the mechanisms of pleasure, and it is this uncoupling that makes possible the constitution of a unitary field of aberrations. Pleasure not governed by normal sexuality supports the entire series of abnormal, aberrant, instinctive conducts that are capable of being psychiatrized. In this way, a theory of instinct and its aberrations linked to imagination and pleasure emerges to replace the old theory of alienation centered on representation, interest, and error.

Psychiatry, then, finds itself before this new field of instinct linked to imagination and pleasure, before this new instinct-imagination-pleasure series, which is the only way it has of covering the entire domain allocated to it politically, or at least allocated to it by the organization of the mechanisms of power. Next week I want to talk about the way in which psychiatry, now possessing this instrument for covering the domain, is obliged to elaborate this instrument in a specific theory and conceptual framework. This, in my view, is what the theory of degeneration amounts to. With degeneration, with the figure of the degenerate, we have the general formula for psychiatry to cover the domain of intervention entrusted to it by the mechanics of power.

1. Cf. M. Foucault, "La politique de la santé au XVIII siècle" (1976) in *Les Machines à guérir. Aux origines de l'hôpital modernes. Dossiers et documents* (Paris: s.l., 1976) pp. 11-21 *in Dits et écrits*, vol. 3. pp. 13-27. English translation: "The Politics of Health in the Eighteenth Century" (1980 [1976]) in *Power/Knowledge. Selected Interviews and Other Writings 1972-1977*, edited by Colin Gordon (Brighton: Harvester, 1980), p. 182, which concludes with the following passage: "The reform of the hospitals ... owed its importance in the eighteenth century to the set of problems relating to: the urban space; the mass of the population with its biological characteristics; the close-knit family cell; and the bodies of individuals." See also *Politique de l'habitat (1800-1850)* (Paris: s.l., 1977), a study carried out by J. M. Alliaume, B. Barret-Kriegel, F. Béguin, D. Rancière, and A. Thalamy.

2. G. Deleuze and F. Guattari, *Capitalisme et Schizophrénie. L'Anti-Oedipe* (Paris: Les Editions de Minuit, 1972). English translation: *Anti-Oedipus. Capitalism and Schizophrenia* (New York: Viking, 1977 [1972]).

3. M. Foucault, *La Volonté de Savoir*, pp. 170-173. English translation: *The History of Sexuality*, pp.108-111.

4. See the lecture of February 12, in this volume.

5. See the lecture entitled *Le Pouvoir psychiatrique*; English translation; *Psychiatric Power*, especially November 7 and 14, December 5, 12 and 19, 1973 and January 9, 1974.

6. H. Kaan, *Psychopathia sexualis*, p. 34 and p. 36: "Instinctus ille, qui toti vitae psychicae quam physicae imperat omnibusque organis et symptomatibus suam notam imprimit, qui certa aetate (pubertate) incipit certaque silet, est nisus sexualis. Uti enim cuique functioni organismi humani, quae fit ope contactus cum rebus externis, inest sensus internus, qui hominem conscium reddit de statu vitali cuiusvis organi, ut sitis, fames, somnolentia, sic et functio procreationis gaudet peculiari instinctu, sensu interno, qui hominem conscium reddit de statu organorum genitalium et eum ad satisfaciendum huic instinctui incitat. ... In toto regno animale instinctus sexualis conducit ad copulationem; estque copulatio (coitus) naturalis via, qua ens instinctui sexuali satisfacit et munere vitae fungitur, genus suum conservans."

7. Ibid., p. 37: "Etiamsi in homine nisus sexualis se exolit tempora pubertatis tamen et antea eius vestigia demonstrari possunt; nam aetate infantili pueri amant occupationes virorum, puellae vero feminarum. Et id instinctu naturali ducti faciunt. Ille instinctus sexualis etiam specie curiositatis in investigandis functionibus vitae sexualis apud infantes apparet; infantes octo vel novem annorum saepe sive invicem genitalia examinant et tales investigationes saepe parentum et pedagogorum curam aufugiunt (haec res est summi momenti et curiositas non expleta validum momentum facit in aetiologia morbi quam describo)."

8. Ibid., p. 38, 40: "Eo tempore prorumpit desiderium obscurum, quod omnibus ingenii facultatibus dominatur, cuique omnes vires corporis obediunt, desiderium amoris, ille animi adfectus et motus, quo quivis homo saltem una vice in vita adficitur et cuius vis certe a nemine denegari potest. ... Instinctus sexualis invitat hominem ad coitum, quem natura humana exposcit, nec moralitas nec religio contradicunt."

9. Ibid., p. 43: "Nisus sexualis, ut ad quantitatem mutationes numerosas offert, ita et ad qualitatem ab norma aberrat, et diversae rationes extant nisui sexuali satisfaciendi et coitum supplendi."

10. Ibid., pp. 43-44: ("Onania sive masturbatio"); p. 44 ("Puerorum amor"); p. 44 ("Amor lesbicus"); p. 45 (Violatio cadaverum); p. 45 ("Concubitus cum animalibus"); p. 43 ("Expletio libidinis cum statuis").

11. In fact, it is A. Voisin, J. Socquet and A. Motet, "État mental de P., poursuivi pour avoir coupé les nattes de plusieurs jeunes filles," *Annales d'hygiène publique et de médicine-légale*, 23 (1890), pp. 331-340. See also V. Magnan, "Des exhibitionnistes, *Annales d'hygiène publique et de médicine-légale*, 24 (1890), pp. 152-168. [Gilles Deleuze, in *Sacher-Masoch*.

An Interpretation (London, 1971; Paris, 1967), p. 29, n. 1, attributes the description of this perversion to Krafft-Ebing, *Psychopathia Sexualis*, revised by Moll.]

12. H. Kaan, *Psychopathia sexualis*, pp. 47-48. The connection between aberration and fantasy is established in the short chapter, "Quid est psychopathia sexualis?"

13. Ibid., p. 47: "In omnibus itaque aberrationibus nisus sexualis phantasia viam parat qua ille contra leges naturae adimpletur."

14. This concerns J. C. Prichard's *A Treatise on Insanity* (London, 1835).

15. W. Griesinger, *Die Pathologie und Therapie*, p. 12.

16. See the lecture of February 12 in this volume.

17. The main sources for this case are the article already cited by C. F. Michéa, "Des déviations maladives de l'appétit vénérien", and the article by L. Lunier, "Examen médico-légale d'un cas de monomanie instinctive. Affaire du sergent Bertrand," *Annales médico-psychologiques* vol. 1 (1849), pp. 351-379. In the *Factums* of the Bibliothèque nationale de France (8 Fm 3159) can also be found *Le Violateur des tombeaux. Détails exacts et circonstanciés sur le nommé Bertrand qui s'introduisait pendant la nuit dans le cimetière Montparnasse où il y déterrait les cadavres des jeunes filles et des jeunes femmes, sur lesquels il commettait d'odieuses profanations*, [no date or place of publication]. See also de Castelnau, "Exemple remarquable de monomanie destructive et érotique ayant pour objet la profanation de cadavres humains," *La Lancette française* 82, (14 July 1849), pp. 327-328; A. Brierre de Boismont, "Remarques médico-légales sur la perversion de l'instinct génésique," *La Lancette française* 30 (28 July 1849), pp. 555-564; F.-J., "Des aberrations de l'appétit génésique," *La Lancette française* 30 (28 July 1849), pp. 575-578; L. Lunier's summary in *Annales médico-psychologiques*, vol. 2 (1850), pp. 105-109 and 115-119; H. Legrand du Saulle, *La folie devant les tribunaux*, pp. 524-529; A. Tardieu, *Études médico-légales sur les attentats aux mœurs*, seventh edition (Paris, 1878), pp. 114-123.

18. See the lecture of January 29, in this volume.

19. On the role in the trial of the military doctor Marchal (de Calvi), who also presented a document written by Bertrand, cf. L. Lunier, "Examen médico-légale d'un cas de monomanie instinctive," pp. 357-363.

20. Ibid., p. 356.

21. Ibid., p. 362: "What we have before us is then an example of destructive monomania complicated by erotic monomania; and this all initiated by a monomania of sadness, which is very common and actually frequently the case."

22. The Troyes case to which Foucault refers was not disclosed by Marchal. It concerned an earlier case of A. Siméon, reported by B. A. Morel in the first of his letters to Bédor: "Considérations médico-légales sur un imbecile érotique convaincu de profanation de cadavres," *Gazette hebdomadaire de médecine et de chirurgie*" 8 (1857), pp. 123-125 (Siméon case); *Gazette hebdomadaire* 11, pp. 185-187 (Bertrand case); *Gazette hebdomadaire* 12, pp. 197-200; *Gazette hebdomadaire* 13, pp. 217-218. Cf. J. G. F. Baillarger, "Cas remarquable de maladie mentale."

23. C. F. Michéa, "Des déviations maladives de l'appétit vénérien," p. 339a: "I think that erotic monomania was the basis of this monstrous madness; and that it was anterior to the destructive monomania." But B. A. Morel, *Traité des maladies mentales*, p. 413, under the title "Perversion des instincts génésiques," explains Bertrand's case as an effect of lycanthropy.

24. C. F. Michéa, "Des déviations," pp. 338c-339a: "Vampirism . . . was a variety of nightmare, nocturnal delirium, extended in the waking state and characterized by this belief that men who have been dead for a more or less considerable length of time leave their graves in order to suck the blood of the living."

25. *Ibid.*, p.338c: "In the event of such a strange and extraordinary fact I hope you will permit me to communicate to you some reflections suggested to me by the close reading of trial documents, specific reflections to which I will add some general considerations of pathological psychology which are closely connected to them and are their logical complement and natural corollary."

26. Ibid., p. 339a.

27. Foucault summarizes the following passage from Michéa, "Des déviations:" "By reha-bilitating the woman, Christianity carried out an immense revolution in morals. It makes physical love a means and not an end; it assigns it the exclusive end of the propagation of the species. Any venereal act performed outside of this expectation became in the eyes of Christianity a violation that often passed from the domain of Christian morality into that of civil and criminal law sometimes receiving an atrocious and capital punish-ment.... Some modern philosophers, [Julien de] La Mettrie among others [*Œuvres phi-losophiques,* vol. 2 (Paris, 1774), p. 209, vol. 3, p. 223], think the same.... The physiologists of the school of La Mettrie say that if the sexual organs were, in the designs of divine wisdom, exclusively intended for the reproduction of the species, the sensation of pleasure arising from the exercise of these organs would no longer exist, when man did not still find himself or no longer found himself in the conditions desired for him to reproduce."

28. C. F. Michéa, "Des déviations."

29. See the analysis of the four genres, ibid., p. 339 a–c.

30. F. Leuret's analyses are outlined in *Fragments psychologiques sur la folie* (Paris, 1834), and developed at greater length in *Du traitement moral de la folie* (Paris, 1840), pp. 418–462. See also the end of the course entitled *La Societé punitive* (lecture of December 19, 1972), and the course *Le Pouvoir psychiatrique*; (December 19, 1973).

eleven

19 March 1975

A mixed figure: the monster, the masturbator, and the individual who cannot be integrated within the normative system of education. ~ The Charles Jouy case and a family plugged into the new system of control and power. ~ Childhood as the historical condition of the generalization of psychiatric knowledge and power. ~ Psychiatrization of infantilism and constitution of a science of normal and abnormal conduct. ~ The major theoretical constructions of psychiatry in the second half of the nineteenth century. ~ Psychiatry and racism: psychiatry and social defense.

I WOULD LIKE TO close the problem I have dealt with this year, that is to say, the appearance of the abnormal individual and of the domain of abnormalities as the privileged object of psychiatry. I began by promising a genealogy of the abnormal individual on the basis of three characters: the great monster, the little masturbator, and the recalcitrant child. The third figure is missing from my genealogy and I hope you will forgive me for this. You will see its outline appear in today's exposition. I have not had time for its genealogy, so we leave it in outline.

By looking at a particular case, today I want to show the quite precisely compound and mixed figure of the monster, the little masturbator, and, at the same time, the recalcitrant individual, or anyway, the individual who cannot be integrated within the normative system of education. The case is from 1867 and you will see that it is extremely banal. However, if this case does not enable us to mark the exact date of birth of the figure of the abnormal as an individual who can be psychiatrized, at least it indicates roughly the period in which and the way in which the figure of the abnormal individual was psychiatrized.

Quite simply it is the case of an agricultural worker of the Nancy region who, in the months of September and October in 1867, was denounced to the mayor of his village by the parents of a little girl he had almost, partly, or more or less raped. He is charged. He undergoes a first psychiatric examination by a local doctor and is then sent to Maréville, which was and still is, I believe, the major asylum for the Nancy region. Here, over several weeks, he undergoes a thorough psychiatric examination by two psychiatrists, at least one of whom, Bonnet, was a prominent figure.[1] What does this individual's file reveal? He was about forty years old at the time of the events. He was an illegitimate child and his mother died when he was still very young. He lived as best he could, a bit on the margins of the village, poorly educated, a bit drunk, solitary and badly paid. In short, he is more or less the village idiot. And I assure you that it is not my fault that this character is called Jouy. The questioning of the little girl reveals that Charles Jouy first got her to masturbate him in the fields. In fact, Charles Jouy and the little girl, Sophie Adam, were not alone. There was another young girl who watched them, but when her young friend asked her to take over she refused. Afterward, they recounted what had happened to a peasant who was returning from the fields, boasting of having, as they said, made *maton*, the local dialect word for curdled milk, with Jouy.[2] The peasant seems not to have worried about it further, and it is only a bit later, the day of the village festival, that Jouy dragged young Sophie Adam (unless it was Sophie Adam who dragged Charles Jouy) into the ditch alongside the road to Nancy. There, something happened: almost rape, perhaps. Anyway, Jouy very decently gives four *sous* to the little girl who immediately runs to the fair to buy some roasted almonds. She says nothing to her parents, of course, for fear, she says later, of getting a couple of slaps. It is only some days later that the mother, when washing the little girl's clothes, suspects what happened.

The fact that legal psychiatry took responsibility for a case like this—that it sought in the depths of the countryside for someone accused of an offense against public decency (and, I would say, a quite commonplace accused and a quite everyday offense), that it then took this individual and subjected him to a first psychiatric assessment and then to a second, much deeper, very thorough and meticulous examination, that it placed him in an asylum, that it easily got the investigating magistrate to declare that there were no grounds for prosecution, and finally that it obtained the definitive "confinement" of this character (if the text is to be believed)—represents not merely a change of scale in the domain of objects with which psychiatry is concerned, but actually a completely new way in which it functions. What is this new way for psychiatry to function that we see in this kind of case?

I would like to recall the first model case with which I started some months ago: the Henriette Cornier case.[3] As you know, Henriette Cornier was the servant who decapitated a little girl without a word or explanation, without the trappings of any kind of discursive support. An entire social landscape appears in the Henriette Cornier case. She, too, naturally, was a peasant girl, but the peasant girl who had moved to the town. She was a lost girl in many senses of the term since she had wandered from place to place; her husband or lover had abandoned her; she had had several children whom she had abandoned in turn; she had more or less been a prostitute. A lost girl, but a silent figure who, without explanation, committed a monstrous act that simply irrupted in the urban environment in which she found herself and passed before the eyes of the spectators like a fantastic, black, enigmatic meteor that no one can say anything about. Nobody would have said anything if the psychiatrists had not been interested in her for a number of theoretical and political reasons.

The Charles Jouy case has certain similarities, but he occupies a quite different landscape. In a sense, Charles Jouy is the fairly familiar figure of the village idiot: He is the simpleton, the mute. He has no origins; he is an illegitimate child. He, too, is unsettled and goes from place to place. When he is asked, "What have you done since you were fourteen years old?" he answers, "I have been in one place and then another." He was also thrown out of school: "Were they pleased with you ... at school?" Answer: "They didn't want to keep me." He was excluded from games: "Did you sometimes play with the other boys?" Answer: "They didn't want me." He was also excluded from sexual games. With regard to the masturbation, the psychiatrist quite sensibly asks him why he did not approach older girls. Charles Jouy answers that they mocked him. He was equally rejected in his home: "What did you do when you returned [from work; M.F.]?" Answer: "I stayed in the stables." He is, then, a marginal figure, but he is far from being a stranger in his village. He is firmly inserted within the social configuration in which he moves and circulates, and he has a function within it. He fulfills a quite precise economic function since he is the last of the workers in the strict sense. That is to say, he does the worst jobs that no one wants to do and he is paid at the lowest rate: "How much do you earn?" He answers: "One hundred francs, food and a shirt." The going rate for an agricultural worker in this region at that time was four hundred francs. He is the internal immigrant who has a role and lives in the marginal society of the low paid.[4]

His floating, unsettled character has a very precise economic and social function. From what we can gather from the text, even the sexual games he engages in, and which are the object of this case, seem to be as firmly established as his economic role. When the two young girls masturbate the simpleton in a corner of the woods or along the side of a road, they boast about it to an adult without difficulty; they laugh and say they have been making curdled milk, to which the adult merely replies: "Oh, you little horrors!"[5] The matter goes no further. All this clearly formed part of a social landscape and practices that were very familiar. The young girl more or less lets it happen; she seems to receive a few *sous* quite naturally and runs to the fair to buy some roasted almonds. She says nothing to her parents simply to avoid being given a couple of wallops. Moreover, during his questioning, Jouy says that he had done it only twice with Sophie Adam but had often seen her doing it with other boys. Besides, the whole village knew it. Once he had come across Sophie Adam masturbating a boy of thirteen or fourteen along the side of the road while another young girl was doing the same thing with another young boy beside them. The psychiatrists themselves recognized that this was part of a social landscape that until then was quite familiar and tolerated, since in their report Bonnet and Bulard say: "He acted . . . in a way that one often sees children of different sexes behave with each other; we mean [they add as a precaution; M.F.] those badly brought up children whose bad tendencies are not [sufficiently; M.F.] restrained by supervision and good principles."[6] We have here a village infantile sexuality of the open air, the side of the road, and the undergrowth that legal medicine is cheerfully psychiatrizing. And it is doing so in a carefree way that, it must be said, raises a problem if we think of the difficulties encountered some years earlier in psychiatrizing something so enigmatic and monstrous as Henriette Cornier's crime or Pierre Rivière's crime.

The first thing to note is that we are dealing with a psychiatrization of practices and individuals that essentially seem to be well established in the social landscape of the village at that time. The first thing to keep in mind, I think, is that this psychiatrization does not come from above, or not only from above. It is not a codification imposed from outside with psychiatry fishing in troubled waters because of a problem, a scandal, or an enigma, the enigmatic figure of Jouy. Not at all: From the very start we begin to make out a real mechanism of appeal to psychiatry. We should not forget that it is the little girl's family who discovers the facts through the famous inspection of the dirty linen that I have spoken about in connection with masturbation and which I told you was one of the hygienic and moral instructions given to families from the end of the eighteenth century.[7] It is the family, then, that becomes aware of it and it is the family that asks the mayor to do something about it. The little girl expected to be walloped, but in fact the family had already given up this kind of reaction and was already plugged into another system of control and power. The first expert, the doctor Béchet, hesitated. Faced with this known and familiar figure he might very well have said: OK, yes, he did it, he is responsible. Now this doctor Béchet says in his first report: Of course, legally, judicially, he is responsible. However, in a letter attached to the report and addressed to the investigating magistrate, he says that the "moral sense" of the accused "is insufficient to resist animal instincts." It is a case in fact of a "dim-witted person who can be forgiven because of his abstruseness."[8] The meaning of this fine phrase is mysterious but essentially it suggests that this doctor (who is no doubt a country doctor or the doctor of the canton) is clearly appealing to the possibility of a more serious and thorough psychiatrization. It seems, moreover, that the village itself had taken responsibility for the affair and had transferred it to a completely different level from that of the slaps expected by the young girl. The mayor was gripped by the case, and it is the mayor who called in the public prosecutor. Furthermore, after the report of the psychiatric experts, the entire population of Loupcourt, the name of the village, keenly desired that little Sophie Adam to be confined in a house of correction until she came of age.[9] What perhaps we see emerging here, and at a relatively deep level, is the concern of adults, of a family and a village, about this peripheral, floating sexuality that brings children and marginal adults together. Then, again at a relatively deep level, we see resort to an agency of control that branches out in different directions since what the family, village, mayor, and, up to a point, the first doctor demand is a house of correction for the little girl and either a court or the psychiatric asylum for the adult.

Faced with something that a few years earlier would doubtless have seemed perfectly commonplace and anodyne, the whole village makes an appeal, a somewhat confused, indifferent, and combined reference to higher authorities of technical, medical, and judicial control. How does psychiatry react to this appeal? How does a psychiatrization that is requested, rather than imposed, take place? To understand how a character like this was psychiatrized we need to look a bit more at the model I referred to a short while ago, that is to say, Henriette

Cornier. What did one look for when one sought to psychiatrize Henriette Cornier, or, more simply to demonstrate her madness, her mental illness? First of all, one looked for a physical correlation, that is to say, a physical element that could at least serve as the triggering cause of the crime, and one found, quite simply, her periods.[10] Above all, and more seriously and fundamentally, one tried to inscribe Henriette Cornier's decapitation of a child within an illness that was naturally very difficult to see but whose signs a practiced eye at least could detect. And this was how, not without difficulty and much subtlety, one came to refer all this back to a change of mood that affected Henriette Cornier at a certain time of her life and marked the insidious invasion of this illness that remained practically without any other symptom except the crime, but which was already signaled by this little crack in her mood. Then one tried to assign to this change a certain instinct that is monstrous, sick, and pathological in itself, which passes through conduct like a meteor, an instinct to murder that resembles nothing, corresponds to no interest, and is not inscribed within any system of pleasure. It is present as an automatism that passes through Henriette Cornier's behavior like an arrow and that nothing can justify except, precisely, a pathological basis. The sudden, partial, discontinuous, heterogeneous, senseless character of the act with regard to the whole of the personality is what enables Henriette Cornier's act to be psychiatrized.

Now the psychiatrization of Jouy's actions and behavior proceeds quite differently in Bonnet and Bulard's report. First of all, his behavior is not psychiatrized by situating it within a definite chronological process, but rather by inserting it in a sort of permanent physical constellation. What the psychiatrists look for in order to demonstrate that they are dealing with someone who can be psychiatrized, what they identify in order to claim Jouy's conduct for their competence, what they need, is not a process but permanent stigmata that brand the individual structurally. And it is in this way that they make the following observations: "The face and cranium do not present the standard symmetry that one should normally find. There is a lack of proportion between trunk and limbs. The cranium is faultily developed; the forehead recedes, which, with posterior flattening, makes the head into a sugarloaf; the lateral sides are also flattened, which raises the parietal bones more than is usual."[11] I stress all these descriptions that indicate what should be normal, the arrangement one usually finds. The accused is subjected to a series of measurements of the occipital-frontal, occipital-chin, frontal-chin, and bi-parietal diameters, of the frontal-occipital circumference and of the anterior-posterior and bi-parietal semi-circumferences, and so on. In this way it is ascertained that the mouth is too wide and that the palate has an arch that is typical of imbecility. You can see that none of these elements given by the examination constitutes either a cause of or even a principle for triggering the illness, as when it was observed that Henriette Cornier was menstruating when she committed her act. In actual fact, all these elements, together with the act itself, form a sort of polymorphous constellation. The act and its stigmata refer—all of them, and in some way on the same plane, even if their nature is different—to a permanent, constitutive, congenital condition. The deformities of the body are, as it were, the physical and structural outcomes of this condition, and the aberrations of conduct, those precisely that earned Jouy his indictment, are its instinctual and dynamic outcomes.

Broadly speaking, we can say that for Henriette Cornier, and at the time of the mental medicine of monomania, starting from a crime that one wanted to turn into a symptom, one constructed beneath it a pathological process. In the case of Charles Jouy and in this new kind of psychiatry, the offense is instead integrated within a schema of permanent and stable stigmata. A psychiatry of the permanent condition that guarantees a definitively aberrant status replaces a psychiatry of pathological processes that create discontinuities. What is the general form of this condition? In the case of Henriette Cornier and what was called "instinctual madness," which was more or less constructed around cases like this, the pathological process that was supposed to support the criminal act had two characteristics. First of all, it was like the inflation, the turgescence, the looming up of the instinct and the proliferation of its dynamism. In short, it is an excess

that marks the pathological functioning of the instinct. The consequence of this excess was a blindness such that the mentally ill person
could not even conceive of the consequences of his action; the force
of instinct was so irresistible that he could not integrate its mechanisms within a general calculation of interest. So the pathological core
is fundamentally the looming up, inflation, and exaggeration of an
instinct that has become irresistible. As a result, there is blindness,
absence of interest, and absence of calculation. This is what was called
"instinctual delirium." In the case of Charles Jouy, however, the signs
that are put together to constitute the condition that allows the act
to be psychiatrized reveal a very different configuration in which it
is not the excess and exaggeration of an instinct that suddenly wells
up that is fundamental and takes precedence (as in the case of monomania and instinctual madness). What is primary, fundamental, and
the very core of the condition in question is deficiency, lack, and
arrested development. That is to say, Bulard's and Bonnet's description of Jouy does not look for an intrinsic exaggeration as the origin
of his conduct but rather a sort of functional imbalance that means
that in the absence of inhibition or control, or in the absence of the
higher levels that secure the establishment, domination, and subjection of the lower levels, these lower levels will develop on their own
account. Not that there is a sort of pathological bacillus in these lower
levels that would suddenly throw them into turmoil and multiply
their strength, dynamic, and effects. It is not at all a case of this, and
these lower levels remain what they are; but they begin to dysfunction
only when what should have integrated, inhibited, and controlled
them is put out of play.[12]

There is no illness intrinsic to instinct. Rather, there is a sort of
functional imbalance of the whole, a sort of bad setup in the structures
that ensures that the instinct, or a certain number of them, is made
to function "normally" in terms of their own regime, but "abnormally" in the sense that this regime is not controlled by levels whose
function is precisely to take charge of the instincts, put them in their
place, and delimit their action. A number of examples of this new
type of analysis can be found in Bonnet and Bulard's report. I will

look at just a few of them. They are important, I believe, for a good understanding of the new interlocking or the new functional filter in terms of which one tries to understand pathological behavior. There is the way in which adult genital organs are described, for example. Bonnet and Bulard conduct a physical examination of the accused; they examine his genital organs. They note: "Despite the very small size [of the accused; M.F.] and his marked arrested physical development, his [genital; M.F.] organs are normally developed like those of an ordinary man. This phenomenon is found in imbeciles."[13] What is seen in imbeciles is not the abnormal development of the genital organs but a contrast between perfectly normal genitals and a lack of the enveloping structure that should restore the role of such organs to their proper place and proportions.[14]

The entire clinical description is carried out in the same way. Consequently, the reality of lack is the first spur, the point of departure of the behavior to be analyzed. Exaggeration is only the visible consequence of this primary and fundamental lack, the opposite of what we found with the alienists when they sought the pathological core in the irresistible violence of instinct. Thus in the analysis of Jouy there are a number of statements such as: He is not wicked, they say, and is even "gentle," but "the moral sense has failed." "He does not have sufficient mental self-possession to resist by himself certain tendencies that he may . . . regret later, without this however allowing us to conclude that he will not start again. . . . These bad instincts . . . are due to his original arrested development, and we know that sometimes their irresistibility is greater in imbeciles and degenerates. . . . Fundamentally affected by arrested mental development, lacking the benefit of any education . . . he does not possess what is needed to counterbalance the tendency to evil and to resist successfully the tyranny of the senses. . . . He does not possess the mastery of 'self' that would enable him to contain the incitements of his thoughts and carnal drives. . . . The mastery of such powerful animality . . . does not have the support of faculties that can soundly appraise the value of things."[15]

As you can see, what calls for psychiatrization and what characterizes the condition is not an excess in quantitative terms or an absurdity in terms of satisfaction (as was the case, for example, with the psychiatrization of Henriette Cornier); rather, it is a lack in terms of inhibition, a spontaneity of lower and instinctual processes of satisfaction. Hence the importance of "imbecility," which is functionally and essentially linked to aberrations of behavior. We can say then that the condition that enables Jouy to be psychiatrized is precisely what caused his arrested development: It is not a process that plugs into or grafts itself onto him, or which passes through his organism or behavior; it is an arrested development, that is to say, quite simply his infantilism. The psychiatrists constantly refer to his childish behavior and intelligence: "We cannot liken his behavior better than to that of a child who is happy when he is praised."[16] Here is the infantile character of Jouy's morality: "Like children who have done wrong . . . he is frightened of being punished. . . . He will understand that it is wrong because he is told so; he will promise not to do it again, but he does not appraise the moral value of his actions. . . . We find him puerile, with no moral consistency."[17] His sexuality is also infantile. I have just quoted the text in which the psychiatrists say: "He acted like a child and, in this case, as one often see children of different sexes behave with each other," but "badly brought up children whose tendencies are not restrained by supervision," et cetera.[18] This, it seems to me, is the important point. At any rate, I do not know if it is important, it is just where I wanted to get to: a new position of the child is being defined vis-à-vis psychiatric practice. It is a matter of establishing continuity with childhood, or rather of immobilizing life around childhood. It is this immobilization of life, conduct, and performance around childhood that essentially makes psychiatrization possible.

In the analysis of the alienists (those of Esquirol's school who were concerned with Henriette Cornier), what really allowed one to say that the subject was ill? It was precisely that, as an adult, she did not resemble in any way the child she had been. What was said to demonstrate that Henriette Cornier was not responsible for her act? You recall that it was: When she was a child she was smiling, cheerful, kind, and affectionate. Then, at a certain point, when she became an adolescent or adult, she became gloomy, melancholic, taciturn, not saying a word. Childhood, then, must be separated from the pathological process so that the latter can effectively function and play its part in the deresponsibilization of the subject. You can see why the signs of infantile wickedness were a stake and the object of an important struggle in the medicine of mental alienation. You recall, for example, the concern and perseverance manifested in the struggle over the signs of childhood wickedness in the Pierre Rivière case.[19] With these signs one could ultimately arrive at two conclusions. One could say: Look, when he was very young he was already torturing frogs, killing birds, and burning the soles of his brother's feet. That shows that the conduct that would one day lead him to kill his mother, his brother, and his sister was already being prepared in his earliest childhood. So, with this crime we are not dealing with something pathological, since from earliest childhood his whole life resembles his crime. You can see, then, that when the psychiatrists wanted to psychiatrize the affair and remove Rivière's guilt, they had to say: But these signs of wickedness are precisely paroxysmal signs of wickedness, and besides they are so paroxysmal that we only find them at a certain period of his childhood. Before he was seven years old there was no trace of them; it is only afterward that everything begins. This means that the pathological process that ten or thirteen years later will end up with the crime was already at work. Hence the legal-psychiatric battle around childhood wickedness, a battle whose echoes and traces will be found throughout the legal psychiatry of 1820, 1860-1880, and even beyond.

With this new mode of psychiatrization, with this new problematic that I am trying to define, signs of wickedness function in a completely different way. It is precisely inasmuch as an adult resembles what he was as a child and continuity can be established between childhood and the adult condition, that is to say, inasmuch as one can rediscover an earlier wickedness in today's act, that one can then identify that condition (*état*), along with its stigmata, that is the condition (*condition*) of psychiatrization. The alienists essentially said to Henriette

Cornier: You were not then what you later became, and for this reason we cannot convict you. The psychiatrists say to Charles Jouy: If we cannot convict you, it is because when you were a child you were already what you are now. You can see precisely why, from the beginning of the nineteenth century, the biographical history was required both by Esquirol's type of medicine of mental alienation and also by the new psychiatry I am now talking about. However, this history is made up of completely different lines, traces entirely different paths, and produces completely different effects of exoneration. In the medicine of mental alienation of the beginning of the century, one indicted when one said: He was already this; he was already what he is. Now, however, one exonerates when one says: What he is now he already was. In general terms, in the psychiatric assessment of Jouy we see childhood becoming an essential element in the new way in which psychiatry functions.

To sum up, Henriette Cornier murdered a child and she could be considered mentally ill only on the condition that she was radically separated from childhood in two ways. She was separated from the child she killed by showing that there were no bonds between her and this child whose family she hardly knew: There was no relationship of hatred and no bond of love between her and the child she scarcely knew. So the first condition for Henriette Cornier's psychiatrization is a minimum of relationships with the child she killed. The second condition is that she was herself separated from her own childhood. Her past, as a child and as a young girl, must resemble as little as possible the act she commits. Consequently there is a radical break between childhood and madness. Charles Jouy, however, can be psychiatrized only by establishing that he remains extremely close to and almost fused with his own childhood and the child with whom he had relationships. Charles Jouy and the young girl he more or less raped must be shown to have been so close to each other as to be of the same grain, of the same ilk, and—the word is not used but you will see it emerge—at the same level. It is their profound identity that will give psychiatry its hold. In the end, Charles Jouy could be psychiatrized because childhood and infantilism are features shared by the criminal and his victim. Childhood as a historical stage of development and a general form of behavior becomes the principal instrument of psychiatrization. Moreover, I would say that it is through childhood that psychiatry succeeded in getting hold of the adult and the totality of the adult. Childhood has been the principle of the generalization of psychiatry; childhood has been, in psychiatry as elsewhere, the trap for adults.

I would like to say a few words now about how the child functions, about his or her place and role, in psychiatry. I think that with the introduction, not so much of the child, as of childhood as the central and constant point of reference for psychiatry, we can grasp quite clearly the new way in which psychiatry functions in comparison with the medicine of mental alienation, a new mode of functioning that will last for about a century, that is to say, until today. First of all, with regard to the discovery of childhood by psychiatry I would say that if I am right, then the discovery of the child or of childhood is not a belated phenomenon but takes place very early on. We have an example of it from 1867, but we could certainly find it earlier. Not only is it an early phenomenon but it also seems to me (and this is what I would like to show) that it is far from being the consequence of a broadening of psychiatry. Consequently, far from considering childhood as a new territory that is annexed to psychiatry at a certain point, it seems to me that it is by taking childhood as the target of its action, both of its knowledge and its power, that psychiatry succeeds in being generalized. That is to say, childhood seems to me to be one of the historical conditions of the generalization of psychiatric knowledge and power. How is the central position of childhood able to bring about this generalization of psychiatry? Summarizing things considerably, I think it is fairly easy to grasp the generalizing role of childhood in psychiatry. When childhood or infantilism becomes the filter for analyzing behavior, then to psychiatrize any conduct it is no longer necessary to insert it within an illness, to situate it within a coherent and recognized symptomatology (as had been the case in the period of the medicine of mental illness). It is no longer necessary to discover that little scrap of delirium that psychiatrists, even at the time of Esquirol, sought with such frenzy behind what seemed to them to be a dubious action. The presence of any kind of trace of infantilism is enough for conduct to fall within the jurisdiction of psychiatry, for it to be possible to psychiatrize it. As a result, inasmuch as it is capable of fixing, blocking, and halting adult conduct and of being reproduced within it, all of the child's conduct is in principle subject to psychiatric inspection. Conversely, all adult conduct can be psychiatrized inasmuch as it can be linked to the child's conduct in one way or another, whether through resemblance, analogy, or a causal relationship. Consequently, all of the child's conduct is thoroughly scoured since it may contain an adult fixation within it. Conversely, adult conduct is scrutinized for any possible trace of infantilism. This is the first effect of generalization that the problematization of childhood introduces into the psychiatric field. The second effect arising from this problematization of childhood and infantilism will be the possibility of integrating three previously separated elements. These three elements are: pleasure and its economy; instinct and its mechanism; imbecility, or at least backwardness, with its inertia and insufficiencies.

Psychiatry during the Esquirol period (from the beginning of the nineteenth century until around 1840) was, as I have emphasized before, strongly marked by its failure to find a way of hitching together pleasure and instinct. It was not that pleasure could not figure in the Esquirol type of psychiatry, but that it figured only when invested in delirium.[20] That is to say, it was admitted that an individual's delirious imagination might well carry the direct and immediate expression of a desire (and this theme, moreover, goes back well beyond Esquirol to the seventeenth and eighteenth centuries).[21] Thus there are the classical descriptions of those who, when disappointed in love, imagine in their delirium that the person who has left them showers them with affection and love.[22] Classical psychiatry certainly accepted the presence of desire in delirium. However, instinct must be freed from pleasure if it is to function as a pathological mechanism because instinct ceases to be automatic if there is pleasure. An individual will necessarily recognize an instinct that is accompanied by pleasure and will register it as liable to induce a pleasure. Therefore, because an instinct accompanied by pleasure naturally figures in a calculation, it cannot be regarded as pathological no matter how violent its movement. Pathologization through instinct excludes pleasure. As for imbecility, it was sometimes pathologized as the final consequence of the development of delirium or dementia and sometimes as a sort of fundamental instinctual inertia.

Now you can see that with someone like Charles Jouy, who has been subjected to this kind of psychiatrization, the three elements or three characters are brought together: the little masturbator, the great monster, and then the individual who rejects all discipline. Henceforth, instinct may well be a pathological element as well as bringing pleasure. The sexual instinct and Charles Jouy's pleasures are actually pathologized at the level of their appearance without the disconnection between pleasure and instinct that instinctual monomania required. It is enough to show that the process, the mechanism of instinct, and the pleasures that it gives, belongs to an infantile level and are marked by infantilism. Pleasure-instinct-backwardness, pleasure-instinct-retardation now constitutes a unified configuration in which these three characters are brought together.

When the major and privileged form of individuals who can be psychiatrized is defined by childhood, infantilism, and the blockage and immobilization around childhood, psychiatry is able to connect with neurology, on the one hand, and general biology on the other. This is the third way in which the problematization of childhood makes possible the generalization of psychiatry. Here again we could say that the Esquirol type of psychiatry could really become a medicine only though a number of what I would call imitative processes. It had to establish symptoms as in organic medicine; it had to name, classify, and organize different illnesses in relation to each other; it had to produce the same kind of etiologies as found in organic medicine, by looking in the body or in predispositions for elements that could explain the formation of the illness. The Esquirol type of mental medicine is medicine as imitation. However, when childhood becomes the focal point around which the psychiatry of individuals and behavior is organized, you can see how psychiatry can be made to function through correlation rather than imitation; the neurology of development and of arrested development, just as general biology with the analysis of evolution at the level of individuals or species, provides both the gap in which and the warranty with which psychiatry can function as scientific knowledge and as medical knowledge.

Finally, the fourth and, I think, most important way in which childhood is a factor of generalization for psychiatry is that childhood and infantilism of conduct offer psychiatry an object that is not so much, and perhaps even not at all, an illness or pathological process, but a certain unbalanced condition, that is to say, a condition whose elements do not function pathologically and that is not the basis of disease, but a condition that is nonetheless not normal. The system of reference of psychiatry, or at least the domain of objects that it tries to divide up and control, now comprises the emergence of an instinct that is not ill in itself, that is healthy in itself, but which it is abnormal to see appearing here and now, so early or so late and with so little control; the appearance of a type of conduct that is not pathological in itself but that should not normally appear within the constellation in which it figures. It is a hitch or a scramble in the structures that contrasts with normal development and constitutes the general object of psychiatry. Illnesses appear only secondarily, as a sort of epiphenomenona, with regard to this condition that is fundamentally a condition of abnormality.

Psychiatry became the science of normal and abnormal behavior by becoming a science of behavioral and structural infantilism. Two consequences can be drawn from this. The first is that psychiatry was able to constitute itself as a general authority for the analysis of conduct through a kind of angled trajectory that increasingly focused on the little confused corner of life that is childhood. Consequently, it was not by capturing the whole of life and surveying the whole development of individuals from birth to death that psychiatry made itself a kind of general controlling body of conduct, the titular judge, if you like, of behavior in general, but rather by confining itself to childhood and digging ever more deeply into childhood. This enables us to see why and how psychiatry was so relentless in putting its nose into the nursery or into childhood. It is not because it wanted to add an additional piece to its already immense domain. It was not because it wanted to colonize yet another little bit of life that it had not yet touched. Rather, psychiatry found in childhood the instrument of its possible universalization. However, the consequence that I want to underline is that by seeing psychiatry focusing on childhood in this way and making it the instrument of its universalization, we can, I think, if not remove, at least disclose, in any case quite simply draw attention to what could be called the secret of modern psychiatry, of the psychiatry inaugurated around 1860.

In fact, if we say that around 1850-1870 a new psychiatry is born that is different from the old medicine of the alienist (symbolized by Pinel and Esquirol),[23] we should nonetheless note that this new psychiatry dispenses with something that previously was essential for the justification of mental medicine. Quite simply, it dispenses with illness. Psychiatry ceases then to be a technique and knowledge of illness, or becomes such only secondarily and as a last resort. Around 1850-1870 psychiatry gave up at once delirium, mental alienation, reference to the truth, and then illness. What it considers now is behavior with its deviations and abnormalities; it takes its bearings from a normative development. Fundamentally, therefore, it no longer deals with illness and the person who is ill; psychiatry is a medicine that purely and simply dispenses with the pathological. And you can see that, starting in the middle of the nineteenth century, it finds itself in a paradoxical situation since mental medicine was essentially constituted as a science around the beginning of the nineteenth century by redefining madness as illness. It constituted madness as illness through a number of procedures, including those analogical procedures I referred to a moment ago. This was how psychiatry was able to constitute itself as a special science alongside and within medicine. By pathologizing madness through the analysis of symptoms, the classification of forms, and the search for etiologies, it could at last constitute a specific medicine of madness: This was the medicine of the alienists. Now from the period 1850-1870 psychiatry had to defend its status as medicine since the effects of power that it was trying to generalize derived, in part at least, from this status. However, these effects of power and the status as medicine from which they derive are now applied to something that, even within the discourse of psychiatry itself, no longer has the status of illness but rather of abnormality.

To put things more simply, when psychiatry was constituted as the medicine of mental alienation, it psychiatrized a madness that was not, perhaps, an illness, but a madness that psychiatry was obliged to consider and assert as such in its own discourse if it was to be an authentic medicine. It could establish its power relation over the mad only by instituting an object relation that was one of medicine to illness: You will be ill for a knowledge that will then authorize me to function as medical power. Broadly speaking, this is what psychiatry said at the beginning of the nineteenth century. However, starting in the middle of the nineteenth century, there is a power relation that only holds fast (and still does so today) inasmuch as it is a medically qualified power, but a medically qualified power that brings under its control a domain of objects that are defined as not being pathological processes. Depathologization of the object was the condition for the generalization of psychiatric power that was nonetheless still medical power. This gives rise to a problem: How can a technological apparatus, a knowledge-power, function in such a way that, from the outset, the knowledge depathologizes a domain of objects that it nonetheless hands over to a power that can exist only as medical power? I think the central problem of psychiatry, perhaps you will say the obvious problem of psychiatry, is this medical power exercised over the nonpathological. In any case, this is where the problem is formed, and it is formed precisely around this investment of childhood as the central point on the basis of which generalization can take place.

I want now to reconfigure very schematically the history of what took place at that moment and starting from that moment. In the second half of the nineteenth century, to get these two differently orientated and even heterogeneous relations to work together, that is to say, a medical power relation and a relation to depathologized objects, psychiatry had to construct a number of what could be called major theoretical edifices that are not so much the expression or reflection of this situation as its functional requirements. I think we should try to analyze the grand structures and theoretical discourses of psychiatry at the end of the nineteenth century in terms of technological advantages, starting from the point at which it became a question of maintaining or even increasing the power effects and knowledge effects of psychiatry through these theoretical or speculative discourses. I would like just to present schematically these grand theoretical constructions starting with three aspects of the constitution of a new nosography.

The first aspect involves organizing and describing a series of aberrant and deviant behaviors merely as syndromes of abnormalities, as abnormal syndromes valid in their own terms rather than as symptoms of an illness. In the second half or last third of the nineteenth century there is what could be called the consolidation of eccentricities into well-specified, autonomous, and recognizable syndromes. In this way the psychiatric landscape comes alive with a population that is completely new for psychiatry: the population of those who do not have symptoms of an illness but are the bearers of intrinsically abnormal syndromes, of eccentricities consolidated into syndromes. They form a long dynasty. I think that one of the first of these syndromes of abnormality is the well-known agoraphobia described by Krafft-Ebing, which is then followed by claustrophobia.[24] In 1867 Zabé writes a French medical thesis devoted to mentally ill arsonists.[25] There are the kleptomaniacs described by Gorry in 1879,[26] and the exhibitionists of Lasègue in 1877.[27] In 1870, in the *Archives de neurologie*, Westphal described the inverts. This is the first time that homosexuality appears as a syndrome within the psychiatric field.[28] Then the masochists appear around 1875-1880. In short, there is an entire history of these little people of abnormal individuals, of these syndromes of abnormality almost all of which emerge in psychiatry around 1865-1870 and populate it until the end of the twentieth [*rectius*: nineteenth] century. When, for example, a society for the protection of animals conducts a campaign against vivisection, Magnan, one of the big names in psychiatry at the end of the nineteenth century, discovers a syndrome: the antivivisectionist syndrome.[29] I want to emphasize that, as you can see, there is nothing here that is the symptom of an illness: It is a syndrome, that is to say, a partial and stable configuration referring to a general condition of abnormality.[30]

The second characteristic of the new nosography being formed at this time is what could be called the return of delirium, that is to say, the reevaluation of the problem of delirium. Delirium was traditionally the core of mental illness. It is understandable, then, that psychiatrists should try to superimpose delirium on the abnormal when this becomes their domain of intervention, because with delirium they would have a medical object. The abnormal could be reconverted into illness if they could rediscover the traces or threads of delirium in all these abnormal behaviors whose grand "syndromatology" was being constituted by psychiatry. The medicalization of the abnormal thus implied or required, or in any case made desirable, the adaptation of the analysis of delirium to the analysis of the interplay between instinct and pleasure. Linking the effects of delirium to the mechanism of the instincts and the economy of pleasure would allow the formation of a true mental medicine, a true psychiatry of the abnormal. So, again in the last third of the nineteenth century, we see the development of the major typologies of delirium. However, these typologies of delirium are no longer organized around the delirious object or thematic, as in the time of Esquirol, but rather around its instinctual and affective root, around the interplay of instinct and pleasure underlying the delirium. It is in this way that the major classifications of delirium appear: persecution delirium, delirium of possession, the virulent crises of erotomania, and so on.

The third characteristic of this nosography, and this I think is the fundamental point, is the appearance of the curious notion of "condition" (*état*) introduced by Falret around 1860-1870 and which is then reformulated a thousand times, mainly in the term *mental background (fond psychique)*.[31] What is a "condition"? As a privileged psychiatric object, a condition is not exactly an illness with a starting point, causes, and processes; indeed, it is not an illness at all. The condition is a sort of permanent causal background on the basis of which illness may develop in a number of processes and episodes. In other words, the condition is the abnormal basis upon which illnesses become possible. You may wonder what difference there is between this notion of condition and the old, traditional notion of predisposition. The difference is that a predisposition was first of all a simple virtuality that did not mean that the individual was not normal: It was possible to be normal *and* predisposed to an illness. Second, predisposition meant that someone was predisposed to a particular type of illness and not another. The distinctive feature of the notion of a condition, as Falret and his successors use it, is that it is not found in normal individuals. A condition is not a more or less pronounced characteristic. The condition is a real, radical discriminant (*discriminant*). The individual who suffers from a condition, who has a condition, is not a normal individual. However, the peculiarity of this condition that is typical of so-called abnormal individuals is that it has an absolute, total etiological value. A condition can produce absolutely anything, at any time, and in any order. Both physical illnesses and psychological illnesses can be linked with a condition: dysmorphia, a functional disorder, a drive, an act of delinquency or drunkenness can all be linked to a condition. In short, anything that is pathological in the body or deviant in behavior may be a product of a condition. A condition does not consist in a more or less pronounced trait but essentially in a sort of general deficiency of the individual's levels of coordination. A condition is defined by a general disturbance in the play of excitations and inhibitions, by the discontinuous and unpredictable release of what should be inhibited, integrated, and controlled, and by the absence of a dynamic unity.

This notion of condition offers two big advantages. The first is that it allows any physical element or deviant behavior whatever, however disparate and distant they may be, to be connected with a sort of unified background that accounts for it—a background that differs from the state of health but nevertheless is not an illness. Consequently, this notion of condition has a formidable capacity for integration: It refers to nonhealth, but it can also bring into its field any conduct whatsoever as soon as it is physiologically, psychologically, sociologically, morally, and even legally deviant. The notion's capacity for integration in this pathology, in this medicalization of the abnormal, is clearly marvelous. At the same time, the second big advantage is that the notion of condition makes possible the rediscovery of a physiological model. This model was put forward successively by Luys, Baillarger, and Jackson, et cetera.[32] What is the condition? It is precisely the characteristic structure or structural whole of an individual who has either been arrested in his development or who has regressed from a later to an earlier state of development.

The nosography of syndromes, delirium, and conditions at the end of the nineteenth century corresponds to the major task that psychiatry could not avoid taking on and in which it could not succeed: that of promoting a medical power over a domain whose unavoidable expansion precluded it from being organized around illness. The paradox of a pathology of the abnormal gave rise to these grand theories or structures in order to function. However, if this notion of condition is isolated and developed as a sort of causal background that is an abnormality in itself, as it was by all the psychiatrists from Falret or Griesinger to Magnan or Kraepelin,[33] then this condition must be set within a sequence that can produce it and confirm it. What kind of body can produce a condition that definitively marks the whole of an individual's body? This gives rise to the need to discover the background-body, so to speak, that by its own causality confirms and explains the appearance of an individual who is the victim, subject, and bearer of this dysfunctional state (and here we open onto another immense theoretical edifice of the end of the nineteenth century). What is this background-body, this body behind the abnormal body? It is the parents' body, the ancestors' body, the body of the family, the body of heredity.

The study of heredity, or the attribution of the origin of the abnormal condition to heredity, constitutes the "metasomatization" required by the whole theoretical construction. This metasomatization and this study of heredity offer in turn a number of advantages to psychiatric technology. First of all, it allows an indefinite causal permissiveness characterized by the fact that anything can be the cause of anything else. The theory of psychiatric heredity establishes that not only can a certain type of illness cause an illness of the same type in descendants, but also that with equal probability it can give rise to any other kind of illness of any type whatsoever. Furthermore, it is not necessarily an illness that causes another illness; it may be something like a vice or a defect. For example, drunkenness may be the cause of no matter what other form of behavioral deviation in descendants, whether this is alcoholism, of course, or an illness like tuberculosis, a mental illness, or even delinquent behavior. The causal permissiveness of heredity makes it possible to establish the most fantastic or, anyway, the most supple hereditary networks. Finding a deviant element at any point in the hereditary network will be sufficient to explain the emergence of a condition in an individual descendant. I will give just one example of this ultraliberal functioning of heredity and of etiology in the field of heredity. It is a study by Lombroso of an Italian murderer called Misdea.[34] He had a very large family so its genealogical tree was established in order to identify the point at which the "condition" was formed. His grandfather was very active but not very intelligent. One uncle was an imbecile, another was odd and irascible, a third was lame, and a fourth was a semi-imbecile, irascible priest. His father was odd and a drunkard. The murderer's eldest brother was obscene, epileptic, and a drunkard; his younger brother, the third in the line, was healthy; the fourth brother was impulsive and a drunkard; and the fifth brother was disobedient. Our murderer, then, was the second in the line.[35] As you can see, heredity functions—at the level of this metabody, this meta-somatization—as the fantastic body of physical or functional or behavioral abnormalities that is the origin of the appearance of the "condition."

Another moral, rather than epistemological, advantage of this hereditary causality is that when the analysis of childhood and its abnormalities clearly shows that the sexual instinct is not naturally tied to the function of reproduction (you recall what I said last week),

heredity allows responsibility for aberrations appearing in descendants to be shifted back to previous mechanisms of reproduction in
the ancestors. In other words, the theory of heredity allows psychiatry
of the abnormal to be not just a technique of pleasure or the sexual
instinct, and in truth not to be a technology of pleasure and the sexual
instinct at all, but rather a technology of the healthy or unhealthy,
useful or dangerous, profitable or harmful marriage. As a result, psychiatry focuses on the problem of reproduction precisely when it was
integrating within its field of analysis all the aberrations that reveal
a nonreproductive function of the sexual instinct. The consequence is
a remoralization at the level of this fantastic etiology.

Finally, we can say that the nosography of abnormal states—
reassigned to the great polycephalic, unstable, floating, and slippery
body of heredity—is formulated in the theory of degeneration. "Degeneration" is formulated in 1857 by Morel,[36] that is to say, at the
same time as Falret was getting rid of monomania and constructing
the notion of condition.[37] It is the period in which Baillarger, Griesinger, and Luys put forward neurological models of abnormal behavior and Lucas scours the domain of pathological heredity.[38]
Degeneration is the major theoretical element of medicalization of the
abnormal. In a word, the degenerate is the abnormal mythologically—
or, if you prefer, scientifically—medicalized.

On the basis of the constitution of the degenerate, set in place in
the tree of heredity and bearing a condition that is not a condition
of illness but one of abnormality, we can see that the theory of degeneration enables psychiatry, with its divergent power relation and
object relation, to function. Even better, the degenerate gives a considerable boost to psychiatric power. In fact, you can see that when
it became possible for psychiatry to link any deviance, difference, and
backwardness whatsoever to a condition of degeneration, it thereby
gained a possibility of indefinite intervention in human behavior.
However, by giving itself the power to dispense with illness, by
giving itself the power to dispense with the ill or the pathological
and to connect a deviation of conduct directly with a definitive and
hereditary condition, psychiatry gave itself the power of dispensing

with the need to find a cure. Certainly, at the beginning of the century
mental medicine had made a great deal of incurability, but incurability was defined as such precisely in virtue of what was the necessary
major role of mental medicine, namely, to cure. Moreover, incurability
was only the current limit of the essential curability of madness. However, as soon as psychiatry becomes a technology of the abnormal, of
abnormal conditions fixed by heredity through the individual's genealogy, it is easy to see that the project of curing has no meaning.
In fact, this therapeutic meaning disappears along with the pathological content of the domain covered by psychiatry. Psychiatry no longer
seeks to cure, or in its essence no longer seeks to cure. It can offer
merely to protect society from being the victim of the definitive dangers represented by people in an abnormal condition (and this is what
actually occurs at this time). With the medicalization of the abnormal
and by dispensing with the ill and the therapeutic, psychiatry can
claim for itself the simple function of protection and order. It claims
a role of generalized social defense and, at the same time, through the
notion of heredity, it claims the right to intervene in familial sexuality.
It becomes the discipline of the scientific protection of society; it
becomes the science of the biological protection of the species. I would
like to halt here, at the point at which psychiatry takes on what for
the time was its greatest power as the science and management of
individual abnormalities. At the end of the nineteenth century it
could claim to replace justice itself, and not only justice but also
hygiene, and not only hygiene but eventually most social interventions
and controls, so as to become the general body for the defense of
society against the dangers that undermine it from within.

With this notion of degeneration and these analyses of heredity,
you can see how psychiatry could plug into, or rather give rise to, a
racism that was very different in this period from what could be called
traditional, historical racism, from "ethnic racism."[39] The racism that
psychiatry gave birth to in this period is racism against the abnormal,
against individuals who, as carriers of a condition, a stigmata, or any
defect whatsoever, may more or less randomly transmit to their heirs
the unpredictable consequences of the evil, or rather of the non-

normal, that they carry within them. It is a racism, therefore, whose function is not so much the prejudice or defense of one group against another as the detection of all those within a group who may be the carriers of a danger to it. It is an internal racism that permits the screening of every individual within a given society. Certainly, there were very quickly a series of interactions between this racism and traditional Western, essentially anti-Semitic racism, without, however, the two forms ever being coherently or effectively organized prior to Nazism. We should not be surprised that German psychiatry functioned so spontaneously within Nazism. The new racism specific to the twentieth century, this neoracism as the internal means of defense of a society against its abnormal individuals, is the child of psychiatry, and Nazism did no more than graft this new racism onto the ethnic racism that was endemic in the nineteenth century.

I think, then, that these new forms of racism, which took hold in Europe at the end of the nineteenth century and the beginning of the twentieth century, should be linked historically to psychiatry. Nevertheless, it is clear that although it gave rise to this eugenics, psychiatry is far from being reducible to this form of racism, which covered or took over only a relatively limited part of it. However, even when psychiatry has got rid of this racism or when it did not activate these forms of racism, starting at the end of the nineteenth century, it nonetheless always essentially functioned as a mechanism and body of social defense. The three well-known questions currently put to psychiatrists who testify in court are: "Is the individual dangerous? Is the accused indictable? Is the accused curable?" I have tried to show how little meaning these three questions have with regard to the juridical edifice of the penal code that is still in force today. They are questions without meaning with regard to law, and they have no more meaning with regard to a psychiatry that really did focus on illness. However, they are questions that have a quite precise meaning when they are put to a psychiatry that essentially functions as social defense or, to adopt the terms of the nineteenth century, which functions as a hunt for "degenerates." The degenerate is someone who is a danger. The degenerate is someone who cannot be reached by any kind of penalty. The degenerate is someone who, at all events, cannot be cured. These three questions with no medical, pathological, or juridical meaning have a very precise meaning in a medicine of the abnormal, which is not a medicine of the pathological and of illness. They consequently have a precise meaning in a medicine that essentially continues to be a medicine of the degenerate. This allows us to say that the questions the judicial apparatus still puts to psychiatrists today constantly revive and reactivate the problematic of the psychiatry of the degenerate at the end of the nineteenth century. Those well-known Ubu-esque descriptions that we still find today in medico-legal expert opinions, in which such an incredible picture is given of the individual's heredity, ancestry, childhood, and behavior, have a perfectly precise historical meaning. They are the remains (once, of course, the great theory and systemization of degeneration produced from Morel to Magnan has been abolished), the outcrops of the theory of degeneration that quite naturally find their home in answers to questions put by the court, but whose historical origin is the theory of degeneration.

I have tried to show that this seemingly tragic and crazy literature has its historical genealogy. It is bound up with the functioning, with the technology of psychiatry in the second half of the nineteenth century whose procedures and notions are still active today. I would like to take up again the problem of psychiatry as social defense at the end of the nineteenth century, starting with the problem of anarchy and social disorder. So, there is work to be done on political crime, social defense, and the psychiatry of order.[40]

1. Cf. H. Bonnet and J. Bulard, *Rapport médico-légal sur l'état mental de Charles-Joseph Jouy, inculpé d'attentats aux mœurs* (Nancy, 1868). Bonnet and Bulard were head doctors of the public insane asylum of Maréville where Jouy was confined after the declaration that there were no grounds for prosecution. Foucault refers to this case in *La Volonté de savoir*, pp. 43-44; English translation: *The History of Sexuality*, pp. 31-32.

2. Cf., H. Bonnet and J. Bulard, *Rapport médico-légal*, p. 3.

3. See the lecture of February 5, in this volume.

4. H. Bonnet and J. Bulard, *Rapport médico-légal*, pp. 8-9.

5. Ibid., p. 3.

6. Ibid., p. 10.

7. See the lecture of March 12, in this volume.

8. Béchet's report is found in H. Bonnnet and J. Bulard, *Rapport médico-légal*, pp. 5-6.

9. Ibid., p. 4: "The little girl's father complains a great deal about his daughter who is most undisciplined despite all the beatings she has been given. The population of Loupcourt . . . keenly desire that the little Adam girl be confined in a house of correction until she comes of age. . . . It would seem that the morals of the children and young people of Loupcourt are very lax." Cf. the lectures given by J. Bulard as president of the Société pour la protection de l'enfance (carton Rp. 8941-8990 of the Bibliothèque nationale de France).

10. See the lecture of February 5, in this volume. Cf. J. E. D. Esquirol, *Des maladies mentales*, vol. 1, pp. 35-36; vol. 2, p. 6, p. 52; A. Brierre de Boismont, *De la menstruation considérée dans ses rapports physiologiques et pathologiques avec la folie*, (Paris, 1842) summarized in "Recherches bibliographiques et cliniques sur la folie puerpérale, précédées d'un aperçu sur les rapports de la menstruation et de l'aliénation mentale," *Annales médico-psychologiques* 3 (1851), pp. 574-610; E. Dauby, *De la menstruation dans ses rapports avec la folie* (Paris, 1866).

11. H. Bonnet and J. Bulard, *Rapport médico-légal*, p. 6.

12. Ibid., p. 11: "Jouy is a natural child, and he has been congenitally warped. His arrested mental development has gone hand in hand with organic degeneration. He does possess faculties, however their strength is very limited. If from childhood he had been educated and been in contact with the general principles that govern life and society, if he had been subjected to a moralizing force, he could have made some progress; developing his reason, learning to organize his thoughts in a more relevant way, improving a debased moral sense that leaves him prey to drives appropriate to backward members of his kind, perhaps learning by himself the value of an action. Nonetheless, he still would have remained imperfect, but medical psychology would have been able to attribute him with a limited responsibility in regard to civil matters."

13. Ibid., pp. 10-11.

14. Ibid., p. 11: "This fact is seen in imbeciles and accounts in part for their tendencies because they possess organs that incite them, and as they do not have the faculty for judging the value of things or the moral sense to restrain themselves, they allow themselves be suddenly carried away."

15. Ibid., pp. 9-12.

16. Ibid., p. 7.

17. Ibid., p. 9.

18. Ibid., p. 10.

19. Cf., M. Foucault, editor, *Moi, Pierre Rivière*: English translation: *I, Pierre Rivière*.

20. Foucault is referring to those authors who, prior to the turning point represented by Griesinger and Falret (see the lecture of February 12, in this volume), applied Esquirol's ideas, *Note sur la monomanie homicide* (Paris, 1827).

21. The theme is already present in works such as those of T. Fienus, *De viribus imaginationis tractatus* (Louvain, 1608).

22. The first volume of R. Burton's *The Anatomy of Melancholy* (Oxford, 1621), and J. Ferrand's *De la maladie d'amour ou mélancolie érotique* (Paris, 1623), are devoted to "love melancholy."

23. See, for example, J. P. Falret, *Des maladies mentales et des asiles d'aliénés. Leçons cliniques et considérations générales* (Paris, 1864), p. iii: "The sensualist doctrine of Locke and Condillac then dominated with almost absolute mastery.... This doctrine of the philosophers ... was imported into mental pathology by Pinel." Even more radical is the perception of distance ("The doctrines of our masters, Pinel and Esquirol, dominated mental medicine absolutely.... It is rare to see scientific doctrines so firmly consolidated that they are able withstand the successive efforts of three generations") and the awareness of a break starting in the 1850s, in J. Falret, *Études cliniques sur les maladies mentales et nerveuses* (Paris, 1890), pp. v-vii.

24. According to H. Legrand du Saulle, *Étude clinique sur la peur des espaces (agoraphobie des Allemands), névrose emotive* (Paris, 1878), p. 5, the term was not invented by Krafft-Ebing but by C. Westphal, "Die Agoraphobie. Eine neuropathische Erscheinung," *Archiv für Psychiatrie und Nervenkrankheiten*, 3/1 (1872), pp. 138-161, on the basis of a request from Griesinger in 1868.

25. E. Zabé's thesis, *Des Aliénés incendiaries devant les tribunaux* (Paris, 1867), was preceded by C. C. H. Marc, *De la folie*, vol. 2, pp. 304-400 (initially published under the title, "Considérations médico-légales sur la monomanie et particulièrement sur la monomanie incendiaire," *Annales d'hygiène publique et de médecine légale*, 10 (1833), pp. 388-474); H. Legrand du Saulle, *De la monomanie incendiaire* (Paris, 1856); (cf. Marc, *De la folie devant les tribunaux*, pp. 461-484).

26. T. Gorry, *Des aliénés voleurs. Non-existence de la kleptomanie et des monomanies en géneral comme entités morbides* (Paris, 1879). See also C. C. H. Marc, *De la folie*, vol. 2, pp. 247-303.

27. Ch. Lasègue, "Les exhibitionnistes," *Union médicale* 50 (May 1, 1877), pp. 709-714 (then in *Études médicales*, vol. 1 [Paris, 1884], pp. 692-700). Cf. the article cited, "Des exhibitionnistes" by V. Magnan.

28. J. C. Westphal, "Die conträre Sexualempfindung," (French transation: "L'attraction des sexes semblables," *Gazette des hôpitaux* 75 [29 June 1878]); Cf. H. Gock, "Beitrag zur Kenntniss der conträren Sexualempfindung," *Archiv für Psychiatrie und Nervenkrankheiten*, 5 (1876), pp. 564-574; J. C. Westphal, "Zur conträre Sexualempfindung," *Archiv für Psychiatrie und Nervenkrankheiten*, 6 (1876), pp. 620-621.

29. V. Magnan, *De la folie des antivivisectionnistes* (Paris, no date, 1884).

30. M. Foucault, *La Volonté de savoir*, pp. 58-60; English translation: *The History of Sexuality*, pp. 43-44.

31. Cf. J.-P. Falret, *Des maladies mentales et des asiles*, p. x.: "Instead of going back to the initial lesion of the faculties in mental illnesses, the specialist doctor must devote himself to the study of complex mental conditions (*états psychiques*) as they exist in nature."

32. J. G. F. Baillarger's studies are cited in the lecture of February 12, in this volume. The work of J. Luys to which Foucault refers are collected in *Études de physiologie et de pathologie cérébrales. Des actions réflexes du cerveau, dans les conditions normales et morbides de leurs manifestations* (Paris, 1874). Between 1879 and 1885, J. H. Jackson edited the review of neurology *Brain*. See in particular his essay, "On the Anatomical and Physiological Localisation of Movements in the Brain" (1875) in *Selected Writings* (London: s.l., 1931). Foucault's interest in Jackson's *Croonian Lectures* and in Jacksonism goes back to *Maladie Mental et Psychologie* (Paris: P.U.F., 1954). English translation: *Mental Illness and Psychology* (New York: Harper Colophon, 1976), translated by Alan Sheridan.

33. To the authors already cited must be added E. Kraepelin, *Lehrbuch der Psychiatrie*, (Leipzig, 1883) and *Die psychiatrischen Aufgaben des Staates* (Jena: s.l., 1900); French translation: *Introduction à la psychiatrie clinique* (Paris: s.l., 1907), especially pp. 5-16, 17-28 and 88-89. Cf., *Clinical Psychiatry*, abstracted and adapted from the sixth German edition of *Lehrbuch der Psychiatrie* by A. R. Defendorf (New York: s.l., 1902).

34. On the Misdea case, see C. Lombroso and A.G. Bianchi, *Misdea e la nuova scuola penale* (Turin, 1884), pp. 86-95.

35. Cf. the genealogical tree of Misdea, ibid., p. 89.

36. B. A. Morel, *Traité des dégénérescences*.

37. J. P. Falret, "De la non-existence de la monomanie" and "De la folie circulaire," in *Des maladies mentales et des asiles d'aliénés*, pp. 425-448 and pp. 456-475 (the two articles first appeared in 1854).

38. P. Lucas, *Traité philosophique et physiologique de l'hérédité naturelle*.

39. Cf. M. Foucault, *Il faut défendre la société*, p. 230; English translation: *Society must be defended.*

40. Foucault's seminar at the Collège de France in 1976 was devoted to "the study of the category of "the dangerous individual" in criminal psychiatry. The notions connected with the theme of "social defense" were compared with the notions connected with the new theories of civil responsibility, as they appeared at the end of the nineteenth century in *Dits et Écrits*, vol. 3, p. 130. (*The Essential Works*, vol. 1, p. 64.). This seminar brought to an end the series of investigations devoted to psychiatric expertise that began in 1971.

COURSE SUMMARY*

THE LARGE, ILL-DEFINED, AND confused family of "abnormal individuals," the fear of which haunts the end of the nineteenth century,
does not merely mark a phase of uncertainty or a somewhat unfortunate episode in the history of psychopathology. It was formed in
correlation with a set of institutions of control and a series of mechanisms of surveillance and distribution, and, when it is almost entirely
taken over by the category of "degeneration," it gives rise to laughable
theoretical constructions that nonetheless have harshly real effects.

The group of abnormal individuals was formed from three elements
that were not constituted at exactly the same time.

1. The human monster. This is an old notion whose frame of reference is the law. It is a juridical notion, therefore, but in a broad
sense since it concerns the laws of nature as well as the laws of society;

* Published in the *Annuaire du Collège de France, 76ᵉ année. Histoire des systèmes de pensée, année
1974-1975*, (1975), pp. 335-339, and in *Dits et écrits, 1954-1988* vol. 2, no. 165 (Paris, 1994),
pp. 822-828. An earlier translation of this summary appears in M. Foucault, *The Essential
Works of Foucault, 1954-1984.* Vol. 1: *Ethics, Subjecivity and Truth*, ed. Paul Rabinow, trans.
Robert Hurley and others (New York, 1997), pp. 51-57.

the monster's field of appearance is a juridico-biological domain. This double transgression was represented successively by the figure of the being that is half human and half animal (given prominence especially in the Middle Ages), the double individual (given prominence in the Renaissance), and the hermaphrodite (who gives rise to so many problems in the seventeenth and eighteenth centuries): What makes a human monster a monster is not only that it is an exception to the form of the species but also that it introduces disorder into the legal system (whether it is a question of marriage laws, canons of baptism, or laws of inheritance). The major trials of hermaphrodites in which jurists and doctors confront each other—from the Rouen case at the beginning of the seventeenth century to the trial of Anne Grandjean in the middle of the following century—as well as works such as Cangiamila's *Embryologie sacrée*, published and translated [into French; *trans*.] in the eighteenth century, should be studied from this perspective.

This enables us to understand a number of ambiguities that continue to haunt the analysis and status of the abnormal man even after he has subdued and appropriated the monster's features. At the forefront of these ambiguities is the never wholly mastered interplay between the exception of nature and the breach of the law. These are no longer superimposed but continue to be interrelated. The "natural" deviation from "nature" modifies the legal effects of the transgression but does not completely obliterate them. It does not refer purely and simply to the law, nor does it suspend the law either; it ensnares the law, giving rise to effects, triggering mechanisms, and calling in parajudicial and marginal medical institutions. Following this line we have been able to study the evolution of medico-legal expert opinion in penal matters, from the problematization of the "monstrous" act at the beginning of the nineteenth century (with the Cornier, Léger, and Papavoine cases) to the appearance of the notion of the "dangerous" individual that cannot be given either a medical meaning or a legal status but is nonetheless the fundamental notion of contemporary expert opinion. By asking doctors today the strictly absurd question "Is this individual dangerous?"—a question that contradicts a penal law founded on the principle that one can only be sentenced for actions and a question that postulates a natural kinship between illness and transgression—the courts, through transformations that must be analyzed, have renewed the ambiguities of the age-old monsters.

2. The individual to be corrected. This character appears more recently than the monster. He corresponds less to legal constraints and canonical forms of nature and more to techniques of training with their specific requirements. The "incorrigible" appears in the seventeenth and eighteenth centuries at the same time that disciplinary techniques are being established in the army, schools, workshops, and then, a little later, in families themselves. The new practices for training bodies, behavior, and abilities open up the problem of those who escape a system of norms that has ceased to be that of the sovereignty of law.

"Interdiction" was the judicial measure by which an individual was at least partially disqualified as a legal subject. This juridical and negative framework is partly filled and partly replaced by a set of techniques and practices for training individuals who resist training and for correcting the incorrigible. The "confinement" widely practiced from the seventeenth century on appears as a kind of intermediate formula between the negative practice of judicial interdiction and the positive practices of rectification. Confinement actually excludes and it operates outside the law, but it justifies itself in terms of the need to correct and improve individuals, to get them to see the error of their ways and restore their "better feelings." Starting from this jumbled but historically decisive form, we should study the appearance, at precise historical moments, of different institutions of rectification and the categories of individuals for whom they are intended, that is to say, the technico-institutional births of blindness and deaf-muteness, of imbeciles and the retarded, of the nervous and the unbalanced.

The abnormal individual of the nineteenth century—a faded monster who has been rendered commonplace—is also a descendant of those incorrigible individuals who appeared on the fringes of modern "training" techniques.

3. The onanist. This is a completely new figure in the eighteenth century. The onanist is the correlate of new relations between sexuality and the organization of the family, of the child's new position at the center of the parental group, and of the new importance accorded to the body and health. The onanist marks the appearance of the child's sexual body.

There is, in fact, a long prehistory to this appearance: the linked development of techniques of spiritual direction (in the new pastoral arising from the Reformation and the Council of Trent) and institutions of education. From Gerson to Alfonso de Liguori, the obligation of penitential confession and a highly codified practice of subtle questioning provide a discursive subdivision of sexual desire, the sensual body, and the sin of *mollities*. Schematically, we can say that the traditional control of forbidden relationships (adultery, incest, sodomy, bestiality) was coupled with control of the "flesh" in the elementary impulses of concupiscence.

However, the crusade against masturbation represents a break with this background. It starts clamorously, first in England around 1710 with the publication of *Onania*, and then in Germany before being launched in France with Tissot's book around 1760. Its raison d'être is enigmatic, but its effects are innumerable. These can only be determined by considering some of the essential features of the campaign. It would be inadequate, in fact, to see this campaign—in a perspective close to Reich that has inspired recent works by Van Ussel—as no more than a process of repression linked to the new requirements of industrialization, setting the productive body against the body of pleasure. Actually, in the eighteenth century at least, this crusade does not take the form of a general sexual discipline: It is aimed primarily, if not exclusively, at adolescents or children, and even more specifically at those from rich or well-off families. It places sexuality, or at least the sexual use of one's own body, at the origin of an indefinite series of physical disorders whose effects may be felt in every form and at every age of life. The unlimited etiological power of sexuality at the level of the body and illnesses is one of the most constant themes not only in the texts of this new medical ethics but also in the most serious works of pathology. Now while the child thereby becomes responsible for his own body and his own life, parents are denounced as the real culprits for the child's "abuse" of his sexuality: It is the absence of supervision, the neglect, and especially that lack of interest in the bodies and conduct of their children that leads parents to entrust their children to wet nurses, servants, and private tutors, that is to say, to all those intermediaries regularly denounced as initiators into debauchery (Freud will take his first "seduction" theory from this). The need for a new relationship between parents and children and, more broadly, for a new system of relationships within the family emerges from this campaign: the solidification and intensification of father-mother-children relationships (at the expense of the multiple relationships that characterized the large "household"); the reversal of the system of family obligations (which previously went from children to parents but now tend to make the child the primary and ceaseless object of parental duties that extend to their moral and medical responsibility for their descendants); the appearance of the principle of health as a fundamental law of family ties; the distribution of the family cell around the body—and the sexual body—of the child; the organization of an immediate physical bond, of a physical struggle between parents and children in which desire and power form a complex knot; and finally, the need for an external medical control and knowledge to arbitrate and govern these new relationships between the obligatory vigilance of parents and the child's fragile, irritable, and excitable body. The crusade against masturbation reflects the development of the restricted family (parents and children) as a new apparatus of knowledge-power. One of the ways in which this new apparatus was constituted was by putting in question the child's sexuality and all the abnormalities for which it was held responsible. The small incestuous family that is characteristic of our societies, the tiny, sexually saturated family space in which we are raised and in which we live, was formed from this.

The "abnormal" individual that so many institutions, discourses, and knowledges have been concerned with since the end of the nineteenth century derives from the juridico-natural exception of the monster, the multitude of incorrigible individuals caught in the apparatus of rectification, and the universal secret of childhood sexuality. In fact, the three figures of the monster, the incorrigible, and the onanist do not merge. Each is inscribed within autonomous systems of scientific reference: the monster in a teratology and embryology that achieves its first major form of scientific coherence with Geoffroy Saint-Hilaire; the incorrigible in a psychophysiology of sensations, motor functions, and abilities; the onanist in a theory of sexuality that is developed slowly starting from Kaan's *Psychopathia sexualis*.

However, the specificity of these references should not lead us to forget three essential phenomena that partly negate or at least modify it: the construction of a general theory of "degeneration" that, starting from Morel's book in 1857, serves for more than fifty years as simultaneously both the theoretical framework and the social and moral justification for all the techniques of identification, classification, and intervention concerning abnormal individuals; the setting up of a complex institutional network on the borders of medicine and justice that serves both as a structure for the "reception" of abnormal individuals and as an instrument for the "defense" of society; and, finally, the movement by which the problem of childhood sexuality, historically the most recent element to appear, covers the other two and becomes in the twentieth century the most productive explanatory principle for every abnormality.

The *Antiphysis*, which terror of the monster once brought to the light of an exceptional day, is now slipped under small everyday abnormalities through the universal sexuality of children.

Since 1970, the series of courses has focused on the slow formation of a knowledge and power of normalization based on traditional juridical procedures of punishment. The course for 1975-1976 will bring this cycle to an end with the study of the mechanisms with which, since the end of the nineteenth century, we sought to "defend society."

The seminar this year was devoted to the analysis of the transformations of expert psychiatric opinion in penal matters from the major cases of criminal monstrosity (the prime case being that of Henriette Cornier) to the diagnosis of "abnormal" delinquents.

COURSE CONTEXT

Valerio Marchetti and Antonella Salomoni*

ABNORMAL COMPRISES ELEVEN LECTURES delivered between 8 January and 19 March 1975 that intended to study and link together the different elements that made possible the formation of the concept of abnormality in the history of the modern West.

The summary published in the *Annuaire du Collège de France* for 1974-1975, reproduced elsewhere in this volume,[1] provides a good synthesis of the course with regard to the clarity of its structure and its rigorous description of the "three elements" constituting the "group of abnormal individuals," a set whose "status" and "scale" was fixed only at the end of the nineteenth century: the *monster*, the *undisciplined*, and the *onanist*. However, it should be noted that with regard to the program Foucault presents in the first session, the second category (that of "individuals to be corrected"), squeezed be-

---

* Valerio Marchetti is professor of modern history at the University of Bologna. Antonella Salomoni teaches social history at the University of Sienna (Arezzo section). They wrote this Context together. In the preparation of the text, V. Marchetti was responsible for the sessions of 19 and 26 February and 5, 12, and 19 March. A. Salomoni was responsible for 8, 15, 22, and 29 January and 5 and 12 February.

tween the other two, has almost disappeared completely as an object with its own autonomous documentation and is in some respects dissolved within the general exposition as a figure of "the individual who cannot be integrated within the normative system of education" (19 March).

In the tenth session, that is to say, almost at the end of the course, Foucault takes stock of his work and reports that a change has taken place. After having delimited the importance of the theme of the undisciplined individual with regard to "how the problematic of the monster and instinct and the problematic of the masturbator and infantile sexuality are brought together," Foucault tries as far as possible to make good the gap. On 19 March he presents the case of a "recalcitrant child" subject to a process of "psychiatrization," but states that he has "not had time" for its genealogy and that it exists only "in outline." It remains in outline also in *The History of Sexuality*, where it is summarized even more concisely and is not supported by the complex discussion that is found in the course.[2] Here, Foucault presents the problematization as arising not only from a family now plugged in to a "system of control and power" different from that of the village culture, and from the assertion of a new "concern" that emerges with regard to a "sexuality that brings children and marginal adults together," but above all from an important step taken at this time in the "discovery of the child or of childhood" by psychiatry. Because, when the child's "infantilism" (that is to say, its retarded development) becomes a criterion for the analysis of deformed behavior, then signs of this infantilism must be found in conduct if it is to be psychiatrized. Henceforth, "all adult conduct can be psychiatrized" when signs of infantilism are detected.

If we establish a field—as announced in the first session and referred to in the course summary—within which we find not only the human monster ("exception" to the norm of reproduction), first of all in a "juridico-natural" and then a "juridico-biological" sense, but also the individual to be corrected (who is "regular in his irregularity") and the masturbating child (an "almost universal character"), archaeology and genealogy show that the abnormal individual, as he was defined by the institutions that assumed responsibility for dealing with him at the end of the nineteenth century, is the descendant of these three figures. It is true that, for Foucault, each of these figures has a completely different origin and history. For a long time they remain distinct and separate because the "systems of power and systems of knowledge" that are responsible for them are also distinct and separate. Moreover, a complete and sometimes chaotic "reversal of importance" in their hierarchy has been carried out in the modern age. However, what matters is that the *great monster* (henceforth inscribed in a "scientifically coherent" teratology and embryology), the *incorrigible* ("the individual resistant to all discipline" whose behavior is often described in terms of a "psychophysiology of sensations") and the *little masturbator* (around whom a real sexual psychopathology is constructed) come together in the abnormal individual.

While the case reported in the eleventh session revealed the "disturbing profile" of a child who is seen to be recalcitrant because the family and community are integrated into a different logic of control, the lectures on the human monster (who has become a judicial monster) and the onanist (who is linked up to the constellation of perversions) provide a systematic treatment of these two fundamental figures in the formation of the abnormal individual. The research is deeper and the evidence almost exhaustive. The reason for this discrepancy is probably due to the fact that Foucault develops here the content of dossiers that were already prepared and that he intended to publish, at least in part, and then also that he summarizes the substance of manuscripts intended to take the form of a book. *The Abnormal* offers not only a very clear trace of these dossiers and manuscripts but it also allows us to reconstitute what has been lost.

THE "DOSSIERS"*

1. *The Dossier of Medico-Legal Expert Opinion*

In "Prison Talk" Foucault says that in 1975 he was preparing for publication a study on expert psychiatric opinion in penal matters.[3] In fact, this work appears at several points in the course of the lectures in the form of dossiers already prepared and almost ready for publication (the box file is preserved with the papers inherited by Daniel Defert). It exists in two large blocs. Some of the dossiers, those Foucault analyzed more deeply, go back to the beginning of the nineteenth century, to the moment of the birth of judicial psychiatry whose discourse exists only in embryo. Others date from the second half of the twentieth century.[4] Between the two groups there is a series of cases that are evidence of important transformations in the process of the integration of psychiatry within legal medicine.

(a) Contemporary Expert Opinion. The first part of the dossier opening the session of 8 January is made up from a set of expert opinions submitted to French justice by psychiatrists who enjoyed great renown between 1954 and 1974. They were chosen from innumerable documents that Foucault took from contemporary organs of information. They refer to trials still in process or trials that had ended a few years before. The material collected, information taken from news items or from articles in specialist publications (legal journals), allows Foucault to read out long passages wherever they appear to contain problems that then form the framework for a part of the course. Fundamental questions emerge in this way: questions such as that of statements with "a power of life and death" that "function in the judicial institution as a discourse of truth," and themes like the grotesque ("grotesque sovereignty") or Ubu-esque ("Ubu-esque terror") that should be included among the categories of "historico-political analysis" since they show the high point of "effects of power based

---

* We call "dossiers" the collections of notes classified by Michel Foucault and preserved by Daniel Defert.

on the disqualification of the person who produces them." Usually, it is with these kinds of observations, with analyses that at first seem to be purely interstitial and often develop arguments already broached or hypotheses tested in previous sessions, that Foucault suddenly leaves the "present," buries himself in "history," and then suddenly returns to the "present." He makes an expedition that in an unusual and unexpected way links necessary general or even superficial information to the set of problems on which he was working (for example, in the first lecture, the question of those discourses whose power effects are greater than others and which have a "demonstrative value" linked to the subject who utters them).

(b) Expert Opinion of the First Decades of the Nineteenth Century. The second part of the dossier, used in the session of 5 February and taken up several times in the following lectures, is made up of a series of expert opinions called for by French justice and given by famous psychiatrists from 1826 on, that is to say, from when the application of Article 64 of the penal Code of 1810 ("There is neither crime nor offense when the defendant was in a state of dementia at the time of the action or when he was constrained by a force that he could not resist"[5]) requires the medical institution to take over from the judicial institution in cases of madness. The most important problems that Foucault raises here—which, judging from the fairly frequent references, involve the courses of the three preceding years (*Penal Theories and Institutions, The Punitive Society,* and *Psychiatric Power*[6])—are scattered, sometimes in a form that is barely changed, in his earlier works or works of the same time (particularly *Discipline and Punish,* which appeared in February 1975) and later (notably, *The History of Sexuality.* Vol. 1: *An Introduction,* which appeared in October 1976). The same problems run through Foucault's teaching at the Collège de France from 1970-1971 (some of the lectures in *The Will to Knowledge*[7]) to 1975-1976 (some of the lectures in "*Society Must Be Defended*"[8]). That is to say, they date from the period when Foucault, after having posed the question of the "traditional juridical procedures of punishment," broached the study of the "slow formation of a knowledge and power of normalization," until, having identified "the mechanism with

which, from the end of the nineteenth century, one sought to 'defend society,' " he judged that his research had reached its end.[9] In the courses that bear on the involvement of psychiatry in legal medicine there are some remarkable anticipations of themes studied *in extenso* in the following years (for example, in *The Birth of Biopolitics* of 1978-1979[10] and *On the Government of the Living* of 1979-1980[11]) and in some respects there are also some early signs here of later studies (the course *Subjectivity and Truth* is from 1980-1981[12]). However, the problems raised in this course are often developed only for their pedagogical value. They are therefore destined to disappear with the reorganized plan of work that follows the first volume of *The History of Sexuality*. The change of perspective entailed by the turning point of 1981 (*The Hermeneutic of the Subject*[13]) confirms this and is also clear from the pieces in the fourth volume of *Dits et écrits* and the final published work of 1984: *The Use of Pleasure* and *The Care of the Self*.

   (c) Expert Opinions from between the Early Nineteenth Century and the Present Day. The first (still limited and provisional) "field of abnormality," overwhelmingly dominated by the "judicial monster," is run through from the start (session of 12 March) by the problem of sexuality. For Foucault, this field can be crossed in two ways: by means of the notions of heredity and degeneration or by means of concepts of deviance and perversion, aberration and inversion. The main transitional expert opinion concerns a soldier who was first diagnosed by a military doctor (of Esquirol's school, we could say) as suffering from monomania. He is then seen by a psychiatrist who introduces the notion, but still in an embryonic state, of an "unhealthy deviation of the generative appetite," thus opening the way for the phase in which pleasure becomes a "psychiatric object" or an object that can be "psychiatrized" and a "theory of instinct" and its "aberrations linked to imagination." These theories dominate the whole of the second half of the nineteenth century.

2. *The Dossier on the Human Monster*

On the basis of the material collected, it is clear that Michel Foucault did not intend to study the question of the monster in the sense this term is given in Cesare Taruffi's last great teratogical *summa* of European literature.[14] He chose instead the extremely original sense put forward by Ernest Martin's *Histoire*,[15] that enabled him to establish the framework for his research: a cone of shadow of Western discourse that Foucault calls a "tradition that is both juridical and scientific."

(*a*) *The Juridico-Natural and Juridico-Biological Monster*. Probably following the suggestion of Martin, at the summit of the tradition evoked by Foucault, is the *Embryologia sacra* of Francesco Emanueles Cangiamila.[16] Foucault, who uses the French translation, but in its final, considerably expanded edition approved by the Royal Academy of Surgery,[17] reads this work as a treatise in which, probably for the first time, there is a merging of two previously quite distinct theories: the juridico-natural theory and the juridico-biological theory of the monster.

(*b*) *The Moral Monster*. This represents the reversal, brought about at the end of the eighteenth century, of the idea of the *juridico-natural* and *juridico-biological monster*. Whereas previously "monstrosity . . . brought with it an indication of criminality," now "monstrosity is systematically suspected of being behind all criminality." The first figure of the moral monster that Foucault identifies in the modern history of the West is the political monster. It is elaborated at the time of the French Revolution, at the very moment that the "kinship between the criminal and the tyrant" is being established, since both break the "fundamental social pact" and want to impose their "arbitrary law." In this perspective, "all human monsters are descendants of Louis XVI." Many of the questions raised in the course of the discussions on the sentencing of Louis XVI will be taken up again with regard to all those who reject the social pact (common criminals or political criminals). In any case, between the Jacobin literature that draws up the annals of royal crime, interpreting the history of the monarchy as an uninterrupted chain of offenses, and the anti-Jacobin literature that sees in the history of the Revolution the work of monsters who have broken the social pact through revolt, there is a consensus with serious consequences.

(*c*) *The Founding Monsters of Criminal Psychiatry*. In opening the dos-

sier of expert medico-legal opinions and drawing out those who
founded the discipline (the consultations signed by Jean Étienne Esquirol, Étienne Jean Georget, Charles Chrétien Marc), Foucault ex-
amines some of the most important cases of the first half of the
nineteenth century (particularly those that brought psychiatrists clos-
est to the courts). In the corresponding sessions he excludes only
those major cases that have already been the object of a specific publication.[18] It is a matter of a partition that is very important for understanding the general scheme of the course, for it permits the
presentation of the "huge domain of intervention" (the abnormal)
that opens up before psychiatry.

3. *The Dossier on Onanism*

After the republication of many sources, especially those concerning
its origins, and after the most recent studies undertaken in several
countries, which have contributed an enormous amount of material,
the material presented by Foucault on onanism in *The Abnormal*—and
that he also uses, though to a lesser extent, in *The History of Sexuality*—
seems quite limited. It depends mostly—and sometimes without the
necessary checking—on Léopold Deslandes's *Onanisme* of 1835[19] that
Foucault, on the basis of Claude-François Lallemand's opinion, calls
"the great theorist of masturbation."[20] We should not be surprised by
Foucault's definition. Actually, when pitting Deslandes's work against
Bekker's *Onania* (a book of no importance, Lallemand writes) and
Samuel Tissot's *L'Onanisme* (a modest compilation, Lallemand continues, that has never been highly regarded within the medical profession, despite its enormous success and the excellence of the crusade
undertaken by the author), Lallemand noted that there were much
more interesting sources available in Western culture.[21] For example,
the confessions of Jean-Jacques Rousseau[22] (which enabled him to
sketch a veritable analysis of the sexual problems of the author of
Emile[23]); information on the relation between masturbation and mental
alienation,[24] or on the relation between the testicles and the brain[25];
and the suggested therapy for masturbation (seen as an effect of civilization distancing children from sexuality) that consists in leading

adolescents back to the experience of the opposite sex.[26] Foucault's choice of Deslandes's *Onanisme* was therefore quite appropriate since it enabled him to pass on to the second phase of the crusade against masturbation with some ease: the phase in which, after abandoning the "fiction" or "scientific fabulation" of total illness (the etiology that went by way of the body's exhaustion, the desiccation of the nervous system),[27] and the purely physical concerns of ophthalmologists,[28] cardiologists,[29] bone specialists,[30] and specialists of brain and lung diseases, the idea of a relationship between onanism and sexual psychopathology began to be introduced—with Heinrich Kaan[31]—thus bringing about the emergence "of sexual aberrations in the psychiatric field." It is to Foucault's credit that he studied Kaan's text in depth and discovered in it a theory of the *nisus sexualis* that foregrounds reflection on childhood sexuality and the importance of *phantasia* as the preparatory instrument of the "sexual aberrations." So: "psychiatric genealogy of the sexual aberrations"; "constitution of an etiology of madness or mental illnesses on the basis of the history of the sexual instinct and the imagination linked to it."

THE "MANUSCRIPTS"*

There are at least two: the first concerns the bisexual tradition in medico-legal literature; the second concerns the practice of the confession in Christian treatises on penance.

1. *The Manuscript on Hermaphroditism*

To start with this manuscript seems to be the extension of the dossier on monsters. However, it soon becomes autonomous. Apart from the summary of the course *Abnormal,* there is little trace of this theme in *Dits et écrits*.[32] However, we know that one of the volumes of *The History of Sexuality* was to have been devoted to hermaphroditism. Foucault makes this clear, in 1978, in his presentation of the memoirs of Herculine Barbin: "The question of strange destinies like her own,

---

* We call "manuscripts" the "dossiers" in which the notes and commentaries by Foucault appear, no doubt in preparation for future publications.

which have raised so many problems for medicine and law, especially since the sixteenth century, will be dealt with in the volume of *The History of Sexuality* that will be devoted to hermaphrodites."[33]

Whether it was really a matter of a book devoted entirely to hermaphrodites or rather, according to the plan given in *The History of Sexuality* (1976), of a part of the volume on the *Perverse*,[34] it is nonetheless the case that Foucault published nothing else on this theme apart from the Herculine Barbin dossier (the first and only volume of the collection "Les Vies parallèles" published by Gallimard) because he radically changed the project of *The History of Sexuality*. He acknowledges this in the "Modifications" written on the occasion of the publication of *The Use of Pleasure*,[35] in which he lets it be understood that henceforth the "general recentering" of his studies "on the genealogy of the man of desire," limited to a period going from "classical antiquity to the first centuries of Christianity" no longer comprises *The History of Sexuality* as we know it.[36] The observations on the two big trials brought against Marie (Martin) Lemarcis (1601) and Anne (Jean-Baptiste) Grandjean (1765) derive from a wide collection of data, bibliographies, and transcriptions preserved in a box file that we have been able to consult thanks to the generosity of Daniel Defert, and which clearly indicate the plan of publication of an anthology of texts. The two cases inserted into the course *Abnormal* represent the most important emphases with regard to medico-legal discussion of bisexuality in the Modern Age.

2. *The Manuscript on the Practices of Confession and Spiritual Direction (Direction de conscience)*

Daniel Defert has pointed out to us that Michel Foucault destroyed his manuscript on the practices of confession and spiritual direction entitled *The Body and the Flesh*,[37] which he used to organize the course *Abnormal*. The last unpublished volume of *The History of Sexuality*—according to the 1984 plan—*Les Aveux de la chair*, is concerned solely with the Church Fathers. However, the 1974-1975 course enables us to reconstitute at least part of the missing work.

Foucault's point of departure is the three volumes of Henry Charles

Lea's great *History of Auricular Confession*, which is still indispensable for any researcher.[38] Even the material cited almost never goes beyond that collected by the American historian.[39] We can establish this thanks to a number of references such as the citations of Alcuin concerning the high Middle Ages;[40] the rule formulated by Angiolo de Chivasso according to which the confessor must not look the penitent in the eyes if the penitent is a woman or a young man;[41] Pierre Milhard's stipulation for traditional manuals;[42] and the Strasbourg measures of 1722.[43] However, once he has selected the texts needed to construct his discourse, centered essentially on the end of the seventeenth and the beginning of the eighteenth century, Foucault embarks on a truly penetrating reading.

The decision to examine, for the French territory, the work on confession of the "rigorist" Louis Habert (1625-1718) was certainly suggested to Foucault by Lea—the first historian to study the *Pratique du sacrament de pénitence ou méthode pour l'adminstrer utilement.*[44] The *Pratique*—a rare example of a book that remained in circulation among moral tracts even though its author was progressively distanced from the teaching of the doctrine and marginalized in the theological milieu—was chosen from the innumerable manuals available because it shows, although in seventeenth-century terms, the old juridical and medical conception of confession. In fact, all of Habert's theological language seems deeply contaminated by this fusion so that every metaphor and every *exemplum* includes a reference to the two disciplines.

The History of Sexuality demonstrates the importance of the pastoral—a term that designates in general the ministry of the hierarchy to the faithful for whom they are responsible and over whom they exercise authority—for Foucault's research,[45] both for the Catholic field[46] and, with appropriate variations, for Protestant countries.[47] In these lectures Foucault follows the transition from the "practice of confession" to "spiritual direction (*direction de conscience*)" in accordance with the wish of Carlo Borromeo,[48] and without addressing at the same time what takes place in reformed Europe.[49] The great *Methodus* of Tommaso Tamburini—a Jesuit subjected to the Inquisition and condemned by Pope Innocent XI for his "probabilist" position—is the object of the same thorough treatment as Habert's *Pratique*.[50] This extremely important text is taken as a product of the religious output preceding the turn to "discretion" in confessional practices (the *"how to say"* becomes vital) and enables Foucault to follow the different lines that fight over spiritual direction. Foucault's work on the *Homo apostolicus* of Alfonso Maria de Liguori (1696-1787)[51]—the famous *Praxis et instructio confessariorum* that "gives a series of rules that define modern and contemporary confession,"[52] bringing other disciplines along with it[53] and producing the first "pansexual" interpretation of the sacrament of penance, the major example of which is Leo Taxil's collection[54]—is no less thorough. Much more than in *The History of Sexuality*, Foucault emphasizes the sudden appearance of the clamorous campaign against masturbation in the major transformation of confession and spiritual direction provoked by the Liguorian "stylistics of discretion." He also attempts to explain the early appearance of the "discourse of masturbation in Protestant countries" in which the Catholic form of spiritual direction did not exist. The important thing, however, is that in contrast with the earlier Christian literature, the literature on onanism produces "a discourse from which desire and pleasure are totally absent."

The comments on the "new forms" of mysticism and the "new forms" of religious discourse that appeared at the summit of Christian society in virtue of the stress on the direction of the soul and the propagation of its techniques among the faithful are barely sketched out but very persuasive. Others are more bold, such as the thesis that the practice of the government of consciences produced "below" a series of behaviors that—prepared by the installation of the new "apparatus of control" and "systems of power" in the Church—led over time to *possessions* (phenomena both confused with and "radically" distinct from witchcraft),[55] *convulsions* (as "the plastic and visible form of the struggle in the body of the possessed"), and finally *visions* (that "absolutely exclude physical struggle" and impose the rule "that there should be no contact, no physical struggle and no mixing of the Virgin's spiritual body with the material body of the person who is miraculously cured").

Foucault reaches these conclusions as a result of his familiarity with the major episodes of possession, convulsion, and visions presented in the nineteenth-century psychiatric literature that was developing the notion of a pathology of religious feeling. With regard to possession and convulsions, we refer particularly to the implicit presence of the work of L. F. Calmeil in the lecture of 26 February.[56] But the thread of this discourse can also be reconstituted by carefully analyzing the articles that historians have devoted to the two phenomena in dictionaries and encyclopedias.[57] In Foucault's reading we should not forget the research that Bénédict Auguste Morel included in his *Traité* of 1866.[58] It is still essentially based on the works of Calmeil, but already contains signs of a transformation that was under way: a process by which convulsions become a "privileged medical object."

We could even summarize the situation of the reflux of medical discourse toward religious discourse through the words of a pastor in a thesis on the *Inspirés des Cévennes* presented at the Protestant faculty of theology of Montauban: "These phenomena of inspiration have been seriously and thoroughly studied by several distinguished alienist doctors and in particular by L. F. Calmeil [*De la folie, vol. 2*, pp. 243-310] and A. Bertrand [*Du magnétisme animal en France et des jugements qu'en ont portés les sociétés savants*, (Paris, 1826), p. 447]. We recall here . . . the various explanations they have given. Calmeil connects the ecstatic theomania of Calvinists to pathological disorders, to hysteria in the simplest cases and to epilepsy in the more serious cases. Bertrand speaks of 'a particular condition that is neither waking nor sleeping nor an illness, a condition that is natural to man, that is to say, that always appears essentially the same under certain conditions' and that he calls *ecstasy*"; "Who, when reading the well-known and interesting history of the convulsionary mystics of Saint-Médard, of the devils of Loudon, of turning tables and animal magnetism, has not been struck by the similarity between these phenomena and the phenomena recounted in the *Théâtre sacré*?" [M. Misson, *Le Théâtre sacré des Cévennes ou Récit des diverses merveilles opérées dans cette partie de la province de Languedoc* (London, 1707)]; "The convergence, without arriving at absolute identity, is really indisputable and, I venture to assert, undisputed. Consequently, if we cannot attribute a supernatural cause to the phenomena of animal magnetism, to the possessions of the Ursuline nuns of Loudon, to the nervous crises of the Jansenist convulsionary mystics... can we do so to the ecstasies of the Cévennes prophets?"[59]

We could say, then, that the paradigm imposes itself in the specialist literature after a series of complex convergences and at the end of the therapeutic appropriation of the phenomenon by the magnetists,[60] with the theses of Calmeil; that it enters Salpêtrière in 1872 with Jean Martin Charcot and remains firmly installed there with Désiré Magloire Bourneville, P. Vulet, P. M. L. Regnard, and P. Richer.[61] At the end of this series of shifts there is another intervention by Charcot that enables Foucault to pass from the theme of the medically discredited convulsions to that of visions.[62]

EDITORIAL CRITERIA FOR THE TEXT

The transcript of the course is based on the general rules of this edition presented in the Foreword: the transposition of Michel Foucault's voice from magnetic tape to visual representation, to writing, has been carried out as faithfully as possible.

However, writing has its own requirements with regard to oral expression. It requires more than just a punctuation that makes reading fluent, a subdivision of ideas that ensures their adequate logical unity, and a separation into paragraphs suited to the form of the book. It also demands completing sentences with deviations or breaks in the chain of syntactical relationships, joining a principal proposition to a subordinate proposition that, for whatever reason, has been left autonomous, correcting grammatical constructions that are unacceptable to the expositional norm, reversing an order or arrangement dictated by oratorical brio, and adapting certain inexact agreements (usually between singular and plural) of personal pronouns and verbal inflexions. Writing also demands—but the requirement here is much weaker—the suppression of disagreeable repetitions caused by the speed and spontaneity of oral expression, of the summaries that do not conform to the stylistic modulation of the discourse, and of the innumerable interjections and exclamations or formulae of hesitation and locutions of liaison and stress ("let us say," "if you like," "also").

We have always acted with great prudence and many precautions. At any rate, we have acted only after checking that the speaker's intentions have not been betrayed. It seemed to us appropriate, for example, to put in quotes certain expressions in order to highlight or give a specific meaning to some words. The changes that are an integral part of the transition from the oral to the written are not indicated; the responsibility for this rests with the editors of the text whose first concern has been to render completely readable what they were hearing through the live voice of Foucault.

The general rules that apply to all the courses of the Collège de France have been adapted to the particular necessities of *Abnormal*.

The many transcriptions of French of the Classical Age have in principle been carried out according to modern criteria. However, in the notes, the written forms of the names of individuals have been reproduced in the different forms in which they appear on the frontispiece of the books cited (for example: Borromée, Boromée, and Borromeus; Liguori, Liguory, and Ligorius).

Most of the small material errors we have detected have been corrected, as have those caused by a failure of memory, a lack of attention, or by a passage omitted from the reading of a text. In these cases, we have not hesitated to replace, for example, a false "second" by the correct "third." Occasionally we have introduced "on the one hand" when there is only the correlative "on the other hand." We have not indicated self-corrections, neither the simplest (a vague "in some way" after a peremptory "precisely"), nor the more complex ("according to the regulation of the Châlons diocese, eh! not the regulation of the diocese, of the Châlons seminary, excuse me" becomes obviously "according to the regulation of the Châlons seminary"). In cases where it is only a question of adapting the oral to the written we have not indicated our interventions or our choices.

In other circumstances we have proceeded differently. For example, when Foucault presents the dossier on the Rouen hermaphrodite, Marie Lemarcis (lecture of January 22), he confuses the year of the trial (1601) with that of the publication of certain texts that relate it (1614-1615). This ambiguity is reproduced on several occasions but does not affect the meaning of the discourse. We have noted the error on its first occurrence and then we have corrected it automatically whenever Foucault refers to the trial. When, however, we have come across errors (names, dates, titles) that only appear once, we have introduced the correction in square brackets preceded by the term *rectius*, following current publishing norms.

The problem of quotations has raised many difficulties. Foucault is fairly faithful to the texts he reads to his auditors. However, he takes the liberty of adjusting tenses so as to offer a correct *consecutio*, makes stylistic inversions, and suppresses secondary words and phrases. Having found almost all the sources quoted, it would be very useful to reproduce in the notes the complete original documents. This would have helped to make Foucault's way of working better known and the selections made better appreciated. We have given a number of specimens by offering, for example, several passages from Louis Habert's treatise (*Pratique du sacrement de pénitence*) on which an important part of the Christian discourse of confession was constructed. However, usually it seemed to us appropriate, so as to avoid an unwieldy infrastructure, to indicate where the relevant passage can be found (which enables immediate consultation of the source) and we have put in quotes only extracts actually quoted.

Nonetheless, Foucault's alterations are sometimes so extensive that it was necessary to compare the original. In some cases, through the use of parentheses and quotes, it has been possible to bring out the original from the text. In others (more rarely) it has been necessary to resort to the critical apparatus. With fairly long quotations where the complementary or modifying intervention of Foucault has been suggested by the need to make the context more comprehensible, we have indicated between square brackets the addition or explanation, followed by the initials M.F. For example: "Hardly eight hours had passed [after the marriage; M.F.] when ..."; "these impulsive tendencies found in recent events [that is to say, the Commune; M.F.] an opportunity . . ." However, restrictive interventions are usually indicated by corresponding ellipsis points. For example, in the phrase: "The young woman's sacrificed virtue was worthy of a different end . . .", the ellipsis points simply indicate a break.

With regard to translations or paraphrases of Latin texts we have acted completely differently. Both in the case of the commentary on a section of the *Methodus expeditae confessionis* (the work of Tommaso Tamburini, an important moral theologian of the seventeenth century) and in the case of one the last treatises of sexology written in the common language of European learning (the *Psychopathia sexualis* of Heinrich Kaan), we have reproduced the passages in their entirety. The reason is simple: these Latin versions demonstrate the care Foucault took in preparing his course.

The cassettes we have used are not of a high quality. However, listening has never presented insurmountable problems. Mechanical gaps have been restored.[63] In the event of interpretative ambiguities that could not be resolved, we have used large single quotes ($<$ . . . $>$). For example: instead of choosing between a possible "persuasion" and a possible "percussion," we have opted for $<$persuasion$>$. Reconstituted sentences are indicated by square brackets. For example: "We will understand why the possessed, the convulsionary mystics [appeared]". We have used the same procedure to reintroduce breaks in words or phrases in the quotations.

We have not indicated some extrinsic interventions. For example, in the sixth session we have cut the following observation without noting it: "Since everyone is changing their little machine [the cassette recorders] I will take the opportunity to give you another purely recreational example," an example that was recorded perfectly. Furthermore, we have not indicated the laughter in the amphitheater that often accompanied Foucault's reading of texts and that he provoked moreover—with respect to the first expert opinions—by stressing certain details (particularly the grotesque and the puerility of psychiatric language in penal matters).

Editorial Criteria for the Critical Apparatus

The published work of Michel Foucault is quite meager in literal quotations and references to the set of sources used in the work. With some exceptions, the traditional system of notes tracing the history of the question being studied and calling on current studies on the subject is completely absent. The courses, which always maintain a profile and a value linked to the public report of research, are oral. They often present improvised passages based on material that the author has not revised for publication. Moreover, because of the approximate references and vague citations (sometimes given from memory), the course editors have a great responsibility for checking: Not only must they offer the present-day reader—who is no longer the Collège de France auditor—an exact and practical reference to the different documents that Foucault has already explored, indeed copied out in his notes, they must also indicate the traces, imperceptible at first sight, of the books that made up his library. Our critical apparatus, by strongly emphasizing the sources (sometimes presented in their entirety) at the cost of a current bibliography, seeks to demonstrate the validity of a judgment by Georges Canguilhem that has served as our guide: Foucault cited only original texts as if he wished to read the past through the thinnest possible "grid."[64]

With regard to the implicit sources (some more obvious, others less so), it should be noted that our references constitute only tracks for research and in no way seek to imply that they were suggested by Foucault himself. The editors, who have followed the principle of never citing works later than 1975 (except for republications without variations or anastatic reprints), assume entire responsibility for the references.

With regard to the secondary historical literature, we have privileged work that bears essentially on the historical production of psychiatrists and on the history of medicine. Foucault had a deep knowledge of this literature, especially from research published in specialist journals (for example, the *Annales d'hygiène publique et de médecine légale* or the *Annales médico-psychologiques*) and in the big collections (like the Ballière medical editions). He used this literature as a sort of layout that was sufficiently clear to draw the map of questions to be problematized in genealogical terms. One only needs to examine the growing interest of nineteenth-century medical literature in questions concerning monstrosity or onanism (the two main dossiers of the course), in hermaphroditism or confession (the two manuscripts supporting the course), and in possessions-convulsions-visions, to be aware of this particularity of Foucault's work.

It could also be argued, for example, that the very lively perception of the political importance of measures against plague is much more an effect of reading a number of nineteenth-century *Histoires médicales* than of the use of contemporary research. This does not mean that Foucault was not abreast of the existing bibliography and that he did not follow the work of historians of his time. But the historical position of nineteenth-century psychiatry, through its assembling and ordering of material, stimulates Foucault's problematization much more than the orientations predominant in the years 1970 to 1976. In this regard we can cite, upstream, *Discipline and Punish* and, downstream, *The History of Sexuality*, in which in order to study the complex question of the "power of normalization" Foucault accords an important place to the techniques of control of sexuality introduced after the seventeenth century. He acknowledges the existence of a remarkable production of books in this period on the repression of sexuality and on its history and he admits the necessity of adopting a different theory of power that puts the previous analyses of *Madness and Civilization* in question (and these analyses were actually modified, at several points, by the results of *Discipline and Punish*).

We find here the opposition between the model of exclusion (the leper) and that of placing under control (the plague). In *Discipline and Punish* Foucault referred to a regulation at the end of the seventeenth century from the military archives of Vincennes. But he adds: "This regulation is broadly similar to a whole series of others that date from the same period and earlier."[65] This series of regulations is present in the course we publish here. If we examine the similarities

("I refer," says Foucault in the lecture of 15 January "to a series of regulations, all absolutely identical moreover, that were published from the end of the Middle Ages until the beginning of the eighteenth century"), it seems unlikely that to undertake his research and synthesize its content Foucault did not use at least the description of the *quadrillage* left to us by Antoine François Ozanam's famous *Histoire médicale générale et particulière des maladies épidémiques*.[66]

What is important is that the conclusions are very forceful and more comprehensive relative to *Discipline and Punish*: "Reaction to the leper is a negative reaction" (*exclusion*); "reaction to the plague is a positive reaction" (*inclusion*). However, it seems that in *The History of Sexuality* the obviously forced outcome of the course is not integrated into the section on "The Repressive Hypothesis" that was intended to accommodate it. Finally, it should be noted that in the session of 15 January Foucault also abandons, quite quickly, the traditional "literary dream" of the plague (for which there was a considerable literature at the time) in order to emphasize the much more important "political dream" when power is exercised to the full. It is precisely Ozanam who offers a different thread by taking as his model for studying "the measures of sanitary police" the regulations "full of wisdom and foresight" adopted by the town of Nola in the Kingdom of Naples in 1815 "that can serve as the type and example to be followed in such a calamity."[67] Ozanam recalls that "one of the best works to consult for this end is that of Ludovico Antonio Muratori entitled *Del governo in tempo di peste*" in which "we find a very good summary of all the sanitary measures taken in the different plagues of Europe up to that of Marseille," and he appreciates the large documentation collected in the work of Cardinal Gastaldi, *De avertenda peste*, and in Papon's *Traité historique de la peste* "the second volume of which is devoted to recounting all the precautions that must be taken to prevent the spread and introduction of plague."[68]

The example of the vast and important political literature on the plague (*Du gouvernement en temps de peste*) referred to here via Ozanam's *Histoire médicale* finally leads us to recall that between the notes of the critical apparatus of *The Abnormal*, as we have presented them on the basis of obvious traces, and Course Context, there is a contiguity that aims at continuity. In fact, in the Course Context we have cited a series of references that it would have been imprudent to include in the critical apparatus because they should not be attributed to Michel Foucault in any way. Nevertheless, it seemed to us that they could contribute to the understanding and explanation of the text.

1. M. Foucault, *Dits et écrits, 1954-1988*, vol. 2, (Paris: Gallimard, 1994), pp. 822-828.
2. Cf. M. Foucault, *La Volonté de Savoir* (Paris: Gallimard, 1976), pp. 43-44. English translation: *The History of Sexuality* vol. 1, (London: Allen Lane, 1979), pp. 31-32.
3. M. Foucault, *Dits et écrits, 1954-1988*, vol. 2, (Paris: Gallimard, 1994), p. 746. French translation: "Prison Talk," in *Power/Knowledge. Selected Interviews and Other Writings 1972-1977*, edited by Colin Gordon, translated by Colin Gordon and others (Brighton: Harvester, 1980). In fact, at this time Foucault was working on expert psychiatric opinion in his seminar at the Collège de France.
4. Ibid.
5. Cf. E. Garçon, *Code pénal annoté*, vol. 1 (Paris: s.l., 1952), pp. 207-226; R. Merle and A. Vitu, *Traité de droit criminel*, sixth edition, vol. 1 (Paris: s.l., 1984), pp. 759-766.
6. Summaries in M. Foucault, *Dits et écrits, 1954-1988*, vol. 2, (Paris: Gallimard, 1994), pp. 389-393, pp. 456-470, pp. 675-686. English translation: *The Essential Works of Michel Foucault, 1954-1984*, vol. 1: *Ethics: Subjectivity and Truth*, edited by Paul Rabinow and translated by Robert Hurley and others (New York: New Press, 1997), pp. 17-21; pp. 23-37 and pp. 39-50.
7. Summary in *Dits et écrits, 1954-1988*, vol. 2, pp. 240-244; English translation: *The Essential Works of Michel Foucault, 1954-1984*, vol. 1, pp. 11-16. This was Foucault's first lecture course at the Collège de France and its title was taken from the (French) title, *La Volonté de savoir*, the first volume of *The History of Sexuality*.
8. M. Foucault, *Il faut défendre la société: Cours au Collège de France (1975-1976)*, edited by M. Bertani and A. Fontana (Paris: Gallimard/Seuil, 1997); English translation: "*Society Must Be Defended*": *Lectures at the Collège de France (1975-1976)*, (New York: Picador, 2003).
9. M. Foucault, *Dits et écrits*, vol. 2, p. 828.
10. Summary in *Dits et écrits*, vol. 3, pp. 818-825; English translation: *The Essential Works*, vol. 1, pp. 73-79.
11. Summary in *Dits et écrits*, vol. 4, pp. 125-129; English translation: *The Essential Works*, vol. 1, pp. 81-85.
12. M. Foucault, *Dits et écrits*, vol. 4, p. 214: "We have undertaken the history of subjectivity by studying the divisions carried out in society in the name of madness, illness, delinquency and their effects on the constitution of a reasonable and normal subject."
13. Summary in *Dits et écrits*, vol. 4, pp. 353-365; English translation: *Essential Works*, vol. 1, pp. 93-106.
14. This eight volume work by C. Taruffi, *Storia dell teratologia* (Bologna, 1881-1894), reconstitutes in the smallest details the library and museum of monsters with which a number of doctors and surgeons of the Modern Age were occupied.
15. E. Martin, *Histoire des monstres depuis l'Antiquité jusqu'à nos jours* (Paris, 1880). The first chapter ("Les législations antiques et les monstres," pp. 4-16) offers a synthetic framework of the evolution from the old Roman law on the *monstra* that begins with this observation: "In Rome we find a teratological legislation that proves that the judicial spirit of this nation did not neglect any subject susceptible to regulation," p. 4.
16. F. E. Cangiamila, *Embriologia sacra ovvero dell'uffizio de' sacerdoti, medici e superiori circa l'eterna salute de' bambini racchiusi nell'utero libri quattro* (Palermo, 1745). The spread of this text in Europe only begins with its translation into Latin, in a considerably revised and expanded edition: *Embryologia sacra sive de officio sacerdotum, medicorum et aliorum circa aeternam parvulorum in utero existentium salutem libri quatuor* (Panormi, 1758).
17. F. E. Cangiamila, *Abrégé de l'embryologie sacrée, ou Traité des devoirs des prêtres, des médecins, des chirurgiens, et des sages-femmes envers les enfants qui sont dans le sein de leurs mères* (Paris, 1766). The first French edition appeared under a title closer to the Latin—*Abrégé de*

l'embryologie sacrée ou Traité des devoirs des prêtres, des médecins et autres, sur le salut eternal des enfants qui sont dans le ventre de leur mère—and was published in 1762.

18. M. Foucault, editor, *Moi, Pierre Rivière, ayant égorgé ma mère, ma soeur et mon frère . . . Un cas de parricide de XIXe siècle* (Paris: Gallimard/Julliard, 1973); English translation: *I, Pierre Riviére, Having Slaughtered My Mother, My Sister, and My Brother . . . A Case of Parricide in the Nineteenth Century* (New York: s.l., 1975).

19. Cf. L. Deslandes, *De l'onanisme et des autres abus vénériens considérés dans leurs rapports avec la santé* (Paris, 1835).

20. Cf. C. F. Lallemand, *Des pertes séminales involontaires*, vol. 1 (Paris-Montpellier, 1836), pp. 313-488 (chapter six, on "abuses," devoted entirely to the effects of masturbation).

21. In particular, he noted the intermediary phase represented by J. L. Doussin-Dubreuil, *Lettres sur les dangers de l'onanisme, et Conseils relatifs au traitement des maladies qui en résultent. Ouvrage utile aux pères de famille et aux instituteurs* (Paris, 1806), and by J.-B. Téraube, *Traité de la Chiromanie* (Paris, 1826). For the definition of the term and the proposal of a new name, see pp. 16-17.

22. C. F. Lallemand, *Des pertes séminales*, vol. 1, pp. 403-488.

23. Ibid., vol. 2, pp. 265-293.

24. Ibid., vol. 3, pp. 182-200. This is a commonplace of contemporary psychiatric literature. Cf., for example, C. C. H. Marc, *De la folie considérée dans ses rapports avec les questions médico-judiciaires*, vol. 1 (Paris, 1840), p. 326.

25. Cf. chapter three of J. L. Doussin-Dubreil, *De la gonorrhée bénigne ou sans virus vénérien et des fleurs blanches* (Paris, VI [1797-1798]).

26. C. F. Lallemand, *Des pertes séminales*, vol. 3, pp. 477-490.

27. Foucault uses J. B. T. Serrurier "Masturbation," in *Dictionnaire des sciences médicales*, vol. 31 (Paris, 1819), pp. 100-135; "Pollution," ibid., vol. 44 (1820), p. 114 *et sq.* In the second edition of the *Dictionnaire*, the two articles disappear and are replaced by "Spermatorrhée" and "Onanisme," respectively in *Dictionnaire de médecine ou Répertoire général des sciences médicales considérées sous les rapports théorique et pratique*, vol. 22 (Paris, 1840), pp. 77-80. The article "Onanisme" is particularly interesting since in it, the medico-legal experience of mental pathology is already integrated.

28. L. J. Sanson, "Amaurose" in *Dictionnaire de médecine et de chirurgie pratiques*, vol. 2 (Paris, 1829), p. 98; A. Scarpa, *Saggio di osservazione e di esperienza sulle principali malattie degli occhi* (Pavia, 1801); French translation: *Traité pratique de maladies des yeux, ou Expériences et Observations sur les maladies qui affectent ces organes*, vol. 2, (Paris, 1802), pp. 242-243; English translation: A. Scarpa, *A Treatise on the principal diseases of the eyes,* translated by J. Briggs (London, 1818). Cf., A. L. M. Lullier-Wimslow, "Amaurose," in *Dictionnaire des sciences médicales*, vol. 1 (1812), pp. 430-433 and J. N. Marjolin, "Amaurose," in *Dictionnaire de médecine*, vol. 2 (Paris, 1833), pp. 306-334.

29. P. Blaud, "Mémoire sur les concrétions fibrineuses polypiformes dans les cavités du cœur," *Revue médicale française et étrangere. Journal de clinique*, 4 (1833), pp. 175-188 and pp. 331-352.

30. A. Richerand, the editor of A. Boyer, *Leçons sur les maladies des os rédigées en un traité complet de ces maladies*, 1, 9 (1802-1803), p. 344, notes: "Masturbation is sometimes the cause of caries of the vertebrae and of abscesses through congestion. Citizen Boyer's practice has provided him with several examples of this."

31. H. Kaan, *Psychopathia sexualis* (Leipzig 1844).

32. M. Foucault, *Dits et Écrits*, vol. 3, pp. 624-625, pp. 676-677.

33. *Herculine Barbin, dite Alexina B*, introduced by M. Foucault (Paris: Gallimard, 1978), p. 131. English translation: *Herculine Barbin. Being the Recently Discovered Memoirs of a Nineteenth-Century French Hermaphrodite*, introduced by Michel Foucault, translated by Richard McDougall (Brighton: Harvester, 1980), p. 119.

34. See also the chapter "L'implantation perverse", in M. Foucault, *La Volonté de Savoir*, pp. 50-67; English translation: "The Perverse Implantation," in M. Foucault, *The History of Sexuality*, pp. 36-49.

35. M. Foucault, *L'Usage des Plaisirs* (Paris: Gallimard, 1984), pp. 9–39; English translation: *The Use of Pleasure*, translated by Robert Hurley (New York: Viking, 1985).

36. Loose sheet inserted in the first (French) edition published by Gallimard of *L'Usage des plaisirs* (Paris, 1984).

37. The title was indicated by Foucault in *La Volonté de Savoir*, p. 30; English translation: *The History of Sexuality*, p. 21 n. 4.

38. H. C. Lea, *A History of Auricular Confession and Indulgences in the Latin Church* (Philadelphia, 1896).

39. Foucault, at least in this phase of his research, appears not to have referred to the rich material in the *Dictionnaire de théologie catholique*, 3/1 (Paris, 1923), cols. 838-894, 894-926, 942-960, 960-974 (sections of the article "Confession" written by E. Vacandard, P. Bernard, T. Ortolan, and B. Dolhagaray); 12/1 (Paris, 1933), cols. 722-1127 (sections of the article "Pénitence" written by E. Amann and A. Michel). Nor does he appear to have used the two volumes of selections translated and presented by C. Vogel: *Le Pécheur et la Pénitence dans l'Église ancienne* (Paris: s.l., 1966); *Le Pécheur et la Pénitence au Moyen Age* (Paris: s.l., 1969). The remarkable essay of T. N. Tentler, *Sin and Confession on the Eve of Reformation* (Princeton, 1975), was published in the same year that Foucault was discussing the question of confession in the framework of *The Abnormal*.

40. F. Albinus seu Alcuinus [Alcuin], *Opera omnia*, vol. 1: *Patrologiae cursus completus*, second series, tome 100 (Paris, 1851); cols. 337-339.

41. A. de Clavasio, *Summa angelica de casibus conscientiae*, with additional material by I Ungarelli (Venice, 1582), p. 678.

42. P. Milhard, *La Grande Guide des curés, vicaires et confesseurs* (Lyon, 1617). The first edition, known under the title of *Le Vrai Guide des curés*, is from 1604. Made obligatory within his jurisdiction by the archbishop of Bordeaux, it was withdrawn from circulation in 1619 following condemnation by the Sorbonne.

43. Given their rarity, Foucault was certainly not able to consult the *Monita generalia de officiis confessarii olim ad usum dioceses argentinensis* (Strasburg, 1722). His translation is based on Lea's transcription in *A History of Auricular Confession*, vol. 1, p. 377.

44. The first edition of the *Pratique du sacrament de pénitence ou méthode pour l'administrer utilement* was published anonymously in 1689 in Blois and Paris. The preface incorporates the *Avis touchant les qualités du confesseur* and the text comprises four parts: penitence, contrition, absolution, and satisfaction. The second edition appeared in 1691 with the same title but revised and considerably expanded. The eight editions that followed between 1700 and 1729 should be considered reprints of the third edition (Paris, 1694), but only the 1722 edition carries the author's name. The editions of 1748 and 1755 were completed by an extract from the penitential canons drawn from Carlo Borromeo's *Instructions* to confessors and printed for the French clergy. Louis Habert was involved in a major controversy because of his *Theologia dogmatica et moralis* published in Paris in seven volumes, four editions of which are known up to 1723. See in particular the *Défenses de l'auteur de la théologie du séminaire de Châlons contre un libelle intitulé "Dénonciation de la théologie de Monsieur Habert,"* (Paris, 1711), and *Réponse à la quatrième lettre d'un docteur de la Sorbonne à un homme de qualité* (Paris, 1714).

45. On the complexity of this theme, cf. M. Foucault, *Dits et Écrits*, vol. 4, pp. 134-161.

46. The organization of the Catholic pastoral in the post-Tridentine period developed from the *Acta ecclesiae mediolanensis* (Mediolani, 1583). The *Reliqua secundae partis ad instructionem aliqua pertinentia* (pp. 230r-254r) are in the vernacular and include *Le avvertenze ai confessori* (p. 230r-326r). The in-folio for France was published in Paris by J. Jost in 1643.

47. M. Foucault, *La Volonté de savoir*, p. 30; English translation: *The History of Sexuality*, p. 21, n. 4: "The reformed pastoral also laid down rules, albeit in a more discreet way, for putting sex into discourse."

48. The revival of the term appears after publication in the Netherlands of C. Borromeus [Carlo Borromeo] *Pastorum instructiones ad concionandum, confessionisque et eucharistiae sacramenta ministrandum utilissimae* (Antwerp, 1586). The pastoral was disseminated in France thanks to the translation of Charles Borromée [Carlo Borromeo], *Instructions aux confesseurs*

de sa ville et de son diocèse. Ensemble: la manière d'administrer le sacrement de pénitence, avec les canons pénitentiaux, suivant l'ordre du Décalogue. Et l'ordonnance du même saint sur l'obligation des paroissieurs d'assister à leurs paroisses (Paris, 1648, fourth edition: Charles Borromée, Paris, 1665) and *Règlements pour l'instruction du clergé, tirés des constitutions et décrets synodaux de saint Charles* Borromée (Paris, 1663). However, it should also be noted that well before the translations of the archbishop of Milan, the treatise of the archbishop of Cosenza, J. B. Constanzo, had been made known: *Avertissements aux recteurs, curés, prêtres et vicaires qui désirent s'acquitter dignement de leur charge et faire bien et saintement tout ce qui appartient à leurs offices* (Bordeaux, 1613), that took at the end of the century the title *La Pastorale de saint Charles Borromée* (Lyon, 1697 and 1717). Book five, "De l'administration du sacrement de pénitence," is divided into "The Office of the Confessor as Judge" [pp. 449-452], "Master" [pp. 457-460], and "Doctor" [pp. 462-463].

49. M. Foucault, *La Volonté de savoir*, p. 30; English translation: *The History of Sexuality*, p. 21, n. 4: "This . . . will be developed in the next volume, *The Body and the Flesh*." It is this manuscript that Foucault destroyed.

50. T. Tamburinus [Tommaso Tamburino], *Methodus expeditae confessionis tum pro confessariis tum pro poenitentibus* (Rome, 1645). Book seven of the *Explicatio decalogi, duabus distincta partibus, in qua omnes fere conscientiae casus declarantur* (Venice, 1694), pp. 201-203, summarizes the content of the *Methodus*, pp. 388-392, with important additions and explanations. The main opposition to the "probabilism" of Tamburini's *Methodus* was organized by Paris priests who in 1659 presented a petition in the form of a pamphlet to the archbishop, the Cardinal of Retz, in order to obtain a condemnation.

51. A. de Ligorius [de Liguori], *Homo apostolicus instructus in sua vocatione ad audiendas confessiones sive praxis et instructio confessariorum* (Bassani, 1782); French translation: A. de Liguori, *Praxis confessarii ou Conduite du confesseur* (Lyon, 1854).

52. We should note its use in the *Manuel des confesseurs*, seventh edition, composed by J. J. Gaume (Paris, 1854). See J. J. Gaume, *Advice for Those Who Exercise the Ministry of Reconciliation through Confession and Absolution* (London, 1878). This was abridged and adapted for the use of the English Church.

53. On the shift of Liguorism into the medical field, see J. B. de Bourge, *Le Livre d'or des enfants ou Causeries maternelles et scolaires sur l'hygiene* (Mirecourt, 1865).

54. The French version of the *Praxis et instructio confessariorum*, published in Paris without date by P. Mellier, was inserted in *Les Livres secrets des confesseurs dévoilés aux pères de famille*, through the efforts of L. Taxil [G. J. Pagès] (Paris, 1883), pp. 527-577.

55. "Who says *possession* does not say *witchcraft*. The two phenomena are distinct and one is subsequent to the other, even though many treatises combine them and even confuse them," writes M. de Certeau in the introduction to *La Possession de Loudon* (1970; Paris: Gallimard/Julliard, 1980), p. 10.

56. L. F. Calmeil, *De la folie considérée sous le point de vue pathologique, philosophique, historique et judiciaire* (Paris, 1842).

57. For example, A. F. Jenin de Montegre, "Convulsion," in *Dictionnaire des sciences médicales*, vol. 6 (1813), pp. 197-238.

58. B. A. Morel, *Traité de la médecine légale des aliénés dans ses rapports avec la capacité civile et la responsabilité juridique des individus atteints de diverses affections aiguës ou chroniques du système nerveux* (Paris, 1866).

59. A. Kissel, *Les Inspirés des Cévennes* (Montauban, 1882), pp. 70-71. Misson's book was reprinted at the time that psychiatry was discovering convulsions, with the title: *Les Prophètes protestants* (Paris, 1847).

60. J. P. Deleuze, *Histoire critique du magnétisme animal* (Paris, 1913).

61. J. M. Charcot, *Œuvres complètes*, vol. 1 (Paris, 1886); D. M. Bourneville and P. Vulet, *De la contracture hystérique permanente* (Paris, 1872); D. M. Bourneville and P. M. L. Regnard, *L'Iconographie photographique de la Salpêtrière* (Paris, 1876-1878), and P. Richer, *Études cliniques sur l'hystéro-épilepsie, ou la grand hystérie* (Paris, 1881).

62. J. M. Charcot, *La Foi qui guérit* (Paris, 1897). To understand the allusion to the emphasis on visions it is useful to know the point of view of the Roman Church expressed by an

author who followed the evolution of psychiatry. See the articles of R. Van der Elst, "Guérisons miraculeuses" and "Hystérie," in *Dictionnaire apologétique de la foi catholique contenant les épreuves de la vérité de la religion et les réponses aux objections tirées des sciences humaines*, vol. 2 (Paris, 1911), pp. 419-438, 534-540.

63. We have used the cassettes recorded by Gilbert Burlet and Jacques Lagrange.

64. G. Canguilhem, "Mort de l'homme ou épuisement du cogito?" *Critique* 242 (July 1967).

65. M. Foucault, *Surveiller et Punir. Naissance de la prison* (Paris: Gallimard, 1975), p. 197. English translation: *Discipline and Punish. The Birth of the Prison*, translated by Alan Sheridan (London: Penguin, 1977), p. 316, n. 1.

66. J. A. F. Ozanam, *Histoire médicale générale et particulière des maladies épidémiques, contagieuses et épizootiques, qui ont régné en Europe depuis les temps les plus reculés jusqu'à nos jours*, second edition, vol. 4 (Paris, 1835), pp. 5-93.

67. Ibid., pp. 64-69.

68. Ibid., pp. 69-70. Cf. H. Gastaldus, *Tractatus de avertenda et profliganda peste politico-legalis, eo lucubratus tempore quo ipse loemocomiorum primo, mox sanitatis commissarius generalis fuit, peste urbem invadente, anno 1656 e 57 ac nuperrime Goritiam depopulante typis commissus* (Bologna, 1684); L. A. Muratori, *Del governo della peste e della maniera di guardarsene. Trattato diviso in politico, medico et eclesiastico, da conservarsi e aversi pronto per le occasioni, che dio tenga sempre lontane* (Modena, 1714), and J.-P. Papon, *De la peste ou époque mémorable de ce fléau et les moyens de s'en preserver*, vols. 1-2 (Paris VIII [1799-1800]).

INDEX OF NOTIONS AND CONCEPTS

INDEX OF NAMES